Microdevelopment
Transition Processes in Development and Learning

Microdevelopment is the process of change in abilities, knowledge, and understanding during short time-spans. This book presents a new process-oriented view of development and learning based on recent innovations in psychology research. Instead of characterizing abilities at different ages, researchers investigate processes of development and learning that evolve through time, and explain what enables progress in them. Four themes are highlighted: variability, mechanisms that create transitions to higher levels of knowledge, interrelations between changes in the short time scale of microdevelopment and the life-long scale of macrodevelopment, and the crucial effect of context. Learning and development are analyzed in and out of school, in the individual's activities and through social interaction, in relation to simple and complex problems, and in everyday behavior and novel tasks. With contributions from the foremost researchers in the field, *Microdevelopment* will be essential reading for all interested in cognitive and developmental science.

NIRA GRANOTT is an assistant professor at the School of Human Development, University of Texas at Dallas, and director of the Microdevelopmental Lab at the UT Dallas. She has worked as an educational software designer, producer of multimedia projects in educational television, and consultant for software design projects.

JIM PARZIALE is a part-time professor at the Graduate School of Education at the University of Massachusetts, Boston, and a classroom teacher and science resource teacher for Brookline Public Schools, Brookline, Massachusetts.

Cambridge Studies in Cognitive Perceptual Development

The aim of this series is to provide a scholarly forum for current theoretical and empirical issues in cognitive and perceptual development. As the new century begins, the field is no longer dominated by monolithic theories. Contemporary explanations build on the combined influences of biological, cultural, contextual and ecological factors in well-defined research domains. In the field of cognitive development, cultural and situational factors are widely recognized as influencing the emergence and forms of reasoning in children. In perceptual development, the field has moved beyond the opposition of "innate" and "acquired" to suggest a continuous role for perception in the acquisition of knowledge. These approaches and issues will all be reflected in the series which will also address such important research themes as the indissociable link between perception and action in the developing motor system, the relationship between perceptual and cognitive development to modern ideas on the development of the brain, the significance of developmental processes themselves, dynamic systems theory, and contemporary work in the psychodynamic tradition, especially as it relates to the foundations of self-knowledge.

Microdevelopment

Transition Processes in Development and Learning

edited by

Nira Granott and Jim Parziale

CAMBRIDGE
UNIVERSITY PRESS

PUBLISHED BY THE PRESS SYNDICATE OF THE UNIVERSITY OF CAMBRIDGE
The Pitt Building, Trumpington Street, Cambridge, United Kingdom

CAMBRIDGE UNIVERSITY PRESS
The Edinburgh Building, Cambridge CB2 2RU, UK
40 West 20th Street, New York, NY 10011-4211, USA
477 Williamstown Road, Port Melbourne, VIC 3207, Australia
Ruiz de Alarcón 13, 28014 Madrid, Spain
Dock House, The Waterfront, Cape Town 8001, South Africa

http://www.cambridge.org

First published 2002

Printed in the United Kingdom at the University Press, Cambridge

Typeface Plantin 10/12 pt.   *System* LATEX 2$_\varepsilon$ [TB]

A catalogue record for this book is available from the British Library

Library of Congress Cataloguing in Publication data
Microdevelopment: transition processes in development and learning / edited
by Nira Granott & Jim Parziale.
    p.   cm. – (Cambridge studies in cognitive perceptual development)
Includes bibliographical references and index.
ISBN 0 521 66053 X
1. Child psychology.   2. Developmental psychology.   3. Child development.
I. Granott, Nira, 1946– II. Parziale, Jim.   III. Series.
BF721.M533   2002
153.1′5 – dc21   2001043127

ISBN 0 521 66053 X hardback

Contents

v

Figures

Tables

Contributors

Martha Wagner Alibali, Department of Psychology, University of Wisconsin-Madison

Daniela Corbetta, Department of HKLS & Department of Psychological Sciences, Purdue University

Kurt W. Fischer, Harvard Graduate School of Education

Wendy S. Francis, Department of Psychology, University of Texas at El Paso, El Paso

Rochel Gelman, Psychology and Cognitive Science, Rutgers University

Susan Goldin-Meadow, Department of Psychology, University of Chicago

Nira Granott, School of Human Development, University of Texas at Dallas

Annette Karmiloff-Smith, Neurocognitive Development Unit, University College London

Deanna Kuhn, Teachers College, Columbia University

Kang Lee, Department of Psychology, Queen's University, Kingston

Marc D. Lewis, Department of Human Development and Applied Psychology, Ontario Institute for Studies in Education, University of Toronto

Jim Parziale, University of Massachusetts at Boston

Laura Romo University of California Los Angeles

Robert S. Siegler, Department of Psychology, Carnegie Mellon University

Esther Thelen, Department of Psychology, Indiana University

Paul van Geert, Department of Psychology, University of Groningen

Zheng Yan, Harvard Graduate School of Education

Microdevelopment: A process-oriented perspective for studying development and learning

Nira Granott and Jim Parziale

This book presents a new, process-oriented view of development and learning focusing on microdevelopment. Microdevelopment is the process of change in abilities, knowledge, and understanding during short time spans. The defining attributes of microdevelopment are embedded in its name. "Micro-" pertains to short time scales, periods ranging from months to just a few minutes. "Development" indicates the evolving nature of the process, the real-time (on-line) evolution of skills and abilities of development and learning. Studies of cognitive, motor, and emotional microdevelopment commonly focus on processes in which lower-level abilities are reorganized into higher-level ones (Werner, 1957). In this way abilities are examined as they are constructed and before they become automatic reactions (Vygotsky, 1978; Werner, 1957). The microdevelopmental perspective allows researchers to follow the evolution and modification of the functional models that people use (Inhelder et al., 1980). When observing microdevelopment, researchers examine processes within specific task contexts, while people solve problems, perform assignments, or make discoveries. They analyze the process of change, identify its attributes and patterns, and look for the processes that underlie quantitative and qualitative change (Miller & Coyle, 1999; Siegler, 1996). Researchers focus, then, on the "how" of development and learning, on giving explanations, which is the ultimate goal of science (Flavell, 1984).

As editors, we are grateful to all the authors who contributed to this book their outstanding and pioneering work on microdevelopment. We are honored by the opportunity to put together the first collected work in this new and developing area. We are also grateful for the diligent effort and support of Sarah Caro, Senior Commissioning Editor, Sophie Read, the superb copy-editing of Virginia Catmur, and to the Cambridge University Press production team for their splendid work in publishing this book.

Editing this book and writing the editorial chapter were supported by National Science Foundation (Grant SBR-9818959), Texas Higher Education Coordination Board TARP grant, Timberlawn Psychiatric Research Foundation grant, and University of Texas at Dallas to the first author, and University of Massachusetts at Boston to the second author.

1

State-oriented vs. process-oriented approaches

Although development and learning are evolving processes, their understanding has been based on comparing knowledge and abilities at different ages. In pre- and posttests or cross-sectional designs, researchers compare abilities at different time points. Even longitudinal studies only provide a series of snapshots taken at different points in time. Using these approaches, researchers can compare the product of change, but not its process (Miller & Coyle, 1999). These approaches make inferences about processes by comparing static states, which is similar to inferring motion from still pictures.

Comparisons of static states can indicate global developmental trends and provide an understanding of a person's abilities at specific ages. However, such comparisons leave a significant gap in understanding how change occurs (Siegler & Crowley, 1991). The gap is a necessary by-product of state-based methods, because change is inherently dynamic. It occurs throughout time, during a process, not at a point in time but *across* points in time (Granott, this volume).

With technological innovations that have made video technology accessible, simple, and inexpensive to use, researchers can easily document processes. Availability of computers and specialized software has also facilitated the analysis of videotaped data, as did the development of new analytic methods, such as those provided by the dynamic systems approach. These innovations have supported a natural evolution in psychology from analysis of *what* develops to analysis of *how* people learn and develop, and from general identification of structures that characterize developmental stages to analysis of processes of real-time activity within specific contexts.

As the different chapters in the book demonstrate, when using a process-oriented perspective, researchers explore how people learn, adapt to new circumstances and environments, change their behavior, discover new strategies, solve unfamiliar problems, create new understanding, and develop new abilities. Process-oriented researchers ask new questions and change research procedures. They look for innovative analytic methods and devise different prediction techniques. Microdevelopmental researchers are developing new theories that account for a wide variety of findings that have not been predicted nor explained by state-oriented theories. The changes in the study of development and learning are so substantial, that several researchers view process-oriented approaches as marking a paradigm shift in these areas (Granott, 1998a; Lee & Karmiloff-Smith, this volume; Thelen & Smith, 1994).

Microdevelopmental research provides educators and other practitioners with powerful tools that extend the understanding of learning practices and enrich assessment methods. Microdevelopmental research is especially promising for validating performance-based assessment in education, which has triggered much interest in the last few years (Baker, O'Neil, & Linn, 1993). Microdevelopment-based methods may prove to be more valid and informative than conventional methods of evaluation or standardized achievement tests. Better understanding of the process of change in school can help educators make classroom practices more effective and efficient. They can restructure approaches to support better learning, design empowering curricula, and create programs that stimulate development. To improve education, more needs to be known about how progress occurs during learning.

Development and learning

The study of microdevelopment unites the areas of development and learning. In the past, views about the relationship between development and learning have covered a wide range. Some approaches collapsed one into the other, viewing development as nothing but learning, or learning as nothing but development (Kuhn, 1995b). Other approaches considered development and learning as separate processes, substantially different from each other. For example, Piaget (1964) identifies development with a spontaneous process and learning with a process provoked by another person, a teacher or an experimenter. In this view, development was characterized by inventive construction, whereas learning by exogenous acquisitions and repeated responses, not structured or reorganized (Piaget, 1970). The extreme approach, which divides learning and development into two distinct processes, maintains that development is deep, fundamental, irreversible, and mostly internally controlled, whereas learning is superficial, simplistic, reversible, automatic, and externally driven (see, for example, review in Kuhn, 1995b; Halford, 1995; Zimmerman, 1995).

The degree of distinction between learning and development depends on the theoretical frameworks that define these processes. If every form of cognitive acquisition were defined as learning, development would have consisted only of a succession of learning situations (Piaget, 1970, p. 112). When behaviorism declined and other approaches, such as constructivist learning, emerged, researchers expected effective learning to create cognitive restructuring, internalization, and transfer. Recently the distinction between development and learning has been examined again with theories and models that make a wide range of claims (see the collected work in Kuhn, 1995a; Liben, 1987; Strauss, 1993).

Research on microdevelopment is based on tasks that traditionally have been related to development as well as learning. Researchers also use tools that apply to both development and learning and serve as "arching methodologies" (Granott, 1998b). Because these methodologies make it possible to compare processes in development and learning, it is not surprising that many of the findings of microdevelopment have highlighted the similarities between development and learning.

Similarities between development and learning

Studies of microdevelopment show that attributes of development are similar to those expected from learning processes and vice versa. On the one hand, development is like learning: it includes much variability and reversibility. New research on microdevelopment shows that variability is one of the most consistent attributes of developmental processes. Correspondingly, variability is a most prominent issue in this book and appears in each of its chapters (see below).

On the other hand, learning is similar to development. Studies of microdevelopment show learning processes with trend of growth (see, for example, the chapters of Gelman et al., Granott, and Parziale). Learning does not necessarily require external support from another person, but rather can evolve through self-scaffolding (Granott, Fischer, and Parziale, this volume) and an internal feedback loop between meta-level operators and strategies (Kuhn, this volume). Reversibility in learning processes is reinterpreted as a facet of progress. For example, Goldin-Meadow & Alibali (this volume) show that increased mismatch between information expressed in speech and gesture (which could have been presented as reversibility in matched information) is related to progress toward more correct understanding. Similarly, Siegler (1996, this volume) shows that use of less advanced strategies is part of a progress defined in terms of increasing frequency of more advanced strategies. Granott (this volume) shows that recurrent regressions and backward transitions (which could be seen as reversibility in knowledge during learning) have important developmental roles, serving as a major mechanism for creating progress. Granott (1998b) demonstrates that learning processes can have fundamental developmental attributes: a high growth rate, qualitative restructuring of knowledge, and shifts to higher levels of thinking that are neither guided nor supported by a more capable person. As Siegler (this volume) indicates, this is the generative attribute of learning.

Microdevelopment, then, refers to processes of change in both learning and development. Not all learning processes show microdevelopment, just as there may be plateau-like periods in development. Processes of "developing learning" or "developmental learning" (i.e., learning that has developmental attributes; see Granott, 1998b), as well as periods of progress in abilities in development, are periods of microdevelopment.

By analyzing microdevelopment, researchers gain increasing understanding of processes of change. Their findings shed light on the common attributes that underlie development and learning and can promote progress in both.

Studying microdevelopment: The microgenetic and dynamic systems approaches

Microdevelopment can be studied with different methods. We use the term "microdevelopment" to refer to a developmental phenomenon of changes in abilities across short time spans. This book focuses on two approaches for studying microdevelopment: the microgenetic and dynamic systems approaches.

Terminology: Microdevelopment, the microgenetic method, and dynamic systems approach

The terms "microdevelopment" and "microgenesis" have been used interchangeably. The term "microgenesis" was coined by Werner (1956) as referring to processes that unfold during a short time span (Flavell & Draguns, 1957). A year later, Flavell and Draguns reviewed studies based on this approach and used both the terms "microgenesis" and "microdevelopment." Since then, researchers have used either the term "microgenesis" (e.g., Brown, 1982; Kuhn, 1995c; Siegler & Crowley, 1991) or "microdevelopment" (e.g., Fischer, 1980; Karmiloff-Smith, 1979) or both (e.g., Metz, 1993). In this book, researchers use both terms to indicate development during short time spans.

However, we find that the modern use of the term "microgenesis" is somewhat ambiguous. During Werner's time, "genesis" was used to signify "development." For instance, Werner (1948, p. 38) discusses "genetic experiments," referring to experiments on development. Today, "genetic experiments" would be understood as experiments on genes, and the term "genetic" usually refers to phenomena related to the genes. By contrast, the term "microdevelopment" is more easily and intuitively understood as indicating a micro time scale of development.

Therefore, we suggest the use of the term "microdevelopment" for the developmental phenomenon.

On the other hand, we use the term "microgenetic method" to refer to a specific method for studying microdevelopment, as is currently well accepted in the literature (e.g., Kuhn, 1995c; Siegler, 1996; Siegler & Crowley, 1991).

The microgenetic method

The microgenetic method is defined by three main attributes (Siegler & Crowley, 1991). (1) It spans a period from the beginning of a process of change until a stable state. (2) The density of observations is high relative to the period of change. (3) Intensive trial-by-trial analysis focuses on inferring processes that triggered quantitative or qualitative change. Some studies are even based on continuous documentation, which captures an entire process of change (Granott, 1998c, this volume; Parziale, this volume). By making continuous or nearly continuous observations, researchers obtain data that can capture developmental transitions and give direct access to the actual process of change.

Dynamic systems approach

The other approach for studying microdevelopment is based on application of tools and concepts developed through mathematical analyses of dynamic and especially nonlinear systems: the dynamic systems approach. Thelen and Corbetta (this volume) suggest that dynamic systems theory is a metatheory that provides rationale for studying microdevelopment, which involves real, dynamic, process-based data. The dynamic systems approach offers powerful concepts that help in explaining the developmental process. For example, the concept of self-organization denotes processes in which existing components of a system are interrelated and assembled into new forms of organization (see the chapters by Granott; Lee & Karmiloff-Smith; Lewis; and Thelen & Corbetta). Emergence, another concept discussed in the dynamic systems literature, refers to system-induced creation of new structures out of existing structures. The concept of attractor – a stable state toward which the system tends to evolve – is very useful for describing developmental stages (Thelen & Smith, 1994) or the stability that a system approaches during microdevelopment (Lewis, this volume; Granott, Fischer, & Parziale, this volume).

As this book demonstrates, the combination of the microgenetic method and dynamic systems approach, when used for studying microdevelopment, makes an important contribution for understanding the nature of change in development and learning. Process-oriented research makes this contribution through a rich pool of diverse types of studies.

Types of microgenetic studies

Microgenetic studies vary along five dimensions. These dimensions are independent of each other and all of them appear in this book.

1. Natural vs. novel task Researchers can focus on a natural occurrence or familiar task that children or adults use in the normal course of development. Such are, for example, spontaneous mismatches between speech and gesture (Goldin-Meadow & Alibali, chapter 3). Other examples include infants' reaching and interlimb coordination (Thelen & Corbetta, chapter 2), interrelations between emotion and cognition (Lewis, chapter 7), and infants' crying (van Geert, chapter 12).

By contrast, a novel task is one that participants are unlikely to encounter in circumstances other than experimental settings. Examples of novel tasks in this book are infants' treadmill stepping (Thelen & Corbetta, chapter 2) and the wuggle study, in which participants were asked to explore unfamiliar robots (Granott, chapter 8). Another example is Karmiloff-Smith's (1981) experiment, in which children devised a notational system with directions for driving an ambulance to a hospital (see Lee & Karmiloff-Smith, chapter 9). Similarly, the evolution of Darwin's theory can be classified as a novel task, uncharacteristic of regular, everyday life (Fischer & Yan, chapter 11).

Natural and novel tasks are two opposite ends of a continuous dimension (Granott, 1993). Many tasks fall in between these extreme cases. For example, although a conservation task is contrived, children do encounter issues of conservation in everyday life. By the same token, the task of explaining the experimenter's reasoning is induced by experimental conditions (Siegler, chapter 1), but children do develop the ability to consider another person's way of thinking in the natural course of development. Similarly, tasks that are part of children's learning experiences at school may be planned by teachers or researchers (see Gelman, Romo, & Francis, chapter 10; Parziale, chapter 6), yet to various degrees they blend with other learning activities that have become part of children's everyday experience at school. Another example is children's reasoning about causality in relation to the features of a boat or a car (Kuhn, chapter 4), which is devised by a researcher, yet children may encounter other tasks that require similar reasoning when playing with some educational toys.

The last examples correspond to tasks that fall in between the extremes of natural or novel tasks. These tasks can be grouped into one or more categories if this dimension is treated as a categorical or ordinal scale. Alternatively, it can be treated as a continuum, with weights assigned to values between the two extremes of the dimension, much like the fuzzy-logic-based method suggested by van Geert (chapter 12).

2. Intensive and concentrated vs. routine or interspersed experience
Microgenetic studies vary along another dimension – the intensity and concentration of the targeted experience. Some studies focus on an intensive experience that is concentrated within a relatively short period of time. Some examples for such activities in this book are solving conservation problems (Siegler, chapter 1) or boat/race-car problems (Kuhn, chapter 4); treadmill stepping (Thelen & Corbetta, chapter 2); building bridges (Parziale, chapter 6); or exploring a robot (Granott, chapter 8). This type of study often promotes accelerated microdevelopment.

Other tasks correspond to more routine or interspersed experience. Such are, for example, the science-into-ESL activity (Gelman et al., chapter 10), theory development (Fischer & Yan, chapter 11), and, fortunately for parents, babies' crying (van Geert, chapter 12). Such activities often correspond to a slower rate of change.

Like the previous dimension, the intensity of experience can be a continuous dimension with tasks' intensities corresponding to various values along the dimension. For example, Goldin-Meadow & Alibali (chapter 3) report studies that differ on this dimension, varying from weekly experience over a period of weeks to a concentrated experience during one hour. Lewis (chapter 7) discusses emotional experiences that vary in their time scales from seconds (microdevelopment of emotional appraisal and action), through minutes, hours, or days (mesodevelopment related to moods), and to months and years (macrodevelopment of personality dispositions).

3. Individual vs. socio-interactive experience Some microgenetic studies focus on an individual and examine changes in the individual's behavior across time. In this book, infants' crying (van Geert, chapter 12), babies' reaching and stepping (Thelen & Corbetta, chapter 2), children's notational systems (Lee & Karmiloff-Smith, chapter 9), students' science-into-ESL learning (Gelman et al., chapter 10), and Darwin's theory development (Fischer & Yan, chapter 11) are examples for such studies.

Other studies focus on interactive processes. Interactive processes themselves comprise diverse types of interactions (Granott, 1993). Studies can include interactions among peers (as in Granott, chapter 8; Granott, Fischer, & Parziale, chapter 5; Kuhn, chapter 4; and Parziale, chapter 6). Other studies focus on interaction between a child and a more capable partner, such as an experimenter (as in Siegler's chapter) or teacher (as in Goldin-Meadow & Alibali's chapter).

This dimension can be treated as dichotomous categories (either individual or interactive), as an ordinal scale, or as a continuous dimension. In the latter two cases, the dimension can measure the degree of collaboration or the asymmetry of expertise (Granott, 1993).

4. Spontaneous vs. training or guided activity Another dimension on which microgenetic studies vary is a distinction between spontaneous, unconstrained activity and an activity that provides guidance or training. Spontaneous activities can evolve without a corrective feedback from another (e.g., gesturing while solving equations in Goldin-Meadow & Alibali's chapter; designing a notational system, reviewed in Lee & Karmiloff-Smith's chapter).

At the other end of the dimension, activities involve interaction that provides guidance or training. As Thelen & Corbetta (chapter 2) note, researchers can deliberately facilitate discoveries through coaching, training, practice, or scaffolding support. For example, Siegler (chapter 1) presents an activity in which the child gets feedback from the experimenter. By the same token, Gelman, Romo, and Francis (chapter 10) describe activities with teaching–learning interactions between the teacher and the students.

As in the previous dimensions, there are studies that map on values between these two extreme ends. For instance, during spontaneous activities, participants may receive feedback from the task materials, by observing how the latter change as a result of their own actions or by adjusting to changes in the materials. Such are the cases of the boat and race-car problems in Kuhn's chapter; treadmill stepping in Thelen & Corbetta's chapter; bridge building in Parziale's chapter; and robot exploration in Granott's chapter. Darwin's theory building (Fischer & Yan, chapter 11) may be considered in this category, as Darwin continually developed his theory by comparing its predictions or implications with ongoing observations. In a similar vein, spontaneous activities in real-life situations may involve varying degrees of feedback from the social environment, and sometimes no feedback at all. Such may be studies involving babies' crying (as in van Geert's chapter) or emotional development (Lewis, chapter 7).

The examples demonstrate that this dimension too can be treated either as categorical/ordinal or as a continuous dimension with varying degrees of feedback.

5. Natural vs. laboratory setting The fifth and last dimension for comparing microgenetic studies is the environment in which the data are collected. On the one hand, there are natural, familiar settings from the participants' everyday life. Such settings are used in Gelman et al.'s (chapter 10) and Parziale's (chapter 6) studies. Both of these studies take place within school, in the students' regular learning environments. On the other hand, many studies are performed in the laboratory. Most of the studies presented in the book fall under this category.

Unlike the previous dimensions, this one appears to be dichotomous. However, if studies simulate and blend aspects of the natural and laboratory settings, this dimension can become continuous too.

Advantages of studying microdevelopment

The study of microdevelopment makes an important contribution for understanding development, learning, and change. Its unique attributes manifest in the type of data collected, analyses performed, explanations offered, and implications inferred for both learning and development.

1. Data Dense data that are collected by using the microgenetic method have several benefits not obtained through state-oriented methods.

(i) Access to a process. Owing to dense sampling throughout a process of change, microgenetic data allow direct observations of processes. Microgenetic data give access to the process by documenting participants' actions (see the chapters by Thelen & Corbetta; Siegler), gestures (Goldin-Meadow & Alibali's chapter), vocalization (van Geert's chapter), conversations (the chapters by Granott; Granott, Fischer, & Parziale; Kuhn; Parziale), explanations to the experimenter (Goldin-Meadow & Alibali; Siegler), notes (Fischer & Yan; Gelman, Romo, & Francis), and concrete products (Parziale).

Microgenetic data are more detailed than data obtained through other methods (Siegler, this volume). These data provide access to the on-line process of learning and allow observations of people constructing new knowledge (Gelman et al., this volume; Kuhn, this volume). Such data make it possible to identify characteristic attributes, patterns, and mechanisms of change, which manifest in the *process* and cannot be detected in cross-sectional or conventional longitudinal data (Granott, this volume). Microgenetic data are a key factor for facilitating the analysis and identification of developmental transitions (Granott, Fischer, & Parziale, this volume). The opportunity to study the process of development and learning may be one of the potentially richest advantages of the microgenetic method (Kuhn, this volume). The method makes it possible to identify not only scattered structures, but processes of change that are dynamic, distributive, and self-constructive (Parziale, this volume).

(ii) Valid data. Microgenetic studies may provide more valid data than those obtained through traditional cross-sectional or longitudinal studies. The latter data may be misleading, since participants' behavior on subsequent encounters with a task may reveal different actions or ways of thinking from a first encounter (Kuhn, this volume). Moreover, measures taken at different points in time may correspond to different microdevelopmental sequences, related to somewhat different conditions (Granott, this volume). Comparison of such points, therefore, may not be valid.

(iii) Rich raw data. Microgenetic data are usually captured on videotape, and as such they provide rich, high-textured, raw data that can be analyzed in different ways. Such data lend themselves to analytic discovery. By observing the data, researchers may identify new interrelated variables they did not foresee or expect previously. The videotaped data yoke these variables to the time line and allow researchers to observe and analyze the way they change in relation to each other. By the same token, researchers can define new measures of previously identified variables, unveil new patterns in these variables, and discover related underlying transition mechanisms. In addition, as Siegler (this volume) indicates, such data are essential for modeling change. Microgenetic data therefore open many options for innovative findings.

2. Analysis Studies of microdevelopment also offer a powerful potential in the types of analyses they afford. In this respect too they have several benefits.

(i) Attributes of change. Microgenetic analyses can identify periods of developmental transitions. Researchers can examine change that involves a wide variety of tasks and age groups and identify similarities and dissimilarities in processes of change across tasks and ages (Siegler, chapter 1). As Siegler (1996) indicates, such analyses can reveal five attributes of change – its path (sequence of progress); rate (pace); breadth (generalization); variability (individual differences); and sources (causes). Behavior and change can be understood as patterns over time (Thelen & Corbetta, chapter 2), and analyses of microdevelopment indicate specific patterns of change (Granott, chapter 8).

(ii) Identifying processes. Analyses of microdevelopment can apply to processes that researchers are unlikely to identify by using other methods and time scales. Microgenetic analyses can reveal how instructional approaches exercise their effects and what strategies children develop

in response to instruction (Siegler, chapter 1). These analyses reveal not only what children know, but also how they get there (Goldin-Meadow & Alibali, chapter 3). Examination of the process indicates how people create structures that bridge toward higher levels of knowledge (Granott, Fischer, & Parziale, chapter 5). Researchers can identify how people construct meaning *about* knowing and how this meaning evolves (Kuhn, chapter 4). Researchers can also identify continuity and changes in ways of thinking, as processes create series of consecutive sequences, each evolving with microdevelopmental growth (Granott, chapter 8). As Parziale (chapter 6) notes, microgenetic analyses show the creative nature of knowledge construction and its spontaneous path. They indicate shifts in thinking that would not have been noticed with conventional methods.

(iii) Differentiation between processes. Process-oriented studies show that development is not monolithic, but rather consists of interweaving different paths. When analyzing microdevelopment, researchers can differentiate between evolution paths of various developmental variables. Every chapter in this book demonstrates this differentiation. Siegler distinguishes between different strategies that participants use to solve the same problems at different times, under similar or different conditions. Thelen and Corbetta differentiate between multiple behavioral dimensions and demonstrate this distinction in their analysis (e.g., infants' kicking, reaching, and stepping). They also indicate that differentiated locomotor patterns are assembled in relation to different contexts and task constraints. Goldin-Meadow and Alibali distinguish between two modalities through which participants express their knowledge – gesture and speech. Kuhn highlights the differentiation between the development of performance strategies and meta-level operators. Granott, Fischer, and Parziale make a distinction between current levels of thinking and target levels that function as a transition mechanism. They also differentiate between different aspects of an activity that can show different developmental levels. Parziale makes a distinction between three mechanisms that operate in microdevelopment: shifts of focus, distributed cognition, and bridging. Lewis distinguishes between mechanisms of intention, emotion, and action; and between time scales in cognitive and emotional processes. Granott makes a distinction between three types of variability that operate in microdevelopment – backward transitions, ordered fluctuations within a developmental range, and reiterations. Lee and Karmiloff-Smith distinguish between types of organizational processes within a system. Gelman, Romo, and Francis indicate that different measures can diverge, conflict, or disagree. They specify different aspects in learning paths – those related to understanding scientific ideas vs. the

command of language used when expressing those ideas. They also indicate a differentiation between learning paths of different students. Fischer and Yan distinguish between sources of prior knowledge and the ways they serve for bridging into new ideas in Darwin's theory construction. Van Geert builds on differentiation of abilities in contexts and funnels it into fuzzy-logic-based formulations. All these analyses demonstrate that different developmental indicators can have different developmental profiles. These analyses imply that lumping together developmental indicators without differentiating among them obscures the nature of development.

(iv) Patterns and interrelations between processes. While differentiating between evolution paths of developmental variables, process-oriented researchers also examine interrelations among these paths and their patterns. Siegler (chapter 1) indicates that strategic evolution generates a pattern of overlapping waves. This pattern appears in Kuhn's findings as well (chapter 4). Kuhn analyzes a feedback loop between meta-level operators and strategies. Goldin-Meadow and Alibali (chapter 3) report on a U-shape pattern of matched-mismatched-matched information conveyed in gesture versus speech. The initial matching is consistently incorrect, the subsequent matching is consistently correct, and the mismatch serves as a transition that is led by correct gesture-based information. Granott (chapter 8) demonstrates that microdevelopment consists of reiterative sequences that start with backward transition and then progress within a delimited range. Fischer and Yan (chapter 11) analyze scalloping patterns in microdevelopmental progress.

Specific paths in microdevelopment may be related to a global organization. Thelen and Corbetta (chapter 2) show that overall improvement in arm control consists of changing patterns, alternating between periods of one-handed and two-handed reaching. Patterns of specific developmental variables correspond to systemic response; their transitions reflect developmental milestones. Gelman et al. (chapter 10) indicate a somewhat similar relation between specific paths and systemic organization, stating that domain-relevant paths lead learners to knowledge construction that is consistent with the domain's structure.

Other researchers compare the different paths or patterns and highlight their interrelations or integration. Lee and Karmiloff-Smith (chapter 9) compare models of reorganization and self-organization and their corresponding shapes. Lewis (chapter 7) analyzes the interrelations between developmental scales and complementarities (probabilistic patterns of activation) among them. Parziale (chapter 6) specifies triangular interrelations between processes of shift of focus, distributed cognition, and bridging. Van Geert (chapter 12) integrates diverse abilities-in-contexts within one formula. Granott, Fischer, and Parziale (chapter 5) show how higher and lower levels are integrated within a shell created through specific formulations.

As Werner (1957) and Fischer (1980) suggested, differentiation and integration are complementing processes that serve the developmental process. The chapters of this book support this suggestion and highlight the many ways in which different developmental indicators are interrelated or integrated to create progress and change.

3. Explanations The process of building new knowledge can seem mysterious, and the study of microdevelopment has a great promise for unpacking some of that mystery (Fischer & Yan, this volume). When studying microdevelopment, researchers attempt to uncover the source of developmental processes. They try to find the underlying processes that give rise to change (Siegler, 1996) and the mechanisms that underlie developmental transitions (a theme that appears in all the book chapters). Thus, researchers simultaneously track changes in knowledge and in the strategies used to construct and modify that knowledge (Kuhn, chapter 4). Studies of microdevelopment, which investigate the kinds of hypotheses, language, and strategies children use across time, contribute to understanding concept development (Gelman et al., chapter 10). These studies can lead to detecting the different trajectories along which knowledge change occurs (Goldin-Meadow & Alibali, chapter 3). They open a window to understanding the interactionist nature of development (Lee & Karmiloff-Smith, chapter 9). Studies of microdevelopment can reveal the tight interactions between the state of the organism at a given point in time, previous times, and the conditions induced by the task, which create soft-assembly of new forms (Thelen & Corbetta, chapter 2). These studies illuminate the sources of variability in development and indicate when it reflects meaningful struggle to construct understanding of observed phenomena (Granott, chapter 8). They are useful for probing whether patterns are modifiable or resilient to changing environmental constraints (Thelen & Corbetta, chapter 2).

As Siegler (chapter 1) suggests, studies of microdevelopment are useful for addressing a wide variety of theoretical issues and for producing general theories. This book lays out several theories that explain development and learning in new ways (see the preview of the chapters below).

4. Implications Studies of microdevelopment have a wide application for a variety of concepts and theoretical perspectives (Miller & Coyle, 1999). Using this approach, researchers can identify when interventions may work and when teaching may become beneficial; they can provide more accurate predictions, and contribute to improved teaching.

(i) Predicting when teaching and intervention can be beneficial. Participants are ready to change when they lose stability (Thelen and Corbetta, chapter 2), show more variability in pretests (Siegler, chapter 1), and indicate mismatched information in gesture and speech (Goldin-Meadow & Alibali, chapter 3). Readiness to construct higher levels of knowledge manifests in bridging structures (Granott, Fischer, and Parziale, chapter 5) and may have a precursor of backward transition (Granott, chapter 8). At these times, participants are more likely to benefit from instruction (Goldin-Meadow & Alibali, chapter 3).

(ii) More accurate predictions. Microdevelopmental studies allow researchers to describe cognitive change more precisely (Siegler, chapter 1) and make more accurate predictions (Goldin-Meadow & Alibali, chapter 3; Thelen & Corbetta, chapter 2).

(iii) Improved teaching. When studying microdevelopment, researchers gain understanding of how instructional procedures work, which allows them to improve teaching in other contexts as well (Siegler, chapter 1).

Thus, studies of microdevelopment make an important contribution in the type of data they provide, analyses they make possible, theoretical explanations they suggest, and their academic and practical implications. In all these ways, they shed important light on the nature of learning and development. Studies of microdevelopment highlight specific attributes that characterize development and learning, and which cannot be easily studied in other ways. Four of these attributes serve as the main themes that organize the book.

The main themes of this book

This book addresses four main themes that are crucial for understanding development and learning: (1) The nature of variability in development and learning. (2) Mechanisms that create transitions to higher levels of knowledge in both processes. (3) Interrelations between changes in the short time scale of microdevelopment and the longer, life-long scale of macrodevelopment. (4) The crucial effect of context on microdevelopment. Almost all the chapters in the book address more than one theme and many address all four. In dividing the book into parts, we considered the issue that was most prominent in each chapter. However, the themes cut across chapters. Therefore, first we discuss the four main themes, building on the contribution of all the chapters.

Variability

One of the most consistent findings about microdevelopment is variability in behavior. As Miller and Coyle (1999) note, variability seems to be a general attribute that characterizes human behavior and not only a symptom of children in transitional states. Siegler (1996) shows variability across domains, across tasks within a domain, across items within a task, across presentations within an item, and even within a single presentation of a single item. Coyle & Bjorklund (1997) find variability in recall strategies when a mixture of strategies is used even within each trial. Many process-oriented researchers find much variability and suggest explanations for its occurrence (see review in Granott, this volume).

Siegler's wave theory explains change through variability. Siegler suggests that using more varied ways of thinking increases the opportunities to discover unknown aspects of a task, and his findings indicate that variability is the best predictor for development and effective learning (chapter 1). Thelen and Corbetta (chapter 2) maintain that variability is the harbinger of change – it is a manifestation of change itself. During periods of variability, the developing system can override previously obligatory patterns. Their analysis indicates that variability in coordination of different developmental dimensions is a result of pervasive systemic reorganization. Goldin-Meadow and Alibali (chapter 3) focus on concrete manifestation of variability in thinking, which is displayed in mismatches between knowledge conveyed in gesture and in speech. Goldin-Meadow and Alibali indicate that in these mismatches, learners articulate two ideas about the same problem. Both ideas are conveyed within a single response.

Variability reflects important developmental attributes, as several authors indicate. High intra-subject variation implies that qualitative developmental changes may be taking place (Lee & Karmiloff-Smith, chapter 9). Understanding development requires recognition of the enormous variability in the complexity of skill level in each individual (Fischer & Yan, chapter 11). Variability between a current skill level and a shell of a future level serves as a mechanism that creates developmental progress (Granott, Fischer, & Parziale, chapter 5). Variability appears in three interrelated processes that engender progress and change (Parziale, chapter 6). Different types of variability that operate in microdevelopment – backward transitions, ordered fluctuations, and reiterations – appear across and within sequences and explain the construction of knowledge in development and learning (Granott, chapter 8).

All the chapters of the book indicate substantial variability in process. Variability is prevalent in self-explanation strategies (Siegler, chapter 1), in infants' kicking, stepping, and reaching (Thelen and Corbetta, chapter 2), gesture–speech mismatches (Goldin-Meadow and Alibali, chapter 3), and in strategies and meta-operators (Kuhn, chapter 4). Variability appears in adults' and children's scientific reasoning (Granott,

Fischer, & Parziale, chapter 5) and in children's scientific products (Parziale, chapter 6). Prevalent variability appears in recurring patterns in cognitive and personality development (Lewis, chapter 7). Variability is treated fundamentally differently by traditional methods and when studying microdevelopment (Lee & Karmiloff-Smith, chapter 9). Variability appears in adults' collaborative problem solving (Granott, chapter 8), in children's learning curves (Gelman, Romo, & Francis, chapter 10), in Darwin's understanding of the principle of evolution through natural selection (Fischer & Yan, chapter 11), and in a person's attributes across conditions at a particular period (van Geert, chapter 12). All the analyses and theoretical arguments presented in this book attest to the importance and prevalence of variability in developmental and learning processes.

Transition mechanisms

One of the main goals of researchers who study microdevelopment is understanding *how* change occurs. Researchers attempt to uncover the mechanisms that underlie progress and change in development and learning and create transitions to higher levels. Kuhn (chapter 4) presents a transition mechanism through which people get from a current state to a goal state. The mechanism involves more than is observable in performance: it involves meta-level operators that select strategies, and manage and monitor strategy applications. Interconnections between the meta-level operators and the application of strategies stimulate progress and change. Granott, Fischer, and Parziale (chapter 5) propose a transition mechanism called "bridging." When using bridging, people operate on two levels: current, more established knowledge, and a still-vague target level. The target level creates a marker for the content of the missing knowledge and directs the activity toward discovering it. Parziale (chapter 6) suggests a mechanism operating through bi-directional relations between three microdevelopmental processes. Bridging provides target levels for development and coordinates structures into a more complex one. Shift of focus introduces sources of variability and fleshes out the target levels provided through bridging. Distributed cognition confirms shared ideas generated and elaborated through the other processes by off-loading them onto objects.

Other researchers too highlight important transition mechanisms and processes. Siegler suggests that development occurs through change in the distributions of ways of thinking and strategies (chapter 1). Siegler also proposes specific mechanisms through which explaining other people's reasoning operates: increased probability of trying to generate an explanation, deeper search for an explanation, increased accessibility of effective strategies, and increased engagement with the task. Thelen and Corbetta (chapter 2) analyze shifts and transitions in coordination and demonstrate the flexibility of behavior during these periods. They highlight the interrelation between these transitions and new developmental milestones. Goldin-Meadow and Alibali (chapter 3) indicate that gesture is an index of transitional knowledge. Their analysis demonstrates how instruction can create transitions, lead children to consider multiple strategies and then to integrate a new strategy. Lewis (chapter 7) proposes mechanisms by which developmental scales influence one another. Lewis identifies common mechanisms of intention, emotion, and action in personality and cognitive development and defines tensions between goals and obstacles as a transition mechanism that operates across domains and scales. Granott (chapter 8) proposes that similar mechanisms operate in micro- and macrodevelopment and analyzes different types of transition processes. Lee and Karmiloff-Smith (chapter 9) discuss and analyze mechanisms of re-organization and self-organization. Gelman, Romo, and Francis (chapter 10) study students' notes as an indication of their transitional knowledge states. They also use as their underlying assumption a mechanism according to which skeletal knowledge in a domain influences subsequent learning paths. Fischer and Yan (chapter 11) analyze the way the transition mechanism of bridging operates to create fundamental change in Darwin's theory construction. Van Geert (chapter 12) indicates that a forthcoming transition may be preceded or characterized by an increase in variability and demonstrates such a transition in the use of pronomina. Overall, the book presents a major contribution in understanding the nature and the specific operation of transition mechanisms in development and learning.

Relationships between micro- and macrodevelopment

The relationships between microdevelopment – development during short time spans – and macrodevelopment across the life span are one of the intriguing issues in the study of microdevelopment, yet an issue that is still puzzling. In this book, several researchers portray and specify these interrelations. Lewis (chapter 7) presents a groundbreaking theory that explains the way processes in micro-, meso-, and macrodevelopment are interrelated. Lewis uses a dynamic systems analysis to identify the principles of interscale relationships. He indicates how self-organization in movement to an attractor in real-time microdevelopment influences and is influenced by change and consolidation in macrodevelopment. Mesodevelopment funnels orderliness from microdevelopment and mediates its emergence in macrodevelopment. However, macrodevelopment also influences favored patterns in real-time microdevelopment. Granott (chapter 8) proposes a theory that explains how microdevelopment creates and is influenced by macrodevelopment. Granott specifies processes that create progress and change in microdevelopment. She also suggests that similar processes appear in macrodevelopment, with the same underlying mechanisms that operate on structures in both scales. The highest macrodevelopmental level sets an upper bound on microdevelopment, while during discoveries breakthroughs in microdevelopment expand this macrodevelopmental upper bound. Lee and Karmiloff-Smith (chapter 9) state that while the studies of micro- and macrodevelopment have some similar underlying assumptions, there are major differences between them. The differences manifest in research focus, the nature of the relations between the developmental and independent variable, the models researchers use for specifying these relations, and the way they treat measurement errors. Lee and Karmiloff-Smith also indicate the benefit of integrating both the micro- and macrodevelopmental approaches.

Other researchers in the book also discuss the link between micro- and macrodevelopment. Siegler (chapter 1) notes that findings on microdevelopment parallel findings of cross-sectional studies that compare different age groups. Thelen and Corbetta (chapter 2) indicate that the general principles underlying behavioral change work at multiple time scales. Kuhn (chapter 4) maintains that findings on microdevelopment are essential to understanding macrodevelopment. Granott, Fischer, and Parziale (chapter 5) suggest that bridging is a general transition mechanism that operates in microdevelopment as well as macrodevelopment. Fischer and Yan (chapter 11) maintain that when distinguishing between micro- and macrodevelopment, the time frame is less important than the processes involved. They suggest that macrodevelopment begins with changes that evolve in microdevelopment. What is added in macrodevelopment involves long-term changes in capacity and framework.

A substantial step is taken, then, in this book for proposing a conceptual framework that specifies the interrelations between micro- and macrodevelopment. This step is important for creating a link between more traditional studies and studies of microdevelopment. The step is also crucial for understanding the long-range effect of microdevelopment in its contribution for development and learning.

The effect of context

One of the major breakthroughs of the study of microdevelopment is in changing the status of context from a nonessential instantiation to a factor that has a major effect on the corresponding process. Studies of microdevelopment indicate that in different contexts, the developmental process may be substantially different. Studying processes of microdevelopment with a focus on context, therefore, may shed light on processes that may have substantial effects on development and learning.

Gelman, Romo, and Francis (chapter 10) highlight the importance of creating a science-based context for ESL learning. They maintain that understanding science requires acquisition of scientific language, with specialized terms and meanings. They indicate the multi-directional relations between acquiring scientific knowledge, understanding and recall of salient science-based features, and the use of scientific language. Gelman, Romo, and Francis provide a science-based context in which students make active use of notebooks to prepare graphs, record data and scientific vocabulary, make reviews, and ask questions. They analyze the students' learning curves, scientific understanding, and mastery of English grammar skills within the specific context.

Fischer and Yan (chapter 11) analyze the way Darwin bridged across substantially different contexts to construct his theory of evolution. Darwin's starting point was understanding variation in the social context. Darwin then used sophisticated ideas about biology and geology to create for himself microdevelopmental bridges for the new ideas about evolution. His knowledge about the death of deviant organisms and about breeding served as bridging shells for the new theory. Whether through successful explanations or productive mistakes, the construction of the new theory was based on a principle that tied together knowledge from different contexts. Van Geert highlights context as an integral part of personal properties. Van Geert indicates that what has been conventionally viewed as a confounding effect is intrinsic to meaning making and cannot be separated from abilities. Hypothetically, there is an infinite range of contexts and each affects the measured abilities in a particular way. For example, when solving a problem with an adult's help, the child shows different abilities from when trying to solve the problem independently. Instead of attempting to identify a "true" score, Van Geert proposes a context-based scheme for analyzing abilities. According to this scheme, abilities are defined across contexts by considering how characteristic each context is for a given person.

The importance of context is discussed in other chapters too. Siegler (chapter 1) analyzes the effect of different task contexts on children's understanding. Asking children to explain the reasoning of an experimenter triggers higher-level explanations than asking children to explain their own reasoning and giving them feedback on their answers. By the same token, asking children to explain both correct reasoning and why wrong explanations are incorrect triggers better learning than just explaining correct reasoning. Thelen and Corbetta (chapter 2) claim that differences in the task have a profound effect on performance. When a system is especially susceptible to change, different environmental conditions can engender particularly adaptive or maladaptive choices. Thelen and Corbetta describe findings that show different performances across different contexts and indicate that specific environmental interventions can facilitate the discovery of new patterns. Goldin-Meadow and Alibali (chapter 3) underscore the facilitating effect that teachers' matching gestures have on children's understanding. Kuhn (chapter 4) analyzes the strengthening effect of collaborative context on meta-level knowledge. Granott, Fischer, and Parziale (chapter 5) highlight the importance of analyzing activities within their social and environmental context and specify the way such an analysis can detect transitional knowledge in learning and development. Parziale (chapter 6) underscores the importance of the task context (its specific materials) in carrying part of the cognitive load and coordinating ideas. Lewis (chapter 7) indicates that the dynamic systems approach can take into account the effect of context, as in environmental continuity vs. discontinuity. Granott (chapter 8) suggests that microdevelopmental sequences are context-specific. Granott demonstrates that when the task context changes, a microdevelopmental sequence stops and another starts, creating backward transition to lower levels. The extent of backward transition and the subsequent progress depend on the social and task contexts. Lee and Karmiloff-Smith (chapter 9) propose that any particular developmental pattern is affected by the ever-changing environments of the child.

Although the chapters cover different time-ranges of microdevelopment, age groups, domains, tasks, procedures, and methods of analysis, they paint a similar picture in which the context has an intrinsic effect on abilities in microdevelopment. Findings on variability, transition mechanisms, interrelations between processes operating at different time scales, and context specificity all shed a new light on the nature of processes. They make a major contribution for understanding development and learning.

Preview of chapters

In chapter 1, Siegler describes the overlapping wave theory, according to which development proceeds as a series of overlapping waves. Each wave corresponds to a different way of thinking. Change, which is puzzling when viewed as sudden, discontinuous stage shifts, becomes intuitively understood when explained as orderly, gradual, and continual change, emanating from changes in weights (percentage distribution) of different ways of thinking across time. Siegler examines the effects of instructional approaches and how they encourage generating self-explanations (explanation to oneself). Specifically, Siegler asks children to explain the experimenter's reasoning ("how do you think I knew that?"). This task combines the effectiveness of a didactic approach with the motivation created by a discovery-oriented approach. Siegler also examines the effect of explaining both correct and incorrect reasoning. Siegler's findings illuminate the attributes of successful learning, indicate the predictive function of variability in learning and development, and offer an effective way of examining the outcomes of interventions.

In chapter 2, Thelen and Corbetta suggest that changes of patterns in infants' spontaneous kicking are not hard-wired, but rather self-assemble through interaction between the organism current state, past history, and the specific task constraints. Fluctuations in a specific developmental dimension reflect the system's organization in response to newly developing behaviors. Thelen and Corbetta demonstrate these principles in analyses of the emergence of early motor skills in infancy. They show that infants discover and switch patterns of kicking or stepping coordination in response to environmental interventions, such as tying a ribbon attached to a mobile around one ankle, or being supported on a treadmill. They demonstrate that changes in interlimb coordination often match (and may be affected by) the development of new postural milestones. Their findings lead to an innovative explanation of development based on the interrelations of multiple behavioral and contextual dimensions.

In chapter 3, Goldin-Meadow and Alibali examine longer- and shorter-term microdevelopmental changes in understanding, based on mismatches between information expressed in gesture and in speech. Mismatches reflect transitional knowledge, activate two ideas on the same problem, and give access to participants' implicit knowledge. Goldin-Meadow and Alibali highlight an important developmental trajectory, starting from matching, consistent, and incorrect responses, continuing with a transitional state of gesture–speech mismatch, and leading to matching, correct responses. They show that without instruction on a task, behavior tends to become less variable. By contrast, instruction introduces a new strategy, leads children to consider multiple options and then to abandon old, incorrect strategies. Goldin-Meadow and Alibali explore the effect of mismatches on teaching, on information exchanged between the teacher and the student, and on the role of gesture, particularly in communication about wrong strategies.

Kuhn (chapter 4) analyzes phases in performance and the corresponding processes in meta-level operators. The meta-level operators are developmental mechanisms that function in relation to understanding the task goals and how to get there. Kuhn analyzes a feedback loop between performance and the meta-level. Meta-knowledge mediates, supervises, and evaluates performance, and is also modified by it. Kuhn suggests that meta-operators lead development, because sometimes the improvement in the meta-level exceeds improvement in performance, whereas performance does not exceed the meta-operation. Kuhn's explanation of meta-level operators and their interrelation with performance helps in the understanding of how learning and development occur. It is especially revealing in studying collaborative learning and analyzing the differences between unsuccessful, successful, and super-successful pairs who work collaboratively.

Granott, Fischer, and Parziale (chapter 5) present a new transition mechanism, called "bridging," that generates progress in development and learning. In bridging people create partially defined shells for future skills at higher knowledge levels. They operate simultaneously on two levels: a lower level of existing knowledge and a higher target level of still undefined knowledge. Bridging shells provide scaffolds that guide the construction of new knowledge by outlining an advanced perspective for processing new experiences. Granott, Fischer, and Parziale suggest that bridging occurs within individuals as well as between people in social interaction. Their analysis details the way a dynamical system's attractor functions from its initial emergence in real-time activities in context and until the formulation of well-established structures. Examples from children's and adults' activities demonstrate several forms of bridging, in which shells set tentative targets for development and learning through the use of terms, sentence format, questions, intentions, and reformulation (recast).

Parziale (chapter 6) suggests three types of developmental mechanisms that operate, with alternating emphasis, to create change during learning. The mechanisms involve bridging, in which incomplete ideas operate as target levels for learning; shifts of focus, in which attention switches from one aspect of a task to another; and distributed cognition, in which physical attributes of a current configuration of the task materials carry part of the cognitive process. Parziale analyzes students' science activity in the classroom, in which pairs of students collaborate to solve a construction design problem. Parziale shows how new design ideas emerge, are elaborated, and are tested through the interaction between these three mechanisms. He demonstrates that the physical structures that children build in their design solutions imply knowledge at a higher level than they actually express in their speech. Parziale's analysis offers a more sensitive method for evaluating the effectiveness of learning at school than the current prevailing methods.

Lewis (chapter 7) proposes an innovative interscale theory that explains personality and cognitive development. Lewis suggests that processes occurring at different time scales (micro-, meso-, and macrodevelopment) influence one another. Self-organization in microdevelopment creates connections among elements that have acquired complementarities in macrodevelopment. These connections replace competing organizations on other time scales. Interscale relations are bi-directional. Large-scale patterns emerge from lower-order elements, but also shape patterns at shorter-term scales, creating cascading constraints on developmental outcomes. Lewis explains that common mechanisms define parallel processes in personality and cognitive development. He shows how tensions between goals and actions operate as a fundamental mechanism of emergence on different scales in both personality and cognitive development. Lewis' theory is groundbreaking in explaining development through interrelations among different scales in a way that encompasses two major psychological domains.

Granott (chapter 8) proposes a theory that relates micro- and macrodevelopment by explaining development as a series of reiterated microdevelopmental sequences. Even slight changes in the problem parameters, which alter the problem context, can stimulate a new sequence. Granott suggests several types of variability that operate across and within sequences to create development: (1) Backward transition (BT), where regression appears either when participants initiate a new sequence (initial BT), or within a progressive process (intermediate BT), or after leaps forward (posterior BT); (2) fluctuations within a developmental zone, which Granott labels a "Zone of Current Development"; (3) reiterations, appearing within and across sequences and within and across people. Granott indicates the developmental functions of these types of variability. A study on collaborative explorations of robots demonstrates the theory and the developmental functions of variability.

Lee and Karmiloff-Smith (chapter 9) make a systematic comparison between the study of macrodevelopment, which uses traditional research methods, and that of microdevelopment, which uses the microgenetic and the dynamical systems approaches. Lee and Karmiloff-Smith indicate fundamental differences among these approaches not only in data collection, but also in fundamental assumptions, research strategies, methods, and methodological constraints derived from the assumptions and the research strategies. They also show each approach's benefits for explaining developmental change. Lee and Karmiloff-Smith view the approaches as complementing and make suggestions about sequencing them in research designs. They analyze three types of change that occur during development: (1) cumulative; (2) re-organizational, which follows a qualitative change in at least one independent variable; and (3) self-organizational change, when qualitative change emerges in the developmental (dependent) variable.

Gelman, Romo, and Francis (chapter 10) build on the idea that existing (even skeletal) knowledge structures of a domain lead learners to domain-relevant learning paths, and they explore it by testing learning paths of novice learners. Novice learners have to develop domain-relevant structures as well as content and therefore may move onto wrong learning paths. Gelman, Romo, and Francis employ the microgenetic method to analyze the learning paths of ninth-grade students (around fifteen years of age) in a project that integrates science instruction with ESL. They use the students' notebooks as windows through which they probe the students' transitional states of knowledge and "on-line" learning. Gelman, Romo, and Francis examine the students' conceptual knowledge and learning curves, showing improvement in understanding scientific concepts and in using complex causal formulations. Their findings of the acquisition of scientific knowledge, English grammar skills, and the interrelations among conceptual and language variables indicate the multi-faceted nature of knowledge acquisition.

Fischer and Yan (chapter 11) examine microdevelopment within a longer-term process of theory construction. They focus on one of the major conceptual revolutions of the last centuries – Darwin's theory of evolution by natural selection, which was documented in detail in Darwin's notebooks. Fischer and Yan highlight the lengthy microdevelopment of component skills, which involves combining, differentiating, reorganizing, and generalizing specific skills in particular tasks and contexts. The microdevelopmental components still need to undergo longer-term cognitive reorganization. Fischer and Yan indicate the variability in microdevelopment between an upper limit of optimal level in high-support contexts, and lower functional levels in less supportive contexts, and show this variability in Darwin's thinking. Their analysis illuminates how new knowledge is constructed, showing how Darwin used cross-contextual concepts, such as concepts from geology, and previously discovered components, like the theory of coral reefs, as bridging shells to bootstrap his understanding of the evolution of living organisms.

Van Geert (chapter 12) proposes a theoretical framework and method for defining a person's attributes or skills in all possible contexts. His proposal transforms theoretical definitions of abilities as well as views about the nature of psychological measurement, and offers an innovative approach for analyzing variability in microdevelopment. Van Geert maintains that variability in a person's psychological abilities is not due to the medium of measurement, but to the contexts in which these properties manifest. A person's attributes have a range of possible scores that cannot be meaningfully reduced to a single representative one. Instead, scores in the possible range differ in their degree of characteristicness for the person and are related to the corresponding contexts in which they may appear. Scores become, then, a continuous-set membership function. By using fuzzy logic, these scores can be formulated by attributing a certain weight to each score. The power of the method is in its ability to formalize natural statements and quantify linguistic qualifiers such as "highly," "likely," "fairly good," "relatively rare," and so forth.

Together all these chapters present an innovative approach for studying processes that underlie development and learning. The book highlights the similarities between these processes, illuminates their nature in a new light, and suggests explanations for how progress occurs during the construction of new knowledge. The book also raises questions that outline directions for further research, in a continuing effort to explain how change occurs in development and learning.

References

Baker, E. L., O'Neil, H. F., & Linn, R. L. (1993). Policy and validity prospects for performance-based assessment. *American Psychologist, 48(12)*, 1210–1218.

Brown, A. L. (1982). Learning and development: The problem of compatibility, access, and induction. *Human Development, 25*, 89–115.

Coyle, T. R., & Bjorklund, D. F. (1997). Age differences in, and consequences of, multiple- and variable-strategy use on a multitrial sort-recall task. *Developmental Psychology, 33*, 372–380.

Fischer, K. W. (1980). A theory of cognitive development: The control and construction of hierarchies of skills. *Psychological Review, 87*, 477–531.

Fischer, K. W., & Yan, Z. (this volume). Darwin's construction of the theory of evolution: Microdevelopment of explanations of variation and change in species.

Flavell, J. H. (1984). Discussion. In R. J. Sternberg (Ed.), *Mechanisms of cognitive development* (pp. 187–209). New York: Freeman.

Flavell, J. H., & Draguns, J. (1957). A microgenetic approach to perception and thought. *Psychological Bulletin, 54(3)*, 197–217.

Gelman, R., Romo, L., & Francis, W. S. (this volume). Notebooks as windows on learning: The case of a science-into-ESL program.

Goldin-Meadow, S., & Alibali, M. W. (this volume). Looking at the hands through time: A microgenetic perspective on learning and instruction.

Granott, N. (1993). Patterns of interaction in the co-construction of knowledge: Separate minds, joint effort, and weird creatures. In R. Wozniak & K. W. Fischer (Eds.), *Development in context: Acting and thinking in specific environments* (pp. 183–207). Hillsdale, NJ: Erlbaum.

Granott, N. (1998a). A paradigm shift in the study of development. *Human Development, 41(5–6)*, 360–365.

Granott, N. (1998b). We learn, therefore we develop: Learning versus development – or developing learning? In C. Smith & T. Pourchot (Eds.), *Adult learning and development: Perspectives from educational psychology* (pp. 15–34). Mahwah, NJ: Erlbaum.

Granott, N. (1998c). Unit of analysis in transit: From the individual's knowledge to the ensemble process. *Mind, Culture, and Activity: An International Journal, 5(1)*, 42–66.

Granott, N. (this volume). How microdevelopment creates macrodevelopment: Reiterated sequences, backward transitions, and the Zone of Current Development.

Granott, N., Fischer, K. W., & Parziale, J. (this volume). Bridging to the unknown: A transition mechanism in learning and development.

Halford, G. S. (1995). Learning processes in cognitive development: A reassessment with some unexpected implications. *Human Development, 38*, 295–301.

Inhelder, B., Blanchet, A., Boder, A., de Caprona, D., Saada-Robert, M., & Ackermann-Valladao, E. (1980). Procédures et significations dans la résolution d'un problème concret. *Bulletin de Psychologie, 33(345)*, 645–648.

Karmiloff-Smith, A. (1979). Micro and macrodevelopmental changes in language acquisition and other representational systems. *Cognitive Science, 3*, 91–118.

Karmiloff-Smith, A. (1981). Getting developmental differences or studying child development? *Cognition, 10*, 151–158.

Kuhn, D. (Ed.). (1995a). Development and learning: Reconceptualizing the intersection [Special issue]. *Human Development, 38(2)*.

Kuhn, D. (1995b). Introduction. *Human Development, 38*, 293–294.

Kuhn, D. (1995c). Microgenetic study of change: What has it told us? *Psychological Science 6(3)*, 133–139.

Kuhn, D. (this volume). A multi-component system that constructs knowledge: Insights from microgenetic study.

Lee, K., & Karmiloff-Smith, A. (this volume). Macro- and microdevelopmental research: Assumptions, research strategies, constraints, and utilities.

Lewis, M. D. (this volume). Interacting time scales in personality (and cognitive) development: Intentions, emotions, and emergent forms.

Liben, L. S. (Ed.). (1987). *Development and learning: Conflict or congruence?* Hillsdale, NJ: Erlbaum.

Metz, K. E. (1993). Preschoolers' developing knowledge of the pan balance: From new representation to transformed problem solving. *Cognition and Instruction, 11(1)*, 31–93.

Miller, P. H., & Coyle, T. R. (1999). Developmental change: Lessons from microgenesis. In E. K. Scholnick, K. Nelson, S. A. Gelman, & P. H. Miller (Eds.), *Conceptual development: Piaget's legacy* (pp. 209–239). Mahway, NJ: Erlbaum.

Parziale, J. (this volume). Observing the dynamics of construction: Children building bridges and new ideas.

Piaget, J. (1964). Development and learning. In R. Ripple & V. Rockcastle (Eds.), *Piaget rediscovered* (pp. 7–19). Ithaca: Cornell University Press.

Piaget, J. (1970). Piaget's theory. In P. H. Musssen (Ed.), *Carmichael's manual of child psychology* (pp. 103–128). New York: Wiley.

Siegler, R. S. (1996). *Emerging minds: The process of change in children's thinking.* New York: Oxford University Press.

Siegler, R. S. (this volume). Microgenetic studies of self-explanation.

Siegler, R. S., & Crowley, K. (1991). The microgenetic method: A direct means for studying cognitive development. *American Psychologist, 46,* 606–620.

Strauss, S. (1993). Theories of learning and development for academics and educators [Special issue]. *Educational Psychologist, 28(3),* 191–203.

Thelen, E., & Corbetta, D. (this volume). Microdevelopment and dynamic systems: Applications to infant motor development.

Thelen, E., & Smith, L. B. (1994). *A dynamic systems approach to the development of cognition and action.* Cambridge, MA: MIT Press.

van Geert, P. (this volume). Developmental dynamics, intentional action, and fuzzy sets.

Vygotsky, L. S. (1978). *Mind in society: The development of higher psychological processes.* Cambridge, MA: Harvard University Press.

Werner, H. (1948). *Comparative psychology of mental development.* New York: International Universities Press.

Werner, H. (1956). Microgenesis and aphasia. *Journal of Abnormal and Social Psychology, 52,* 347–353.

Werner, H. (1957). The concept of development from a comparative and organismic point of view. In D. B. Harris (Ed.), *The concept of development: An issue in the study of human behavior* (pp. 125–148). Minneapolis: University of Minnesota Press.

Zimmerman, B. J. (1995). Attaining reciprocality between learning and development through self-regulation. *Human Development, 38,* 367–372.

Part I

Variability

1　Microgenetic studies of self-explanation

Robert S. Siegler

Microgenetic methods are useful for many purposes. They can yield more precise descriptions of cognitive change than would otherwise be possible, can reveal both similarities and dissimilarities in change processes across tasks and age groups, and can provide the type of detailed data that are essential for constructing formal models of cognitive change. Further, as is amply demonstrated in this volume, they are useful for examining change involving a wide variety of tasks and age groups and for addressing a wide variety of theoretical issues.

In the present chapter, I pursue two main goals, one quite general and one relatively specific. The more general goal is to describe a theory of cognitive change – the overlapping waves approach – that has arisen from my own and other investigators' microgenetic studies. The more specific goal is to illustrate a use to which the microgenetic method is just beginning to be put, but one that it can serve very effectively: Helping us understand how instructional approaches exercise their effects. The particular instructional approach used to illustrate this function is encouragement to generate self-explanations, that is, encouragement to explain how or why events occurred. I first describe the general theory, then the specific application.

Overlapping waves theory

Implicit metaphors shape our thinking about many topics. A common implicit metaphor underlying traditional views of cognitive development was made explicit by the title of Robbie Case's (1992) book *The mind's staircase*. As shown in figure 1.1, the staircase metaphor suggests that children think in a given way for an extended period of time (a tread on the staircase); then their thinking undergoes a sudden upward shift

Robert Siegler gratefully acknowledges the help of a grant from the Spencer Foundation and a grant from the National Institutes of Health (HD 19011) for supporting the research on which this chapter is based.

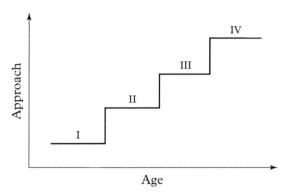

Figure 1.1 The staircase model.

(a riser on the staircase); then they think in a different, "higher" way for another extended period (the next tread); and so on.

Although this depiction of development is most closely associated with the Piagetian and neo-Piagetian traditions, it also underlies many other approaches to development. For example, theory-theory approaches rest on a similar metaphor. Two-year-olds are said to have a desire theory of mind, whereas three-year-olds are said to have a belief-desire theory of mind; five-year-olds are said to have a psychological theory of biology until around age ten when they generate a truly biological theory; and so on (Carey, 1985; Wellman & Gelman, 1998). Information processing descriptions also often reflect the staircase metaphor. Thus, five-year-olds are said to solve simple addition problems by counting from one, seven-year-olds by counting from the larger addend, and nine-year-olds by retrieving the answer from memory (Ashcraft, 1987).

Most staircase depictions have been based on data aggregated across many children and many trials. They describe the main trend in the data. Microgenetic analyses, in which strategy use is assessed on a trial-by-trial basis, have allowed finer-grained examination of the change process. The results yielded by such trial-by-trial assessments of changing competence have been both consistent and surprising. Regardless of whether the tasks have involved problem solving, reasoning, language, memory, attention, or motor activity, and regardless of whether the children have been infants, toddlers, preschoolers, elementary schoolers, or adolescents, children use a variety of strategies (Adolph, 1997; Alibali & Goldin-Meadow, 1993; Coyle & Bjorklund, 1997; Granott, 1998; Kuhn, Garcia-Mila, Zohar, & Andersen, 1995; Miller & Aloise-Young, 1996; Schauble, 1996; Thelen & Ulrich, 1991; Thornton, 1999). Older, less advanced strategies continue to be used long after newer, more advanced strategies have been discovered.

The variability also is present at every level of analysis, as can be seen through microgenetic studies of strategic development. It is present at the level of individuals as well as groups. Individual children have been found to use at least three strategies in such varied domains as arithmetic, spelling, scientific experimentation, and recall of previously presented information (Siegler, 1996). Variable strategy use also exists within a child solving a single problem on two occasions, close in time. Presented with a single addition problem, or a single analog clock time on two successive days, roughly one-third of children used a different strategy on the second day from the first (Siegler & McGilly, 1989; Siegler & Shrager, 1984). Variable strategy use is even evident within a single trial. A single presentation of a problem can elicit one strategy in speech and a different one in gesture (Alibali & Goldin-Meadow, 1993).

The fact that children use a variety of strategies over prolonged periods of time does not mean that strategy choices are random or that strategic development is directionless. Even infants and toddlers choose quite adaptively among strategies (Adolph, 1997; Chen & Siegler, 2000). For example, from the beginning of their experience with ramps, toddlers adjust their descent strategies to the steepness of the ramp. They use quicker but riskier strategies on the shallower ramps and slower but surer strategies on the steeper ones. With age and experience, their and older children's strategy choices become even more adaptive. Thus, toddlers' descent strategies become increasingly finely calibrated to the ramp's angle (Adolph, 1997).

Such findings indicate that the overlapping waves depiction, shown in figure 1.2, may be a more useful way of thinking about strategic development than the staircase metaphor. Within the overlapping waves depiction, children typically know and use a variety of strategies at any one time. With age and experience, the relative frequency of each strategy changes, with some strategies becoming less frequent (Strategy 1), some becoming more frequent (Strategy 5), some becoming more frequent and then less frequent (Strategy 2), and some never becoming very frequent (Strategy 3). In addition to changes in relative frequencies of existing strategies, new strategies are discovered (Strategies 3 and 5), and some older strategies cease to be used (Strategy 1).

At times, all or almost all of these changing patterns of strategy use are evident within a single study. Consider a study of number conservation (Siegler, 1995) in which five-year-olds were given a pretest and four training sessions. During the training sessions, children needed to

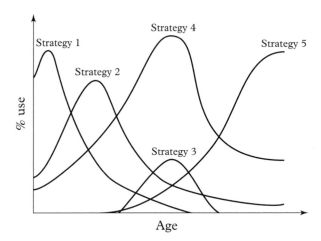

Figure 1.2 The overlapping waves model.

explain the logic underlying the experimenter's answer on each trial. As shown in figure 1.3, over the course of the experiment, reliance on the relative lengths of the two rows of objects decreased, reliance on the type of transformation that had been performed increased, reliance on counting and on the observation that the experimenter just moved the objects back and forth stayed at a constant low level throughout the experiment, and answering "I don't know" first increased and then decreased.

These descriptions of strategic change fit adults as well as children. Adults also use multiple strategies over prolonged periods of time; they continue to use earlier-formulated strategies, even after superior alternatives are available; and they choose adaptively among the strategies. Such findings have emerged in individual problem solving (Perry & Elder, 1999), collaborative problem solving (Granott, 1993), single-digit arithmetic (LeFevre, Bisanz, & Sadesky, 1996), spatial reasoning (Marquer & Pereira, 1990), and other domains. Also, as with children, adults' new strategies often involve recombination of subprocedures from previous ones (Anzai & Simon, 1979).

Thus, as Granott (1998) has emphasized, findings from microgenetic studies suggest that the traditional distinction between learning and development is, at minimum, overstated. Both children's learning and adults' learning in such studies display characteristics that are supposed to be on the developmental side of the dichotomy: Knowledge moves consistently from less to more advanced, rather than oscillating aimlessly; knowledge often is reorganized, rather than shifting in superficial ways; and learning is generative, in the sense that early advances form the foundation

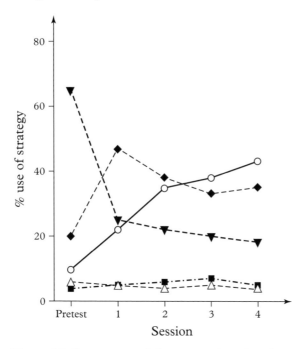

Figure 1.3 Percent use of five types of explanations on the number conservation task. ─○─, Type of transformation; --▼--, Length; ----△----, Counting; ---■---, Back and forth; --◆--, Don't know.

for later ones. The findings that emerge from microgenetic studies also parallel those that arise from detailed cross-sectional studies of different age groups. Both types of studies reveal prolonged variability of strategy use, both within and between subjects, and increasingly adaptive choices among strategies as subjects gain experience in the domain. Thus, despite differences in the time spans of the changes, developmental and microgenetic change seem to be more similar than different.

The overlapping waves approach to strategic development has several advantages over staircase approaches. Most obviously, it fits the data better. Studies that have examined strategy use on a trial-by-trial basis have consistently revealed substantial variability. Older strategies continue to be used long after more advanced, newer strategies are also available. As illustrated in figure 1.3, this is true even when the tasks are ones that have been viewed as classic illustrations of staircase approaches, such as number conservation. Relying on the type of transformation yields consistently correct performance, relying on length does not, yet children continue to rely on length even after they are also relying on the type of transformation. The overlapping waves approach also better captures the dynamic, continually changing character of development and focuses attention on discovery of new approaches as well as on choices among existing ones. Yet another advantage of microgenetic approaches is just beginning to be appreciated: It can help us understand how instructional approaches exercise their effects. The remainder of this chapter focuses on this application of microgenetic methods.

Analyzing instructional manipulations

Designing effective instructional procedures is a major challenge. Even after effective procedures have been designed, however, an equally large challenge remains: To understand how the procedures exercise their effects. Gaining such understanding is crucial to being able to improve the instructional techniques further and to utilizing them successfully in contexts other than the ones in which they were formulated.

Microgenetic methods have the potential to play a large role in addressing this problem. Examining the way that children learn under various instructional procedures, contrasting the characteristics of more and less successful learners, and identifying where learning goes awry when it goes awry – all can contribute to improving instructional procedures. Such analyses also can help us better understand learning and development. Once children enter school, much of the most important cognitive development occurs in the context of instruction. Understanding the types of instruction that benefit children of different ages, and understanding why older children often learn more effectively than younger ones, can deepen our theories regarding this crucial aspect of development.

A particular advantage of microgenetic studies for understanding how instruction exercises its effects lies in its ability to reveal the strategies that children develop in response to the instruction. Often, there are a variety of correct strategies for approaching a class of problems and a variety of incorrect strategies as well. Both classes of strategies vary in the range of problems to which they can be applied, in their ease of execution, and in the conceptual underpinnings needed to understand their functioning. As will be seen, children who are presented with the same instructional procedure often construct quite different strategies. Microgenetic studies can help us understand how and why this occurs.

The particular instructional approach that my colleagues and I have examined through microgenetic studies is encouragement to generate self-explanations. We next examine why encouraging children to generate such explanations is a potentially valuable instructional approach, and what is known about its effectiveness.

Background on self-explanations

Self-explanations are inferences about causal connections among objects and events. The inferences can concern how procedures cause their effects, how structural aspects of a system influence its functioning, how people's reasoning leads to their conclusions, how characters' motivations within a story lead to their behavior, and so on. In short, they are inferences concerning "how" and "why" events happen.

Ability to infer such causal connections is present from very early in life. Infants in their first year sometimes infer connections between physical causes and their effects (Leslie, 1982; Oakes & Cohen, 1995). Infants and toddlers also remember events that reflect a coherent causal sequence better than ones in which the causality is unclear (Bauer & Mandler, 1989). Thus, ability to explain the causes of events seems to be a basic property of human beings and influences many aspects of cognition including memory, problem solving, and conceptual understanding.

Although very young children can generate causal connections, even older children and adults often fail to do so. This poses a particular problem in math and science instruction. Math and science teachers frequently lament the fact that their students can execute procedures but have no idea why the procedures work. Such situations reflect failures of self-explanation. The problem can be illustrated in the context of buggy subtraction (van Lehn, 1983). On problems requiring subtraction across a zero, such as 704 – 337, second- through fifth-graders (seven- to eleven-year-olds) generate a variety of incorrect answers. These answers usually reflect misunderstandings of how the procedure works, rather than carelessness. For example children often subtract across a zero without decrementing the number from which the borrowing was done. On 704 – 337, this would produce the answer 477. Such procedures reflect children knowing the superficial form of the long subtraction algorithm but not understanding why it generates the answers that it does.

Another type of evidence for the importance of self-explanations comes from studies of individual differences in learning. One difference between better and worse learners is the degree to which they try to explain what they are learning. In a wide range of areas, including physics, biology, algebra, and computer programming, frequency of explaining the logic underlying statements in textbooks is positively related to learning the material covered in the textbook (Chi, Bassok, Lewis, Reimann, & Glaser, 1989; Chi, de Leeuw, Chiu, & LaVancher, 1994; Ferguson-Hessler & de Jong, 1990; Nathan, Mertz, & Ryan, 1994; Pirolli & Recker, 1994). The kinds of explanations that seem most effective involve constructing causal connections between procedures and their effects, as well as between structural, functional, and behavioral aspects of systems and sub-systems (Chi, 2000).

The positive relation between learning and generation of self-explanations is not entirely attributable to people of higher ability generating a greater number of explanations than those of lower ability. Both high and low scorers on standardized achievement tests who generate a greater number of such explanations learn more than those who do not (Chi et al., 1994). Nor is it attributable to those who generate a greater number of explanations spending more time on the task. Generating explanations does take time, but equating the time spent on the task by having a control group read the textbook material twice did not result in as much learning as generating the explanations on a single reading (Chi et al., 1994).

Another type of evidence for the positive effects of self-explanations on learning comes from studies of math teaching practices in Japan (Stigler & Hiebert, 1999). Levels of math learning in Japan are at consistently high levels. For example, in one comparison of fifth-graders, the mean level of math achievement in all ten Minneapolis schools that were examined was below the mean level of any of the schools examined in a comparable community in Japan (Stevenson, Lee, Chen, Stigler, Hsu, & Kitamura, 1990). One contributing factor to these differences seems to be differing degrees of emphasis on generating explanations for why mathematical algorithms work. In Japanese classrooms, both teachers and students spend considerable time trying to explain why solution procedures that differ superficially generate the same answer, and why seemingly plausible approaches yield incorrect answers. Encouraging children to explain why the procedures work appears to promote deeper understanding of them than simply describing the procedures, providing examples of how they work, and encouraging students to practice them – the typical approach to mathematics instruction in the US (Stigler & Hiebert, 1999).

Thus, when my colleagues and I began the present series of investigations, we knew that amount of self-explanation and amount of learning were correlated. We did not know, however, whether there was a causal relation between the two. It might be the case, for example, that more intelligent and more highly motivated children might learn more and generate more explanations, but the self-explanatory activity might not cause the greater learning. Only by randomly assigning children to conditions under which they were or were not encouraged to engage in explanatory activity could causal linkages between the two be drawn.

The particular form of self-explanation instruction that we have examined involves asking children to explain the reasoning of another person. In particular, children are presented with a problem, they advance an answer, they are given feedback concerning the correct answer, and then the experimenter asks them, "How do you think I knew that?" This instructional procedure was of particular interest because it can be used on virtually any task, it is easy to execute, and it can be used with a wide range of age groups.

The detailed data about learning that is yielded by microgenetic methods provides a means for finding out not only whether such encouragement enhanced learning but also why it did or did not work for individual children. The investigations have been aimed at answering six main questions:

1) Is self-explanation causally related to learning as well as being correlated with it?
2) Do young children, as well as older individuals, benefit from encouragement to provide explanations?
3) Is explaining other people's reasoning more useful than explaining your own reasoning?
4) What individual difference variables influence ability to benefit from self-explanations?
5) Is explaining both correct and incorrect reasoning more useful than just explaining correct reasoning?
6) How does encouragement to explain generate its effects?

The remainder of this chapter reports our efforts to answer these six questions. More generally, it illustrates how microgenetic studies can help reveal the workings of instructional approaches.

Explaining number conservation

The first context in which we examined the causal influence of self-explanations involved five-year-olds performing number conservation problems (Siegler, 1995). The task closely resembled the classic Piagetian procedure. Children were shown two parallel rows, each with the same number of objects (seven, eight, or nine, depending on the item), arranged in 1:1 correspondence. At the beginning of each trial, children readily agreed that the two rows had the same number of objects. Then, one of the rows was transformed spatially (by lengthening the row, shortening it, or leaving the length unchanged) and quantitatively (by adding an object, subtracting an object, or doing neither). The experimenter called attention to both spatial and numerical transformations, by saying (for example) "Now I'm spreading this row out and I'm taking an object away from it." Children in all groups were then asked whether they thought the transformed row had more objects, fewer objects, or the same number of objects as the untransformed row.

Children in all groups were first given a pretest. Those whose performance indicated that they did not yet know how to solve number conservation problems then spent four sessions participating in one of three training procedures. One group of children received feedback alone; they advanced their answer and were immediately told whether it was correct or incorrect (*feedback-only condition*). A second group of children advanced their answers, were asked, "Why do you think that?" and then were given feedback on their answer, as in the feedback-only condition (*explain-own-reasoning condition*). In collaborative learning experiments, the children who learn the most tend to be those who advance elaborate explanations of their own reasoning to other children (King, 1991; Webb, 1989). Examining this condition allowed us to determine whether describing one's own reasoning was causally related to learning.

A third group of children advanced their answers, received feedback from the experimenter concerning which answer was correct and then were asked by the experimenter "How do you think I knew that?" (*explain-correct-reasoning condition*). This last condition, in which the child needed to explain the experimenter's reasoning, was of greatest interest. Having children explain another person's correct reasoning combines advantages of discovery and didactic approaches to instruction. It is like discovery-oriented approaches in that it requires the child to generate a relatively deep analysis of a phenomenon without being told how to do so. It is like didactic approaches in that it focuses the child's attention on correct reasoning. Thus, it combines some of the efficiency of didactic instruction with some of the motivating properties of discovery.

Trying such instruction with young children was of particular interest. Although young children can and do try to explain other people's reasoning, their frequent egocentrism and lack of reflection seem to lead them to do so less often than older individuals. If this is the case, then instructions to try to explain to oneself the reasoning of a more knowledgeable individual may be especially useful for young children.

The results indicated that, as hypothesized, encouraging children to explain the reasoning underlying the experimenter's answer resulted in their learning more than feedback alone or feedback in combination with requests to explain their own reasoning (figure 1.4). The differential gains were largest on the most difficult problems, those in which relying on the length cue led to the wrong answer.

These findings, though interesting, could have been obtained in a conventional training study. Other results from the study, however, could not have been obtained without the trial-by-trial analysis of change made

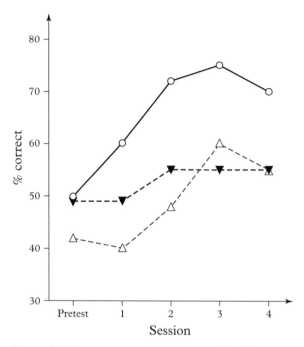

Figure 1.4 Percent correct on pretest and training sessions of number conservation task. –◯–, Explain experimenter's answer; --▼--, Explain own answer; ----△-----, Feedback only.

possible by microgenetic methods. The advantages of the microgenetic data were especially evident in analyzing performance and learning of children in the explain-correct-reasoning group, the group that showed the greatest learning.

One such finding was that even in a logical domain such as number conservation, a variety of ways of thinking coexisted both before and while the instruction was presented. As shown in figure 1.3, children explained the experimenter's reasoning in five qualitatively distinct ways: the type of numerical transformation, the relative lengths of the rows, counting the objects in each row and choosing the row with the greater number, saying the objects were just moved back and forth, and saying that they didn't know why the experimenter had answered as she had.

Variability of reasoning was evident in all phases of the experiment. On the pretest, only 7% of children relied on a single strategy on all trials. Of the other children, 20% used two approaches, 47% used three approaches, and 27% used four approaches. Thus, the large majority of children used three or more strategies on the pretest.

A surprising aspect of the pretest results was the fact that most children explicitly cited the type of transformation at least once. The overall percentage of citations of the type of transformation was low – 9%. The low percentage was logically necessary, because children who used transformational explanations on more than 25% of pretest trials were excluded from further participation in the experiment. Despite this restriction, most children showed some knowledge of the influence of the type of transformation on the number of objects. Thus, even before the training session began, the sophisticated transformational explanation coexisted with less sophisticated strategies, such as those based on length and counting.

This diversity of strategy use continued during the four training sessions. In each of these sessions, only about 10% of children relied on a single strategy.

The microgenetic design also made possible detailed analysis of the way in which the request to explain the experimenter's reasoning produced its effects. As shown in figure 1.3, the pattern of change clearly was more akin to that envisioned in the overlapping waves model than in the stair-step model. On the pretest, the children explained most of their answers by saying that the row they chose was longer (or by saying that the two rows had the same number of objects because the rows were equally long). When they initially needed to explain the experimenter's reasoning, in the first training session, most children could not generate a good explanation; their most frequent response was that they didn't know why the experimenter had answered as she had. This explanation was used more than twice as often as explanations in which they cited the type of transformation. However, by the second training session, they were citing the type of transformation just as often as saying that they did not know, and in the third and fourth training sessions, their most frequent explanation was to say that the experimenter had based her judgment on the type of transformation. Thus, the group-level data suggested that the major source of change was children de-emphasizing length and emphasizing the type of transformation that was performed.

The dense sampling of changing performance yielded by the microgenetic analysis allowed examination of individual children's change patterns as well as those of the group as a whole. The analyses of individual children indicated that the group-level change pattern corresponded to the single most common pattern of change at the individual level, but that two other patterns of change also occurred. In particular, identifying for each child the type of explanation that underwent the largest increase from the pretest to the last training session and the type of explanation that underwent the largest decrease over the same period indicated three distinct patterns of change: large increases in reliance on transformations and large decreases in reliance on length (53% of children), large increases in saying "I don't know" and large decreases in reliance on length (27%), and idiosyncratic change patterns (20%).

These changes in explanations proved highly predictive of changes in percentage of correct answers. Children in the decreased-length/increased-transformation sub-group progressed from 49% correct on the pretest to 86% correct in the final session of the training period. Children in the other two sub-groups did not increase their accuracy at all over the same period; they answered correctly 52% of pretest items and 50% of items in the last training session. This result left little question that the source of learning from explaining the experimenter's reasoning came from recognizing the rule of the type of numerical transformation in her reasoning. Those children who came to explain the experimenter's reasoning in terms of transformations substantially increased the accuracy of their own judgments. Those children who did not showed little or no improvement in the accuracy of their own judgments.

How did the children who benefited from the requests to explain the experimenter's reasoning differ from those who did not benefit? To answer this question, a regression analysis was conducted in which several characteristics of children and their pretest performance were used to predict amount of learning (defined as percent correct answers over the four training sessions). Three predictors accounted for 65% of the variance in learning: number of different explanations that the child used on the pretest (right or wrong), whether the child ever advanced two explanations on a single pretest trial, and the child's age. The first two predictors – number of different explanations and use of multiple explanations on a single trial – both indicated that the children who learned the most were the children whose pretest performance was the most variable.

Thus, variability of children's thinking prior to training was positively related to learning. This finding is consistent with results in which rats, pigeons, and adult humans have been presented with experimental procedures that increased their behavioral variability (Baer, 1993; Neuringer, 1993; Stokes, Mechner, & Balsam, 1997). It also is consistent with results from microgenetic studies in which children's understanding is assessed on each trial via both gesture and speech. Children whose gestures and speech on a pretest frequently reflect divergent reasoning are more likely to learn (Alibali & Goldin-Meadow, 1993; Church & Goldin-Meadow, 1986). Verbal inarticulateness, as reflected in false starts and long pauses, also is positively related to learning (Perry & Lewis, 1999).

The positive relation between initial variability and later learning makes sense; use of more varied approaches increases opportunities to explore the task environment and to discover heretofore unexpected aspects of it. Relatively great initial variability also may be indicative of an openness to new approaches. In addition, part of the effectiveness of many forms of instruction may lie in their leading children to try more varied approaches. In the Siegler (1995) study, for example, children who were asked to explain the experimenter's reasoning advanced more different types of explanations than did peers asked to explain their own reasoning. Thus, part of the reason for the effectiveness of requests to explain the experimenter's reasoning may have been that it encouraged generation of varied possibilities, some of which were more effective than the approaches that children usually used.

The findings from the Siegler (1995) study of number conservation provided answers to four of the six questions about self-explanation posed earlier in this chapter. With regard to the first question, encouraging children to explain other people's reasoning is causally related to learning. Children who were randomly assigned to explain the experimenter's reasoning learned more than children who explained their own reasoning. Studies conducted in other laboratories have shown that the people whose reasoning is being explained need not be present for the positive effects to emerge. Encouraging children and adults to explain the reasoning that they encounter in textbooks has similar benefits (Chi et al., 1994; Bielaczyc, Pirolli, & Brown, 1995).

The results also indicated positive answers to the second and third questions. Children as young as five years, as well as older children and adults, benefited from being asked to explain other people's reasoning, and explaining other people's correct reasoning was more beneficial than explaining the mix of correct and incorrect reasoning that children themselves generated. With regard to the fourth question, individual differences in learning were positively related to variability of initial reasoning. Additional experiments were necessary, however, to address the fifth and sixth questions.

Explaining mathematical equality

Within recent computer simulation models of strategy choice, such as ASCM and SCADS (Shrager & Siegler, 1998; Siegler & Shipley, 1995), the likelihood of a strategy being used on a problem is a positive function of its own effectiveness and a negative function of the effectiveness of competing approaches. For example, although children can solve $2 + 2$ very quickly and accurately by counting from 1, they rarely use that approach, because they can solve $2 + 2$ even more quickly, and just as accurately, by retrieving the answer from memory. Similarly, a strategy that is not particularly fast and accurate will be used often if alternative approaches are even less effective. Thus, the likelihood of using a given strategy can be increased in two ways: increasing its own strength or decreasing the strength of alternative strategies.

This issue arises frequently in instructional contexts in which less-advanced previous approaches continue to be used after more advanced new approaches are also employed. The computer simulations suggest that the best way to increase the use of the new, more advanced approaches should be to increase their strength and also to decrease the strength of less advanced approaches. In the context of self-explanation, having children explain both why correct approaches are correct and why incorrect approaches are incorrect should be more effective than only explaining why correct approaches are correct. Explaining how correct answers were generated and why they are correct should increase the strength of correct procedures, and explaining how incorrect answers were generated and why they are wrong should decrease the strength of incorrect procedures.

I tested this prediction on a task developed by Perry, Church, & Goldin-Meadow (1988). This task involves problems of the form $A + B + C =$ ___ $+ C$. Third- and fourth-graders find such problems surprisingly difficult. For example, they usually answer $3 + 4 + 5 =$ ___ $+ 5$ by writing "12." This answer reflects an add-to-equal-sign strategy, in which the children add all numbers to the left of the equal sign. The next most common answer to the problem is 17, which reflects an add-all-numbers strategy (see Goldin-Meadow & Alibali, this volume). Both approaches reflect limited understanding of what the equal sign means. The third and fourth graders seem to interpret it as a signal to add the relevant numbers, rather than as an indication that the values on the two sides of the equal sign need to be equivalent.

In the experiment that I ran on this task (Siegler, in preparation), eighty-seven third- and fourth-graders were presented with a procedure that included three phases: pretest, training, and posttest. The pretest and posttest included three types of problems: $A + B + C =$ ___ $+ C$ (*C problems*), $A + B + C =$ ___ $+ B$ (*B problems*), and $A + B + C =$ ___ $+ D$ (*D problems*). These problems differed in the relation of the number after the equal sign to the numbers before it. On "C problems," the number after the equal sign was identical to the rightmost number before it (e.g., $3 + 4 + 5 =$ ___ $+ 5$). On "B problems," the number after the equal sign was identical to the middle number before it (e.g., $3 + 4 + 5 =$ ___ $+ 4$). On "D problems," the number after the equal sign did not match any of the numbers before it (e.g., $3 + 4 + 5 =$ ___ $+ 6$).

The reason for including these three kinds of problems was that they were solvable by different types of strategies. One strategy worked only on C problems: just add the first two numbers. A second strategy worked on both B and C problems, but not on D problems: locate a number that is present on both sides of the equal sign, and add the other two numbers. Two other strategies worked on all types of problems. One of these optimal strategies was to create equal values on the two sides of the equal sign (e.g., on $3 + 4 + 5 = \_\_ + 5$, add the numbers on the left and solve $12 = \_\_ + 5$). The other optimal strategy was to subtract from both sides the number on the right side of the equation (e.g., on $3 + 4 + 5 = \_\_ + 5$, subtract 5 from both sides and solve $3 + 4 = \_\_$). Thus, presenting these three types of problems allowed assessment of children's strategy use before and after training.

The training procedure included ten problems. The ones of greatest interest were the six C problems, such as $3 + 4 + 5 = \_\_ + 5$. The other four items were standard three-term addition problems with no numbers on the right side of the equal sign, such as $5 + 6 + 7 = \_\_$. These four problems were included to prevent children from reflexively adding the first two numbers on all problems. Performance on these foils was virtually perfect in all conditions and will not be described further.

Children received the ten problems under one of three training conditions. Children in the *explain-own-reasoning condition* were asked to answer a problem, then asked to explain why they thought their answer was correct, and then given feedback about the answer (either "You're right, the answer is N" or "Actually, the correct answer is N"). Children in the *explain-correct-reasoning condition* were first presented with a problem, asked to answer it, and given feedback as to the correct answer. They then were told that a child at another school had answered N (the right answer), asked how they thought the child had done so, and asked why they thought that was the right answer. Finally, children in the *explain-correct-and-incorrect-reasoning condition* were presented with the same procedure, except they were asked to explain not only the reasoning of a hypothetical child who had generated the right answer but also the reasoning of a hypothetical child who had generated a wrong answer. The wrong answer that children in this condition needed to explain matched the answer that would have been generated by the procedure that that child had used most often on the pretest.

Pretest performance of this sample closely resembled that described in previous studies in which this task was used. Children usually employed the add-to-equal-sign strategy. A minority of children used the add-all-numbers approach. Percent correct was 0% for children in all three conditions, and mean solution time was around 10 s in all conditions and did not differ among them. (These figures exclude the performance of nine children who answered most pretest items correctly and therefore did not participate further in the study.)

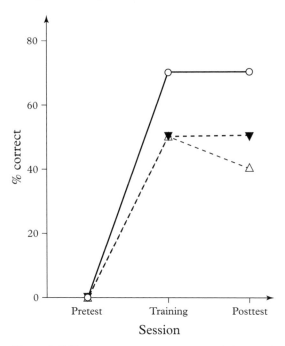

Figure 1.5 Percent correct on pretest, training, and posttest problems on mathematical equality task. –○–, Explain correct and incorrect answer; --▼--, Explain correct answer; ----△----, Explain own answer.

As shown in figure 1.5, children in all conditions learned a considerable amount during training. However, those who were asked to explain both why correct reasoning was correct and why incorrect reasoning was incorrect learned more than those in the other two groups. The differences were maintained on the posttest. Children who were asked to explain both correct and incorrect reasoning improved from 0% correct on the pretest to about 70% correct during training and on the posttest. Children in the other two groups progressed from 0% correct answers on the pretest to about 50% correct during training and on the posttest. The absolute level of learning of children who were asked to explain the correct answer was quite high, but so was that of children who were given feedback and asked to explain their own answer.

As shown in figure 1.6, the superior posttest performance of children who explained both correct and incorrect answers during training was due largely to their being better able to solve the problems that required relatively deep understanding (B and D problems). Analysis of changes in explanations during the training phase made clear the source of this

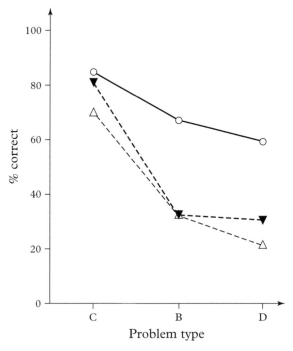

Figure 1.6 Percent correct on posttest of mathematical equality task on three types of problems: trained (C), near generalization (B), and far generalization (D). –○–, Explain correct and incorrect answer; --▼--, Explain correct answer; ----△----, Explain own answer.

effect. Children in all groups greatly decreased their use of the add-to-equal-sign strategy that had predominated on the pretest. The decrease occurred more quickly in the group in which children needed to explain why that strategy was wrong (figure 1.7), but over the six trials it occurred in all three groups to large extents. However, the groups differed considerably in the new strategies that children adopted. Children who only explained their own reasoning largely adopted the simplest strategy, that of adding A + B (figure 1.8). In contrast, children who explained both why correct answers were correct and why incorrect ones were incorrect were more likely to use the advanced strategies of equalizing the two sides or eliminating the constant on the right side of the equal sign by subtracting its value from both sides (figure 1.9).

The strategies that children adopted to explain correct answers during the training period proved to be very predictive of their own posttest performance. Frequency of adopting one of the two advanced strategies

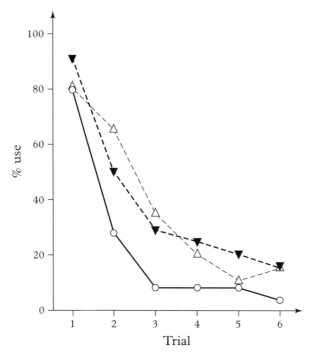

Figure 1.7 Decline in use of main incorrect strategy (A + B + C strategy) during training session of mathematical equality task. –○–, Explain correct and incorrect answer; --▼--, Explain correct answer; ----△----, Explain own answer.

correlated $r = 0.77$ with percent correct on the B problems on the posttest and $r = 0.86$ with percent correct on the D problems on the posttest. In contrast, percent use of the A + B explanations during training correlated $r = -0.70$ with percent correct on the B problems on the posttest and $r = -0.76$ with percent correct on the D problems. Thus, asking children to explain why correct answers were correct and why incorrect answers were incorrect led to deeper understanding of the problems, as indicated by adoption of strategies that would solve a broader range of problems rather than just the problems in the initial training set.

Changes in solution times over the six trials of the training period shed additional light on the change process for children in the three groups. As shown in figure 1.10, on Trial 1, times for children in all three groups were around 12 s. The lack of difference made sense, because children in all groups had been treated identically up to this point. However, for those children who were asked to explain either correct reasoning or correct and

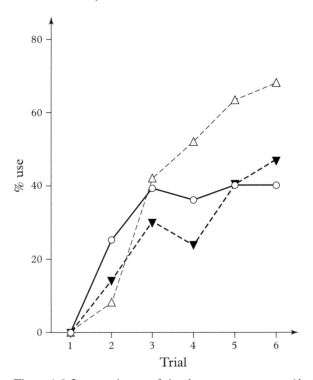

Figure 1.8 Increase in use of simplest correct strategy (A + B) during training session of mathematical equality task. –○–, Explain correct and incorrect answer; --▼--, Explain correct answer; ----△----, Explain own answer.

incorrect reasoning at the end of Trial 1, solution times approximately doubled on Trial 2. On Trial 3, solution times of children who were asked to explain both correct and incorrect reasoning started to decline and the times continued to decline thereafter. In contrast, mean solution times of children who were asked to explain only correct answers increased to 26 s on Trial 3, before decreasing substantially over the remaining trials.

Why did the solution times of children asked to explain another child's reasoning show these changes? Consideration of data on each child's trial of last error during the training phase suggested a simple explanation. Most children who were asked to explain both correct and incorrect reasoning made their last error on Trial 2. The next most common outcome was for their last error to occur on Trial 3. Thus, their solution times for explaining the correct reasoning increased from Trial 1 to 2, when they became confused about how the correct answer was generated, and

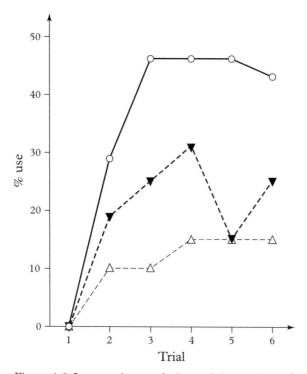

Figure 1.9 Increase in use during training session of mathematical equality task of most advanced strategies ("equalize values" and "subtract C from both sides"). –O–, Explain correct and incorrect answer; --▼--, Explain correct answer; ----△----, Explain own answer.

the times decreased thereafter as the children increasingly understood how to generate the correct answer. In contrast, most children who were asked only to explain the correct answer did not make their last error until Trial 3, and a number of them made their last error on Trial 4. This suggested that one or more incorrect procedures continued to compete with the correct procedure for a longer time, resulting in their solution time on Trial 3 being much greater than that of children who explained both correct and incorrect answers.

Thus, requests to explain correct answers, or correct and incorrect answers, led to an initial period of cognitive ferment, characterized by incorrect answers and very long solution times. Then children induced one or more strategies for solving the problems, and thus for explaining correct answers. This led to their consistently answering correctly and to their solution times becoming much shorter. Children who were asked

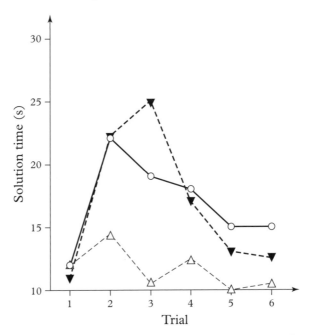

Figure 1.10 Solution times during training session of mathematical equality task. –○–, Explain correct and incorrect answer; --▼--, Explain correct answer; ----△----, Explain own answer.

to explain both correct and incorrect answers tended to cease relying on their previous incorrect approach more quickly than did children who only were asked to explain correct answers, and they tended to settle on more widely applicable new strategies as well.

These findings are reminiscent of previous ones indicating that just prior to discoveries, children show increased solution times (Siegler & Jenkins, 1989), increased verbal disfluencies (Perry & Lewis, 1999), increased gesture-speech mismatches (Alibali & Goldin-Meadow, 1993), and increased cognitive conflict (Piaget, 1952). They also are reminiscent of the previously described number conservation findings from Siegler (1995), in which pretest variability was positively related to subsequent learning. In all cases, learning seems to involve children moving from incorrect approaches to a state of high uncertainty and variability, and then to a period in which the uncertainty and variability gradually decrease as children increasingly rely on more advanced approaches. The process occurs much faster in situations such as number conservation and mathematical equality, in which the less advanced approaches generate wrong answers, than in situations such as addition and time telling, in which the less advanced approaches generate correct answers but do so relatively inefficiently.

Thus, the answer to Question 5 seems to be: Children do learn more from being asked to explain both why correct answers are correct and why incorrect answers are incorrect than from being asked only why correct answers are correct. Findings from a very recent study of the water displacement task (Siegler & Chen, in preparation) yielded converging findings. There too, children learned more from being asked to explain both correct and incorrect answers than from being asked only to explain correct answers. This leaves the last, and most challenging, of the six questions, for final consideration.

How does self-explanation help children learn?

Self-explanation seems likely to generate its effects through several distinct mechanisms. Data from the present studies of number conservation and mathematical equality provide evidence for at least four of them.

One way in which encouragement to explain exercises its effects is to increase the probability of the learner seeking an explanation at all. When people are told that an answer is wrong, they often simply accept the fact without thinking about why it is wrong or how they might generate correct answers in the future. The number conservation data provide evidence regarding this source of effectiveness. Children who were told that their answer was wrong and which answer was right, but who were not asked to explain why the correct answer was correct, did not increase the accuracy of their answers over the course of the four sessions. In contrast, children who received the same feedback but who also were asked to explain how the experimenter had generated the correct answer, did increase their accuracy. Further, those children who showed the largest increases in successfully explaining the experimenter's reasoning also showed the largest increases in generating correct answers on their own. Thus, encouragement to generate self-explanation seems to work partially through encouraging children to try to explain observed outcomes.

Even when children try to explain what they have seen or been told, they vary in the depth of their search for an explanation. A second way in which encouragement to explain exercises its effects is through increasing the depth of explanatory efforts. The study of the mathematical equality task provides relevant evidence. Children in all three groups succeeded in finding ways to solve the problems by the second half of the training period. However, children who were asked to explain correct and incorrect answers appeared to search considerably more deeply. They more often generated conceptually more sophisticated solutions, such as balancing the values on the two sides of the equal sign. In contrast, children who were only given feedback usually generated solutions to the training problems that happened to work on those problems but were not generally applicable (the A + B strategy). Thus, encouraging generation of explanations also seems to promote a deeper search than might be undertaken otherwise.

It should be noted that both of these mechanisms also have the effect of increasing the variability of the procedures that children attempt. For example, in the number conservation study, children who were asked to explain the experimenter's answer generated a greater number of strategies than did children who were only given feedback concerning their own answers. This difference was present despite feedback per se often increasing variability of responses (Neuringer, 1993). Thus, increasing the likelihood of searching for an explanation and the depth of the search if one is undertaken seem to operate in part by increasing the range of strategies that children attempt.

A third likely mechanism involves changing the accessibility of effective and ineffective ways of thinking. The most directly relevant evidence here comes from the mathematical equality study. Children who were asked to explain why incorrect answers were incorrect as well as why correct answers were correct showed more rapid decreases in use of their previous A + B + C strategy than did children who were only asked to explain why correct answers were correct. This was what models such as ASCM and SCADS would predict. Instructional approaches that not only strengthen effective approaches but that also weaken ineffective ones should increase the likelihood of retrieving the effective approaches and decrease the likelihood of retrieving ineffective ones.

A fourth set of mechanisms involves more general processes related to degree of engagement with the task. One concerns motivational effects. Learning is more enjoyable when what you are learning makes sense. By encouraging children to make sense of their observations, encouragement to generate explanations achieves this motivating effect. A second, related benefit involves depth of processing; encouraging children to explain what they see or are told leads them to process the information more deeply than they otherwise might. A third general benefit involves increased time spent actively engaged in thinking about the problem. The more time that children spend trying to understand why correct answers are correct and why incorrect answers are incorrect, the more they are likely to learn.

Thus, the two microgenetic studies yielded answers to all six questions posed earlier in the chapter. They demonstrated:

1) Encouragement to explain other people's statements is causally related to learning;
2) Five-year-olds as well as older children can benefit from encouragement to explain;
3) Explaining other people's answers is more useful than explaining your own, at least when the other people's answers are consistently correct and your own answers include incorrect ones;
4) Variability of initial reasoning is positively related to learning;
5) Explaining why correct answers are correct and why incorrect answers are incorrect yields greater learning than only explaining why correct answers are correct;
6) The mechanisms through which explaining other people's reasoning exercises its effects include increasing the probability of trying to explain observed phenomena; searching more deeply for explanations when such efforts are made; increasing the accessibility of effective strategies relative to ineffective ones; and increasing the degree of engagement with the task.

Thus, microgenetic studies are useful for both general and specific purposes. At a general level, they have provided much of the underpinning of the overlapping waves model, a broad framework for thinking about development. At a more specific level, they have proved useful for understanding how instructional procedures, such as encouragement to explain other people's reasoning, exercise their effects. As amply documented in other chapters in this volume, they have many additional uses as well.

References

Adolph, K. E. (1997). Learning in the development of infant locomotion. *Monographs of the Society for Research in Child Development, 62* (Serial No. 251).

Alibali, M. W., & Goldin-Meadow, S. (1993). Gesture-speech mismatch and mechanisms of learning: What the hands reveal about a child's state of mind. *Cognitive Psychology, 25,* 468–523.

Anzai, Y., & Simon, H. A. (1979). The theory of learning by doing. *Psychological Review, 86,* 124–140.

Ashcraft, M. H. (1987). Children's knowledge of simple arithmetic: A developmental model and simulation. In J. Bisanz, C. J. Brainerd, & R. Kail (Eds.), *Formal methods in developmental psychology* (pp. 302–338). New York: Springer-Verlag.

Baer, J. (1993). *Creativity and divergent thinking: A task-specific approach.* Hillsdale, NJ: Erlbaum.

Bauer, P. J., & Mandler, J. M. (1989). One thing follows another: Effects of temporal structure on 1- to 2-year-olds' recall of events. *Developmental Psychology, 25,* 197–206.

Bielaczyc, K., Pirolli, P. L., & Brown, A. L. (1995). Training in self-explanation and self-regulation strategies: Investigating the effects of knowledge acquisition activities on problem solving. *Cognition and Instruction, 13,* 221–252.

Carey, S. (1985). *Conceptual change in childhood.* Cambridge, MA: MIT Press.

Case, R. (1992). *The mind's staircase: Exploring the conceptual underpinnings of children's thought and knowledge.* Hillsdale, NJ: Erlbaum.

Chen, Z., & Siegler, R. S. (2000). Across the great divide: Bridging the gap between understanding of toddlers' and older children's thinking. *Monographs of the Society for Research in Child Development, 65* (2, Whole No. 261).

Chi, M. T. H. (2000). Self-explaining expository texts: The dual processes of generating inferences and repairing mental models. In R. Glaser (Ed.), *Advances in instructional psychology, Vol. 5* (pp. 161–237). Mahwah, NJ: Erlbaum.

Chi, M. T. H., Bassok, M., Lewis, M., Reimann, P., & Glaser, R. (1989). Self-explanations: How students study and use examples in learning to solve problems. *Cognitive Science, 13,* 145–182.

Chi, M. T. H., de Leeuw, N., Chiu, M.-H., & LaVancher, C. (1994). Eliciting self-explanations improves understanding. *Cognitive Science, 18,* 439–477.

Church, R. B., & Goldin-Meadow, S. (1986). The mismatch between gesture and speech as an index of transitional knowledge. *Cognition, 23,* 43–71.

Coyle, T. R., & Bjorklund, D. F. (1995). The development of strategic memory: A modified microgenetic assessment of utilization deficiencies. *Cognitive Development, 11,* 295–314.

Coyle, T. R., & Bjorklund, D. F. (1997). Age differences in, and consequences of, multiple- and variable-strategy use on a multitrial sort-recall task. *Developmental Psychology, 33,* 372–380.

Ferguson-Hessler, M. G. M., & de Jong, T. (1990). Studying physics texts: Differences in study processes between good and poor solvers. *Cognition and Instruction, 7,* 41–54.

Goldin-Meadow, S., & Alibali, M.W. (this volume). Looking at the hands through time: A microgenetic perspective on learning and instruction.

Granott, N. (1993). Patterns of interaction in the co-construction of knowledge: Separate minds, joint effort, and weird creatures. In R. Wozniak & K. W. Fischer (Eds.), *Development in context: Acting and thinking in specific environments* (pp. 183–207). Hillsdale, NJ: Erlbaum.

Granott, N. (1998). A paradigm shift in the study of development: Essay review of *Emerging Minds* by R. S. Siegler. *Human Development, 41,* 360–365.

King, A. (1991). Effects of training in strategic questioning on children's problem-solving performance. *Journal of Educational Psychology, 83,* 307–317.

Kuhn, D., Garcia-Mila, M., Zohar, A., & Andersen, C. (1995). Strategies of knowledge acquisition. *Monographs of the Society for Research in Child Development, 60* (Serial No. 245).

LeFevre, J. A., Sadesky, G. S., & Bisanz, J. (1996). Selection of procedures in mental addition: Reassessing the problem-size effect in adults. *Journal of Experimental Psychology: Learning, Memory, and Cognition, 22,* 216–230.

Leslie, A. M. (1982). The perception of causality in infants. *Perception, 11,* 173–186.

Marquer, J., & Pereira, M. (1990). Reaction times in the study of strategies in sentence-picture verification: A reconsideration. *Quarterly Journal of Experimental Psychology, 42A,* 147–168.

Miller, P., & Aloise-Young, P. (1996). Preschoolers' strategic behaviors and performance on a same-different task. *Journal of Experimental Child Psychology, 60,* 284–303.

Nathan, M. J., Mertz, K., & Ryan, B. (1994). *Learning through self-explanation of mathematical examples: Effects of cognitive load.* Paper presented at the 1994 Annual Meeting of the American Educational Research Association.

Neuringer, A. (1993). Reinforced variation and selection. *Animal Learning & Behavior, 21,* 83–91.

Oakes, L. M., & Cohen, L. B. (1995). Infant causal perception. In C. Rovee-Collier & L. P. Lipsitt (Eds.), *Advances in infancy research, Vol. 9.* Norwood, NJ: Ablex.

Perry, M., Church, R. B., & Goldin-Meadow, S. (1988). Transitional knowledge in the acquisition of concepts. *Cognitive Development, 3,* 359–400.

Perry, M., & Elder, A. D. (1999). Knowledge in transition: Adults' developing understanding of a principle of physical causality. *Cognitive Development, 12,* 131–157.

Perry, M., & Lewis, J. L. (1999). Verbal imprecision as an index of knowledge in transition. *Developmental Psychology, 25,* 749–759.

Piaget, J. (1952). *The child's concept of number.* New York: W. W. Norton.

Pirolli, P., & Recker, M. (1994). Learning strategies and transfer in the domain of programming. *Cognition and Instruction, 12,* 235–275.

Schauble, L. (1996). The development of scientific reasoning in knowledge-rich contexts. *Developmental Psychology, 32,* 102–119.

Shrager, J., & Siegler, R. S. (1998). SCADS: A model of children's strategy choices and strategy discoveries. *Psychological Science, 9,* 405–410.

Siegler, R. S. (1995). How does change occur: A microgenetic study of number conservation. *Cognitive Psychology, 28,* 225–273.

Siegler, R. S. (1996). *Emerging minds: The process of change in children's thinking.* New York: Oxford University Press.

Siegler, R. S., & Jenkins, E. A. (1989). *How children discover new strategies.* Hillsdale, NJ: Erlbaum.

Siegler, R. S., & McGilly, K. (1989). Strategy choices in children's time-telling. In I. Levin & D. Zakay (Eds.), *Time and human cognition: A life span perspective* (pp. 185–218). The Netherlands: Elsevier Science Publishers.

Siegler, R. S., & Shipley, C. (1995). Variation, selection, and cognitive change. In T. Simon & G. Halford (Eds.), *Developing cognitive competence: New approaches to process modeling.* Hillsdale, NJ: Erlbaum.

Siegler, R. S., & Shrager, J. (1984). Strategy choices in addition and subtraction: How do children know what to do? In C. Sophian (Ed.), *The origins of cognitive skills*. Hillsdale, NJ: Erlbaum.

Stevenson, J. W., Lee, S. Y., Chen, C., Stigler, J. W., Hsu, C. C., & Kitamura, S. (1990). Contexts of achievement: A study of American, Chinese, and Japanese children. *Monographs of the Society for Research in Child Development, 55* (1–2, Serial No. 221).

Stigler, J. W., & Hiebert, J. (1999). *The teaching gap*. New York: The Free Press.

Stokes, P. D., Mechner, F., & Balsam, P. D. (1999). Effects of different acquisition procedures on response variability. *Animal Learning and Behavior, 27*, 28–41.

Thelen, E., & Ulrich, B. D. (1991). Hidden skills. *Monographs of the Society for Research in Child Development, 56* (Serial No. 223).

Thornton, S. (1999). Creating the conditions for cognitive change: The interaction between task structures and specific strategies. *Child Development, 70*, 588–603.

van Lehn, K. (1983). On the representation of procedures in repair theory. In H. P. Ginsburg (Ed.), *The development of mathematical thinking*. New York: Academic Press.

Webb, N. M. (1989). Peer interaction and learning in small groups. In N. Webb (Ed.), Peer interaction, problem-solving, and cognition: Multidisciplinary perspectives. [Special issue.] *International Journal of Education Research, 13*, 21–39.

Wellman, H. M., & Gelman, S. A. (1998). Knowledge acquisition in foundational domains. In W. Damon (Series Ed.), & D. Kuhn & R. S. Siegler (Vol. Eds.), *Handbook of child psychology, Vol. 2: Cognition, perception, and language* (5th edn., pp. 523–574). New York: Wiley.

2   Microdevelopment and dynamic systems: Applications to infant motor development

Esther Thelen and Daniela Corbetta

For many years, the primary occupation of developmental psychologists has been to document the ages at which infants and children reached various cognitive, social, and perceptual-motor milestones. One legacy of Gesell and of Piaget (although not necessarily endorsed by these pioneers) has been elaborate catalogues of "ages and stages" by which to gauge developmental progress and to compare children from different cultures, backgrounds, and family or medical circumstances. A more recent corollary of this tradition is the concern with documenting the earliest evidence of a particular competence. Do three-month-old infants have the object concept? When can babies count?

While we can hardly imagine a developmental psychology not anchored by "age" on the x-axis, a different approach has surfaced in the last decade or so, and is now the topic of this volume. The focus has shifted from "when" to "how." Microdevelopment is the study of the processes of change, not only the endpoints. It represents a shift in thinking, but also in methods. And it requires new theory, or at least new looks at old theory.

We contend in this chapter that the study of motor development in infancy has been a particularly successful example of microdevelopmental thinking and methods. There are two reasons why this is so. First, the particular theoretical stance that has gained wide acceptance in this domain – dynamic systems – provides both rationale and means for such a genuinely process approach. And second, the data – real-time series of movements in time and space – are particularly amenable to asking process questions. What follows in this chapter is, first, our understanding of the essentials of a microdevelopmental approach. We then describe the larger theory of dynamic systems as a compelling rationale for the study of microdevelopment and the use of microgenetic methods. Finally, we illustrate these points with a review of two issues in the emergence of early motor skills: the problem of how change in infants' upper and lower limbs coordination occurs, and the problem of how infants learn to walk.

The research reported here was supported by NIH R01 HD22830, which is gratefully acknowledged.

What is microdevelopment?

As discussed by others in this volume as well, microdevelopment is the study of processes of change and, in particular, the changes in behavior that can be documented over relatively small time scales. The goal of microdevelopmental studies is to understand change itself: what are the mechanisms by which people forgo old ways of behaving and adapt new ones. Often microdevelopmental studies include *microgenesis* experiments, where the researcher deliberately facilitates (or even retards) the discovery of these new ways within one or several experimental sessions through coaching, training, practice, or scaffolding support.

There are several core assumptions, we believe, that underlie a microdevelopmental stance. The first is that processes of change can be made transparent. This reflects a belief that there are moments in the continuous evolution of behavior where we can directly observe events as they happen over time. In the traditional approaches, change is not directly observed, therefore it can only be inferred from specific endpoints or definite times of observation. Of course, the problem with such approaches is that children (or adults) can use multiple routes to the same outcome and the routes may be equally, or more, interesting than the endpoint per se. The second is that these observable, microdevelopmental small-scale changes have something to do with developmental changes over a longer time scale. In particular, we study microdevelopment because we believe that the processes that cause change in a matter of minutes or hours are the same as those working over months or years. In other words, the general principles underlying behavioral change work at multiple time scales. Finally, a microdevelopmental approach assumes that the system – at least at times – is open to influences from the environment such that we can manipulate certain variables and see effects. Along with this is the assumption that our manipulation also has something to do with what happens outside the laboratory, indeed that we are simulating real agents of change.

As microdevelopmental assumptions become more widely accepted, and microgenetic methods more highly elaborated, there is the promise of addressing some long-standing issues in human ontogeny. First, we may come to understand the puzzling dips and regressions that seem to be the signature of developmental change in so many domains. When development is depicted as continuous progress or inevitable sequential stages toward higher function, such seeming backward steps pose a theoretical and empirical challenge. Are regressions just noise in the process or are they the inevitable accompaniment of change? As we will see later in this chapter, microgenetic methods do offer some real tools to answer such questions.

Likewise, developmentalists must deal with context variability. Even subtle differences in a task can affect performance profoundly. How does context variability fit into a picture of improving competence? Does the child have the competence or not? Is context variability a measure of unstable performance or a particularly adaptive strategy? Related to this is the issue of both intra- and inter-individual variability. Conventionally, tasks are chosen to minimize variability. If a child cannot give the same performance over several days of testing, what does this tell us about either the child or the task? Here again, we will provide examples of microdevelopmental research to illustrate that we alternatively may consider this variation as an important harbinger of change, or indeed the manifestation of the very process of change.

A dynamic systems approach to development

These very issues – nonlinearity, context variability, continuity, and change – are directly addressed by the general theory of dynamic systems as applied to development. Indeed dynamic systems theory really stands as a metatheory that provides a rationale for studying human development using microgenetic approaches and methods. Central to this theory is the assumption that developing systems really *are* dynamic and obey the same principles as other physical and biological systems.

The basic assumptions of a dynamic systems approach to development are now fairly well known (e.g. Thelen & Ulrich, 1991; Thelen & Smith, 1994, 1997; van Geert, 1994). Here we will summarize the main points. In the next section, we will provide examples from our own research to illustrate and explain how these assumptions motivate microdevelopmental studies.

1. Self-organization from multiple components The first assumption is that behavior, at any level of analysis, is the cooperative assembly of multiple, contributing components, including both those that are part of the organism and those that constitute the environment in which the organism resides. Critically, in dynamic systems, these multiple components *self-organize* to produce complex behavior through the mutual interaction (cooperation) of the disparate parts. This is done without the necessity of a pre-existing structure or pattern that "commands" all the pieces to work together. No component is thus privileged over the others. Behavior is just as much a product of the nervous system and of the muscles and bones as it is of the world, which provides physical and social support. Indeed, such self-organizing systems can only exist because they are "open," that is, continually exchanging energy and information with their surroundings.

2. Systems exist in time A second fundamental assumption is that these self-organized patterns exist continually in time such that a behavioral configuration seen, say, at time t_0 is a product of all the patterns that preceded it at t_{-1}, t_{-2}, t_{-3} and so on, at whatever time scale is measured. Likewise, the pattern at t_0 contributes to the behavior of the system in the future at t_{+1}, t_{+2}, t_{+3} and so on, again, whether time is measured in seconds, minutes, or years. This means that behavior and its changes can only be understood as patterns over time, at a scale appropriate to the dimensions of change that we are interested in. Often, developmental studies that offer "snapshots" of performance at widely spaced ages fail to elucidate how children improved or changed because the processes that intervened between the snapshots are unknown and unknowable.

A consequence of both the principles of self-organization of multiple components and of the issue of time is that the system may be sensitive to seemingly small changes in one or more elements. This feature of *nonlinearity* – system-wide reconfiguration from sometimes nearly imperceptible differences in a contributing part – has important implications for prediction. Nonlinearity means that our success at prediction diminishes as time passes because the opportunity for small changes accumulates. Accordingly, our ability to detect and understand change is greater on smaller time scales. Microgenesis studies, which focus on these short time scales, are thus better windows into actual mechanisms of change than widely spaced snapshots for good theoretical reasons.

3. Stability is an appropriate metric The third dynamic assumption supporting a microgenetic approach is a focus on relative stability. Here the key is: for dynamic systems to change, they must become unstable. That is, the coherence of the current pattern must be somehow disrupted so that the system can seek a new configuration. Stable systems do not change: to allow change the components must be able to reassemble. According to this view, development can be envisioned as times when the current pattern is stable and times when that stability is lost and new patterns emerge.

Microgenesis experiments work best when the system is inherently unstable and thus can be manipulated to effect change (e.g. Siegler & Jenkins, 1989). Thus, the researcher must know well the overall landscape of stability of the patterns of interest, so that the points of transition can be identified. It is at these unstable points that the system is more likely to be pushed into new types of behavior.

One important way to detect systems' instability is to look for variability in the behavior of interest. When patterns are stable, they are produced in a relatively similar form over many occasions and over different contexts. For example, and as we will illustrate in the next section, there are times when infants use two hands for reaching. During these times, infants also tend to move both arms together in the same fashion even when they are not reaching. When that occurs, bimanual patterning is more stable. When the patterning is stable, it cannot be easily disrupted and it exhibits less variability. In contrast, at other times, the system seems to be especially sensitive to even minute contextual changes such that infants may use one hand to reach for a small toy at one moment and two hands just a few minutes later. This reflects overall increased variability. It is at these times when it appears that the system has choices that the obligatory pattern can be overridden. It is just at these junctures that we can ask about what aspects of the child or the environment engender particular adaptive (or nonadaptive) choices and then, why these new patterns become the ones that are stable.

In sum, a dynamic systems approach dictates that one know the history of the system through appropriate measures of when it is stable and when loss of stability enables the appearance of new forms. It is at these points of transition that the system can be probed. Knowing the history of the system means that observations must be done in the appropriate time scale. If change is rapid and sudden, the time scale of observation may need to be quite dense in order to pinpoint the process underlying that change.

Microdevelopment in patterns of limb coordination in infants

These abstract principles can be best understood through a few well-worked-out examples. In our laboratories, we have been studying patterns of limb coordination as babies develop during the first year or so of life. In this section, we show how a microdevelopmental approach can describe the interesting changes in patterns that occur over that time, but also can help highlight the mechanisms that may be responsible for the change in coordination.

Early patterns of interlimb coordination in infancy, whether between leg or arm movements, typically follow an unstable, non-linear developmental progression, with frequent shifts and transitions in coordination that sometimes may appear as dips or regressions in development. The reason why these developmental fluctuations and instabilities occur are still poorly understood and scientists have been wondering for a long time about the significance of these behavioral fluctuations in the formation of later goal-oriented and functional activity. Why do some behaviors appear and disappear, to eventually reappear again later in similar or altered forms? Are these changing patterns and fluctuations simply the result of the changing neural substrate or are they the result of many confluent developmental factors? And are these patterns modifiable or resilient to changing environmental constraints? As we plan to illustrate in this section, microdevelopmental studies have been particularly useful at addressing some of these questions. They also were successful at providing insights into the processes of change that are underlying these early behavioral fluctuations. Here we present three sets of studies that addressed different issues related to these behavioral fluctuations. We will first examine fluctuations in coordination in infants' spontaneous kicking to illustrate how changes in kicking patterning are the result of the soft-assembled properties of the system in interaction with specific task constraints. Then, we will address changes and fluctuations in interlimb coordination in reaching and discuss how these changes result from the pervasive reorganization of the system in response to newly developing behaviors such as sitting, crawling, and walking. Finally, we use the case of infants' stepping on a treadmill to illustrate how this microdevelopmental experiment helped at identifying both the times of transitions and the possible mechanisms by which these transitions occurred.

Patterns of spontaneous kicking

From the first days of life, infants are able to generate spontaneous, highly rhythmic, and regular alternating kicking movements (Prechtl, 1977; Touwen, 1976). These early patterns, however, soon become quite unstable. Within a few months, different periods of unilateral and bilateral forms of kicking succeed one another. That is, the initial regular alternation of the two legs becomes less prevalent and is replaced by either single-leg kicking or bilateral simultaneous kicks.

Thelen, Ridley-Johnson, and Fisher (1983) provided a detailed longitudinal description of the developmental shifts and fluctuations occurring between different forms of spontaneous kicking in infants from two to twenty-six weeks old. As in other microdevelopmental approaches, this early study used nearly continuous observations to capture changes and transitions in spontaneous kicking as a function of developmental time, and document both a quantitative picture of changes in kicking during early infancy, as well as individual variations in interlimb coordination.

In this first descriptive study, the authors confirmed the existence of a high rate of alternate kicking following birth. Only a very low portion of these neonatal kicks were simultaneous, meaning that very few kicks involved both legs kicking in the same time. In addition, as reported by several previous authors (Gesell, 1939; Thelen, Bradshaw, & Ward, 1981; Touwen, 1976), Thelen et al. (1983) verified that the rate of these early alternate responses strongly declined between four and eight weeks of age. They observed that, during this declining period, asymmetric or single-leg kicking became the more predominant mode of response; however, it depended greatly on the individual. Finally, they discovered that in all infants, the rate of bilateral simultaneous kicking increased over the first six months. Again, this increase in bilateral kicking was more or less marked, or more or less continuous depending on the individual. But overall, the highest peaks of bilateral kicking always occurred some time between four and six months of age, and were always preceded by an important drop-off in alternate kicking activity around three months of age.

Traditionally, the appearance, switch, and developmental successions of these different patterns of spontaneous kicking were believed to reflect autonomous changes in brain maturation (Gesell, 1939; McGraw, 1945). However, recent views, and particularly the microgenetic and dynamic systems views, suggested that these changes in patterning are the result of a process of continuous modifications of current abilities taking place in response to changes occurring in either the organism or the environment or both (Granott, 1998; Siegler, 1996; Thelen & Smith, 1994; Vygotsky, 1978). A now well-known example of how the decline in kicking and stepping reflex, typical of infants aged four to eight weeks, is related to peripheral biological changes occurring in the organism was demonstrated by the work of Thelen and Fisher (1982). Thelen and Fisher found that a rapid modification in the muscle:fat ratio of the infants' leg during the first two months of life was responsible for this early decline in kicking. Here, we provide another example to illustrate how these patterns of spontaneous kicking and their developmental time scale can be modified and soft-assembled microgenetically as a response to changing conditions in the environment.

In a recent study, Thelen (1994) used Rovee-Collier and colleagues' conjugate reinforcement procedure (Rovee-Collier, 1991) to induce changes in spontaneous kicking in three-month-old infants. Many studies have demonstrated that infants' kicking can be reinforced when the ankle of one foot is attached with a ribbon to a mobile hanging over the infant's crib. The perceived sound and motion of the mobile resulting from the kicking activity of the child usually entails an increase in the rate, force, and amplitude of the kicks (Rovee-Collier, Morongiello, Aron, & Kupersmidt, 1978; Thelen & Fisher, 1983a). Thelen (1994) used this conjugate procedure to test whether three-month-old infants could switch and discover new coordination patterns in response to a novel context.

As mentioned above, in absence of particular task conditions, three-month-old infants prefer to kick with one leg or two alternating legs, and only occasionally kick using simultaneous patterns (Thelen et al., 1983). Thelen (1994) created a novel context to see if three-month-olds could discover and select their less preferred response – simultaneous kicking – to activate the mobile more efficiently. To do this, she yoked the infants' legs together with a soft piece of elastic that permitted all of single, alternate-leg, or simultaneous kicking. But because the elastic restrained movement amplitude in single and alternate-leg kicking, only the simultaneous kicks, allowing a full excursion of both legs, permitted the most vigorous activation of the mobile. Thelen predicted that if infants were able to discover the effectiveness of the simultaneous pattern, they would learn to use that new pattern in preference to the other normally predominant patterns. Therefore, this study tested whether initial and naturally occurring spontaneous patterns of kicking could be modified and newly soft-assembled to accommodate changing environmental conditions.

In that study, testing took place using a microgenetic method (Vygotsky, 1978), creating conditions that facilitated discovery of a new form. In particular, after four minutes of baseline kicking (without reinforcement) where infants' movements did not activate the mobile, infants' legs were yoked together and attached to the mobile for a total of ten minutes of acquisition. The leg movements were recorded continuously during baseline and acquisition in order to keep track of the changes in interlimb coordination as a function of time. As predicted, over the course of the ten minutes of acquisition, infants whose legs were yoked together progressively increased their rate of simultaneous kicking. Another group of infants, who served as controls and did not have their legs yoked together during acquisition, increased single-leg kicking and selected the leg that was attached to the mobile. Therefore, this study demonstrated that even at three months, infants can assemble and maintain differentiated patterns of interlimb coordination when given particular task constraints. It showed that changes in kicking patterning are not prescribed or hardwired, but rather soft-assembled, and that this soft-assembly is the result of tight interactions between the state of the organism at a given point in time, its history, and certain conditions brought or induced by the task.

The microgenetic intervention worked, we believe, because infants were tested at an age – three months – when the originally very stable alternate kicking was already losing its dominance in the repertoire and the system was flexible enough to recruit a pattern that was partially available: simultaneous kicking. Thus, the environmental intervention simply pushed the infants, perhaps because they sought an efficient means for making the mobile jiggle, into discovering the new pattern and increasing its use, at least for the time in which it was a preferred solution. Since infants do not ordinarily have their legs yoked together by elastic, it is unlikely that the microgenetic intervention was a substitute for the normal developmental changes. Indeed, we do not yet know why these kicking patterns succeed each other. One possibility is that simultaneous kicking requires strength in the extensor muscles in the back to lift both legs, and that this is gradually developing as infants spend more time upright and rolling over. However, the mobile experiment does illustrate the flexibility of behavior in periods of transition and the use of interventions at that time.

Patterns of spontaneous bimanual coordination, lateral biases, and reaching

Similarly to spontaneous kicking, patterns of reaching in infancy follow an equally unstable developmental course with frequent shifts and transitions in interlimb coordination mostly throughout the first year. Gesell and Ames (1947) were the first to describe these fluctuations. In a longitudinal study, they reported that infants' reaching responses frequently shifted and alternated between periods of predominantly unilateral, one-handed reaching, and periods of predominantly bilateral, two-handed reaching. They also noted that the lateral preferences in hand use during these periods, that is whether infants used their right or left hands, were as unstable and as inconsistent as the fluctuations between one- and two-handed reaching. Finally, and again, similarly to kicking, they observed that despite some broad trends in the order and succession of these early shifts, these patterns of transition were highly individually defined. As infants aged, the fluctuations became less common and more stable patterns emerged.

Again, one may ask why these developmental fluctuations occur. What is particularly puzzling in this reaching scenario is that infants still continue to display shifts and transitions in interlimb coordination and laterality well after they have developed relatively fine and stable arm–hand coordination and control (Corbetta & Thelen, 1999; Hofsten, 1991; Thelen, Corbetta, & Spencer, 1996). Moreover, by the second half of the first year, infants are capable of modulating their reaching and grasping abilities to accommodate many objects' spatial and physical properties such as their orientation and shape (Hofsten & Fazel-Zandy, 1984; Lockman, Ashmead, & Bushnell, 1984) or size (Fagard & Pézé, 1997; Newell, Scully, McDonald, & Baillargeon, 1989). Despite this ability to integrate perceptual information into reaching patterns, infants still display reversals and fluctuations between one- and two-handed reaching later in the first year, even when reaching for small objects (Corbetta & Thelen, 1996; Fagard & Pézé, 1997; Flament, 1975; Goldfield & Michel, 1986a, b).

As with kicking, the traditional view was to consider these fluctuations in interlimb reaching as the expression of autonomous reorganizations of the central nervous system (Gesell, 1956). Recently, however, an extensive longitudinal study on infant reaching from Thelen and collaborators (see Corbetta & Thelen, 1996, 1999; Spencer & Thelen, 2000; Thelen, Corbetta, & Spencer, 1996; Thelen, Corbetta, Kamm, Spencer, Schneider, & Zernicke, 1993; Spencer, Vereijken, Diedrich, & Thelen, 2000) allowed the formulation of an alternative hypothesis in regard to the developmental processes underlying these shifts and transitions in early upper-arm interlimb coordination and reaching; namely, that these changes can result from the pervasive reorganization of the system in response to newly developing behaviors such as sitting, crawling, and walking.

In this longitudinal study, Thelen and collaborators adopted again a microdevelopmental method to track periods of change and stability in the patterns of infants' reaching throughout the first year of life. To gain insights into the processes underlying these periods of change and stability, they observed and mapped out multiple behavioral dimensions at once. In particular, they tracked changes in arm control and trajectory formation (Thelen et al., 1993, 1996), in interlimb coordination and laterality (Corbetta & Thelen, 1996, 1999), in muscle patterns (Spencer & Thelen, 2000), and in posture (Spencer et al., 2000) in four infants whom they followed weekly from three to thirty weeks old and then every other week until fifty-two weeks old. In many of these observations, Thelen and collaborators not only studied how goal-oriented patterns of reaching formed as a function of time but also investigated whether these patterns shared common kinematic characteristics with upper-arm spontaneous activity.

In brief, Thelen and collaborators were able to confirm that goal-oriented patterns of reaching became more stable and better controlled in the second half of the first year (Thelen et al., 1996). However, and as explained above, they found that despite overall improvement in arm control, infants continued to display changing patterns of interlimb activity, with periods of one-handed reaching alternating with periods of two-handed reaching (Corbetta & Thelen, 1996). That is, even though the babies were always presented with small-size toys throughout the year of testing, they sometimes consistently used one hand to grab them, while at other times they used two hands. Moreover, Corbetta and Thelen (1999) found that patterns of lateral instability, instead of decreasing with time, increased. Indeed, lateral instability was especially characteristic of the second half of the first year, suggesting that improvement in arm control played a small role in the development of lateral preferences. Finally, by analyzing patterns of spontaneous upper-arm activity, Corbetta & Thelen (1996, 1999) were able to demonstrate that these patterns of fluctuation in interlimb coordination and lateral biases were not unique to goal-oriented reaching, but corresponded to pervasive responses of the system that affected also patterns of coordination in upper-arm sponta- neous activity.

Figure 2.1 illustrates these developmental changes and fluctuations in reaching patterning (top chart) and spontaneous interlimb activity (bot- tom chart) throughout the first year in one infant, NQ, who began to reach for the first time at twelve weeks of age. The top graph illustrates changes in reaching patterning from twelve to fifty-two weeks old. The y-axis represents the indexed number of one- versus two-handed reaches performed every week. A value of −1 indicates that NQ reached only using one arm, a value of +1 indicates that NQ reached only with two arms, and any value in between indicates a gradual mixture of one- and two-handed reaches, ranging from predominantly one-handed reaches (negative val- ues) to predominantly two-handed reaching (positive values). As shown, NQ had two periods of two-handed reaching: a first one following the onset of reaching, from twelve to twenty-one weeks old, and a second one toward the end of the year, from forty-four to fifty-two weeks old. Indeed, NQ returned to two-handed reaching at the end of the first year, although he was, by that time, quite experienced at reaching for small objects with one arm and was very familiar with the task.

The bottom graph in figure 2.1 represents a frequency landscape of the different patterns of upper-arm interlimb activity generated sponta- neously by NQ during the same developmental period. Interlimb coor- dination in these spontaneous patterns of activity was captured by using a running correlation function applied to the resultant velocity profiles of both arm movements. This is illustrated in figure 2.2. The small charts at the top of figure 2.2 show two examples of spontaneous interlimb ac- tivity during a 9 s time window. The example on the left reveals that the resultant speed profiles of both-arms movements displayed quasi- simultaneous changes in acceleration and deceleration, while the example on the right exhibits quite different speed profiles for each hand. The two smaller charts located underneath each resultant speed chart dis- play the corresponding running correlation functions used to capture these different patterns of interlimb coordination. The left charts show

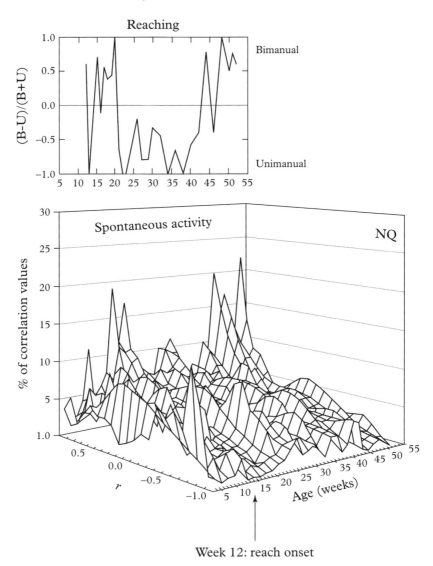

Figure 2.1 Fluctuations in reaching patterning and spontaneous inter-limb activity in infant NQ during his first year of life. *Top graph*: Indexed number of unimanual vs. bimanual reaching by week. *Bottom graph*: Frequency landscape of correlation values expressing various patterns of interlimb coordination by week.

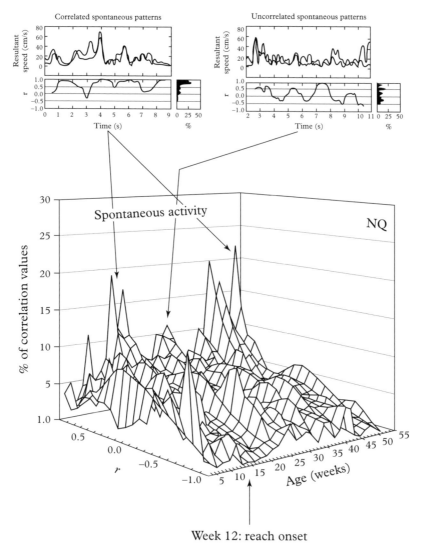

Figure 2.2 Fluctuations in spontaneous interlimb activity in infant NQ during his first year of life. *Top left graph*: Exemplar of highly correlated patterns of interlimb activity. The resultant speed profiles shown on the top chart reveal quasi-simultaneous patterns of acceleration and deceleration. These patterns yielded to a predominantly positive running correlation function (shown on smaller charts underneath). *Top right graph*: Exemplar of uncorrelated patterns of interlimb activity. The resultant speed profiles shown on the top chart reveal different patterns of acceleration and deceleration. These patterns yielded to changing and lower correlation values (shown on smaller charts underneath). *Bottom graph*: Frequency landscape of correlation values expressing various patterns of interlimb coordination by week.

that the running correlation is most of the time positive as a result of the quasi-simultaneous changes in acceleration and deceleration between arms. The charts on the right, on the other hand, reveal that the non-simultaneous patterns of acceleration and deceleration in both arms yielded to lower or negative correlation values. The ensemble of correlation values obtained for each week are reported in the 3D-landscape shown in figure 2.2. This landscape, therefore, summarizes and describes how NQ's spontaneous patterns of coordination changed over the first year. Higher peaks on the landscape mean that some patterns of coordination were produced more frequently than other patterns during certain developmental periods.

As shown in figures 2.1 and 2.2, this landscape revealed two peak periods during which NQ generated a higher rate of interlimb patterns with similar acceleration/deceleration phases. Strikingly, these periods of correlated spontaneous arm activity co-occurred during the same periods during which NQ reached more bimanually (see figure 2.1).

The three other infants in the study also revealed concurrent shifts and fluctuations in spontaneous interlimb coordination and reaching throughout the first year (see Corbetta & Thelen, 1996). However, just as Gesell and Ames (1947) observed, the time at which these fluctuations and transitions occurred was highly individually defined. There was no blueprint or consistent developmental pathway that could be used to predict when and at which age infants shifted their patterns of interlimb coordination.

Why do these fluctuations occur? A better understanding and possible explanation of the origins of these fluctuations in upper-arm coordination became possible when Corbetta and Thelen (1996, 1999) compared the shifts in arm patterning to periods of postural transitions in the first year (Spencer et al., 2000). Consistently with previous findings (Goldfield, 1993; Rochat, 1992), Corbetta and Thelen noticed that transitions in interlimb coordination and lateral biases often matched transitions in the development of new postural milestones. For example, they observed that in some infants, early unimanual and right-handed responses developed following the emergence of hand and knee posture. That was the case for NQ. They also noticed that in all four infants, the later disruption of predominant lateral biases followed the development of crawling. Finally, NQ's return to two-handed reaching toward the end of the first year coincided with the emergence of upright locomotion (Thelen & Smith, 1994). It is indeed possible that shifts in postural development and its control influence and modify the organization of the upper-arm system by strengthening or weakening coupling activity between arms at certain developmental periods. Moreover, linking shifts in interlimb coordination to transitions in postural control may provide a rationale for the individual variations observed in regard to the time at which these fluctuations in interlimb coordination occur. It is well known that the rate at which these postural milestones are developed varies enormously from one infant to another. The fact that these transitions in posture and interlimb coordination co-occur within a same time frame within a same infant developmental history may support the existence of a functional link between posture and upper-arm activity, as already suggested by others (see for example, Rochat & Bullinger, 1994). However, before drawing firm conclusions about the relations between posture and upper-arm activity a cautionary note seems necessary. Given the small sample of four infants in this study, such hypotheses should be tested and verified on a broader population. Nevertheless, the important contribution of this first longitudinal study on reaching that screened multiple behavioral components at a time made possible the formulation of new hypotheses on the origins of the early shifts and fluctuations occurring in infant interlimb coordination: that shifts in interlimb patterning and reaching may not simply result from autonomous changes in the central nervous system, but may rather reflect the pervasive behavioral reorganization of the system in response to changing components in the postural system. Here again, the main idea is that microdevelopmental change takes place as the result of a continuous process of modifications and alterations of current abilities as infants develop and learn new skills as a function of time.

Treadmill stepping as a microdevelopmental experiment

Our third example of microdevelopmental approaches in motor development involves the important milestone of learning to walk. Indeed, the acquisition of upright locomotion, a classic topic in the field, was once again long believed to be under the control of maturational processes in the brain. As with kicking and reaching, the fluctuations and individual differences seen in the developmental course of learning to walk were also thought to reflect waves of brain reorganization (McGraw, 1945). When motor development was conceptualized as largely maturational, research was primarily observational: watching and cataloguing the inevitable stages of change. (The notable exception to this was McGraw's [1935] classic intervention study of the twins, Jimmy and Johnny.) In the last two decades, our theories of the development of upright locomotion have changed from a top-down view of autonomous brain maturation setting the pace of change to a more contemporary notion of dynamic, soft-assembled patterns in systems in continual interaction with the physical properties of the body and the environment. Such a dynamic view opens up the possibility for identifying and experimentally manipulating possible agents of change, using microdevelopmental design.

A good example of this approach is Thelen and Ulrich's (1991) and Vereijken & Thelen's (1997) studies of treadmill stepping in infants. The theoretical issue is: how is upright locomotion – a new pattern – assembled from precursors that themselves are not locomotion? Are there components of the process that are stable and ready before locomotion commences? What are the factors that shift the system into the new form, and can they be experimentally manipulated?

These studies were based on Thelen's (1986) discovery that pre-locomotor infants, indeed infants who did not even show "stepping" movements when held upright, would perform well-coordinated, alternating locomotor-like patterns when they were supported on a small, motorized treadmill. Further research showed that this behavior was not simply a stereotyped reflex, but a flexible and adaptive pattern, although likely not a voluntary one in the accepted sense (Thelen, Ulrich, & Niles, 1987). These authors proposed that the treadmill was itself like a microgenesis experiment: it provided for the infant a component of the behavior that mimicked a longer developmental change. More specifically, the treadmill acted to mechanically stretch the standing legs backward. This is the action that independent walkers normally do when they shift their weight onto the stance leg after the foot has touched the ground. With this weight shift, the trailing leg is stretched. Stretching the leg has two effects. First it provides tension in the muscles that allows the leg to easily swing forward for the next step. And second, a stretched leg appears to signal to the opposite leg to remain in stance. We surmise this because when we switch on the treadmill, both of the infant's legs are pulled back, yet typically only one leg swings forward. There appear to be some neural connections that facilitate this pattern of interlimb coordination. Nevertheless, the treadmill seems to be an efficient apparatus to elicit one important leg response that will likely become a functional component of later independent locomotion, but this response in "pre-locomotor" infants is only expressed when the biomechanical and support conditions are appropriate.

Thelen and Ulrich (1991) traced the developmental course of this pre-locomotor response to understand how it would re-assemble during the first year. They discovered that alternating treadmill stepping could be elicited in infants as young as one month, but that the patterns were variable and unstable. The proportion of well-coordinated movements increased over the next few months such that by six months, all of the infants were performing nicely coordinated stepping. What accounted for this improvement in response to the treadmill? Thelen & Ulrich (1991) compared treadmill stepping to other changes in infants' body build and postural configurations. They found that treadmill performance was associated with changes in the predominant leg postures adopted by the infants at different ages. Specifically, young infants were more likely to have a flexor-dominant posture, that is, to hold their legs more tightly bent toward their bodies. Since treadmill stepping can only be elicited when the legs are stretched back by the treadmill, this response was not easily performed when infants' muscles were tightly flexed. Also, the leg "spring" must have sufficient flexibility to respond to the treadmill. As infants moved their legs more and used them for rolling and sitting, this flexor dominance changed to a more extensor posture (see also Thelen & Fisher, 1983b). This allowed the facilitating effect of the treadmill to provide adequately the missing stretch component and, consequently, promoted smoother and more stable coordination.

An important tenet of both the dynamical systems approach and microgenetic methods is that intervention in a developing system is only effective when the system is in transition. At such times, systems have sufficient instability to be affected by appropriate agents of change. In many cases, experimenters intervene to provide additional training to show that they can shift behavior into a more mature form by practice (e.g. Siegler & Jenkins, 1989).

This is what Vereijken and Thelen (1997) did with treadmill stepping. They saw from the earlier study that at three months, infants were just at the point where rapid improvements in treadmill stepping commenced. Variability was high. At seven months, in contrast, infants' performance was good and also quite stable, both within and between observations. Thus, they initiated a program of month-long intensive home training on the treadmill of infants at these two ages and compared them to babies without daily training. They found that, indeed, trained three-month-olds improved in the number of alternating treadmill steps. Untrained infants also improved, but to a lesser degree. Seven-month-olds, in contrast, did not improve their patterns whether trained or untrained. They were likely at ceiling performance from the start.

Treadmill training might work on several levels which could not be distinguished by this procedure. For example, training may activate and strengthen the neural pathways that produce the stepping pattern when the legs are stretched. Training may also strengthen muscles. Or it may promote a more extended and thus responsive leg posture. Or all of these changes may occur. In any event, these are also likely changes that happen developmentally as infants naturally move on their own and begin to roll, sit, and even crawl, and as parents practice standing with them. These experiments, therefore, have identified times of transitions and possible mechanisms by which those transitions are initiated and resolved.

Conclusions

As discussed throughout this chapter, a major focus of developmental research is to uncover and understand which processes underlie the emergence of new behavioral forms at certain points in time. Although it is widely accepted that such processes take place through the interactions between an organism and its environment, the methods used to study these interactions and related processes have been quite different. We made a distinction between what we called the more traditional methods, which tend to be "anchored" by age and only allow the observation of "snapshots" of performance at the different ages, and the more recent methods used by dynamic systems and microgenesis studies which emphasize the need to study change as a function of continuous timescales. In particular, we explained how the *search* for developmental processes can be better achieved by tracking changes and interactions between organism and environment as a function of continuous and multiple timescales. We illustrated this throughout a series of examples from our research in infant motor development. We showed how screening multiple behavioral levels at once over similar timescales, or providing certain environments during critical developmental times can lead to a novel interpretation and understanding of the processes of underlying behavioral changes. For example, we illustrated how postural transitions may differentially influence patterns of interlimb coordination in reaching or pre-locomotor stepping patterns in infants. We also described how changes induced by the environment, by using a treadmill or a mobile, can modify the history of a system and shift patterns of coordination to a new mode of functioning.

We believe that the general theoretical/methodological stance of dynamic systems and the compatible notions of microgenesis hold for all developmental phenomena, not just those involving coordination and control of the limbs. As illustrated in this book, scientists are now able to apply such methods to teaching in the classroom, theory in evolution, emotional and cognitive development, and the formation of strategies for solving problems, to only cite a few examples. Clearly, studying behavior and systems as a function of time allows a better understanding of the systems themselves, their potential for learning and development, and may help scientists and practitioners to improve intervention by identifying times during which the developing system is more sensitive to learning.

References

Corbetta, D., & Thelen, E. (1996). The developmental origins of bimanual coordination: A dynamic perspective. *Journal of Experimental Psychology: Human Perception and Performance, 22*, 502–522.

Corbetta, D., & Thelen, E. (1999). Lateral biases and fluctuations in infants' spontaneous arm movements and reaching. *Developmental Psychobiology, 34*, 237–255.

Fagard, J., & Pézé, A. (1997). Age changes in interlimb coupling and the development of bimanual coordination. *Journal of Motor Behavior, 29*, 199–208.

Flament, F. (1975). *Coordination et prévalence manuelle chez le nourrisson.* Paris: Editions du C.N.R.S.

Gesell, A. (1939). Reciprocal interweaving in neuromotor development. *Journal of Comparative Neurology, 70*, 161–180.

Gesell, A. (1956). The ontogenesis of infant behavior. In L. Carmichael (Ed.), *Manual of child psychology* (pp. 295–331). New York: John Wiley.

Gesell, A., & Ames, L. B. (1947). The development of handedness. *Journal of Genetic Psychology, 70*, 155–175.

Goldfield, E. (1993). Dynamic systems in development: Action systems. In L. B. Smith & E. Thelen (Eds.), *A dynamic systems approach to development: Applications* (pp. 51–70). Cambridge, MA: MIT Press.

Goldfield, E. C., & Michel, G. F. (1986a). Spatiotemporal linkage in infant interlimb coordination. *Developmental Psychology, 19*, 259–264.

Goldfield, E. C., & Michel, G. F. (1986b). The ontogeny of infant bimanual reaching during the first year. *Infant Behavior and Development, 9*, 81–89.

Granott, N. (1998). Unit of analysis in transit: From the individual's knowledge to the ensemble process. *Mind, Culture, and Activity, 5*, 42–66.

Hofsten, C. von (1991). Structuring of early reaching movements: A longitudinal study. *Journal of Motor Behavior, 23*, 280–292.

Hofsten, C. von, & Fazel-Zandy, S. (1984). Development of visually guided hand orientation in reaching. *Journal of Experimental Child Psychology, 38*, 208–219.

Lockman, J. J., Ashmead, D. H., & Bushnell, E. W. (1984). The development of anticipatory hand orientation during infancy. *Journal of Experimental Child Psychology, 37*, 176–186.

McGraw, M. (1935). *Growth: A study of Johnny and Jimmy.* New York: Appleton-Century Croft.

McGraw, M. (1945). *The neuromuscular maturation of the human infant.* New York: Columbia University Press.

Newell, K. M., Scully, D. M., McDonald, P. V., & Baillargeon, R. (1989). Task constraints and infant grip configurations. *Developmental Psychobiology, 22*, 817–832.

Prechtl, H. F. R. (1977). *The neurological examination of the full-term newborn infant.* London: S.I.M.P and Heinemann.

Rochat, P. (1992). Self-sitting and reaching in 5- to 8-month-old infants: The impact of posture and its development on early eye-hand coordination. *Journal of Motor Behavior, 24*, 210–220.

Rochat, P., & Bullinger, A. (1994). Posture and functional action in infancy. In A. Vyt, H. Bloch, & M. H. Bornstein (Eds.), *Early child development in the French tradition* (pp. 15–34). Hillsdale, NJ: Erlbaum.

Rovee-Collier, C. K. (1991). The "memory system" of prelinguistic infants. In A. Diamond (Ed.),*The development and neural bases of higher cognitive functions. Annals of the New York Academy of Sciences, 608,* 517–536.

Rovee-Collier, C. K., Morongiello, B. A., Aron, M., & Kupersmidt, J. (1978). Topographic response differentiation and reversal in 3-month-old infants. *Infant Behavior and Development, 1,* 323–333.

Siegler, R. S. (1996). *Emerging minds: The process of change in children's thinking.* New York: Oxford University Press.

Siegler, R. S., & Jenkins, E. (1989). *How children discover new strategies.* Hillsdale, NJ: Erlbaum.

Spencer, J. P., & Thelen, E. (2000). Spatially specific changes in infants' muscle co-activity as they learn to reach. *Infancy, 1,* 275–302.

Spencer, J. P., Vereijken, B., Diedrich, F. J., & Thelen, E. (2000). Posture and the emergence of manual skills. *Developmental Science, 3,* 216–233.

Thelen, E. (1986). Treadmill-elicited stepping in seven-month-old infants. *Child Development, 57,* 1498–1506.

Thelen, E. (1994). Three-month-old infants can learn task-specific patterns of interlimb coordination. *Psychological Science, 5,* 280–285.

Thelen, E., Bradshaw, G., & Ward, J. A. (1981). Spontaneous kicking in month-old infants: Manifestation of a human central locomotor program. *Behavioral and Neural Biology, 32,* 45–53.

Thelen, E., Corbetta, D., Kamm, K., Spencer, J. P., Schneider, K., & Zernicke, R. F. (1993). The transition to reaching: Mapping intention and intrinsic dynamics. *Child Development, 64,* 1058–1098.

Thelen, E., Corbetta, D., & Spencer, J. (1996). Development of reaching during the first year: Role of movement speed. *Journal of Experimental Psychology: Human Perception and Performance, 22,* 1059–1076.

Thelen, E., & Fisher, D. M. (1982). Newborn stepping: An explanation for a "disappearing reflex." *Developmental Psychology, 18,* 760–775.

Thelen, E., & Fisher, D. M. (1983a). From spontaneous to instrumental behavior: Kinematic analysis of movement changes during very early learning. *Child Development, 54,* 129–140.

Thelen, E., & Fisher, D. M. (1983b). The organization of spontaneous leg movements in newborn infants. *Journal of Motor Behavior, 15,* 353–377.

Thelen, E., Ridley-Johnson, R., & Fisher, D. M. (1983). Shifting patterns of bilateral coordination and lateral dominance in the leg movements of young infants. *Developmental Psychobiology, 16,* 29–46.

Thelen, E., & Smith, L. B. (1994). *A dynamic systems approach to the development of cognition and action.* Cambridge, MA: MIT Press.

Thelen, E., & Smith, L. B. (1997). Dynamic systems theories. In W. Damon (Series Ed.), & R. M. Lerner (Vol. Ed.), *Handbook of child psychology, Vol. 1: Theoretical models of human development* (5th edn., pp. 563–634). New York: Wiley.

Thelen, E., & Ulrich, B. D. (1991). Hidden skills. *Monographs of the Society for Research in Child Development, 56* (Serial No. 223).

Thelen, E., Ulrich, B. D., & Niles, D. (1987). Bilateral coordination in human infants: Stepping on a split-belt treadmill. *Journal of Experimental Psychology: Human Perception and Performance, 13*, 405–410.

Touwen, B. (1976). *Neurological development in infancy*. London: S.I.M.P. and Heinemann.

Van Geert, P. (1994). *Dynamic systems and development. Change between complexity and chaos*. New York: Harvester Wheatsheaf.

Vereijken, B., & Thelen, E. (1997). Training infant treadmill stepping: The role of individual pattern stability. *Developmental Psychobiology, 30*, 89–102.

Vygotsky, L. S. (1978). *Mind in society: The development of higher psychological processes*. Cambridge, MA: Harvard University Press.

3 Looking at the hands through time: A microgenetic perspective on learning and instruction

Susan Goldin-Meadow and Martha Wagner Alibali

Methods for studying learning typically involve three steps: Assess the learner's knowledge of the task. Provide instruction or some form of intervention on the task. Reassess the learner's knowledge of the task. Any improvement that the learner demonstrates between assessment 1 and assessment 2 is assumed to constitute learning. This method can provide rich information about the effect of intervention on a learner's initial state – it elegantly documents *that* learning has occurred. However, the method tells us very little about *how* the learner arrives at the final state – it tells us little about the process of learning.

Microgenetic methods (Siegler & Crowley, 1991) were developed to investigate the small steps learners take in their acquisition of knowledge, particularly steps taken just prior to apparent progress (Karmiloff-Smith, 1992; Kuhn, Garcia-Mila, Zohar, & Andersen, 1995; Siegler & Jenkins, 1989). The goal of microgenetic studies is to examine the learner, not just before and after instruction as in traditional training studies, but throughout the learning process. Such studies provide a spotlight on the period of transition itself.

The spotlight can, of course, have a wide or narrow beam. We can examine change over a period of minutes, hours, days, weeks, or years. One challenge in microgenetic studies is selecting the appropriate time period over which to view change. The appropriate units and intervals between them depend on the pace at which we expect change to occur. If explicit instruction is given on a task, change is more likely than if no instruction is given – and consequently, our beam can be narrower, focusing on a shorter period of time. One goal of this chapter is to examine short-term change before, during, and after instruction on a task, and contrast such change with longer-term change that takes place in the

We are grateful to Theresa Graham, Martha Scott, Melissa Singer, and San Kim for their contributions to the studies described herein. This research was supported by grants to Susan Goldin-Meadow from the National Institutes of Child Health and Human Development (R01 HD18617) and the Spencer Foundation.

absence of instruction. In both instances, we observe the unfolding of events over time – minutes in one case, weeks in the other.

A second challenge in microgenetic studies of learning is identifying when a learner is undergoing change. It is relatively easy to identify a learner as having been "in transition" after a task has been mastered – the learner who made progress on the task was in transition, whereas the learner who failed to make progress was not. However, such a post hoc measure is of limited use, both for experimenters interested in exploring the process of change, and for teachers interested in identifying learners who might be in a transitional period and therefore particularly receptive to instruction. We need a measure of transition that is not after-the-fact, and that has the potential to capture change as it is occurring.

In our previous work, we have found that gesture, particularly when considered in relation to the accompanying speech, can be used to identify when a child has transitional knowledge about a task. Children (and adults: Alibali, Bassok, Solomon, Syc, & Goldin-Meadow, 1999; Perry & Elder, 1996) frequently gesture when asked to explain how they solved a task. Interestingly, in both children and adults, the information speakers convey in gestures does not always match the information they convey in the accompanying words. For example, a child asked to explain his response to a Piagetian number conservation task said, "they [the two rows of checkers] are different because you moved them," thus focusing, in his words, on the experimenter's actions. However, in his gestures, the child made it clear that he had some understanding of the one-to-one correspondence between the checkers in the two rows – he moved his pointing finger from checker 1 in the first row to checker 1 in the second, then from checker 2 in the first row to checker 2 in the second, and so on (Church & Goldin-Meadow, 1986). The important point for our purposes here is that these "mismatches" between gesture and speech reflect transitional knowledge. Children whose gestures often convey information about a task that is different from the information conveyed in their speech are likely to make progress when given instruction on that task. In other words, these children are "ready" to learn the task and, in this sense, are in transition (Church & Goldin-Meadow, 1986; Perry, Church, & Goldin-Meadow, 1988).

Why might gesture, taken in relation to speech, be a good index of transitional knowledge? By definition, a gesture–speech mismatch involves two ideas, one conveyed in speech and the other in gesture, both articulated on the same problem. Learners who produce gesture–speech mismatches are displaying variability in their problem-solving performance on each problem. Variability plays an important, and perhaps even essential, role in developmental change, as several theorists have recently argued (e.g., Bertenthal, 1996; Siegler, 1996; Thelen, 1989), and gesture–speech mismatches are a concrete manifestation of variability. We suggest that gestures convey knowledge that learners have not yet integrated into their explicitly acknowledged view of a problem. As such, gesture expresses incipient ideas that may, perhaps with instruction, grow into more stable, explicit ones.

Gesture thus provides us with the opportunity to chart variability that might otherwise go unnoticed. In this chapter, we present three studies that use gesture as a window into variability and change. We use this window, not only to observe the learner before and after change has taken place, but also to examine the process of change. In the first pair of studies, we use a microgenetic approach to explore change both in the absence of instruction and in response to explicit instruction. We use gesture and speech to chart children's level of variability and their progress in learning to solve mathematical equations. In the third study, we use a microgenetic approach to explore how unscripted, tutorial mathematics lessons unfold over time. In particular, we focus on the impact of children's gestures on teachers' responses. Before turning to these microgenetic studies, we briefly review the studies that provide support for the claim that gesture reflects transitional knowledge.

Gesture is a reliable and informative index of transitional knowledge

Gesture-speech mismatch reflects openness to instruction

As described above, speakers often gesture when asked to explain their solutions to a task. At times, those gestures convey essentially the same information as conveyed in speech. For example, when asked to solve addition problems involving the concept of mathematical equivalence (i.e., the idea that the two sides of an equation represent the same quantity), e.g., $3 + 5 + 4 = \underline{} + 4$, fourth-grade children (nine- to ten-year-olds) frequently solve the problems incorrectly, and offer incorrect explanations in both speech and gesture for their solutions. A child might say, "I added 3, 5, 4, and 4, and got 16," while pointing at 3, 5, 4 on the left side of the equation, 4 on the right side, and then the blank (an "add-all-numbers" explanation).

At times, however, children produce the same verbal explanation, but along with it produce a very different gestural explanation. For example, while saying "I added 3, 5, 4, and 4, and got 16, and put it in the blank," the child may point at 3 and 5 – the two numbers that can be added to arrive at the correct solution (a "group-two-numbers" explanation).

Some children frequently produce such gesture–speech mismatches when they explain mathematical equivalence problems. When given instruction, such children are significantly more likely to profit from that instruction than children who seldom produce mismatches (Perry et al., 1988). Thus, producing different information in gesture and speech is a signal that the child is open to instruction on that task. Importantly, we have found this same phenomenon with younger children in Piagetian conservation tasks (Church & Goldin-Meadow, 1986) – the phenomenon is not tied to one age, nor to one task.

Gesture–speech mismatch reflects the activation of two ideas on the same problem

By definition, a gesture–speech mismatch incorporates two pieces of information within a single response, one conveyed in speech and another conveyed in gesture. Thus, mismatches are evidence of variability in children's problem solving. However, what we take to be significant is that mismatches provide evidence, not just that the speaker has two ideas available within his or her repertoire, but that the speaker has invoked both of those ideas on a single problem. Put another way, mismatches reflect variability in children's approaches to individual problems. We suggest that concurrently activating two ideas on a single problem may, in fact, be a defining feature of the transitional period.

Note, however, that gesture–speech mismatch is found in problem explanations. Explanations produced "after the fact" may have little to do with how a problem actually was solved (Ericsson & Simon, 1993; Nisbett & Wilson, 1977). Thus, the fact that children exhibit two ideas when *explaining* how they solved a problem does not necessarily mean that the children consider both ideas when *solving* the problem. Mismatches could reflect post hoc reasoning processes rather than on-line problem solving.

To explore this possibility, we conducted a study to determine whether children who produce many mismatches activate more than one idea, not only when they explain their solutions, but also when they solve the problems (Goldin-Meadow, Nusbaum, Garber, & Church, 1993). The approach underlying the study assumes that activating more than one idea when solving a problem takes more cognitive resources than activating a single idea. Thus, a child who activates more than one idea on one task (a math task) should have less capacity left over to simultaneously perform a second task (a word recall task) than a child who activates only a single idea.

Children were initially given six mathematical equivalence problems and asked to solve and then explain the solution to each problem. These explanations were later used to divide children into those who produced many mismatches and those who produced few. Next, on each of twenty-four trials, children were given a list of words to remember and an equation to solve but *not* explain. Note that children were not asked for explanations at any time during this second part of the study, and that the equation and word recall tasks were conducted concurrently, thus presumably *both* drawing upon the limited pool of cognitive resources a child has available.

All of the children, both matchers and mismatchers, solved the equations incorrectly. If explanations are an accurate reflection of the processes that take place in problem-solving, we would expect the mismatching children, who tend to produce two ideas per *explanation* (one in speech and a second in gesture), to also activate two ideas when *solving* each equation. In contrast, matching children, who tend to produce a single idea per *explanation*, would be expected to activate only one idea when *solving* each equation. If this is the case, the mismatching children are, in a sense, working harder to arrive at their incorrect solutions to the equations than are the matching children, and should have fewer resources left over to tackle the word recall task. In other words, because their cognitive capacities are taxed, mismatching children should recall significantly fewer words than matching children, despite the fact that all of the children performed alike on the equation task. This was precisely the pattern of results found in the study.

Mismatching children thus appear to be working harder than matching children to solve the math problems. Intuitively, a child in transition ought to be more advanced and should perform better than the child who has not yet entered the transitional period. However, our data suggest otherwise – the mismatching children, who have been shown to be particularly ready to learn in previous studies, performed *less well* on the word recall task than the matching children. The mismatching children carry the extra burden of too many unintegrated ideas, a burden that appears to demand cognitive resources, leaving fewer resources available for other tasks.

These findings suggest that there may be a cognitive "cost" to being in transition, a cost that may explain why the transitional state is an unstable one. The extra burden carried by the child in transition may make it difficult to remain in a transitional period for long periods. Thus, the variability displayed in the transitional knowledge state may not be long-lasting. The microgenetic studies we describe in later sections directly test this prediction.

Gesture reflects implicit knowledge that is unique to it

When considered in relation to speech, gesture provides a reliable index of the stability of a child's cognitive state. Does gesture also shed light on the knowledge that contributes to that state? The information that a child conveys in gesture is a good candidate for implicit knowledge – knowledge that at some level the child "has," but is not able to articulate (Berry & Broadbent, 1984; Clements & Perner, 1994; Karmiloff-Smith, 1992; Reber, 1993; Stanley, Mathews, Buss, & Kotler-Cope, 1989). There are two steps involved in showing that gesture reflects implicit knowledge.

We first demonstrate that at least some of the knowledge children convey in their gestures is not accessible to speech. We examined the entire set of responses that fourth-grade children produced when asked to explain their solutions to a set of mathematical equivalence problems, and determined which problem-solving strategies were expressed (1) in gesture and never in speech, (2) in speech and never in gesture, or (3) in both gesture and speech. A strategy need not have been produced in gesture and speech on the same problem in order for it to be classified in the third category; it was sufficient for the child to produce the strategy in gesture on one problem and in speech on another problem. Focusing on children who produced gestures on at least three out of six problems (70% of the children), we found that children expressed many strategies uniquely in gesture, and never in speech. However, children expressed very few strategies uniquely in speech, that is, without some expression in gesture even if on another problem. Thus, the children tended to express strategies either in both gesture and speech, or uniquely in gesture (Goldin-Meadow, Alibali, & Church, 1993; Goldin-Meadow, 1999). Most of the information these children possessed about the math problems was accessible to gesture, and some of that information was accessible *only* to gesture.

We next demonstrate that children actually have the knowledge that we impute to them on the basis of their spontaneous gestures. We have assumed that when a string of pointing gestures is produced along with a spoken problem-solving strategy, those pointing gestures are themselves conveying a problem-solving strategy. But it is also possible that the pointing gestures are produced simply to direct the listener's attention to the numbers in the problem. There is evidence, however, that the string of gestures, when taken together, does reflect a strategy in its own right. The evidence comes from cases in which children's gestures do *not* match speech. For example, consider a child responding to the problem $3 + 4 + 7 = \_\_\_ + 7$. The child articulates an "add-numbers-to-equal-sign" strategy in speech, "I added 3, 4, and 7, and put 14 in the blank." In gesture, however, the child produced a string of points that appeared to reflect a completely different strategy – point at 3, 4, left 7, right 7, and the blank, an "add-all-numbers" strategy.

We asked children to rate whether different solutions were acceptable as answers to the math problems. On the whole, children were happy to accept more than one answer for a single problem. A child like the one above would, of course, rate 14 as an acceptable answer to the problem above – 14 is the answer generated by the "add-numbers-to-equal-sign" strategy that she had conveyed in speech. More interesting is her rating of 21 – the answer generated by the "add-all-numbers" strategy that she conveyed in gesture but not speech. In fact, the child is quite likely to give 21 a high rating. Overall, children gave higher ratings to solutions generated by strategies they had expressed uniquely in gesture than to solutions generated by strategies that they had not expressed in either gesture or speech (Garber, Alibali, & Goldin-Meadow, 1998). In other words, children recognized the solutions generated by strategies that they had expressed *only* in their gestures. Thus, gestures can indeed reveal knowledge about problem-solving strategies. Children may not be able to express in speech the problem-solving knowledge that they convey in gesture, but they are able to recognize it on other, gesture-independent tasks, like the rating task. In this sense, the knowledge conveyed uniquely in gesture is implicit knowledge.

Summary

Our previous work suggests that, when in transition with respect to a particular task, children produce frequent gesture–speech mismatches in their explanations of that task. These mismatches are a concrete manifestation of variability in children's thinking, and they reflect the fact that children are activating two ideas on a single problem. These two ideas crop up on the same problem, not only when children are explaining how they solved that problem, but also when solving the problem in the first place. Producing two unintegrated ideas on a single problem appears to exact a cognitive cost, which may be one reason the transitional state is unstable. In the next section, we examine stability and change in the variability of children's knowledge, both with and without instruction.

One of the two ideas that comprise a mismatching response is expressed in speech. That idea is likely to be acknowledged by both the child and those who interact with that child. The other idea is conveyed only in gesture, and therefore may go unnoticed by others. In the final section of the paper, we ask whether the child's gestures do indeed go unnoticed, or whether they play a role in shaping how others (such as teachers) interact with that child.

The effect of instruction on the child: Changes revealed in gesture and speech

Children who perform incorrectly on a task and often produce mismatches on that task are "at risk" for learning – when exposed to instruction on the task, they profit from that instruction, making more progress on the task than children who also perform incorrectly but who seldom produce mismatches (Perry et al., 1988). Thus, the mismatching incorrect state is closer to mastery than the matching incorrect state. These findings suggest a trajectory that learners may follow in mastering a task: They begin by producing incorrect responses in both gesture and speech – a consistent incorrect state. They then enter a transitional state in which they produce gesture–speech mismatches (in which both responses may be incorrect or one, usually gesture, may be correct) – a variable, mismatching state. Finally, they return to a matching state, but this time both responses are correct – a consistent correct state (Alibali & Goldin-Meadow, 1993).

The transitional state is a more advanced state than the matching incorrect state. However, it is also inherently more unstable. The fact that learners in a mismatching state routinely activate two notions that have not yet been integrated (one in speech and the other in gesture) is itself a sign of instability – and our previous work (cf. Goldin-Meadow, Nusbaum et al., 1993) has indicated that being in a state of mismatch has a cognitive cost. We therefore might hypothesize that a mismatching state is one in which learners do not stay for long periods of time – the child will either progress to a consistent correct state if adequate instruction is provided, or regress to a consistent incorrect state if no instruction is available.

We tested this prediction in two microgenetic studies. In the first, we followed a group of children asked to solve mathematical equivalence problems on a weekly basis over a period of weeks, and we observed the progress (or lack of progress) they made in the absence of instruction. In the second study, we followed children over a much shorter period of time, a matter of under an hour, rather than several weeks. Some children received instruction and others did not. This design allowed us to evaluate the effects of instruction on children's trajectories of change.

A long-term microgenetic study: Change in children's understanding of mathematical equivalence in the absence of instruction

In this first study, our goal was to examine change in children's understanding of mathematical equivalence in the absence of instruction. We expected progress to be slow, but we were interested in capturing even small and transient changes in children's problem-solving performance. Hence, we selected weeks as our observation interval. Twenty-one fourth-grade children were asked to solve and explain a set of mathematical equivalence problems on a weekly basis for a period of five weeks.[1]

We predicted that, in the absence of instruction, variability within individual children would decrease over the course of the study. For children who began the study in a variable mismatching state, we expected them to decrease variability over the study because of the cognitive "cost" of maintaining and activating a large number of different strategies. For children who began the study in a consistent state marked by low variability, we expected them to remain in a state of low variability, and not to increase variability, because they received no instructional input. Thus, we expected relatively few children to increase in variability, and we expected many children to decrease in variability.

On average, across all sessions, children expressed 2.29 different strategies ($SE = 0.09$, range 1–4) and produced 1.58 mismatches ($SE = 0.17$, range 0–6) per session. As predicted, overall levels of variability diminished over the five-week period, as indicated by two converging measures: (1) mean number of different strategies (across both gesture and speech) decreased across sessions (open triangles in figure 3.1; $F(4, 76) = 3.71$, $p < 0.01$), and (2) mean number of gesture–speech mismatches decreased across sessions (filled triangles in figure 3.1; $F(4, 76) = 2.38$, $p = 0.06$). Thus, without instruction, children were over time less likely to maintain a large repertoire of different strategies, and less likely to consider multiple strategies on individual problems.

We next examined the particular transitions children made from one session to the next. Following Perry et al. (1988), children were classified as variable if they produced three or more gesture–speech mismatches in any given set of six responses, and children were classified as consistent if they produced two or fewer mismatches. In twenty-five transitions (out of eighty-three), children began in a *variable state*. In thirteen of these transitions (52%), children left the variable state, eleven regressing to a consistent incorrect state (44%) and only two progressing to a consistent correct state (8%). In the remaining fifty-eight transitions, children began in a *consistent state* (i.e., a state in which they rarely produced mismatches). In fifty of these transitions (86%), children remained consistent, and in the remaining eight (14%), children moved into a variable state. Thus, as expected, variability tended either to decrease or to remain low when children were not given instruction.

---

[1] Fourteen of the children also completed a second knowledge assessment task, which will not be discussed here.

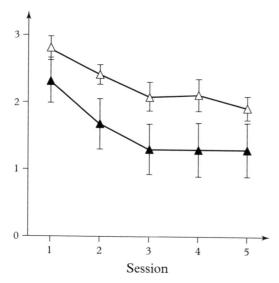

Figure 3.1 Mean numbers of different strategies and gesture–speech mismatches produced at each session in the long-term microgenetic study without instruction. The bars represent standard errors. -△-, Strategies; -▲-, Mismatches.

In sum, evidence from speech and gesture suggests that, for the mathematical equivalence task, children's behavior becomes less variable and more consistent in the absence of instruction. There does appear to be a de facto "cost" to the transitional knowledge state – in the absence of instruction, children are not likely to remain in it. In the next study, we explored whether this pattern held over a shorter time scale, and we also examined the process of change when instruction was provided. We hypothesized that instruction would introduce new ideas into children's thinking. Therefore, we expected variability not to diminish, and perhaps even to increase.

A short-term microgenetic study of the effect of instruction on children's understanding of mathematical equivalence

In this second study, our goal was to examine change in children's understanding of mathematical equivalence, both in the absence and in the presence of explicit instruction. We expected change in response to instruction to be fairly rapid. Hence, we observed children's performance over the course of a single experimental session. Children were asked to solve and explain a set of six mathematical equivalence problems in a pretest. Immediately following this pretest, they were then asked to solve another twelve addition problems in a training set (a subset of the children was also asked to solve six multiplication problems; however, these data will not be discussed here: see Alibali & Goldin-Meadow, 1993). For some children, instruction about equivalence was provided each time they solved one of the training problems incorrectly. For other children, no instruction was provided. For analysis, problems were grouped into three sets of six problems each (the pretest, and two sets of training problems).

We examined children's performance across the pretest and the two sets of training problems in terms of the two measures of variability. On average, across all problem sets and both instruction groups, children expressed 2.25 different strategies ($SE = 0.07$, range 1–7) and produced 1.71 mismatches ($SE = 0.11$, range 0–6) per set. Figure 3.2 presents the mean number of different strategies (top graph) and the mean number of gesture–speech mismatches (bottom graph) produced by children who did vs. children who did not receive instruction on each problem set. On both measures, children in the no-instruction condition (circles, $N = 32$) decreased in variability over the three sets, replicating the five-week study described above. In contrast, and again on both measures, children who received instruction (squares, $N = 58$) increased in variability during the first training set. Overall, children in the instruction group displayed more variability throughout the study than children in the no-instruction group, both in number of different strategies ($F(1, 88) = 10.58$, $p < 0.001$) and in number of gesture–speech mismatches ($F(1, 88) = 6.40$, $p < 0.02$). For many children, instruction served to introduce a new strategy into their repertoires, and also led them to consider multiple strategies for individual problems. By the second set of training problems, many children had integrated the new strategy into their repertoires and abandoned their prior, incorrect strategies – consequently, variability decreased again (figure 3.2).

We next examined the particular transitions that children made from the pretest through the two training sets, focusing on changes in variability as reflected in children's gestures and speech. We first consider transitions that began with children in a *variable state*. As seen at the top of figure 3.3, both with and without instruction, children remained variable in approximately 60% of transitions, moving to a more consistent state in about 40% of transitions. The difference between the groups was in the direction of movement. In the absence of instruction (as in the long-term microgenetic study described above), most of the children who moved regressed to a consistent, incorrect state (left bars). In contrast, when instruction was provided, most of the children who moved progressed to a consistent correct state (right bars).

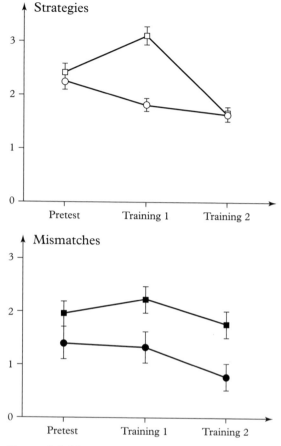

Figure 3.2 Mean numbers of different strategies (*top graph*) and gesture–speech mismatches (*bottom graph*) produced at each session of the short-term microgenetic study with and without instruction. The bars represent standard errors. –□–, Instruction; –○–, No instruction; –■–, Instruction; –●–, No instruction.

We next consider transitions that began with children in a *consistent state*. As seen in the bottom of figure 3.3, without instruction, children remained in a consistent, incorrect state in almost all transitions (93%). Thus, as in the long-term microgenetic study described above, in the absence of instruction, children in a consistent state tended to stay there. When provided with instruction, however, the pattern was quite different: 76% of the children who began in a consistent, incorrect state moved, 29% progressing to a variable mismatching state, and 46% progressing

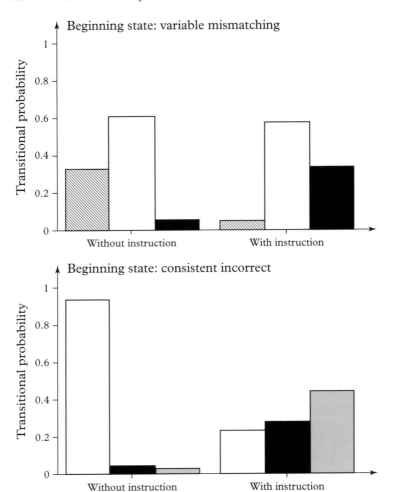

Figure 3.3 The probability that a child will move to a consistent incorrect, variable mismatching, or consistent correct state, given that the child began the transition in a variable mismatching (*top panel*) or in a consistent incorrect (*bottom panel*) state. Probabilities are presented separately for children who received or did not receive instruction during training. *Top panel*: ▨, Regress to consistent incorrect; ☐, Stay variable mismatching; ■, Progress to consistent correct; *bottom panel*: ☐, Stay consistent incorrect; ■, Progress to variable mismatching; ▨, Progress to consistent correct.

directly to a consistent, correct state (i.e., bypassing the variable, mismatching state).[2] Thus, instruction served to introduce new ideas into children's strategy repertoires. In many cases, these new ideas *coexisted* with old ones, resulting in variable behavior. In other cases, new, correct ideas *replaced* old ones, resulting in consistent, correct behavior (replicating Alibali, 1999).[3] These findings raise the question of whether children who progressed to a consistent correct state by *skipping* the variable mismatching state learned the concept of mathematical equivalence as well as children who passed through the variable state.

To explore this question, we examined the children's post-instruction performance as a function of the trajectory they took through the study. All of the children had completed a paper-and-pencil test immediately following the instruction session, and again two weeks later. The test included addition problems similar to those on which the children had received instruction, and multiplication problems which allowed us to determine whether the children had generalized what they had learned. As seen in figure 3.4, children who arrived at the consistent correct state by passing through the variable mismatching state (children who contributed to the black bars in the top of figure 3.3) were more likely to succeed on both types of problems than children who arrived at the consistent correct state by skipping the variable mismatching state (children who contributed to the gray bars in the bottom of figure 3.3). This pattern held for both the posttest (left bars; $\chi^2(1, N = 32) = 6.15$, $p < 0.02$) and the two-week follow-up test (right bars; $\chi^2(1, N = 32) = 6.41$, $p < 0.02$).[4] Thus, gesture–speech mismatch is good for learners. When learners move through a variable, mismatching state on their way

[2] Alibali and Goldin-Meadow (1993) presented the data separately for children who regularly produced gestures, and for children who seldom produced gestures (i.e., children who gestured on two or fewer problems in *all* three sets of six problems). In this paper, we analyzed the data from all children together. As a result, the probabilities presented in the bottom graph in figure 3.3 differ from the transitional probabilities reported by Alibali and Goldin-Meadow (1993).

[3] In thirteen of the twenty transitions in which children progressed directly from a consistent, incorrect state to a consistent, correct state, the children gestured on two or fewer of the six problems both before and after the transition. Note that such children could not be classified as variable on the gesture–speech measure because they gestured so infrequently. It remains an open question whether the absence of gesture in such cases reflects lack of variability, as we have argued here, or whether it reflects a stable disposition not to produce gestures.

[4] This pattern holds for children who skipped the variable mismatching state, regardless of whether or not they produced gestures. Of the five children who often produced gestures but who skipped the variable mismatching state, only one succeeded on both addition and multiplication problems on the posttest, and none on the follow-up. Of the twelve children who rarely produced gestures and who skipped the variable mismatching state, only four succeeded on both addition and multiplication problems on the posttest, and only two on the follow-up.

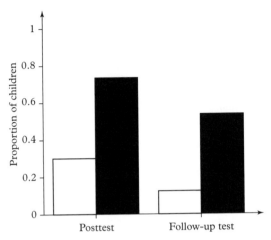

Figure 3.4 Proportion of children who succeeded on both addition and multiplication problems on the posttest, and who maintained that success on the follow-up test, as a function of the child's trajectory during training: Children who passed through the variable, mismatching state on their way to the consistent, correct state vs. children who arrived at the consistent, correct state but did so by bypassing the variable, mismatching state. □, Bypassing the variable state; ■, Passing through the variable state.

to a consistent, correct state, their learning is deeper and more flexible than when they bypass the variable state.

These data also suggest that looking at both speech and gesture is good for experimenters – particularly when a microgenetic perspective is employed. Experimenters would be quite inaccurate at predicting posttest and follow-up test success if they looked only at children's speech, or looked only at their performance immediately before the posttest. To accurately evaluate students' understanding of mathematical equivalence, experimenters must look at both speech and gesture, and must look not only at what children know, but also at how they got there.

The effect of the child on instruction: Do children's gestures influence the course of one-on-one instruction?

We have argued that gesture can provide insight, not only into the stability of the learner's knowledge, but also into the particular notions that the learner is just beginning to entertain. These are the notions that have not yet been integrated into the learner's explicit stance on the problem, and that contribute to performance variability. These same insights are, of course, available to anyone who bothers to look carefully at the learner's gestures. The question is, do participants in an interaction notice, understand, and react to the gestures that speakers produce along with their talk? If so, learners may be able to play a subtle role in shaping the instruction they receive by making their unspoken thoughts accessible to those who interact with them.

Untrained observers can "read" gesture in experimental situations

There are several steps needed to determine whether the gestures children produce in an interaction are "read" by the adults they are interacting with. Our first step was to determine whether adults are able to interpret children's gestures when those gestures have been hand-picked for clarity and when they are presented in an experimental setting (Alibali, Flevares, & Goldin-Meadow, 1997). We selected instances of gesture–speech match and mismatch produced by fourth-grade children on the mathematical equivalence task, and presented them to adult participants on videotape. Each adult saw six children producing mismatches and six children producing matches, and was asked to assess each child's reasoning. The problem used in each videotaped explanation was displayed on a sheet of paper so that the adult could refer to it (in speech and/or gesture) when assessing the child's knowledge.

We found, not surprisingly, that adults accurately repeated or paraphrased virtually all of the *spoken* strategies that the children expressed. The question of interest is whether they were also able to interpret the children's gestures. We found that adults were significantly more likely to add information that the child had *not* articulated in speech when reacting to child mismatches than to child matches, suggesting that the adults' assessments had, indeed, been affected by the children's gestures. The adults appeared to recognize (at some level) that their reiteration of the information conveyed in the child's speech did not capture all that the child knew; they therefore included additional information. Interestingly, the content of about half of these "additions" could be directly traced to the gesture component of the child's gesture–speech mismatch (see also Goldin-Meadow & Sandhofer, 1999; Goldin-Meadow, Wein, & Chang, 1992; Kelly & Church, 1997; 1998).

The adults produced two types of additions that were traceable to children's gestures. In the first, the adult articulated the strategy that the child had produced uniquely in gesture, but denied that the child knew that strategy. For example, one child on the videotape produced a "make-both-sides equal" strategy uniquely in gesture. An adult described this child as follows: "He doesn't understand the equal sign – that the two sides have to – that what's on the left and what's on the right have to be equal." The adult thus described, and denied that the child possessed, the very strategy that the child had expressed in gesture.

In the most common type of addition, adults reproduced the child's gestured strategy in their own gestures without commenting on it at all in speech. For example, one child on the videotape produced an "add-numbers-to-equal-sign" strategy in speech and a "group-two-numbers" strategy in gesture on the problem $4 + 3 + 9 = \underline{\quad} + 9$. In describing this child, one adult reiterated the child's spoken strategy in his own speech (by saying, "she added up all the numbers on the left side and said that it was equal to this blank, again forgetting about the additional sum on the right"), while at the same time reiterating the child's gestured strategy in his own gestures (by pointing at 4 and 3, the two numbers that can be added to obtain the correct answer). In this type of addition, adults neither deny nor attribute the child's gestured strategy to the child, but rather second it in an implicit fashion through their own gestures. As we will see in the next section, this pattern is commonly found in naturalistic interactions between teachers and students.

It is important to note that the adults' "seconded" gestures were not merely unthinking copies of the children's gestures. The adults did not simply mimic the child's forms. Rather, they reproduced the gist of the child's strategy, but did it using different handshapes and motions. For example, a child on the videotape produced a gestured "make-both-sides-equal" strategy by moving his left pointing hand under the left side of the equation and then moving his right pointing hand under the right side of the equation. In describing this child, one adult also expressed the "make-both-sides-equal" strategy in gesture but did so by holding her right hand in a tensed spread-finger handshape first over the left side of the equation and then over the right side of the equation. The "seconded" gestures that the adults produced thus appear to be considered (albeit implicit) renditions of the child's gestures.

Untrained participants can react to gestures in naturalistic teaching situations

The findings described thus far suggest that adults do take in the information that children convey in their gestures – at least in an experimental situation in which the adult is an observer rather than a participant in the interaction. If, however, we are claiming that gesture is a device (albeit unwitting) by which learners can make their unspoken thoughts accessible to their communication partners, it is important to demonstrate that gesture is noticed, interpreted, and reacted to on-line in naturalistic interactions.

We are currently investigating this issue in a study of how teacher–child interaction unfolds over the course of a tutorial lesson (Goldin-Meadow & Singer, in preparation). Thus, we take a microgenetic approach to examining the effects of children's gestures on their teachers' lessons.

We asked seasoned teachers to individually instruct children who had not yet mastered mathematical equivalence. Before instructing each child, the teacher observed the child explaining at the blackboard with the experimenter his or her solutions to a series of pretest problems. This step was designed to give the teacher, who was familiar with none of the children, some idea of each child's understanding of the math problems. The teacher was then asked to instruct the child using any techniques he or she thought appropriate for this particular child. The teaching session was videotaped so that the give-and-take between teacher and pupil could be examined.

Thus far we have analyzed the videotaped interactions of five teachers. We looked first at whether the gestures children produced had any impact on the teacher's next move in the interaction. To do so, we examined all of the strategies that *children* produced during the interactions and classified them into those in which gesture conveyed the same strategy as speech (matches), those in which gesture conveyed a different strategy from speech (mismatches), and those in which no gesture occurred (speech alone). We then examined the next move that the teacher made in response to each of the strategies. Thus, we examined whether children's gestures influenced teachers' next steps in the course of the lesson.

Our analysis focused on whether teachers understood the information expressed in children's *speech*. We reasoned that if teachers were sensitive to the child's gestures, those gestures had the potential to either help or hurt teacher comprehension of child speech. In particular, gestures that match the speech they accompany might be expected to boost the teachers' reiterations of that speech simply because the information conveyed in gesture is redundant with the information conveyed in speech. However, gestures that mismatch the speech they accompany might be expected to depress the teachers' reiterations of that speech because the information conveyed in gesture is not only *not* redundant with speech, but it conveys additional information that can add to the complexity of the message.

The left panel in figure 3.5 presents the findings. As expected, teacher reiterations of child speech were lower when that speech was accompanied by mismatching gestures than when it was accompanied by no gesture at all. Thus, mismatching gestures appear to add to the comprehender's burden in interpreting the child's message. However, teacher reiterations

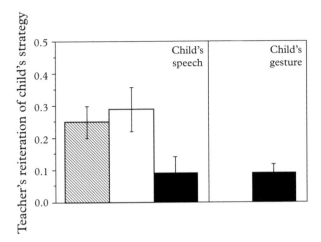

Figure 3.5 Mean proportion of teacher reiterations of child's speech (*left panel*) when accompanied by a matching gesture, by no gesture, or by a mismatching gesture, and teacher reiterations of child's gesture (*right panel*) when accompanied by mismatching speech. The bars represent standard errors. ▨, Speech and gesture match; ☐, Speech without gesture; ■, Speech and gesture mismatch.

of child speech were no higher when that speech was accompanied by matching gesture than when it was accompanied by no gesture at all. Interestingly, a previous study of *child* reactions to *teacher* gesture in individualized math tutorials showed a different pattern (Goldin-Meadow, Singer, & Kim, 1999). Teachers' gestures *both* helped and hurt children's apprehension of the teacher's speech – child reiterations of teacher speech were not only significantly *lower* when it was accompanied by mismatching gesture than by no gesture at all, but they were also significantly *higher* when it was accompanied by matching gesture than by no gesture at all. Teachers' matching gestures may facilitate children's speech comprehension because teachers often communicate content that is new or difficult for children. In contrast, children's gestures may not influence teachers' speech comprehension because child talk is not likely to be difficult for teachers (see McNeil, Alibali, & Evans, 2000).

Thus, children's gestures, when they mismatch speech, appear to affect teachers' comprehension of child speech. But are teachers able to glean substantive information from the gestures children spontaneously produce in instructional interactions? The fact that a mismatching gesture evokes from teachers a different type of response from that evoked by a matching gesture suggests that teachers are sensitive to gesture meaning.

However, it is possible that other aspects of production (timing, fluency) differ between gesture–speech matches and gesture–speech mismatches, and it may be these cues that are influencing the teachers' reiterations.

We therefore asked whether teachers reiterated the message conveyed in a child's gestures in their response to the child. We found that, on average, the five teachers reiterated the strategy that a child conveyed uniquely in gesture (that is, in the gesture component of a gesture–speech mismatch) 9% of the time (see the right panel of figure 3.5). Although a relatively small proportion, note that the teachers were as likely to reiterate the strategy that the child conveyed in the gesture component of a gesture–speech mismatch, 9%, as they were to reiterate the strategy that the child conveyed in the *speech* component of a gesture–speech mismatch, 10% (compare the heights of the two black bars in figure 3.5). Teachers are indeed able to glean substantive information from the gestures children spontaneously produce in teaching interactions.

Gesture plays a role in the give-and-take of information

In our final analysis of these teacher–child interactions, we made use of the fact that we had videotaped the give-and-take between teacher and child across the entire teaching interaction, and we examined the fate of a given strategy across each interaction. We noted which member of a dyad introduced a strategy (and in which modality), and whether that strategy was picked up at some point during the teaching session by the other member of the dyad (and in what modality). We thus broadened our window to look at responses across the entire teaching session in an attempt to see whether gesture played a role in introducing or seconding strategies originally introduced by teacher or child.

Not surprisingly, we found that teachers tended to introduce correct strategies (i.e., strategies that lead to correct solutions to the math problems); 95% of the seventy-six correct strategies expressed during the teaching sessions were introduced by teachers rather than children. Interestingly, teachers tended to present their correct strategies using both gesture and speech (85% of the teachers' seventy-two correct strategies). The children picked up only about half of the teachers' correct strategies (54% of seventy-two). When the children did pick up a correct strategy, they tended to do so in speech alone (56% of thirty-nine) or speech and gesture (28%), and seldom in gesture alone (15%). Note that this assessment of conversational give-and-take is not directly comparable to the systematic assessments of children's problem-solving knowledge in the short-term and long-term microgenetic studies described above. Children may sometimes reiterate strategies presented by the teacher in a conversational setting, though they are unable to produce them on their own.

In contrast to correct strategies, incorrect strategies (i.e., strategies that lead to incorrect solutions) were introduced by both teacher and child, and gesture played a much larger role in the interchange. Across sessions, children introduced 72% of the thirty-six incorrect strategies (ten in both speech and gesture, ten in speech alone, and six in gesture alone), and teachers introduced 28% (four in both speech and gesture, four in speech alone, and two in gesture alone). At first glance, it seems odd that teachers ever introduced incorrect strategies at all. However, we found that they often did so in order to tell children what *not* to do (five instances). In the remaining cases, teachers introduced incorrect strategies in speech without explicitly negating them (three instances), or introduced incorrect strategies, perhaps unwittingly, in gesture alone (two instances).

Overall, teachers picked up 73% of the twenty-six incorrect strategies that the children introduced, and children picked up 60% of the ten incorrect strategies that the teachers introduced. Thus, the uptake rate was higher for incorrect strategies than for correct strategies. Moreover, a great deal of the conversation surrounding incorrect strategies occurred in gesture – for both teachers and children. For teachers, 73% of the nineteen child-introduced incorrect strategies that were picked up involved gesture. Teachers either reproduced the child's gestured strategy in their own gestures (eight instances), or translated the child's spoken strategy into gesture (six). Similarly for children, 83% of the six teacher-introduced incorrect strategies that were picked up involved gesture. Children reproduced the teacher's gestured strategy in their own gestures (one), translated the teacher's gestured strategy into speech (two), or translated the teacher's spoken strategy into gesture (two).

Thus, gesture played an important role in the interchange surrounding incorrect strategies. In one case, teacher and child used gesture to keep an incorrect strategy "alive" over the course of the session. The teacher introduced, and negated, an incorrect strategy in speech. In response, the child translated that spoken strategy into gesture. The teacher then seconded the same incorrect strategy in her own gestures, followed eventually by another child second, again in gesture. As this example shows, gesture may play a role in keeping certain kinds of (perhaps unacknowledged) information alive in conversation. Gesture played a large part in the give-and-take surrounding incorrect strategies – the strategies that were on children's minds.

To summarize, we have shown that gesture can serve as a tool for assessing children's unspoken thoughts – a tool that can be used not only by experimenters, but also by adults who have no expertise in gesture coding. Children thus have a means (perhaps unwitting) by which they can inform those who interact with them about the thoughts that they themselves cannot yet articulate. In this way, children can have an impact on those who instruct them, which in turn may alter the course of instruction.

Why might gesture work as a transitional device?

Our concentrated looks over time at the learning process have shown that gesture can provide insight into a learner's thoughts, particularly at moments of transition. Why should gesture have privileged access to the thoughts learners have during periods of transition? It is likely that, at transitional moments, a learner's ideas are not as well formed as they are at more stable times. Indeed, the budding of ideas that are not easily incorporated into the status quo may be the essence of the transitional period. Gesture is an uncodified system, one that is particularly good at capturing holistic and imagistic notions that have not yet been decomposed into parts (McNeill, 1992). Learners may find it easier to express in gesture an incipient idea at a time when that idea is not sufficiently developed to be articulated in speech.

For example, a child who says that she "added 5, 4, 3, and 3 and got 15" on the problem $5 + 4 + 3 = \underline{} + 3$ displays, in her speech, no awareness that the equation has two sides divided by an equal sign. However, she may move her hand under the left side of the equation, then break the motion and perform precisely the same movement under the right side of the equation. Such a gesture reflects a budding awareness that the two sides are in some way alike, although the child may not have an explicit understanding of the significance of the equal sign. Because the representational formats underlying gesture are mimetic and analog rather than discrete, gesture may permit the learner to represent ideas that lend themselves to these formats and that are not yet developed enough to be encoded in speech.

In addition, because gesture is not codified, it is not susceptible to cultural approbation (speakers are rarely criticized for their spontaneous gestures). It therefore is an ideal modality within which to work out and even consider for the first time notions that are ill formed. In other words, not only does the manual modality make the expression of ill-formed ideas relatively easy, but it also gives the speaker the freedom to be inconsistent – it may be harder for speakers to explicitly articulate in speech an idea that is obviously contradictory with their overall talk than to express that idea in gesture, the unacknowledged modality.

Once having entered the learner's repertoire, ill-formed ideas conveyed uniquely in gesture can begin to change the system. If, for example, the child in the above example notices her own gestures, she may be confronted with the disparity between her explicitly acknowledged system (the unbroken string of numbers articulated in speech) and her newly emerging idea (the two parts to the equation displayed in gesture), and thus may be encouraged to change the system. It may even be sufficient for the learner to produce an idea in the manual modality (without ever taking it in visually), for once produced – even in an unacknowledged medium – the idea may begin to stabilize and affect other ideas.

Finally, as we have shown here, once an idea is articulated in gesture, it is there for all the world to see – and to interpret. The spontaneous gestures that learners produce reflect not only the stability of the learner's knowledge (an index of variability), but also the incipient ideas that presage where the learner may be going next (the proximal zone; cf. Vygotsky, 1978). Gesture therefore provides useful information about learners that can be interpreted by their communication partners.

In sum, we suggest that gesture has the potential to facilitate the process of change in two ways. Gesture can affect the learner directly, by offering an alternative route in which developing ideas can be tried out and expressed. Gesture can affect the learner indirectly by offering a unique view of the learner's thoughts to communication partners who might then use that information to alter their input to the learner.

Microgenetic studies of gesture and speech

Our microgenetic studies have shown that gesture and speech are an important window on knowledge change in response to instruction. We have demonstrated that, in the absence of instruction, children's behavior becomes less variable and more consistent over time – both over weeks and over repeated trials within a single session. Our data support the view that there is a "cognitive cost" to being in a variable knowledge state – and, in the absence of instruction, children are unlikely to remain in it.

Instruction serves to introduce new ideas into children's thinking, and thus, one effect of instruction is to maintain variability at a high level. Our data suggest that the type of variability manifested in gesture–speech mismatches is good for learners. When learners move through a state of variability on their way to a consistent, correct knowledge state, their learning is deeper and more flexible than when they bypass the variable state. These data underscore the value of a microgenetic approach that involves looking at both gesture and speech and how they change over time. The microgenetic approach can lead to an appreciation for the different trajectories along which knowledge change occurs, both in the context of instruction and in its absence. Further, such an approach can lead to a new appreciation for the communicative give-and-take involved in instruction and learning.

We have also shown that both children and teachers are sensitive to the information that their partners express in gesture. Indeed, the microgenetic unfolding of a tutorial lesson depends on how each partner expresses knowledge in both gesture and speech. Through their gestures, children may inform their teachers about ideas that they have but cannot articulate, and in this way, children can have a hand in shaping the course and content of instruction. By the same token, teachers may convey ideas (perhaps inadvertently) through gesture, and their students are likely to pay attention.

In sum, microgenetic approaches have much to offer to the study of knowledge change. As we have argued here, a microgenetic perspective can provide rich information about the role of instruction in the process of change. A microanalytic approach that considers both gesture and speech can provide insights into systematic changes in variability within an individual child, and insights into the "origins" and "fates" of ideas in teacher–student interaction. There is much to be gained from looking at the hands through time.

References

Alibali, M. W. (1999). How children change their minds: Strategy change can be gradual or abrupt. *Developmental Psychology, 35,* 127–145.

Alibali, M. W., Bassok, M., Solomon, K. O., Syc, S. E., & Goldin-Meadow, S. (1999). Illuminating mental representations through speech and gesture. *Psychological Science, 10,* 327–333.

Alibali, M. W., Flevares, L., & Goldin-Meadow, S. (1997). Assessing knowledge conveyed in gesture: Do teachers have the upper hand? *Journal of Educational Psychology, 89,* 183–193.

Alibali, M. W., & Goldin-Meadow, S. (1993). Transitions in learning: What the hands reveal about a child's state of mind. *Cognitive Psychology, 25,* 468–523.

Berry, D. C., & Broadbent, D. E. (1984). On the relationship between task performance and associated verbalizable knowledge. *Quarterly Journal of Experimental Psychology, 36,* 209–231.

Bertenthal, B. (1996). Origins and early development of perception, action, and representation. *Annual Review of Psychology, 47,* 431–459.

Church, R. B., & Goldin-Meadow, S. (1986). The mismatch between gesture and speech as an index of transitional knowledge. *Cognition, 23,* 43–71.

Clements, W., & Perner, J. (1994). Implicit understanding of belief. *Cognitive Development, 9,* 377–395.

Ericsson, K. A., & Simon, H. (1993). *Protocol analysis: Verbal reports as data.* (Revised edn.). Cambridge, MA: MIT Press.

Garber, P., Alibali, M. W., & Goldin-Meadow, S. (1998). Knowledge conveyed in gesture is not tied to the hands. *Child Development, 69,* 75–84.

Goldin-Meadow, S. (1999). The role of gesture in communication and thinking. *Trends in Cognitive Science, 3,* 419–429.

Goldin-Meadow, S., Alibali, M. W., & Church, R. B. (1993). Transitions in concept acquisition: Using the hand to read the mind. *Psychological Review, 100,* 279–297.

Goldin-Meadow, S., Kim, S., & Singer, M. (1999). What the teachers' hands tell the students' minds about math. *Journal of Educational Psychology, 91,* 720–730.

Goldin-Meadow, S., Nusbaum, H., Garber, P., & Church, R. B. (1993). Transitions in learning: Evidence for simultaneously activated strategies. *Journal of Experimental Psychology: Human Perception and Performance, 19,* 1–16.

Goldin-Meadow, S., & Sandhofer, C. M. (1999). Gesture conveys substantive information to ordinary listeners. *Developmental Science, 2,* 67–74.

Goldin-Meadow, S., & Singer, M. (in preparation). Teachers can use gesture to read children's minds in math tutorials.

Goldin-Meadow, S., Wein, D., & Chang, C. (1992). Assessing knowledge through gesture: Using children's hands to read their minds. *Cognition and Instruction, 9,* 201–219.

Karmiloff-Smith, A. (1992). *Beyond modularity: A developmental perspective on cognitive science.* Cambridge, MA: MIT Press.

Kelly, S. D., & Church, R. B. (1997). Can children detect conceptual information conveyed through other children's nonverbal behaviors? *Cognition and Instruction, 15,* 107–134.

Kelly, S. D., & Church, R. B. (1998). A comparison between children's and adults' ability to detect conceptual information conveyed through representational gestures. *Child Development, 69,* 85–93.

Kuhn, D., Garcia-Mila, M., Zohar, A., & Andersen, C. (1995). Strategies of knowledge acquisition. *Monographs of the Society for Research in Child Development, 60* (Serial No. 245).

McNeil, N. M., Alibali, M. W., & Evans, J. L. (2000). The role of gesture in children's comprehension of spoken language: Now they need it, now they don't. *Journal of Nonverbal Behavior, 24,* 131–150.

McNeill, D. (1992). *Hand and mind: What gestures reveal about thought.* Chicago: University of Chicago Press.

Nisbett, R. E., & Wilson, T. D. (1977). Telling more than we know: Verbal reports on mental processes. *Psychological Review, 84,* 231–259.

Perry, M., Church, R. B., & Goldin-Meadow, S. (1988). Transitional knowledge in the acquisition of concepts. *Cognitive Development, 3,* 359–400.

Perry, M., & Elder, A. D. (1996). Knowledge in transition: Adults' developing understanding of a principle of physical causality. *Cognitive Development, 12,* 131–157.

Reber, A. (1993). *Implicit learning and tacit knowledge.* New York: Oxford University Press.

Siegler, R. S. (1996). *Emerging minds: The process of change in children's thinking.* New York: Oxford University Press.

Siegler, R. S., & Crowley, K. (1991). The microgenetic method: A direct means for studying cognitive development. *American Psychologist, 46,* 606–620.

Siegler, R. S., & Jenkins, E. (1989). *How children discover new strategies.* Hillsdale, NJ: Erlbaum.

Stanley, W., Mathews, R., Buss, R., & Kotler-Cope, S. (1989). Insight without awareness: On the interaction of verbalization, instruction and practice in a simulated process control task. *Quarterly Journal of Experimental Psychology: Human Experimental Psychology, 41,* 553–577.

Thelen, E. (1989). Self-organization in developmental processes: Can systems approaches work? In M. Gunnar & E. Thelen (Eds.), *Minnesota symposium on child psychology, Vol. 22: Systems and development* (pp. 77–117). Hillsdale, NJ: Erlbaum.

Vygotsky, L. S. (1978). *Mind in society.* Cambridge, MA: Harvard University Press.

Part II

Transition mechanisms

4   A multi-component system that constructs knowledge: Insights from microgenetic study

Deanna Kuhn

As the appearance of a volume like the present one attests, the growing use of the microgenetic method is in the process of transforming developmental research, focusing it on its true subject – change. Cross-sectional "snapshots" are not just limited in what they portray. More seriously, they may be misleading, since an individual's second encounter with a task may reveal an entirely different approach from a first encounter. The "dynamic assessment" over time that goes back to Vygotsky provides a more informative picture of how an individual functions. Extended over a longer time period, dynamic assessment merges with the microgenetic method. Strategies evolve with the exercise that comes from extended engagement, allowing observation of the change process – a process that presumably would take place in a similar way, although at a slower pace, in the absence of this dense experience.

In this pure form, the microgenetic method allows examination of behavior as it is reorganized simply as a consequence of its own functioning – a process we can assume is a common one in natural settings, since a great many behaviors do change in the absence of instruction or explicit feedback. In this form of the microgenetic method, which my co-workers and I began to use in the early 1980s as a means of studying mechanisms of change (Kuhn & Ho, 1980; Kuhn & Phelps, 1982), the only feedback individuals receive is that arising from their own actions. Other researchers have used the microgenetic method more in the vein of an extended training study, to observe and compare the effects of different kinds of environmental input over an extended period of repeated engagement with a task. In either case, we have the benefit of fine-grained observation of the evolution of behavior over time.

Although the empirical findings that microgenetic research has produced are both interesting and consequential, the single most striking thing about them is their consistency. This consistency has been maintained despite variations in methodology and despite the wide range of content areas to which the method has been applied. Consistency of this sort is unusual in developmental psychology, a field in which, increasingly, researchers have devoted their efforts to specialized topics and sub-topics, with few researchers venturing beyond their own speciality to examine findings in other areas and to assess their implications for, or even connections to, their own areas of expertise.

The major findings that stand out across microgenetic studies are these: Individuals (both children and adults) possess a range of different strategies that they apply variably across time, even when the task environment remains constant. New strategies do emerge and old ones fade away, but the most common developmental change is a gradual shift in the distribution of usage of current strategies, with more effective strategies gradually gaining ascendance and ineffective ones used less often. A major implication of these findings, which I will have more to say about later, is that we must shift attention from performance to a meta-level of functioning that involves strategy selection (rather than strategy execution), if we are to fully explain developmental change. A related implication, and this is about the meta-level of strategy selection, is that the more formidable challenge in the process of developmental change is not mastering new strategies but letting go of old, more familiar, and often seductive ones – a reversal of the way in which development has traditionally been thought about (Kuhn & Phelps, 1982).

With this much in the way of a solid base of empirical findings, ones that extend across domains and have broad implications for the way we conceive of development, the proposal I wish to advance in this chapter is that at this point we are in a position to turn our focus away from the microgenetic method itself, as a research tool for studying change. The power and versatility of the method have been established, in studies as varied as groups of adults exploring unfamiliar robot-like creatures (Granott, 1998, this volume), young children learning the age-old game of tic-tac-toe (noughts and crosses), and infants developing motor skills, as well as such familiar research tasks as conservation and academic staples as spelling. The question we are now ready to ask is this: To what kinds of change phenomena would it be particularly informative to apply the microgenetic method? What kinds of change would we most like to learn about? An answer I propose and describe in this chapter is use of the microgenetic method to study that most generic of cognitive activities that we call knowledge acquisition.

Applying the microgenetic method to the study of knowledge acquisition

Knowledge acquisition, learning, and development

Despite its fundamental importance, the *process* of knowledge acquisition (in contrast to its products) in fact has not been widely studied. The microgenetic method offers an opportunity to study people in the process of acquiring new knowledge, a process some theorists regard as synonymous with learning (Schoenfeld, 1999). The opportunity to study this process may be one of the potentially richest offered by this methodology. It takes advantage of microgenetic analysis at dual levels – in allowing observation of (a) the individual's evolving knowledge structure as new information is coordinated with existing understandings, and (b) the strategies by means of which this knowledge is constructed and the modifications they undergo in the course of their application.

Traditionally, the first type of change might be referred to as learning and the second type as development. It is the microgenetic method itself, however, that has been a major contributor in blurring this traditional distinction. At a theoretical level, microgenetic analysis achieves a reintegration of learning and development as processes that have fewer differences than they do commonalities (Kuhn, 1995a, b; Chen & Siegler, in press). Both are defined by change that is complex, organized, multifaceted, and dynamic, and microgenetic analysis allows us to study those characteristics. Rather than standing in opposition to the study of development, fine-grained studies of learning illuminate, indeed are essential to understanding, the more macro-level phenomena of development. Learning is a change in understanding or capacity (Schoenfeld, 1999), and it is only through such changes that development comes about. From an historical perspective, however, we must keep in mind that the distinction between learning and development has become blurred not because development is "nothing but" learning, as behaviorists (Bijou, 1976) once argued, but because we now recognize learning to be more like development.

Knowledge acquisition in educational settings

Another reason that use of the microgenetic method to study the process of knowledge acquisition is particularly rich in potential is a practical one. "Inquiry learning" is achieving increasingly wide endorsement and use as an educational method (Bransford, Brown, & Cocking, 1999; Brown, 1997; de Jong & van Joolingen, 1998; Eisenhart, Finkel, & Marion, 1996; McGinn & Roth, 1999). The activities involved in inquiry learning, it is argued, are superior to traditional instruction because they involve students in "authentic" investigation, enabling them to develop the skills and disposition to engage independently in learning about what interests them. Since a range of practices have gone by the name of inquiry learning, it should be clarified that the reference here is to an educational activity in which students individually or collectively investigate a set of multivariable phenomena – virtual or real – in an attempt to understand their interrelations. These relationships most often are assumed to be causal, i.e., a change in the level of one variable causes a change in one or more other variables in the system. Students direct their own investigatory activity, although they may be prompted with questions about what they are trying to find out and what conclusions they have drawn.

Unfortunately, we know less about the cognitive strategies that students apply in such activities than might be supposed based on their current educational popularity (Kuhn, Black, Keselman, & Kaplan, 2000). It is just these strategies that are examined in the research described in this chapter, with a goal of understanding more about how they may evolve in the course of knowledge acquisition activities.

Knowledge acquisition as a constructive process

Knowledge acquisition, we noted, can be relabeled with a more commonplace term – learning – but that does not help us a great deal in understanding the process. We know most at this point about what knowledge acquisition is not – namely, the incremental accumulation of facts or associations featured in psychological theories of an earlier era. Nor, to refer to another traditional definition, is it simply a strengthening of behaviors through repetition. One of the findings of microgenetic research noted earlier is that some behaviors are weakened (become less frequent) in the course of their repeated application. We need a theory that explains how and why this happens.

If we regard learning or knowledge acquisition as a change in understanding (Schoenfeld, 1999), what we do know is that such understandings are organized into theory-like entities. Children from an early age construct theories as a means of understanding the world. These theories undergo revision as children interact in the world and encounter evidence bearing on their theories (Wellman & Gelman, 1998). This process of theory–evidence coordination, however, does not necessarily take place at a level of conscious awareness or explicit control. Indeed, it has been my contention that meta-level control over this process is the major dimension in terms of which we see developmental change (Kuhn, 1989, 1999).

Chan, Burtis, and Bereiter (1997) refer to this coordination as a constructive process of "knowledge building." New information must be accessed, represented, compared to what is already known, and, ultimately, in some manner integrated with it. Chan et al. identify differing levels of adequacy in the achievement of this task. New knowledge is the product of the task.

Conceiving of knowledge acquisition as a process of theory–evidence coordination, in my own line of research we have studied people engaged in the process over multiple sessions in a variety of multivariable content domains and formats involving either real objects or computer simulations (Kuhn, Garcia-Mila, Zohar, & Andersen, 1995; Kuhn, Schauble, & Garcia-Mila, 1992). The accumulating data that they access must be coordinated with their evolving theories and inferences made about the causal structure of the domain. In a current version (Kuhn et al., 2000), for example, a computer simulation asks the participant to work as a builder building cabins on sites along a lakefront that is susceptible to flooding. The cabins must be elevated on supports to avoid flood damage, but the supports should be no higher than necessary, to minimize cost. The task, therefore, is to predict the varying degrees of flooding that occur at different sites, which can be done only by analyzing the effects of varying features, such as soil type and depth. In other versions, participants examine variables enabling them to predict how fast a model boat travels down an improvised "canal," or, in the social realm, the variables that influence the popularity of children's TV programs. The multivariable context, we find, has the desirable feature of affording high degrees of freedom in causal attribution. If an outcome conflicts with theory-driven expectations with respect to one variable, the implications can be avoided by shifting to another variable to do the explanatory work. The task is thus a rich one for observing the theory–evidence coordination process.

The microgenetic design allows us to simultaneously track changes in knowledge – the set of beliefs about the causal structure of the system – and in the investigative and inference strategies used to acquire that knowledge. In several different research designs (Kuhn et al., 1992; Kuhn et al., 1995; Schauble, 1990, 1996), these knowledge acquisition strategies have been found to show significant generality across content, justifying the assumption that we are observing some broad "modes of knowing" significant enough to warrant attention and study. The fact that strategies often undergo developmental change in the course of their use allows us to closely observe the process in microgenetic study. Fine-grained microgenetic analysis enables us to observe the emergence of new strategies, and we find that they typically appear at about the same time across domains in studies in which we have participants work on two different tasks during the same period of time (Kuhn et al., 1992; Kuhn et al., 1995). The microgenetic method allows us to answer other fine-grained questions as well, for example whether the appearance of new strategies is more likely to follow a problem-solving success or failure (Kuhn et al., 1995).

These strategies can be categorized according to their adequacy and effectiveness as knowledge acquisition devices. The fact that we observe evolution toward more effective strategies makes our analysis an explicitly developmental one. Comparative study of adults and children has allowed us to identify differences in the knowledge acquisition process at the two different age levels. We could predict that the conflict between the store of feature-related knowledge and new evidence would be greater for adults since they could be presumed to have more "entrenched" feature-related beliefs. In this case we would expect more resistance to belief change in adults than children. In fact, however, the difference is in the reverse direction. Children show greater resistance to abandoning a causal belief in the face of disconfirming evidence than do adults (Kuhn et al., 1995). The implication is that we are observing development of enhanced cognitive flexibility, rather than entrenchment, with development from childhood to adulthood. This flexibility takes the form of (a) increased differentiation of theory and evidence as a source of support for one's beliefs, and, hence, (b) enhanced ability to represent relations between theories and evidence, that is, the implications of one with respect to the other (Kuhn & Pearsall, 2000).

In treating the knowledge acquisition task as one of coordinating theory and evidence, our experimental paradigm raises the question of how to determine the relative weights these two essential components of the process should be given (a question that in fact has long occupied philosophers as well as psychologists; cf. Harman, 1986; Koslowski, 1996). If the process is regarded as one of coordination, strategies that ignore one component or the other are by definition inadequate. In our studies, we have defined coordination as the ability to represent the relations between theory and evidence and in some fashion reconcile them. The tasks we pose are *not* ones that ask the individual to cast aside his or her own evolved beliefs about the world in favor of some arbitrary new information. Rather, these tasks assess an individual's ability to examine and represent new evidence and to appreciate the relation it bears to different theoretical claims. A participant in one of our studies could say, "This is what this evidence implies for these theories, although other sources of support I have for some of these theories leads me to maintain belief in them in the face of your disconfirming evidence." This individual will do perfectly well in our task. More troubling are the many participants in our studies whose beliefs *are* influenced by our evidence but who lack metacognitive awareness that this is so.

A human cognitive system that constructs new knowledge

The major claim I wish to make explicit in this chapter is that it is a multi-component system that is involved in the process of constructing new knowledge when existing beliefs come into contact with new information.

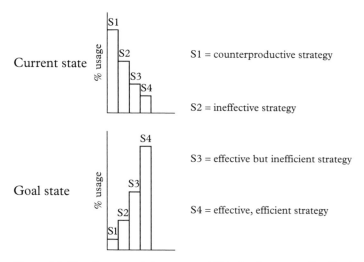

Figure 4.1 Developmental change as a shift in the frequency distribution of strategies applied to a task.

The whole system will take most of the rest of the chapter to fully develop. We begin with the most visible component, performance strategies (figure 4.1) and add from there. The system is meant to apply to a situation in which an individual engages in self-directed activity with the purpose of acquiring knowledge within some domain. The model does not imply that knowledge can only be acquired in such settings, but in other settings – for example, when external or internal motivational constraints limit the individual's knowledge seeking – certain segments of the system may be eclipsed.

Performance strategies

As microgenetic research has repeatedly shown, variability is a fundamental characteristic of the individual (Siegler, 1994). In any situation that elicits action, the individual has a variety of things it can do, with varying probabilities of occurrence (figure 4.1). Moreover, these strategies are of differing degrees of effectiveness, ranging from the counterproductive to the optimal effective and efficient strategy. In the case in which a counterproductive strategy is dominant (upper portion of figure 4.1), what we would like to see, and what we would call development, is a shift in the distribution of usage to one in which the optimal strategy is dominant and others have limited probability of occurrence (lower portion of figure 4.1). Siegler (1996, this volume) refers to such shifts as reflecting

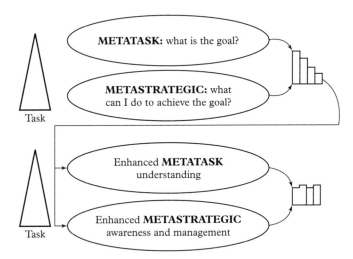

Figure 4.2 Performance feedback enhances meta-level understanding.

an "overlapping waves" model of change, since at any one time one strategy may be increasing in frequency while another is decreasing and a third remains stable.

What is the mechanism that gets one from the current state to the goal state depicted in figure 4.1? In the absence of any obvious mechanism at the level of performance, it must be assumed that something is missing from the diagrams in figure 4.1. In other words, more is going on than what is observable at the level of performance. It is thus necessary to add a number of components to this diagram, the first being a representation of the task in relation to which the individual acts. Strategies don't exist in a void, exercised for their own sake. Rather, they function in relation to a goal, defined by a task that the individual has accepted and engaged. The label *strategy* only has meaning and ought properly only to be used in relation to a goal.

Meta-level operators

To connect the two (task and strategies), and to explain change, something else is needed – another level of operation distinct from strategies, which I will call a *meta-level* of operation. Operators at this level *select* strategies to apply, in relation to task goals, and *manage* and *monitor* their application. I choose the *meta-level* label to emphasize it as a level of operation distinct from and superordinate to the performance level, and I propose that it includes two components (upper portion of figure 4.2), the *metatask* and the *metastrategic* (Kuhn & Pearsall, 1998; Thornton, 1999). The role of one is to represent task goals and the role of the other is to coordinate them with the strategies that are available. In this process, a subset of strategies are recognized as applicable in relation to task goals. These strategies are selected and applied, with probabilities reflecting each strategy's strength, and the application is monitored by the meta-level.

The meta-level directs the application of strategies, and feedback from this application is directed back to the meta-level (lower portion of figure 4.2). This feedback leads to enhanced awareness of the goal and the extent to which it is being met by different strategies, as well as enhanced awareness of the strategies themselves, in particular increased recognition of the power and the limitations associated with each. These enhancements at the meta-level lead to revised strategy selection and hence changes in the distribution of usage observed at the performance level. This modified usage in turn feeds back to enhanced understanding at the meta-level (lower portion of figure 4.2), eventually getting the individual to the performance goal state depicted at the bottom of figure 4.1. Although figure 4.2 suggests a sequence of discrete steps, what is implied of course is a continuous process, one in which the meta-knowing level both guides and is modified by the performance level. (See Sophian, 1997, and Siegler, 1996, for similar conceptions that have appeared in recent literature.)

In this model, then, changes at the performance level are all channeled, or mediated, through the meta-level. This feature of the model thus privileges the meta-level as the locus of developmental change. This is a strong claim. In making it, I do not wish to deny the importance of phenomena that are occurring at other levels – the neurological level, certainly, and also the performance level, which is the level at which behaviors are practiced and perfected. My claim, however, is that it is the meta-level (given that it is sufficiently developed and functioning effectively) that is at all times in charge. It remains in charge even if the choice it makes is to shift to "automatic pilot" because nothing much is going on at the moment that requires higher-level management. In other words, it has the final say in what the individual will be doing at any particular moment. In practice, however, this may not always be the case because the meta-level has not reached a point in its development at which it is able to maintain this high level of control, resulting in behaviors that are inconsistent across occasions and highly vulnerable to situational influence.

Educators frequently make the distinction between performance and understanding and have become increasingly concerned about how to promote the latter (Gardner, 1999). Understanding is a meta-level construct, and its lack of direct observability makes it harder to study than performance. Psychological research, however – much of it micro-genetic – has contributed both theoretically and empirically to more rigorously defining what we mean by understanding. We know, for example, that meta-level understanding of strategies comprises knowledge about wrong strategies as an element at least as important as knowledge about correct strategies. The most important meta-level knowledge about correct strategies is the knowledge that these are the appropriate strategies to apply in order to perform the task successfully. Meta-level knowledge, however, includes more:

Besides knowing what the chosen strategies "buy one," so to speak, in terms of solution attainment and efficiency, such knowledge entails as well knowing what is wrong about every other potential strategy or set of strategies that might be applied to the problem – that they do not work (or work efficiently), why they do not work, and what mistakes they lead to. (Kuhn, 1983, pp. 95–96)

Empirical support for the importance of the latter kind of meta-level knowledge comes from both my own and Siegler's microgenetic studies. The major and most influential (in terms of overall performance) change we observed was the inhibition of invalid inference strategies (Kuhn et al., 1995). In Siegler's research (this volume; Crowley & Siegler, 1999), children who generated justifications regarding why poor strategies were incorrect, as well as why good strategies were effective or correct, showed more change than children who generated only the latter or were not asked to justify their strategies.

Phases of knowledge construction activity

Self-directed construction of knowledge involves several major phases, or tasks, and a set of strategies associated with each. In each of these phases individuals show a range of strategies of varying adequacy and a distribution of usage that evolves over time. In addition, each phase I hypothesize to have its own associated meta-level of operation.

The task in the first phase of knowledge acquisition (top row of figure 4.3) is recognizing that there is a question that can be asked and identifying what that question is. This is the *inquiry* phase. Examined in close-up (figure 4.4), the first challenge of this phase is to recognize that the data base I have the opportunity to access yields information that bears on the theories I hold – a recognition that eludes many young theorists. Once the relevance of the data in this respect is recognized, questions can be formulated of a form that is productive in connecting data and theory (left side of figure 4.4).

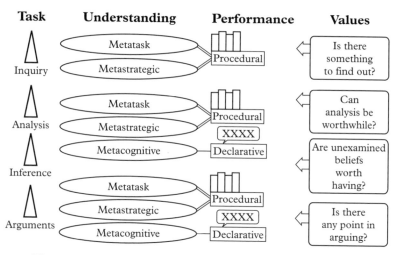

Figure 4.3 Phases and dimensions of knowledge acquisition activity.

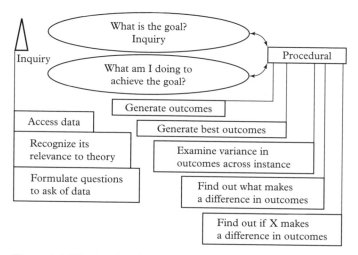

Figure 4.4 The inquiry phase.

The variability and evolution we have observed in strategies in response to this task are portrayed on the right side of figure 4.4. Here (in contrast to the left side of figure 4.5, where objectives are compatible) we have a set of competing strategies which overlap in their usage and are of varying degrees of adequacy (with more adequate strategies appearing further down in the figure). At the lowest level, a strategy for some individuals

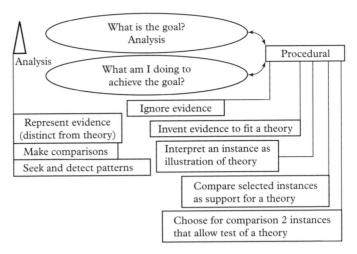

Figure 4.5 The analysis phase.

(or for a particular individual some of the time) may be the simple one of activity, i.e., generating outcomes or producing the phenomenon – a boat's travel down the canal or a flood of the building site. Later, after the phenomenon has been observed many times, the dominant strategy may become one of producing the most desirable outcome (e.g., the fastest boat). The major developmental shift is one from strategies of activity to genuine inquiry, which in its most rudimentary appearance takes the form of "What is making a difference?" or "What will enable me to predict outcomes?" In more advanced forms, inquiry becomes focused on the specific features in terms of which there is variability, and, ultimately, focused on the effect of a specific feature, "Does X make a difference?"

The next phase is *analysis*, a process that leads to the product phase of *inference*. These are depicted in the second and third rows of figure 4.3. To engage in productive analysis (left side of figure 4.5), some segment of the data base must be accessed, attended to, processed, and represented as such, i.e., as evidence to which one's theory can be related, and these data must be operated on (through comparison and pattern detection), in order to reach the third phase, which yields the product of these operations – inference. The strategies we have observed being applied to this task reflect the struggle to coordinate theories and evidence. As seen on the right side of figure 4.5, theory predominates in the lower-level strategies, and only with the gradually more advanced strategies does evidence acquire the power to influence theory.

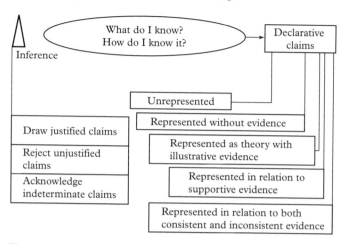

Figure 4.6 The inference phase.

The task of *analysis* requires procedural strategies, or a procedural form of knowing. *Inference*, in contrast, requires one to make knowledge claims that are a declarative form of knowing. Correspondingly, the form of knowing at the meta-level is also different (figure 4.6). This distinction is made by referring to procedural meta-knowing as *metastrategic* (and *metatask*) and declarative meta-knowing as *metacognitive*. Unlike procedural knowing, which generates feedback in the course of its operation (making individuals aware that they are doing something), declarative knowing is more a state of being than doing, and as such the knowing itself does not generate any feedback. We have little occasion to say to ourselves, "This is what I know."

This difference between metastrategic and metacognitive knowing (Kuhn, 1999) is reflected in the absence of a reciprocal arrow from the performance level to the meta-level in the case of the declarative knowing generated at the inference phase (figure 4.3). In recent work (Kuhn & Pearsall, 2000), we have shown preschoolers to be indifferent in identifying as the source of their knowledge that an event occurred either (a) a theory that makes the event plausible, or (b) evidence showing that the event did occur. These weaknesses in metacognitive knowledge regarding a simple event parallel those observed among older children and adults in the research discussed here involving more complex meta-knowing about causal relations.

As shown in the left side of figure 4.6, the inference phase involves inhibiting claims that are not justified, as well as making those that are.

The inferential processes we observe being applied to this task (right side of figure 4.6) range in adequacy from no processing of the evidence and no conscious awareness of one's theories (so-called "theories in action") to the skilled coordination of theory and evidence, which entails understanding the implications of evidence as supporting or disconfirming one's theories.

A fourth and final phase of knowledge acquisition is its application, specifically in the service of an argument that one wishes to justify (final row in figure 4.3). Argument entails debate of multiple claims, in a framework of alternatives and evidence (Kuhn, 1991). The same structure identified in the preceding tasks of analysis and inference applies in the case of argument. A range of argumentive strategies can be identified, strategies that an individual draws on with varying degrees of probability. Given sustained exercise, these strategies undergo development (Kuhn, Shaw, & Felton, 1997; Felton & Kuhn, in press). The products of the argumentive process are revised and strengthened *claims*, strengthened in the sense of being better supported as an outcome of the argumentive process.

Values as a final component of the knowledge acquisition process

The other dimension I wish to add to this picture is a final column (figure 4.3) representing a different kind of cognitive operation, one that I will call *values*. Values – intellectual values, in this case – are slippery phenomena to pin down precisely and psychologists have shied away from studying them. They are anchored, however, by both antecedents and consequences. Feeding into and shaping intellectual values are a person's beliefs about knowing, which have been studied under the heading of *epistemological beliefs* (Hofer & Pintrich, 1997; Kuhn & Weinstock, in press). Intellectual values, in turn, give rise to dispositions (a term I prefer to "habits") to behave in a particular way. Epistemological understanding, however, remains the critical foundation on which intellectual values and dispositions rest. Attainment of a mature level of epistemological understanding is a necessary condition to allow for any of the more specific intellectual values portrayed in figure 4.3 to prevail. Unless one believes that analysis and argument are essential, indeed the only route, to knowing (a belief representative of the highest, *evaluativist* level of epistemological thought; Kuhn & Weinstock, in press; Hofer & Pintrich, 1997), one is unlikely to hold (and to behave in accord with) the values that analysis is worthwhile, that unexamined beliefs are not worth having, and that there is a point to arguing (figure 4.3). In the end, then, we cannot fully understand the kinds of knowing and knowledge acquisition that people engage in without understanding their beliefs about knowing.

Empirical studies of meta-level knowing

The variability in strategies portrayed in figure 4.3, and the gradual evolution that we see in their frequency distribution as they are applied to a task, are empirical facts. The meta-levels of operation portrayed in the second column ("understanding") of figure 4.3 are not. They are theoretical constructs. Do we have any evidence that they exist, that they develop along with the strategies that constitute the performance level, and that they mediate strategic development? To obtain this kind of evidence, we need to be able to assess the meta-level components independent of the performance components.

Externalization of meta-knowing in social discourse

It is not obvious how one might do this, but the approach that Pearsall and I (Kuhn & Pearsall, 1998) took was to externalize meta-level knowing of the procedural type by asking children to explain to another child – who had not participated in the activity – what was to be done and how to do it. Like the participants described earlier (Kuhn et al., 1995), fifth-grade children (ten- to eleven-year-olds) in the main task selected multivariable instances for examination (cars or boats in this case), made predictions, observed outcomes, and drew inferences regarding the causal status of the various features in affecting outcome (speed of the car or boat). We added the metastrategic assessment at two points, first when the participating child had just begun the activity (session 2 of seven sessions) and again after the final session. The observing child had been instructed not to ask questions or otherwise intervene, and so the participating child's verbal communication gave us an indication of his or her understanding of the task and the strategies for accomplishing it. (The latter was not as complete as we would have liked, since it encompasses the child's understanding only of preferred or recommended strategies; it would be worthwhile to know as well what the child understood about other, non-recommended strategies and what the child understood to be wrong with them.) Metatask understanding (the task goal) was assessed separately from metastrategic understanding (how to achieve the goal) and levels of understanding were coded for each. (These two forms of meta-level knowing, note, are independent: Knowing goals does not confer knowledge of strategies, nor does awareness of strategies guarantee that they will be connected to an appropriate goal.)

The results, briefly, were that for most participants meta-level understanding, like performance, shows improvement over time, during a period when strategies are being exercised (as the model in figure 4.2 would predict). Most important, correspondences are apparent in the improvements that occur at the two levels. The relationship is one of the meta-level playing a gatekeeper, or necessary-but-not-sufficient, role with respect to the performance level. Preferred strategies observed at the performance level rarely exceeded the level of understanding exhibited in assessment of the meta-level, although the reverse was not true – meta-level understanding sometimes exceeded what was realized in performance. Typically this happened when individuals understood what was to be accomplished (identification of the causal status of each of the features) but knew no strategies for accomplishing it.

In each of our studies, regardless of the age of the participants, it has been the case that exercise of strategies has been sufficient to induce change (at both performance and meta-knowing levels, when both have been assessed) in a majority, but not all, of the participants. In the cases in which change does not occur, meta-level functioning is perhaps too weak to utilize the feedback generated by the performance level. Whether or not this is exactly the right explanation, the recurring minority of cases in which change fails to occur led us to consider the possibility of doing something to stimulate the meta-level directly (rather than depend on the feedback from strategic performance). How might this be done? Although we have gone on in current work to experiment with other approaches, the first approach we tried was collaborative activity.

Collaboration as a vehicle for strengthening meta-level knowing

The benefits of collaborative cognition typically are construed at the performance level and center around two constructs that the sociocultural literature has made popular , *distributed cognition* and *scaffolding* (figure 4.7). Distributed cognition divides the cognitive workload, allowing the pair to accomplish jointly what neither could manage alone. It is particularly advantageous when each partner contributes competencies not in the repertory of the other. Scaffolding occurs when the competency of the less able partner is enhanced through the guidance provided by the more able partner.

What if we extend this analysis of potential benefits of collaboration to the meta-knowing level, where it has received much less attention? Two effects might be predicted (figure 4.7). First, verbal communication

How does collaboration enhance cognition?

At the performance level

• Cognitive work is *socially distributed.*
• My performance is *scaffolded* by an able partner.

At the meta-knowing level

• Meta-knowing is *externalized.*
• My partner's meta-knowing *scaffolds* my
  meta-knowing and performance.

Figure 4.7 Potential effects of collaboration on performance-level and meta-level cognition.

of my meta-level understanding externalizes it, making it more explicit. The benefit here is well captured in the orangutan theory. If I have some new ideas and I go into a room with an orangutan and explain them, the orangutan will simply sit there and eat its banana. I will come out of the room, however, knowing more than I did before.

Second, my explicit communication of meta-knowing to a partner, or a partner's explicit communication of his or her meta-knowing to me, may influence and guide the recipient of this communication, particularly if the communicator is more capable. This is scaffolding at the meta-knowing level. When both partners have some competence, we can predict the most powerful effect – one in which both partners benefit, since each guides the meta-knowing of the other. In other words, each partner serves as the other's meta-knowing operator, helping to monitor and manage their partner's strategic operations, in a way that the partner is not yet able to do as competently for him- or herself.

In a doctoral dissertation by Andersen (1998), each of these processes was observed, although there are almost as many occasions where they fail to occur as occasions where they do. In other words, conditions have to be just right for them to work. The design of Andersen's study, it should be noted, works against demonstrating the benefits of peer collaboration, the typical goal of researchers who have studied the process. Each of the fifth-grade participants in his study worked on two problems over the course of seven weeks (the boat and car problems), one of them alone and the other with a partner (who remained the same over the seven weeks). It would of course be anticipated that the competencies individuals bring to the task will affect performance in the collaborative setting. This research design, however, leaves open the additional likelihood that whatever a child does in collaboration with a peer will influence his or her performance in the solo condition, thus diminishing the difference between the two conditions. If we wished to maximize the difference between the two conditions, we would design the study as a between-subject comparison of groups representing each of the conditions. In this case, however, we were willing to accept the disadvantage of the within-subject design because the objective was not to maximize difference but rather to be able to precisely compare a child's performance over time in the solo condition to that same child's performance in collaboration with a peer.

Despite the likely diffusion of gains from one condition to the other, the superiority of performance in the peer condition over the solo condition did still appear in overall comparisons. Offering the greatest insight, however, were the individual summaries of how a child performed over the seven weeks when working alone versus with his or her partner. These case studies proved categorizable into roughly equal-sized categories of (a) unsuccessful pairs, in which neither partner progressed, (b) successful pairs, in which the less able partner benefited in the collaborative setting (relative to his or her performance alone), and (c) "super-successful" pairs, in which both members appeared to benefit from the collaboration and both contributed to the collaborative performance, with the result that collaborative performance exceeds the performance of either partner alone. The emergence of this latter group testifies to the power of collaborative cognition, a power that we believe is most readily explained in metastrategic terms. Management of strategic operations becomes externalized, with each partner helping to monitor and manage the other's strategic operations, in a way that the partner cannot yet accomplish alone.

Direct exercise of meta-knowing operations

By externalizing meta-knowing operations, microgenetic studies of social collaboration make these operations easier to observe and highlight their role as managers of performance. Our data show, however, that this managerial role is not always actualized. This fact led us to explore whether there may be other, more direct, perhaps more powerful ways to strengthen meta-knowing operations. One that has now proven successful in two studies (Pearsall, 1999; Kuhn et al., 2000) is to promote at least the evaluative aspect of meta-level operation by requiring participants to evaluate the performance of others in the kind of task that we have described (an evaluation that includes assigning and justifying a grade for the performance).

In the Kuhn et al. (2000) study, sixth- through eighth-graders (eleven- to fourteen-year-olds) participated for several months in an inquiry activity centered around the flood problem described earlier, as part of their science curriculum. In one of the two comparable classrooms that participated in the study, students engaged in a metastrategic evaluation exercise, in addition to their activity working in pairs on the flood problem. (Students in the other classroom worked only on the flood problem.) In the metastrategic exercise, which took place twice each week for six weeks, students were presented with the situation of two individuals who disagree as to the effect of a particular feature, with one individual, for example, claiming that soil type makes a difference and the other one claiming that it does not. Working in pairs, the students must then consider and evaluate the strategies that could be used to resolve the conflict.

Comparisons of the progress made by the two classes revealed several effects of the meta-level exercise. The group who engaged in this exercised exhibited: (a) at the meta-level, better metatask understanding of the object of the activity as identification of effects of individual features; (b) also at the meta-level, superior metastrategic understanding of the need to control the influences of other features (the controlled comparison strategy); (c) at the performance level, a higher incidence of successful use of the controlled comparison strategy and resulting valid inferences regarding the status of causal and noncausal features in the system, and (d) superior acquisition of knowledge about the system, reflected in correct conclusions about its causal structure.

Conclusions

The preceding findings are consistent with the general claim that meta-level understanding, reflected in the ability to explain why a strategy is more effective than its alternatives, is a strong predictor of performance. In particular, it is likely to predict whether a newly emerging strategy will generalize and be applied in other situations in which it is appropriate (Kuhn, 1995a; Crowley & Siegler, 1999). If it is indeed a strong predictor, the goal of microgenetic research should be to trace this evolving understanding, not only evolving performance. Indeed, this is the most important message that I wish the multi-component system presented in figure 4.3 to convey. More is developing than just the performance we see.

It remains to note that, in this chapter, I have not given the final column in figure 4.3, representing values, the full attention it deserves. It is of critical importance to understand how people construct new knowledge, I have argued, and the microgenetic method can help us to do that. But it is at least as critical to know whether people will invest the effort it takes to do so. The latter is a matter of values and the beliefs that support them. In addition to studying knowledge construction, then, we will have to study the process through which beliefs and values surrounding knowledge construction evolve (Kuhn & Weinstock, in press) – in other words just how people construct meaning *about* knowing and how that meaning evolves. Microgenetic methodology promises to be an important tool in that enterprise.

References

Andersen, C. (1998). A microgenetic study of science reasoning in social context. Unpublished doctoral dissertation. Teachers College, Columbia University, New York.

Bijou, S. (1976). *Child development: The basic stage of early childhood.* Englewood Cliffs, NJ: Prentice-Hall.

Bransford, J., Brown, A., & Cocking, R. (Eds.). (1999). *How people learn: Brain, mind, experience, and school.* Report of the National Research Council. Washington, DC: National Academy Press.

Brown, A. (1997). Transforming schools into communities of thinking and learning about serious matters. *American Psychologist, 52,* 399–413.

Chan, C., Burtis, J., & Bereiter, C. (1997). Knowledge-building as a mediator of conflict in conceptual change. *Cognition and Instruction, 15,* 1–40.

Chen, Z., & Siegler, R. (in press). Across the great divide: Bridging the gap between understanding of toddlers' and older children's thinking. *Monographs of the Society for Research in Child Development.*

Crowley, K., & Siegler, R. (1999). Explanation and generalization in young children's strategy learning. *Child Development, 70,* 304–316.

de Jong, T., & van Joolingen, W.R. (1998). Scientific discovery learning with computer simulations of conceptual domains. *Review of Educational Research, 68*(2), 179–201.

Eisenhart, M., Finkel, E., & Marion, S. (1996). Creating the conditions for scientific literacy: A re-examination. *American Educational Research Journal, 33,* 261–295.

Felton, M., & Kuhn, D. (in press). The development of argumentive discourse skills. *Discourse Processes.*

Gardner, H. (1999). *The disciplined mind.* New York: Simon & Schuster.

Granott, N. (1998). We learn, therefore we develop: Learning versus development – or developing learning? In C. Smith & T. Pourchot (Eds.), *Adult learning and development: Perspectives from educational psychology* (pp. 15–34). Mahwah, NJ: Erlbaum.

Granott, N. (this volume). How microdevelopment creates macrodevelopment: Reiterated sequences, backward transitions, and the Zone of Current Development.

Harman, G. (1986). *Change in view: Principles of reasoning.* Cambridge, MA: MIT Press.

Hofer, B., & Pintrich, P. (1997). The development of epistemological theories: Beliefs about knowledge and knowing and their relation to learning. *Review of Educational Research, 67,* 88–140.

Koslowski, B. (1996). *Theory and evidence: The development of scientific reasoning.* Cambridge, MA: MIT Press.

Kuhn, D. (1983). On the dual executive and its significance in the development of developmental psychology. In D. Kuhn & J. Meacham (Eds.), *On the development of developmental psychology.* Basel: Karger.

Kuhn, D. (1989). Children and adults as intuitive scientists. *Psychological Review, 96,* 674–689.

Kuhn, D. (1991). *The skills of argument.* New York: Cambridge University Press.

Kuhn, D. (1995a). Microgenetic study of change: What has it told us? *Psychological Science, 6,* 133–139.

Kuhn, D. (Ed.). (1995b). *Development and learning: Reconceptualizing the intersection. Human Development (Special issue), 38(6).*

Kuhn, D. (1999). Metacognitive development. In L. Balter & C. Tamis Le-Monda (Ed.), *Child psychology: A handbook of contemporary issues.* Philadelphia, PA: Psychology Press.

Kuhn, D., Black, J., Keselman, A., & Kaplan, D. (2000). The development of cognitive skills to support inquiry learning. *Cognition and Instruction, 18,* 495–523.

Kuhn, D., Garcia-Mila, M., Zohar, A., & Andersen, C. (1995). Strategies of knowledge acquisition. *Monographs of the Society for Research in Child Development, 60(4)* (Serial No. 245).

Kuhn, D., & Ho, V. (1980). Self-directed activity and cognitive development. *Journal of Applied Developmental Psychology, 1,* 119–133.

Kuhn, D., & Pearsall, S. (1998). Relations between metastrategic knowledge and strategic performance. *Cognitive Development, 13,* 227–247.

Kuhn, D., & Pearsall, S. (2000). Developmental origins of scientific thinking. *Journal of Cognition and Development, 1,* 113–129.

Kuhn, D., & Phelps, E. (1982). The development of problem-solving strategies. In H. Reese (Ed.), *Advances in child development and behavior, Vol. 17.* New York: Academic Press.

Kuhn, D., Schauble, L., & Garcia-Mila, M. (1992). Cross-domain development of scientific reasoning. *Cognition and Instruction, 9(4),* 285–327.

Kuhn, D., Shaw, V., & Felton, M. (1997). Effects of dyadic interaction on argumentive reasoning. *Cognition and Instruction, 15,* 287–315.

Kuhn, D., & Weinstock, M. (in press). What is epistemological thinking and why does it matter? In B. Hofer & P. Pintrich (Eds.), *Personal epistemology: The psychology of beliefs about knowledge and knowing.* Mahwah, NJ: Erlbaum.

McGinn, M., & Roth, W. (1999). Preparing students for competent scientific practice: implications of recent research in science and technology studies. *Educational Researcher, 28,* 14–24.

Pearsall, S. (1999). The influence of metacognitive reflection on the development of scientific reasoning. Unpublished doctoral dissertation, Teachers College, Columbia University, New York.

Schauble, L. (1990). Belief revision in children: The role of prior knowledge and strategies for generating evidence. *Journal of Experimental Child Psychology, 49,* 31–57.

Schauble, L. (1996). The development of scientific reasoning in knowledge-rich contexts. *Developmental Psychology, 32,* 102–119.

Schoenfeld, A. (1999). Looking toward the 21st century: Challenges of educational theory and practice. *Educational Researcher, 28,* 4–14.

Siegler, R. S. (1994). Cognitive variability: A key to understanding cognitive development. *Current Directions in Psychological Science, 3,* 1–5.

Siegler, R. S. (1996). *Emerging minds: The process of change in children's thinking.* New York: Oxford University Press.

Siegler, R. S. (this volume). Microgenetic studies of self-explanation.

Sophian, C. (1997). Beyond competence: The significance of performance for conceptual development. *Cognitive Development, 12,* 281–303.

Thornton, S. (1999). Creating the conditions for cognitive change: The interaction between task structures and specific strategies. *Child Development, 70,* 588–603.

Wellman, H. M., & Gelman, S. A. (1998). Knowledge acquisition in foundational domains. In W. Damon (Series Ed.), & D. Kuhn & R. S. Siegler (Vol. Eds.), *Handbook of child psychology, Vol. 2: Cognition, perception, and language* (5th edn., pp. 523–574). New York: Wiley.

5 Bridging to the unknown: A transition mechanism in learning and development

Nira Granott, Kurt W. Fischer, and Jim Parziale

How are new abilities created out of existing, less advanced abilities? This question has puzzled researchers for centuries. Various answers have been suggested, yet the mechanisms underlying development have remained enigmatic. In this chapter, we analyze and demonstrate a process called bridging that provides a specific answer to the fundamental question of how more powerful structures can be achieved on the basis of less powerful ones.

Bridging is a process of leaping into the unknown by inserting marker shells that indicate targets for development and learning (Granott, 1993a, 1994, Granott & Parziale, 1996). The marker shells serve as place-holders that people use to direct their own learning and development toward achieving these targets. A shell is like a formula in mathematics, in which the variables represent an unknown whose values can be later defined. Bridging operates as an attractor in dynamic systems and pulls development toward more advanced, relatively stable levels. People use bridging by creating partially defined shells that mark future skills to be constructed at higher knowledge levels. The shells do not contain the relevant knowledge yet, but they outline it. The shells serve as scaffolds that guide the construction of new knowledge by providing a perspective for processing new experiences. A bridging shell serves as a dynamic attractor after its initial emergence in real-time activities within context.

We suggest that bridging is a transition mechanism that people use spontaneously at a wide range of ages. Bridging occurs through self-scaffolding as well as other-scaffolding, within individuals and between people in social interaction. It takes several forms with a similar underlying mechanism, all of which are characterized by setting tentative targets for an unknown skill to be constructed at a developmental level higher than the level of the person's current activity. That is, in bridging, a person functions at two levels simultaneously: the lower level of the ongoing, actual activity and the higher level of the bridging shell that points to future learning.

What creates development? Views about transition mechanisms

Understanding how development is created is an age-old challenge. Researchers have tried to explain it in different ways. Sociohistorical and cultural approaches highlight the ways the social context with its signs, tools, and practices influences development (e.g., Cole, 1988; Leont'ev, 1981; Rogoff, Mistry, Goncu, & Mosier, 1993; Vygotsky, 1978; Wertsch, 1985). Piaget's theory accounts for the development of new structures by constructs such as assimilation, accommodation, equilibration, and reflective abstraction (e.g., Piaget, 1970, 1985). The extreme nativist approach attributes development to maturation of innate abilities (e.g., Gesell, 1940), especially in language development (e.g., Chomsky, 1975, 1980; Fodor, 1975). Today, many researchers agree that both genetic constitution and children's experiences combine forces to create development (e.g., Gottlieb, 1991; Lerner, 1991; Scarr, 1993).

Recently, aspects of innate principles have been interwoven with new approaches to study development, especially in dynamic systems and connectionism (e.g., Elman, Bates, Johnson, Karmiloff-Smith, Parisi, & Plunkett, 1996; Thelen & Smith, 1994). Applications of dynamic systems theory to the study of development suggest processes of self-organization within a developing system that serve as a mechanism of developmental change. According to dynamic systems theory, new forms emerge as a result of nonlinear interaction among the system's components. In development, new behavior is created through nonlinear assembly of multiple components related to the organism and its environment (Lee & Karmiloff-Smith, this volume; Lewis, this volume; Thelen & Corbetta, this volume; Thelen & Smith, 1994; van Geert, 1998a). Self-organization creates new patterns and forms. Owing to its self-organization, the system may settle in a new, more stable pattern – an attractor – which seems to attract the system to it. Several researchers use dynamic modeling to explain and simulate developmental processes (e.g., Case, Okamoto, Griffin, McKeough, Bleiker, Henderson, & Stephenson, 1996; Fischer & Bidell, 1998; Fischer & Rose, 1994; Smith & Thelen, 1993; Thelen & Smith, 1994; van Geert, 1991, 1994, 1998b). Considerable work is based on connectionism and modeling of development after neural network growth (e.g., Elman et al., 1996; Grossberg, 1987; MacWhinney & Leinbach, 1991; Rumelhart & McClelland, 1988) or other computational models (e.g., Klahr, 1992; Simon & Halford, 1995). Models can provide rich hypotheses that can later be studied in human behavior.

In the area of problem solving, many researchers explain the construction of new knowledge in terms of hypothesis testing. The classical theories of learning as hypothesis testing focus on specific contexts, such as behaviorist models of animal learning (Krech, 1932; Tolman, 1948), models of learning as scientific problem solving (Duncker, 1945; Klahr, Fay, & Dunbar, 1993; see also Inhelder & Piaget, 1955/1958), or problem-solving models based on computer programs (Newell & Simon, 1971). Analyses of hypothesis testing examine learning as testing one or more hypotheses until finding a correct solution.

The gamut of the approaches for studying and explaining developmental transitions combines to make important contributions in diverse ways. However, the source of developmental change is still enigmatic. Some answers lead to reformulation of new questions about the sources of development. For instance, what are the ways and the rules under which innate abilities mature? Or, what are the specific mechanisms that assist the individual's development through social interaction? Alternatively, how can the processes of assimilation, accommodation, and equilibration be specified to allow their operational identification in real-time activities? Or, how are hypotheses formed? The solutions of dynamic systems, neural networks, and other computational theories provide a necessary structural background, suggest processes and concepts that explain development, and formulate algorithms to model it. However, rarely do they show these solutions in actual, real-time activities related to higher cognitive functions.

In this chapter, we specify a process that people use at different ages for developing new, higher-level knowledge out of previous, lower-level knowledge. We define operational tools that identify empty shells of missing knowledge and explain how the shells operate as a developmental transition mechanism with the characteristics of an attractor in dynamic systems. Examples of actual activities demonstrate the transitions that people make from missing knowledge, indicated by empty shells, to full-blown, well-defined knowledge.

People often construct their own shells or scaffolds, which is the focus of our analysis; but bridging also occurs in situations where a more knowledgeable person suggests bridges or scaffolds for a less knowledgeable one. Bridging has much in common with processes observed in expert–novice interactions, such as parent–child and teacher–student (e.g., Newman, Griffin, & Cole, 1989; Vygotsky, 1978). For example, in guided participation, parents use techniques to scaffold the knowledge construction of their children (Rogoff, 1990). They build bridges from known to new, linking new knowledge to what their children already know. Caregivers create bridges between their own and their child's knowledge through mutual involvement and by orienting the child to new information (Rogoff et al., 1993). Similarly, teachers and educators scaffold their students' learning by relating new material to what their students have already studied, creating a bridge between the known and the new to facilitate further learning. Case and his colleagues devised a teaching technique that deliberately created a conceptual bridge between children's current level of functioning and a subsequent, more advanced level. Using this technique, teachers designed an animation script, much like a sequence of cartoon drawings. The animation provided external referents, representing the students' current cognitive structures. After practice, when the students familiarized themselves with the cartoon drawings, the teacher expanded the cartoon sequence with referents for more advanced structures, facilitating the students' progress to a higher cognitive level. In this way, the teacher supported students' developmental transitions (Case, 1991; Case & McKeough, 1990).

The bridging analysis that we present here likewise connects known to new, yet it specifies microdevelopmental processes that have not been suggested in the previous literature. (1) Bridging highlights spontaneous ways in which people *self-scaffold their own knowledge*. Scaffolding by a more knowledgeable person is less puzzling than the emergence of knowledge without guidance. In bridging, people spontaneously construct self-scaffolding shells for their own learning and development. (2) Bridging indicates the process from the perspective of the developing person. It focuses on the way in which people create for themselves shells of developmental levels not yet constructed. (3) Bridging occurs in diverse commonly used forms that are readily observable in children's and adults' activities. These bridging forms are based on simple, prevalent, everyday techniques, yet they facilitate significant construction of new, higher-level knowledge.

The bridging mechanism creates transitions that are tentative and partial. Because of their fleeting, under-defined nature, special attention is required for developing methods that can capture these transitions.

Facilitating the identification of transition mechanisms in development

Analysis and identification of developmental transitions can be facilitated in several ways: first, by using methods that give access to the process of change; second, by distinguishing between aspects of activity with different, simultaneous developmental levels; third, by analyzing activities within their social and environmental context; and fourth, by devising methodologies to allow reliable coding of partial, under-defined achievements.

1.   *Getting access to processes of change*

Analyses of long-term development, based on longitudinal or cross-sectional methods, compare abilities at different ages. These analyses compare static states (the "before" and the "after") and can indicate global developmental trends, but cannot capture how change occurs.

In contrast, several recent approaches focus on the developmental process itself, such as those used by researchers in this volume. From the early history of the study of development, research on microdevelopment (development during short time span) analyzed processes of change (Duncker, 1945; Werner, 1948, 1957). Detailed descriptions of developmental processes have been especially common in language development (e.g., Bowerman, 1989; Brown, 1973; Dromi, 1987/1996). Studies that use the microgenetic approach, with dense sampling of data, are especially promising when focusing on a specific period of change (Siegler & Crowley, 1991). Recent research on microdevelopment has produced new findings that highlight variability in developmental processes. Many researchers have found that within a short time span, people shift between more and less advanced strategies or knowledge levels (e.g., Fischer & Bidell, 1998; Fischer & Granott, 1995; Fischer & Yan, this volume; Goldin-Meadow, Nusbaum, Garber, & Church, 1993; Goldin-Meadow & Alibali, this volume; Granott, 1993a, 1998a, this volume; Kuhn, this volume; Kuhn, Garcia-Mila, Zohar, & Andersen, 1995; Miller & Aloise-Young, 1995; Schauble, 1990, 1996; Siegler, 1996, this volume, Siegler & Jenkins, 1989; Smith & Thelen, 1993; Thelen & Smith, 1994; van Geert, 1994, this volume). Analysis of microdevelopment is instrumental for illuminating such processes of change in development and can illuminate the process of learning (e.g., Gelman, Romo, & Francis, this volume; Parziale, this volume). By following microdevelopmental processes instead of focusing on static states, researchers can observe the characteristics of the process of change and highlight its key attributes (Miller & Coyle, 1999).

2.   *Differentiating between aspects of an activity with different developmental levels*

People often function at multiple levels concurrently, especially in relation to indicators for different aspects or components of an activity. Analysis of one indicator may show developmental progress, while other indicators may not. In such cases, identifying change depends on differentiation between developmental indicators.

For example, in a study of collaborative solutions of unfamiliar problems, participants operated on different levels simultaneously, constructing multiple concurrent developmental paths (Fischer & Granott, 1995; Granott, 1993a, 1998a, this volume). Different aspects of the same task showed a different developmental picture. Initially the participants showed high-level skills related to communication and low-level skills related to understanding the new problem. During their activity, their communication levels showed no significant developmental trend while their understanding showed substantial growth. Without differentiating between aspects of the activity, it would be impossible to capture this change. Process-oriented analyses often indicate that people operate simultaneously on different levels (e.g., Damasio & Damasio, 1992; Fischer & Ayoub, 1994; Goldin-Meadow & Alibali, this volume; Kuhn et al., 1995; Marcel, 1983; Siegler, 1996, this volume; Thelen & Corbetta, this volume, Thelen & Smith, 1994), highlighting the need to differentiate aspects of the activity.

Bridging shows the importance of recognizing multiple levels of operation and thinking. Bridging cannot be identified under the assumption that people function at a single level, because bridging itself includes both lower and higher levels – a lower actual level and a higher target level for the current task. Therefore, analysis based on the assumption of a single level cannot identify transition mechanisms like bridging.

3.   *Analyzing activities within context*

Developmental research often focuses on individual participants. However, in real life, behaviors are embedded in context. Interactions with others are part of the developmental reality (e.g., Bronfenbrenner, 1993; Granott, 1993b, 1998b; Mead, 1934; Rogoff, 1990; Vygotsky, 1978). Social interactions affect developmental progress (Fischer, Bullock, Rotenberg, & Raya, 1993; Granott, 1993b, 1998b). Analysis of single individuals will not capture change that evolves through interaction.

Moreover, studying interactions among partners gives a natural access to analyzing how change occurs (Granott, 1993a, 1998b). During collaboration, partners spontaneously share with each other their thoughts and understanding. They talk about their observations, formulate hypotheses, and offer explanations. Their communication provides rich data that exposes thinking and developmental change (Granott, 1993b; Radziszewska & Rogoff, 1988).

To account for this process, Granott (1998b) defined a collective unit of analysis – an ensemble. The ensemble is the smallest group that co-constructs knowledge within a specific activity context. The ensemble can be of different sizes – a dyad, triad, or a larger group. What qualifies a group as an ensemble is that knowledge is a product of the interactive process between the partners. What gives meaning, guides, and constrains the ensemble's activity is the specific context of its operation. Analyzing ensembles' activities, therefore, is not only more ecologically valid, but also more promising for identifying transition mechanisms in development.

4.   *Identifying partial, under-defined steps*

Transitions in development occur through tentative, undetermined steps. They are partial and clumsy, like a child's first steps. Identifying these transitions requires the use of analytic methods that capture ambiguous, partial steps.

Traditionally, coding creates clearly distinct categories, for example for stages or strategies. Researchers devise a coding manual with well-defined criteria for each category. An activity is placed into a category when it meets the category's criteria. Activities, then, are coded as either showing an attribute or not. This practice was developed to assure validity and reliability in coding. However, transitions and partial steps between categories cannot be captured in this way and are ignored and omitted from the analysis. This method discards the exact data that may contain developmental transitions.

To overcome this difficulty, coding systems that define transitions in an objective, reliable, and valid way have to be developed. Such coding systems focus not only on stages, levels, or categories, nor do they merely identify transitions with a global label. Instead, they identify transitions, specify the process of the transitions and the contents of change, code these transitions, and include them in the data. Such coding systems can facilitate the analysis of change and developmental transition mechanisms in development.

Identifying and analyzing bridging

By structuring an experiment and developing a method of analysis that uses the four conditions specified above, Granott (1992, 1993a) discovered the mechanism of bridging in a study on adults' collaborative scientific inquiry and problem solving. Parziale identified the same mechanism in middle-school children's collaborative processes of scientific problem solving (Parziale, 1997, this volume). In both studies, we used the same principles. (1) We focused on processes rather than states by targeting real-time microdevelopment. A whole microdevelopmental process was continuously videotaped to capture change. (2) We distinguished between different aspects of the activity and analyzed microdevelopment of each aspect separately. (3) The activity was collaborative and was studied in relation to its context. Analysis of the participants' activity and conversations gave us access to the microdevelopment of their understanding. (4) Within each study, the coding system defined partial transitory steps as bridging shells. The analysis was based on Fischer's (1980) skill theory and captured partial constructions between skill levels. These transitions were classified and defined in an operational way that showed high reliability between coders.

Although in the two studies the participants' ages and the tasks were different, we found in both the same transition mechanism of bridging. Moreover, the bridging processes of adults and children were similar to processes documented and analyzed in the study of infants in other research, which we describe later. This similarity and the findings of bridging at different ages suggest that bridging is a general transition mechanism that operates across the life span.

What is bridging?

Like an attractor in dynamic systems, bridging indicates a relatively stable state toward which the system gravitates. Three main attributes characterize and define the process of bridging. (1) It is a partial, transitional step that does not constitute a developmental level by itself. Instead, it denotes a search for new knowledge, giving a glimpse of new development. (2) Bridging operates with future, not yet constructed knowledge. It outlines a target level, albeit unknown. Like grappling hooks for mountain climbers, bridging sets an anchor in levels not attained yet and pulls the developmental process toward constructing these levels. (3) During bridging, people function simultaneously on two different levels of knowledge. On the one hand, they work directly on the task at hand, often functioning at a low level, especially in tasks that are novel for them. On the other, they work at a higher level where they construct a bridging shell, albeit still empty of content knowledge. They use the higher-level shell to guide their knowledge construction by gradually filling in the shell's unknown components.

We demonstrate the use of bridging with Fischer's (1980) skill theory formulation. To keep the presentation easily understandable, we use the skill level of mappings of actions for all examples. A skill of mapping interrelates two actions or factors, such as cause-and-effect. For example, a cause (Jack falls down) is related to its result (water in pail spills):[1]

$$\left[\textbf{JACK}_{\textbf{FALLS}} \quad \text{———} \quad \textbf{WATER}_{\textbf{SPILLS}} \right] \qquad (5.1)$$

---

[1] Structure (5.1) uses skill theory notation. Square brackets indicate a skill and a line denotes a mapping between the two parts of the skill.

Bridging occurs when, for example, a child gives some indication of the existence of a cause before constructing the skill for understanding the causality. There is only a glimpse of causality: neither the cause nor the effect is explicitly mentioned. Instead, a partial and ambiguous statement gives a hint for a budding realization that causality may exist. The statement creates a shell,

$$\left[(X_a) \quad \rule{1.5cm}{0.4pt} \quad (Y_b) \right] \tag{5.2}$$

with unknown variables X_a, Y_b, which could be replaced later with specific values, as the content knowledge is constructed.[2] Such bridging shells can be created in a few ways, corresponding to several bridging forms.

Forms of bridging

Bridging shells can occur in different ways, creating several bridging forms, each of which can be used as self-scaffolding tools. For instance, in a bridging term, people create a shell by stating a specific term that implies a causality between two unknown and implied variables:

$$\left[(X_a) \quad \overset{\text{term}}{\rule{1.5cm}{0.4pt}} \quad (Y_b) \right] \tag{5.3}$$

In such a case, the primary indication for understanding the causality is the use of the specific term. There is no other reference to cause and effect (Granott, 1993a). In *bridging term*, then, a single word creates a shell that implies a higher target level with empty slots.

Other ways that people create bridging include using a specific sentence format, asking a question, declaring an intention, or recasting a statement and reiterating it differently (Granott, 1993a). Detailed explanation and demonstration of each of the bridging forms can be found in Parziale (this volume). All the bridging forms are created similarly, by outlining implied shells of more advanced knowledge than previously specified, while leaving out the shells' unknown contents. They all operate by guiding the activity to gradual construction of the missing knowledge. Specifying the different forms of bridging can help to identify the spontaneous use of this mechanism in real-time activities.

In a *bridging format*, the syntax or format of a statement creates a shell with missing content. A person sets up a shell by making an incomplete statement, as in an "if ... then" statement that omits the content of the "if" or the "then" part. Typically, a pause or a gesture marks the omitted

---

[2] In bridging shells, variables are noted in italics, according to mathematical conventions. Implied information (variable or implied specific content) is marked by parentheses.

content. In discourse, people often make partial statements, leaving a sentence incomplete and continuing to make another. They may not finish statements for various reasons, such as skipping obvious content instead of repeating it unnecessarily. Unlike such cases, what distinguishes bridging format is that people leave out information that is still unknown.[3] By outlining a format that indicates missing knowledge, they form a shell that creates access to this knowledge, guides their exploration, and gradually helps them to construct the target knowledge.

In other bridging forms, similar shells are created by other means. In *bridging question*, people ask a question that outlines a shell with unknown components as a target for future development. In *bridging intention*, they state what they intend to do when the way to achieve it is still unknown. In *bridging recast*, they create a shell by a lower-level formulation followed by a higher-level reformulation. Before explaining in more detail how bridging occurs, we demonstrate it by example from real-time activity in microdevelopment.

How bridging operates in real-time activities

The following episode, which demonstrates the use of bridging, is taken from a study on microdevelopmental co-construction of scientific knowledge (Granott, 1993a, 1998a, this volume). Eight graduate students were asked to discover and understand the operation of unfamiliar Lego robots called "wuggles." The wuggles reacted to light, sound, and touch by changing their movement patterns. The participants explored the wuggles in a room especially designed to include diverse stimuli that affected the robots' movement in different ways. The collaborative activity continued for four one-hour sessions. Within the general task, the participants defined their own goals, problems, and strategies.

The participants constructed bridging shells spontaneously in their attempts to bootstrap their understanding of how the wuggles functioned. For example, Kevin and Marvin explored a wuggle that responded to changes in light. When they first encountered the robot, Kevin and Marvin did not know what affected it or even that it had specific sensors. They tried to understand how the wuggle operated by playing with it, placing their hands around it in different ways, and observing its movement. After a brief exploration, they showed their first bridging – a vague, tentative allusion to undefined cause-and-effect. As Marvin was putting his hand around the robot, Kevin commented:

---

[3] In studies of microdevelopment, it is possible to encapsulate and document the process of learning a specific issue, especially when it is related to a new context. Microgenetic data can show, therefore, when specific information is still unknown and when it is acquired.

"Looks like we got a reaction there."

The term "reaction" implied cause and effect, action and response (re-action). Yet Kevin specified neither the cause nor the effect. At this time, it was unclear what was causing the robot's changing movement and how the robot moved differently, because Kevin and Marvin had not identified yet any patterns in its complex movement. Kevin used a bridging term ("reaction"), which merely alluded to an unknown causality:

$$\left[(X_a) \xrightarrow{\text{reaction}} (Y_b) \right] \qquad (5.4)$$

The only explicit component in the shell is the term "reaction," which implies a causal relation between two unknowns – action X_a and response Y_b.

Skill (5.4) demonstrates how bridging operates in real-time activity in context. (1) People spontaneously make a statement that implies a target-level shell of more advanced knowledge than currently specified. (2) Important content of the shell is still missing. In the example, the first condition is fulfilled because the term "reaction" implied a shell of some causal relation, when Kevin and Marvin have not specified any causal relation before. The shell was still empty of content: the causal relation and its components were still unknown. Even though the shell was merely implied, the statement indicated progress and assisted the construction of the missing knowledge (Granott, 1993a).

As the example demonstrates, bridging in development occurs much like the construction of bridges over highways. In actual bridges, pillars are first erected. These pillars do not support anything yet, because the horizontal part of the bridge, on which the road will pass, is still missing. Yet the "empty" pillars mark the future road. Later, horizontal structures are built over the pillars, bridging from one place to another. Similarly, in developmental bridging, people first set up an empty structure, which, like the pillars, sketches the way for building new knowledge. Then, people fill the empty structure with relevant content, thereby reaching the target knowledge. In the example, bridging merely outlined an undefined structure, just like pillars of future bridges. The content of Kevin's statement – the specific cause and effect – was still missing, like the horizontal beams between the pillars. By outlining a target level, the shell guides toward further development, as we demonstrate later.

Bridging as an attractor for future development

Although the bridging shell does not carry content, it is functional, serving as a goal for learning. It is fundamentally different from a statement in which this knowledge is missing without acknowledging its existence. The vacant structure traces a goal for future development and, like an attractor, pulls the process toward it. By directing new experiences toward gradual construction of the shell's target level, the bridging attractor acts as a catalyst of self-organization, leading to self-guided construction of higher-level structures. These structures are more complex and explicit than those that gave rise to the attractor.

In the "reaction" episode, merely outlining a missing causality created a target level that directed the participants' observations and actions. After the bridging statement, Kevin and Marvin focused on discovering the missing causality, as evidenced in their activity and conversation. By playing with the wuggle and observing its movement, they tried to identify its reactions to their actions and its pattern of movement. The shell guided them toward making more elaborate distinctions about their own actions and the robot's movement.

In their progress toward constructing the knowledge outlined by the shell (5.4), Kevin and Marvin created a series of bridging statements that gradually filled in the missing components in (5.4). For instance, they created bridging with the unfinished statement: "You're getting a different reaction when you're putting your hand on it instead of when you put your hand ... " Although this shell included some information, part of the action was not specified (put your hand where?) and neither was the robot's movement (what different reaction?). Kevin and Marvin gradually progressed, continually steering their explorations toward the shell's target. Their observations contributed to increasing specification of the wuggle's movement – "Sometimes it goes one way ... " – and of relevant environmental conditions – "Look, we've got light problems too." They wondered if light and shadow had any effect – "Light and shadows [do] anything?" – but also asked about sound: "Uh, actually, does it have anything [to do] in relation to the sound /of/ the tape-recorder is playing?" This series of statements increasingly specified components of possible cause and effect relations pertaining to the wuggle's movement.

In dynamic systems terms, bridging operates as an attractor – a relatively stable state to which the system gravitates, a state that attracts the system to it. In the process of knowledge construction, bridging shells operate as attractors, pulling skills toward higher developmental levels. An attractor shell functions like a grappling hook for mountain climbers: it pulls knowledge and understanding up, toward the target level.

Bridging takes place not only from existing knowledge toward the new, but also from the shell's target level toward the current skill, in a top-down pull. The target level serves as a magnet, attracting the process of knowledge construction toward a more complex skill. The top-down pull in developing toward the attractor is created because bridging creates a lens for observing and interpreting events. Even when a bridging shell is completely empty, it establishes a new perspective and affects people's ways of thinking. By processing information from the perspective set by the shell, a person considers different parts of the situation, works them through within that perspective, and gradually constructs new, higher-level knowledge that fills the shell. In this way, the pull of bridging as an attractor creates "self-fulfilling" structures for future knowledge.

The initial shell (5.4) created such a lens for Kevin and Marvin. It directed their actions, gave focus to their observations, and guided their processing of new experiences. Through activity directed toward the higher-level attractor, Kevin and Marvin later formulated their first causal mapping when they said: "When it comes over here and as soon as it gets underneath part of the shadow there, it starts changing its behavior." They stated a simple causal relation between the robot's being under shadow and its changed behavior,

$$\left[\text{SHADOW}_{(\text{ON WUGGLE})} \text{ ——— } \text{IT(THE WUGGLE)}_{\substack{\text{CHANGE(S)} \\ \text{BEHAVIOR}}} \right]$$

$$(5.5)$$

which finally gave shell (5.4) full content.

Bridging specifies the way an attractor starts operating when its manifestation just emerges. First, bridging gives an initial indication of missing knowledge in an empty shell. Then, it guides the subsequent activity, which becomes focused on the shell's target level, and increasingly constructs component of the shell. Gradually, the activity fills the shell with content, stimulates hypotheses, and eventually leads to constructing the target level and reaching the attractor. Along the way, unfit shells can also be revised or abandoned, based on results of the activities, so that the target structure changes.

What bridging is and what it is not: Bridging versus hypotheses

The initial bridging statement is not a hypothesis, because it is vague and undefined, only outlining an empty structure. But it is an attractor, fully functioning to guide the activity toward developmental progress. When an undefined shell becomes increasingly specified and more defined, it turns into a hypothesis.

An example from Parziale's study (1997, this volume) demonstrates the difference between bridging and hypothesis testing. Parziale studied the way fifth- and seventh-graders (mean ages about eleven and thirteen years, respectively) constructed marshmallow-and-toothpick bridges. When Mary and Beth, two fifth-graders, first faced their task, they did not know how to begin their construction. Mary asked: "How are we going to do this?" Clearly, Mary's question was not a hypothesis. Yet as a bridging question, it directed further activity. Mary's statement created a shell with missing content related to her and Beth's action (X_a) and an unspecified component related to the bridge structure ("this"):

$$\left[(X_a) \quad \xrightarrow{\text{how?}} \quad \textbf{THIS}_{(b)} \right] \tag{5.6}$$

A statement made during the activity of two other fifth-graders demonstrates even more explicitly that bridging appears before any hypothesis. Josh and Will, who had doubled the toothpicks between every two marshmallows, were running out of toothpicks. Observing their bridge, which was sagging despite the doubled toothpick connections, Will said: "Hey, Josh. Let's not double. Doubling doesn't work as well as if we . . . Actually, I don't know about that."

Will expressed his dissatisfaction with the strategy of doubling and, using bridging format, compared it to a better, yet unknown, strategy. Will explicitly said he did not know what an alternative strategy might be. Because he did not have a hypothesis yet, he left the alternative strategy unspecified in the incomplete sentence.

The pre-hypothesis function of bridging cannot be attributed to age: it appeared also in adults' activities (Granott, 1993a). For example, in the wuggle study, Ann and Donald were observing a robot that was moving on the floor when the robot suddenly stopped. Bewildered, Ann asked: "What caused it to stop?" At this time, Ann did not have any hypothesis. Yet her bridging question directed the continued activity in search of an answer.

An initial bridging often triggers a series of bridging statements that become increasingly specified. As the activity proceeded, participants in our studies created more advanced bridging shells that indeed served as hypotheses. For example, Mary's question provided a scaffold for initiating a plan. Beth answered: "Well, to make it go across we could do something like this." While talking, Beth placed toothpicks next to each other in the form of a letter H. Her answer started filling in the missing components in (5.6):

$$\left[\textbf{DO SOMETHING}_{\substack{\text{LIKE} \\ \text{THIS(H)}}} \quad \text{——} \quad \textbf{IT(THE BRIDGE)}_{\substack{\text{GO(ES)} \\ \text{ACROSS}}} \right]$$

$$\tag{5.7}$$

By placing toothpicks in an "H" shape, Beth traced a proposed structural unit for the bridge construction. Her answer and action provided a hypothesis, suggesting that by using H units, they could construct the desired bridge.

Similarly, in the other bridge-building dyad, Will's bridging shell, albeit empty, directed the dyad's activity toward identifying an alternative strategy. The dyad continued to experiment with doubling the toothpicks. They started filling in the missing components and then explicitly suggested a different strategy when Josh said "Got to make Xs on the base." This statement specified a hypothesis for their continued construction.

Ann and Donald's activity showed a similar pattern with the wuggle. The shell created a focus for their observations, which soon led to discovering the missing causality. When Donald started talking loudly, the robot moved and Ann exclaimed: "Voice start. Voice!" stating a causal mapping between sound (voice) and the wuggle's movement. At this time, the statement "Voice start" became a hypothesis that Ann started testing by clapping and snapping fingers.

These examples demonstrate the way initial bridging differs from hypothesis testing. While a hypothesis indicates an assumed structure of knowledge, a bridging shell marks the lack thereof. It does not state a possible structure to be tested, but outlines a vacant structure. Bridging puts a place-holder for missing knowledge. It is used when there is not enough knowledge to formulate a hypothesis. However, bridging guides the activity and prepares the way for formulating a hypothesis later. The missing shell directs the continued activity toward filling the missing knowledge. As more knowledge is constructed and components of the shell are increasingly specified, a more advanced bridging shell can serve as a hypothesis.

Bridging as a scaffold

An empty bridging shell operates as a scaffold for future knowledge. It gives structure to knowledge that is still unknown, outlines a missing relation between its components, and gives a goal for the following activity. Stating or acting out a shell that outlines missing knowledge is similar to drafting an initial outline before writing a document. Like a bridging shell, the document's outline is still missing its content, which is not spelled out yet. However, when an initial outline is tentatively sketched, it guides the construction of the actual document.

Bridging is a self-scaffolding mechanism that bootstraps one's own knowledge. It is used by individuals or in collaborative co-construction when people work closely together on a task. By sharing with each other their thoughts, questions, and observations, collaborating partners state bridging shells that scaffold their continuing activity. Within these scaffolds, future knowledge and skills can develop.

For instance, some time after defining shell (5.4), Marvin and Kevin watched their wuggle as it moved on the floor, passed under a bridge, continued to the other side of the bridge, and then stopped close to a box. Marvin said: "Let's see if I can make it come back." Marvin expressed an intention to make the robot come back, but did not specify how he would do it. The cause of the wuggle's movement had been the focus of Kevin and Marvin's exploration since their initial shell (5.4). Now, Marvin's statement created the following new shell:

$$\left[\text{MAKE}_{(a)} \quad \overset{\text{let's see if?}}{\rule{2cm}{0.4pt}} \quad \text{IT (THE WUGGLE)}_{\text{COME(S) BACK}}\right]$$
(5.8)

In the shell (5.8), the action was not specified. Still, the statement created a scaffold for constructing the missing knowledge by indicating a target for future activity. Marvin proceeded to play with the lamp, changed its direction in several ways, and indeed made the robot come back.

As a scaffold, bridging can explain construction that is otherwise puzzling. An example from engineering scaffolding can illustrate this point.[4] The Roman or Gothic arches are logically impossible to construct: the central closing stone is needed for keeping the lateral supporting stones in place, and the lateral supporting stones are needed to keep the closing stone in place. Scaffolding solves this "logical impossibility." By constructing a wooden support for the arch, constructors can assemble the stones on the wooden support. When the stone structure is completed, the wooden support can be removed and the stone structure will support itself. Bridging-shell scaffolds assist development similarly. *It seems logically impossible to construct missing knowledge, because one does not know yet what to construct. By outlining the missing knowledge, the shell creates a scaffold that makes the construction possible.*

Bridging as a transition mechanism

As a transition mechanism, bridging operates in several ways. First, it operates through a series of increasingly specified statements and shells that gradually fill an initial shell. The previous examples demonstrate increasing specification of the initial shell (5.4) through a series of statements and shells, like (5.8), until its fulfillment into fully specified structures, as in (5.5). Second, bridging involves a series of shifting target shells at a given level to generalize a skill. People create a succession of shifting

---

[4] We thank Paul van Geert for this example.

shells to deal with different aspects of a task at their current level, as did Kevin and Marvin when exploring the effects of sound as well as light. Third, development consists of successive shells of more complex skills, shifting to increasingly higher levels.

While initial bridging bootstraps skill development from empty shells, more advanced bridging facilitates the emergence of major qualitative reorganizations from partially filled shells. For example, when Josh and Will were building their bridge, they used bridging to progress from a two-dimensional to a stronger three-dimensional structure. They began with two-dimensional hexagon units with toothpick "spokes" leading to a centered marshmallow. Josh used a bridging question by asking if they should continue adding units in the same plane or build upwards, adding a third dimension: "Are we going to make a higher level, or are we going to just keep on building like that?" While speaking, Josh represented the shell visually by holding a toothpick vertically over a unit that was lying flat on the table. His question shell and action outlined two optional strategies – flat or three-dimensional structure – when the way to execute the strategies remained unknown. Later, this shell led Josh and Will's activity to a major advance. They inserted a toothpick in a way that created a third dimension and began building vertically off the flat structure. Testing their bridge provided them with feedback about the effect of their strategies and helped them understand the missing variables in the shell (Parziale, this volume).

An important kind of shell for such major reorganizations is a bridging recast, which reformulates or recasts the structure of understanding into a higher-level shell. For instance, when Ann and Donald were exploring the robot's response to sound, Donald said: "It goes not from the talking but from the difference in the loudness." Later, he reformulated the idea of loudness difference from the perspective of what the wuggle sensed: "See, I think that it must have to sense that there's loudness difference." The recast bridged the way from description of the movement to expla-nation, knowledge that was only implicit in the previous statement.

Another way in which bridging operates as a transition mechanism is by revising and changing content knowledge. Again, the process is similar to the transition from an outline to a written document. When writing the outlined document, an author often makes substantial changes. In bridging, people make similar changes when filling a tentative outline set by a shell. The outline can either be supported by the continuing activity and filled with content or discarded when further activity leads to knowledge incompatible with the shell. In both capacities, bridging leads to further progress.

For example, having made the hypothesis that their robot responded to sound, Ann put forth a new shell, saying: "I think it's directional." The term "directional" indicated that direction was important somehow, though its effect on the robot's movement was undefined because it was still unknown. Ann went on to explore the effect of direction by clapping at one side of the robot and then at the other. Following some further exploration, she and Donald concluded that the sound's direction had no effect on the robot's movement: "So, you don't think it's where the noise comes from." The bridging shell set forth by the term "directional" created a target level that led the activity and was then invalidated. Developing understanding depends as much on such instances of discarding wrong shells as it does on building shells that bridge to correct knowledge and skills.

The prevalence of bridging: Discussion and implications

The developmental mechanism of bridging gives an answer to a question that has puzzled researchers for centuries: How does development occur? Specifically, how do higher-level structures of knowledge in action and speech develop out of lower-level structures? We describe a developmental transition mechanism called bridging that gives an answer to this question. We suggest that the answer can be found in all aspects of life. People routinely formulate undefined bridging shells that use the structure of higher-level skills and knowledge but leave components empty or vague. They then use those shells to guide their learning and problem solving and gradually fill the missing components. As shells are transformed into explicit skills, people continue to use bridging to achieve still higher levels. They create a series of shifting shells, scaffolding their own learning and development to increasingly higher levels of knowledge.

During bridging, people routinely operate at multiple levels simultaneously. They function at established levels of knowledge, where they use explicit, well-defined skills. Yet they also function at higher levels when constructing bridging shells as targets for future knowledge. By working toward filling the shells with content, they bridge the gap between the two levels. Through bridging across levels, people continue to improve their skills and understanding.

Bridging clarifies how people use existing structures to construct new knowledge. They state terms that imply higher-level shells. They use sentence formats that include empty components. They ask questions for which they have no answers. They state intentions to perform an act when the way to do it is still unknown. They recast an idea at a higher, still unknown level. Through these forms of bridging, people create goals for their learning and development and direct themselves to construct new knowledge.

The function of bridging for guiding development explains how people grope toward new knowledge in ways that seem to reflect a goal-oriented process. The phenomenon is paradoxical, since this goal-oriented process is guided by an unknown goal: the target shell represents knowledge that is still missing. A few researchers have noted this puzzle previously. For example, Siegler & Jenkins (1989) conclude that children do not proceed in a haphazard, trial-and-error manner when generating new strategies for solving problems. Siegler suggests that "one possibility is that even before discovering new strategies, children understand the goals that legitimate strategies in the domain must satisfy" (Siegler, 1994, p. 4). Bridging may explain this pattern of development, because when building shells people use vague, tentative, and undefined notions of still-missing knowledge to create goals for their own learning and development.

In our studies too, participants did not make random attempts to understand a robot or build a marshmallow–toothpicks bridge. Instead, their actions and discourse were directed by goals set by their bridging shells. Bridging sheds light on the puzzling attribute of development toward the unknown since in bridging even missing knowledge can be used to set targets to guide future development.

We suggest that bridging operates at all ages, not only at the ages that we studied. Bridging is similar to Piaget's (1936/1952) description of groping behavior in infancy. When infants encounter a new situation, they try out different actions to grope toward a target of effective actions. They produce what Piaget, following Baldwin (1894), called circular reactions – repetitions of similar actions in groping toward a goal. According to Piaget, groping can occur in two ways, corresponding to two extremes of the same phenomenon. Some groping is non-systematic, occurring through fortuitous discovery, chance occurrence, and trial and error. Other groping is systematic, occurring through directed activity that is based on some comprehension, like the use of bridging shells. Piaget argued that infant groping is mostly systematic and directed, albeit at times in a vague and general way. According to Piaget (and Claparède, 1931), groping in infants starts as awareness of a possible relation between actions, such as means–end – like the bridging shell (5.4) described above. Then, groping leads to repetition of similar but varied actions. We suggest that bridging explains this phenomenon: infants use bridging to guide their exploration and pave the way to discovering new relations. Through circular reactions, they fill components and interrelations that were missing in the shell and gradually develop their skills and knowledge. In this way, the shells operate as attractors in dynamic systems, guiding actions and observations for infants, children, and adults. Through a series of shifting, increasingly defined bridging shells, a person constructs new knowledge at levels higher than she or he has constructed in that domain.

Once we discovered bridging, we could see its prevalence in interactive activities, individual knowledge construction, and discovery. Parents, teachers, and employers use bridging techniques intentionally. Bridging appears in diverse contexts, like home, school, or the workplace, and in various activities, including therapy, counseling, and planning.

Parents offer children bridging shells in various ways. In language, for example, they use bridging terms by uttering partial words and letting the children continue them. They use bridging formats by starting a sentence and waiting for the children to complete it. They use bridging questions by asking a question and guiding the children to answer it. They use bridging intentions and prompt the children to participate in translating the intention into action. They use bridging recasts by reformulating children's utterances in order to correct them or to better fit the task demands. Parents use bridging techniques when they collaborate on a task with children, performing part of the task and leaving the rest, partly defined, for the children to do.

At school as well, teachers utilize bridging as learning tools. Using bridging terms, teachers introduce key words that guide the children's activity and discussion. Using bridging questions, they formulate questions that lead students to make statements they have not made before. Using bridging formats, they begin a statement or an activity and ask students to complete it. Using bridging intentions, they indicate intentions that operate as goals for the students' activity. Using bridging recasts, they reformulate students' answers, providing more advanced knowledge. Teachers make comments that suggest problems or hint at solutions in ways that require students to formulate the problems or find the solutions. Through such bridging shells, they lead students to construct new knowledge.

In the workplace, formulation of targets as operational goals is a well-practiced technique. Salespersons have quotas, manufacturing units have production targets, and managers have pre-formulated goals. When these goals are set, the ways to reach them are often unknown. Setting the goals defines targets that guide further growth, just as bridging does in learning and development.

Across settings, especially in middle childhood and beyond, people often ask themselves questions or set for themselves incomplete tasks. These questions and tasks, whether set explicitly or implicitly, serve as bridging for knowledge construction. People raise questions about specific issues and later look for answers to their questions. Sometimes the questions lead to a prolonged process of discovering the answers. At other times, an answer "presents itself": the well-prepared mind, which asked the question, picks the answer from the stream of events.

Bridging appears to be prevalent. Yet the role of partial, vague, and undefined knowledge has often been denied. For example, Vygotsky (1962, p. 163) claimed that a "need is not a sufficient explanation for any developmental change." Yet, as we have demonstrated, a need can guide learning and development through partial, vague definitions of target levels. To trigger bridging, needs must be defined only enough for a person to create an empty shell that guides further activity. Shells can serve as attractors in the dynamics of activity, pulling knowledge toward the goal indicated by the need. A need expressed in a vague statement may be a sufficient trigger for developmental change.

In this chapter we have pointed out the existence of bridging and defined how it occurs. Further extensive research is essential for analyzing bridging and constructing in-depth understanding of its contribution to transitions in development and learning. The description of bridging and the analysis of the way it works, presented in this chapter, may provide a shell for further understanding how bridging functions to create learning and development.

References

Baldwin, J. M. (1894). *Mental development in the child and the race: Methods and processes.* New York: Macmillan

Bowerman, M. (1989). Learning a semantic system: What role do cognitive predispositions play? In M. Rice & R. Schiefelbusch (Eds.), *The teachability of language* (chap. 4). Baltimore: Paul H. Brookes.

Bronfenbrenner, U. (1993). The ecology of cognitive development: Research models and fugitive findings. In R. Wozniak & K. W. Fischer (Eds.), *Development in context: Acting and thinking in specific environments* (pp. 3–44). Hillsdale, NJ: Erlbaum.

Brown, R. (1973). *A first language: The early stages.* Cambridge, MA: Harvard University Press.

Case, R. (1991). A developmental approach to the design of remedial instruction. In A. McKeough & J. Lupert (Eds.), *Toward the practice of theory-based instruction* (pp. 117–147). Hillsdale, NJ: Erlbaum.

Case, R., & McKeough, A. (1990). Schooling and the development of central conceptual structures: An example from the domain of children's narrative. *International Journal of Educational Psychology, 8,* 835–855.

Case, R., Okamoto, Y., Griffin, S., McKeough, A., Bleiker, C., Henderson, B., & Stephenson, K. M. (1996). The role of central conceptual structures in the development of children's thought. *Monographs of the Society for Research in Child Development, 61(1–2)* (Serial No. 246).

Chomsky, N. (1975). *Reflections on language.* New York: Pantheon.

Chomsky, N. (1980). On cognitive structures and their development: A reply to Piaget. In M. Piatelli-Palmarini (Ed.), *Language and learning: The debate between Jean Piaget and Noam Chomsky* (pp. 35–52). Cambridge, MA: Harvard University Press.

Claparède, E. (1931). *L'éducation fonctionnelle*. Paris & Neuchâtel: Delachaux & Niestlé.

Cole, M. (1988). Cross-cultural research in the sociohistorical tradition. *Human Development, 31,* 137–157.

Damasio, A. R., & Damasio, H. (1992). Brain and language. *Scientific American, 267(3),* 89–95.

Dromi, E. (1987/1996). *Early lexical development* (first published 1987). San Diego: Singular Publishing.

Duncker, K. (1945). On problem solving. *Psychological Monographs, 58* (Whole no. 270).

Elman, J. L., Bates, E. A., Johnson, M. H., Karmiloff-Smith, A., Parisi, D., & Plunkett, K. (1996). *Rethinking innateness: A connectionist perspective on development.* Cambridge, MA: MIT Press.

Fischer, K. W. (1980). A theory of cognitive development: The control and construction of hierarchies of skills. *Psychological Review, 87,* 477–531.

Fischer, K. W., & Ayoub, C. (1994). Affective splitting and dissociation in normal and maltreated children: Developmental pathways for self in relationships. In D. Cicchetti & S. L. Toth (Eds.), *Rochester Symposium on dysfunctions of the self* (pp. 149–222). Rochester, NY: University of Rochester Press.

Fischer, K. W., & Bidell, T. R. (1998). Dynamic development of psychological structures in action and thought. In R. M. Lerner (Ed.), *Handbook of child psychology* (pp. 467–561). New York: Wiley.

Fischer, K. W., Bullock, D. H., Rotenberg, E. J., & Raya, P. (1993). The dynamics of competence: How context contributes directly to skill. In R. H. Wozniak & K. W. Fischer (Eds.), *Development in context: Acting and thinking in specific environments.* Hillsdale, NJ: Erlbaum.

Fischer, K. W., & Granott, N. (1995). Beyond one-dimensional change: Multiple, concurrent, socially distributed processes in learning and development. *Human Development, 38,* 302–314.

Fischer, K. W., & Rose, S. P. (1994). Dynamic development of coordination of components in brain and behavior: A framework for theory and research. In G. Dawson & K. W. Fischer (Eds.), *Human behavior and the developing brain* (pp. 3–66). New York: Guilford.

Fischer, K. W., & Yan, Z. (this volume). Darwin's construction of the theory of evolution: Microdevelopment of explanations of variation and change in species.

Fodor, J. A. (1975). *The language of thought.* Cambridge, MA: Harvard University Press.

Gelman, R., Romo, L., & Francis, W. S. (this volume). Notebooks as windows on learning: The case of a science-into-ESL program.

Gesell, A. (1940). *The first five years of life.* New York: Harper & Row.

Goldin-Meadow, S., & Alibali, M. W. (this volume). Looking at the hands through time: A microgenetic perspective on learning and instruction.

Goldin-Meadow, S., Nusbaum, H., Garber, P., & Church, R. B. (1993). Transitions in learning: Evidence for simultaneously activated rules. *Journal of Experimental Psychology: Human Perception and Performance, 19,* 92–107.

Gottlieb, G. (1991). Experiential canalization of behavioral development: Theory. *Developmental Psychology, 27(1),* 4–13.

Granott, N. (1992). Microdevelopmental puzzle and the mechanism of cognitive growth: Alternative pathways, parallel access, and co-existing structures. Paper presented at the *22nd Annual Symposium of the Jean Piaget Society,* Montreal, Canada.

Granott, N. (1993a). Microdevelopment of co-construction of knowledge during problem-solving: Puzzled minds, weird creatures, and wuggles. Doctoral dissertation, Massachusetts Institute of Technology, Cambridge, MA [on line]. Available: *http://theses.mit.edu:80/Dienst/UI/2.0/Composite/ 0018.mit.theses/1993-170/1?nsections=19.*

Granott, N. (1993b). Patterns of interaction in the co-construction of knowledge: Separate minds, joint effort, and weird creatures. In R. Wozniak & K. W. Fischer (Eds.), *Development in context: Acting and thinking in specific environments* (pp. 183–207). Hillsdale, NJ: Erlbaum.

Granott, N. (1994). On the mechanism of cognitive change: Transition mechanism in microdevelopment and the "Zone of Current Development". Paper presented at the *24th Annual Symposium of the Jean Piaget Society,* Chicago, IL.

Granott, N. (1998a). We learn, therefore we develop: Learning versus development – or developing learning? In C. Smith & T. Pourchot (Eds.), *Adult learning and development: Perspectives from educational psychology* (pp. 15–34). Mahwah, NJ: Erlbaum.

Granott, N. (1998b). Unit of analysis in transit: From the individual's knowledge to the ensemble process. *Mind, Culture, and Activity: An International Journal, 5(1),* 42–66.

Granott, N. (this volume). How microdevelopment creates macrodevelopment: Reiterated sequences, backward transitions, and the Zone of Current Development.

Granott, N., & Parziale, J. (1996). Bridges to and from the unknown: The developmental mechanism of bridging. Paper presented at the *26th Annual Symposium of the Jean Piaget Society.* Philadelphia, PA.

Grossberg, S. (1987). *The adaptive brain* (2 vols.). Amsterdam: Elsevier/North-Holland.

Inhelder, B., & Piaget, G. (1955/1958). *The growth of logical thinking from childhood to adolescence* (A. Parsons & S. Seagrim, trans.). New York: Basic Books. (Originally published 1955.)

Klahr, D. (1992). Information-processing approaches to cognitive development. In M. H. Bornstein & M. E. Lamb (Eds.), *Developmental psychology: An advanced textbook* (pp. 273–335). Hillsdale, NJ: Erlbaum.

Klahr, D., Faye, A. L., & Dunbar, K. (1993). Heuristics for scientific experimentation: A developmental study. *Cognitive Psychology, 25,* 111–146.

Krech, D. (1932). The genesis of "hypotheses" in rats. *University of California Publications in Psychology, 6,* 45–64.

Kuhn, D. (this volume). A multi-component system that constructs knowledge: Insights from microgenetic study.

Kuhn, D., Garcia-Mila, M., Zohar, A., & Andersen, C. (1995). Strategies of knowledge acquisition. *Monographs of the Society for Research in Child Development, 60(4)* (Serial No. 245).

Lee, K., & Karmiloff-Smith, A. (this volume). Macro- and microdevelopmental research: Assumptions, research strategies, constraints, and utilities.

Leont'ev, A. N. (1981). The problem of activity in psychology. In J. V. Wertsch (Ed.), *The concept of activity in Soviet psychology* (pp. 37–71). Armonk, NY: Sharpe.

Lerner, R. M. (1991). Changing organism-context relations as the basic process of development: A developmental contextual perspective. *Developmental Psychology, 27(1),* 27–32.

Lewis, M. D. (this volume). Interacting time scales in personality (and cognitive) development: Intentions, emotions, and emergent forms.

MacWhinney, B., & Leinbach, J. (1991). Implementations are not conceptualizations: Revising the verb learning model. *Cognition, 40,* 121–157.

Marcel, A. J. (1983). Conscious and unconscious perception: Experiments on visual masking and word recognition. *Cognitive Psychology, 15,* 197–237.

Mead, G. H. (1934). *Mind, self, and society.* Chicago: University of Chicago Press.

Miller, P. H., & Aloise-Young, P. A. (1995). Preschoolers' strategic behavior and performance on a same-different task. *Journal of Experimental Child Psychology, 60(2),* 284–303.

Miller, P. H., & Coyle, T. R. (1999). Developmental change: Lessons from microgenesis. In E. K. Scholnick, K. Nelson, S. A. Gelman, & P. H. Miller (Eds.), *Conceptual development: Piaget's legacy* (pp. 209–239). Mahwah, NJ: Erlbaum.

Newell, A., & Simon, H. A. (1971). *Human problem solving.* Englewood Cliffs, NJ: Prentice-Hall.

Newman, D., Griffin, P., & Cole, M. (1989). *The construction zone: Working for change in school.* Cambridge, UK: Cambridge University Press.

Parziale, J. (1997). Microdevelopment during an activity based science lesson. Doctoral dissertation, Harvard Graduate School of Education, Harvard University.

Parziale, J. (this volume). Observing the dynamics of construction: Children building bridges and new ideas.

Piaget, J. (1936/1952). *The origins of intelligence in children* (M. Cook, trans.). New York: International Universities Press. (Originally published 1936.)

Piaget, J. (1970). Piaget's theory. In P. H. Mussen (Ed.), *Carmichael's manual of child psychology* (pp. 703–732). New York: Wiley.

Piaget, J. (1985). *The equilibration of cognitive structures: The central problem of intellectual development* (T. Brown & K. J. Thampy, trans.). Chicago: University of Chicago Press.

Radziszewska, B., & Rogoff, B. (1988). Influence of adult and peer collaborators on children's planning skills. *Developmental Psychology, 24,* 840–848.

Rogoff, B. (1990). *Apprenticeship in thinking: Cognitive development in social context.* New York: Oxford University Press.

Rogoff, B., Mistry, J., Goncu, A., & Mosier, C. (1993). Guided participation in cultural activity by toddlers and caregivers. *Monographs of the Society for Research in Child Development, 58(8)* (Serial No. 236).

Rumelhart, D. E., & McClelland, J. L. (1988). *Explorations in parallel distributed processing: A handbook of models, programs, and exercises.* Cambridge, MA: MIT Press.

Scarr, S. (1993). Biological and cultural diversity: The legacy of Darwin for development. *Child Development, 64,* 1333–1353.

Schauble, L. (1990). Belief revision in children: The role of prior knowledge and strategies for generating evidence. *Journal of Experimental Child Psychology, 49,* 31–57.

Schauble, L. (1996). The development of scientific reasoning in knowledge-rich contexts. *Developmental Psychology, 32(1),* 102–119.

Siegler, R. S. (1994). Cognitive variability: A key to understanding cognitive development. *Current Directions in Psychological Science, 3(1),* 1–5.

Siegler, R. S. (1996). *Emerging minds: The process of change in children's thinking.* New York: Oxford University Press.

Siegler, R. S. (this volume). Microgenetic studies of self-explanation.

Siegler, R. S., & Crowley, K. (1991). The microgenetic method: A direct means for studying cognitive development. *American Psychologist, 46,* 606–620.

Siegler, R. S., & Jenkins, E. (1989). *How children discover new strategies.* Hillsdale, NJ: Erlbaum.

Simon, T. J., & Halford, G. S. (Eds.). (1995). *Developing cognitive competence: New approaches to process modeling.* Hillsdale, NJ: Erlbaum.

Smith, L. B., & Thelen, E. (Eds.). (1993). *A dynamic systems approach to development: Applications.* Cambridge, MA: MIT Press.

Thelen, E., & Corbetta, D. (this volume). Microdevelopment and dynamic systems: Applications to infant motor development.

Thelen, E., & Smith, L. B. (1994). *A dynamic systems approach to the development of cognition and action.* Cambridge, MA: MIT Press.

Tolman, E. C. (1948). Cognitive maps in rats and men. *Psychological Review, 55,* 189–208.

van Geert, P. (1991). A dynamic systems model of cognitive and language growth. *Psychological Review, 98,* 3–53.

van Geert, P. (1994). *Dynamic systems of development: Change between complexity and chaos.* New York: Harvester Wheatsheaf.

van Geert, P. (1998a). We almost had a great future behind us: The contribution of non-linear dynamics to developmental-science-in-the-making. *Developmental Science, 1(1),* 143–159.

van Geert, P. (1998b). A dynamic systems model of basic developmental mechanisms: Piaget, Vygotsky, and beyond. *Psychological Review, 105(4),* 634–677.

van Geert, P. (this volume). Developmental dynamics, intentional action, and fuzzy sets.

Vygotsky, L.S. (1962). *Thought and language.* Cambridge, MA: MIT Press.

Vygotsky, L. S. (1978). *Mind in society: The development of higher psychological processes.* Cambridge, MA: Harvard University Press.

Werner, H. (1948). *Comparative psychology of mental development*. New York: International Universities Press.

Werner, H. (1957). The concept of development from a comparative and organismic point of view. In D. B. Harris (Ed.), *The concept of development: An issue in the study of human behavior* (pp. 125–148). Minneapolis: University of Minnesota Press.

Wertsch, J. V. (1985). *Vygotsky and the social formation of mind*. Cambridge, MA: Harvard University Press.

6 Observing the dynamics of construction: Children building bridges and new ideas

Jim Parziale

Perhaps the most useful element of the microdevelopmental approach is its demand for observations that are as direct and as continuous as possible. This use of evidence is in keeping with the successful practices of the natural sciences. Direct and continuous observations have provided the basis for most of the useful ideas of these sciences. What sort of notion would we have about cells if their structures and functions were not closely observed? Weren't centuries of careful observation required before the basic form and dynamics of the solar system were understood? For explanations to be valid in science they must be logical and arise from observations that are as close to the phenomena as possible. It is this emphasis on close observation that gives the microdevelopment approach its great explanatory potential.

Surprisingly, developmental psychology has made only limited use of this power of observation that the natural sciences depend on for so much. The microdevelopmental study described here attempted to re-connect developmental psychology to this potential by directly and continuously observing changes in fifth- and seventh-graders' conversations and actions as they worked in their everyday classroom. (The fifth-graders ranged from 10.8 to 12.1 years of age; the seventh-graders were between 12.7 and 13.7 years old.) During the task pairs of students built marshmallow-and-toothpick bridges across an eleven-inch (28 cm) gap between tables. Two lines of evidence, student conversations and actions, were then used to infer the children's lesson-related ideas and the mechanisms that built these ideas.

These students spontaneously engaged three types of mechanisms in alternating emphasis to make progress on the task: shifts of focus, bridging

The author of this chapter is greatly indebted to the students, teachers, and administrators of the Driscoll School, Brookline, MA, for the generous sharing of their work and ideas. The author would also like to thank Nira Granott and Mike Hardert for their help with earlier versions of this chapter. Partial funding for this study was obtained through grants to Kurt W. Fischer from the Spencer Foundation, Mr. and Mrs. Fredrick P. Rose, and Harvard University.

157

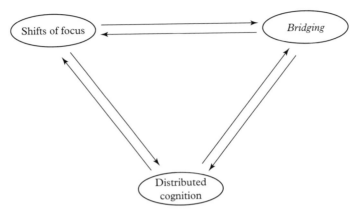

Figure 6.1 Task-solving system outline.

mechanisms, and distributed cognition. Shifts of focus are defined here as simple switches in attention. Bridging mechanisms mainly provide partial ideas that lead to more complete ideas. Distributed cognition is used here to indicate the use of physical things to coordinate ideas in an original way, not in its general sense of ideas shared across people or off-loaded onto objects. The students' use of distributed cognition went beyond any previously described form as student-built bridges showed more complex ideas than the students' conversations did.

These three mechanisms emerged spontaneously and interacted to form a task-solving system. The three mechanisms were mutually supportive through this system by providing input and stimuli for each other as indicated by the arrows in figure 6.1.

None of these mechanisms or the systems they formed would have been observable with the use of probes or pretest-to-posttest comparisons. Without close observation only a scattered few thinking structures could have been inferred of a process of change that was dynamic, distributive, and self-constructive.

This chapter first explores how microdevelopment approaches can satisfy some of the basic needs of developmental psychology and education. The chapter then provides details of this microdevelopmental study of children. Next the three mechanisms of idea construction and the task-solving model are described in greater detail. Finally the educational implications of this study are considered.

Needs and questions

There exists a gap between the questions and methods of researchers and the needs of educators. This gap exists because studies are rarely done in classrooms under the conditions in which children build new ideas. Even though schools are all about fostering change, few researchers are actually watching this change occur. A result of this neglect is research findings and theories that can't be directly applied to the classroom.

The present study found the opportunity to observe change by videotaping children sharing ideas on a shared problem in their everyday environment. As changes were observed, clear evidence of the mechanisms that led to those changes were seen that would have been unnoticed by pretests, posttests and probes. Making our observations in a natural environment meant we could see the creative nature of building ideas along a spontaneous path, unlike the sequences observed in contrived laboratory-based experiments. Many researchers show disdain for such an uncontrolled approach and use experimental controls to narrow their field of observations. This narrowing still needs to occur in data-rich microdevelopmental studies like this one because no one can look at all that actually happens when people solve problems together. The inherent difference between experimental designs and microanalytic studies is when this focus is achieved. During a microanalytic study it is the activity of the coders that must be focused as they watch videotapes. In experimental studies it is generally the activities of the participants that are narrowed in focus. One approach is not better than the other. Each provides important developmental clues, but there are few microanalytic studies to provide the necessary connection with the realities and processes of learning.

Microanalytic studies have the potential of explaining developmental patterns in classrooms for the benefit of teachers and students. However, a second reason for examining process has its roots outside the classroom. In the US, more and more standardized tests are directing classrooms to use lessons that are less focused on the learning process and more focused on the posttest assessment. Teachers and school administrators know that exposing children to extensive experience with the multiple-choice format of these tests is the surest way to improve scores. Teachers, however, widely believe that these tests only assess students' ability to take such tests and that real understanding is something that is more skillful than rote. Research, however, has not explored the learning process enough to support this claim.

In brief, the big question for both educators and researchers is, how do children learn? This is a widely pursued question, but is anyone actually watching the process to see how it happens? This study attempted to observe, as directly and continuously as possible, children working in the constraints of their everyday classroom.

The following two smaller questions directed this study.

> How do children build new understandings during a classroom lesson?
>
> How do children work together and use their environment during this construction process?

The study design

This study was performed in fifth and seventh grades at a well-resourced and respected suburban/urban school that has classes from prekindergarten to eighth grade. The school is part of a public school system that has been considered one of its state's best, offering students generous resources, excellent teachers, and stimulating and diverse curricula. A total of twenty students took part. In order to observe variations in behavior and knowledge construction across children of different ages, children in two different grade levels participated, ten fifth-graders and ten seventh-graders. These two grade levels were chosen because this researcher had also acted as the science resource teacher and classroom teacher of these two grades for the five years leading up to the study. Through this familiarity it was hoped that the questions of education and developmental psychology could be merged.

The participating students were randomly drawn from a pool of thirty-seven students who had their parents' permission to participate. The lesson which the study observed calls for students to work in pairs with members of their own grade. Significant consideration could have been given to the pairing of the students by ability or gender in an attempt to improve learning effectiveness and progress. However, to preserve the natural context of this lesson for the present study, the procedures of the classroom teachers and students were kept as normal as possible and the cooperating teachers for this and other lessons and activities allowed students to match themselves.

In the fifth grade there were two pairs of both females and one pair of both males, leaving two pairs of mixed gender. In the seventh grade there were three pairs of both females, two pairs of both males and no pairs of mixed gender. These children varied considerably in their academic ability. Three of the students who participated in the study had individualized education plans (IEPs), two fifth-graders and one seventh-grader. Both of the fifth-graders' IEPs called for support and remedial tutoring in reading. The seventh-grader's IEP called for organizational assistance from the learning center. Four of the other participating children were in a pull-out program for children gifted in math, two fifth-graders and two seventh-graders.

The task

This study's task was a science problem-solving activity in which students construct a bridge across an eleven-inch (28 cm) gap between tables using only mini-marshmallows and common flat toothpicks. The task was originally used in the town's schools in 1980 during a town-wide science invention convention along with other similar tasks: building the tallest card tower, building the smallest container to safely carry an egg through a four-story fall, and building a rubber-band-powered car that would go the farthest. Many of these activities became part of the standard curriculum across several grades when the convention was discontinued.

This activity was selected from the other activities described above and many other activity-based science lessons used in the classroom for three reasons.

1. This activity consistently stimulated obvious qualitative changes in the way that children built their bridges. Students usually started out with a goal-oriented linear design that did not hold itself up across the eleven inch gap between tables. This design generally would evolve over the period of the activity so that the structure had significant width, and later height. Successful pairs also realized that the small building units that composed the bridge must be stable if the bridge itself was to be stable. To that end students eventually incorporated triangles in most of the building dimensions: vertical, horizontal and cross-sectional. This feature of the lesson ensured a match between the educational emphasis of idea construction with the parallel theoretical conception of constructivism. Other lessons in the workday of these students were much more rote-based and repetitive such as the fifth-graders' memorization of a vocabulary list for a quiz later in English. An analysis of more rote lessons probably would not have demonstrated the increasing complexity of ideas constructed in the lesson chosen for the study.

2. The activity provoked a great amount of idea sharing and discussion. Students needed to not only exchange their ideas about the structure, they also shared strategies and hypotheses about the merits of different ideas. This feature of the lesson allowed us to hear the students build and maintain a joint problem space (Perkins, 1991; Teasley & Roschelle, 1993). This opportunity provided the evidence for us to infer what ideas were constructed and how they came to be built.

3. Other activities that these children were engaged in, such as dissecting squids or determining their own body's density, came to a well-defined endpoint. In contrast to the children in these activities, the children during the building task produced remarkably varied bridges. The diversity of finished designs demonstrated that this task stimulated creativity and had a relatively low amount of task-related constraint.

Successful students learned to build in three dimensions using triangles. Through spontaneous prototype testing, and idea sharing, students usually came to designs that had enough length to account for some sagging, width to support vertical triangles, and height to distribute forces across to the tables.

For this study, the students' own classroom was set up with five pairs of tables each in front of a video camera. The paired tables were placed the "gap distance" of eleven inches apart and provided with marshmallows and toothpicks. Each of the students wore a clip-on microphone to ensure that each student's voice could be separated from the others. Owing to class schedule constraints, the entire activity, including giving instructions and settling down to work, took only forty-five minutes. This meant that the actual time for construction was limited to about thirty-eight minutes. Simple instructions were given: "Build the best bridge that you can using only marshmallows and toothpicks. Work together in pairs of your own choice on just one bridge at a time." The non-recorded participants, those without parents' permission and those not selected by the draw, worked in an adjacent classroom on the same lesson.

Analysis

A skill theory system of analysis (Fischer, 1980) was designed during an earlier preliminary study (Parziale, 1995) to detect conceptual changes in task-related conceptions. The central element of this system of analysis was a skill sequence which defined the levels of idea complexity and was the basis for coding the students' conversations, actions and growing bridge designs. The system grew out of earlier pioneering work which dynamically analyzed the problem-solving of adults (Granott, 1993).

Skill theory permits changing ability to be defined within a hierarchical system of levels. The ability to control variation in specific domains and contexts is a skill. More complex skills are constructed by coordinating skills of the previous levels through interaction with the environment. Transformation rules define the way that skills are coordinated and differentiated leading to orderly sequences for developmental strands that are predictable. The coding system used in this study is described in detail elsewhere (Parziale & Fischer, 1998).

The focus of the skill sequence for this study is one single strand of development out of many that could have been examined in the videotapes, the changing ability of students to control task variables as they design and build a functional bridge. Five levels of skill or idea complexity were necessary to code the videotapes from the pilot study. These range from action 1 through representation 2 in the developmental sequence defined by skill theory.

The complexity of both the student conversations and the marshmallow bridge were coded from the videotapes. There were two reasons for the use of these parallel lines of coding. First, two sources of evidence could better describe and verify the understandings constructed during the activity. Second, the supportive interaction between the activities of the students and the product that they were making could be examined.

Conversation coding was the rating of the complexity of idea structures presented by the participants through conversations, gestures, and actions. Since the coding of ideas depends on task specificity, no off-task activities were coded for skill levels, such as comments on other students' clothing or who picked whom for a partner.

The marshmallow bridge coding used the same skill sequence as the coding described above but focused solely on the student-constructed physical structures. Codes were assigned by examining the videotapes for design changes made to the bridges. For example, the use of a continuous series of vertical triangles is essential for a stable bridge built with these materials. Seeing this feature in a bridge meant that the concept of triangular units was physically coordinated with the concept of using vertical structure to distribute force.

At first it was wrongly assumed by the researchers that the bridge was completely a product of the participants' ability to control variation in thought. In other words, the complexity of this product, the bridge, was taken as direct evidence of the students' ability to coordinate ideas. Consider the example above where triangles are used vertically. Students understanding this design feature should be relating two skill systems: one evidenced by the triangles and the other by their use vertically. These ideas working together would form a level 4 skill when rated on the skill sequence.

After watching the videotapes in a pre-pilot for this study, it was noticed that children only exchanged relatively simple ideas about bridge design. In all the studies done for this project no student ever verbalized, for example, the conception about triangles in the vertical position being essential for a successful bridge. How was it that this conception ended up in about half of the finished bridge structures?

Results

The idea sharing of these twenty students resulted in 2,904 coded events. Each event was a shared idea, question or part of an idea. This microdevelopmental lens revealed that the pairs of children were active participants in a complex system that spontaneously emerged and self-organized to solve the bridge problem. The system was composed of three constructive mechanisms, shift of focus, *bridging*, and distributed cognition.

Shifts of focus

Shift of focus is defined here as the way that students changed their discussions from topic to topic. These shifts sometimes occurred from a detailed topic to another detailed one, such as talking about the stiffness of a toothpick and then the softness of a marshmallow. Other shifts of focus showed shift of level of interest such as talking about the stickiness of a marshmallow and then the arch shape of the bridge that they wanted. Shifts of focus, rather than providing distractions, allowed students to explore new design possibilities. Through shifts of focus ideas were collected that were based on both prior knowledge and current observations. The shifts were, in effect, adding grist for the idea construction mill.

Students stayed with any one topic only momentarily. They often discussed one form of overall bridge design, such as arches, while at the same time they discussed the merits of making a straight bridge with triangles, as two seventh-graders, Scott and Leon, did in the following continuous excerpt.

			Topic
01:02	Scott	*So, why do you need six of them, if you are just going to arch it?*	Arch
01:05	Leon	*So, we can take these, I guess. Can we start? All right. The triangle is like the strongest link to build something. It's like, it has the most support.*	Triangle
01:10	Scott	*Why don't we build it like a real bridge, like an arch?*	Arch
01:13	Leon	*Like, with triangles, it has to have triangles.*	Triangles
01:16	Scott	*So, let's just build some triangles.*	Triangles

01:21	Leon	*Wait, we have to build them, though. So, build six triangles, and then –*	Planning
01:25	Scott	*And see how we go from there.*	Planning
01:31	Leon	*Yeah, we'll see how long it is.*	Length
01:38	Scott	*Some of the marshmallows are crusty and old.*	Marshmallows

Scott and Leon in the above thirty-six-second conversation shifted their focus from a discussion about triangles vs. arches, to planning issues, and then to a comment about length, and the quality of marshmallows. A real arched bridge often is composed of triangles, but these two boys treated them as mutually exclusive ideas. Once Leon mentions using triangles, even though his choice of words indicates a connection to arches, the idea of using arches is not mentioned by these boys again.

In Scott and Leon's conversation the series of topics served an essential constructive function. By shifting focus from one topic to another:

> the students proposed ideas to test the design features of triangles and arches against each other
>
> they started to set up a plan to build the chosen idea of using triangles
>
> they considered the issue of bridge length
>
> they observed a quality of the marshmallows

There is a natural problem-solving sequence here: compare design ideas, think about a plan, remember task constraints, and examine the materials. If it were possible for Scott and Leon to have stayed with just one focus, they might have worked down a blind alley. Instead, they compared designs and then quickly thought about the possibilities of putting the design into practice that met the criteria of the task.

Scott and Leon were maintaining a complex joint problem space while also making progress along several tightly related strands (Fischer & Granott, 1995). Shift of focus was the exploration among these tightly related strands. In fact, Scott and Leon did not follow one line of thought for more than a few sentences since they were tending to several different strands of microdevelopment. Because these shifts in focus were frequent, teachers and researchers examining this task should not expect smooth progression in conversation skill levels. Also, students could be pursuing each strand at a different level of complexity, further leading to irregular patterns of skill levels. Therefore, their conversation skill levels did not show simple trends because they were shifting from one strand to another, maintaining progress on several fronts. This multi-tasking occurred continuously in all ten student pairs.

Two fifth-graders, Sue and Jim, provided another typical example of the extent that shifts of focus were used, how shifts functioned in maintaining progress along multiple strands, and the potential that shifts of focus have in leading to coordinated understandings:

			Topic
05:11	Jim	*So you want to – like sort of build it up?*	Direction
05:13	Sue	*Yeah, but we should probably make it across first, have a foundation.*	Direction
05:27	Jim	*All right. Just stick it in there.*	Component Connections
05:32	Jim	*All right now, we have to go this way. Do you think that's big enough?*	Direction / Length
05:34	Sue	*It's not long enough. Look, it has to go further to this side.*	Length / Direction/length
05:39	Jim	*All right, All right.*	
05:41	Sue	*I'll make a marker.*	Length
05:52	Sue	*Then we have to build it across.*	Length/direction
05:57	Jim	*It's not long enough, is it? One more, all right, that's good enough. One more?*	Length / Length/number of components
06:04	Sue	*Wait a minute; let's see.*	
06:09	Jim	*That's good enough.*	Component Connections
06:10	Sue	*Wait a minute.*	
06:15	Sue	*Maybe one more, I think.*	Number of components
06:21	Jim	*All right, now we have to go this way. How long does it have to be?*	Direction / Length
06:24	Sue	*How long?*	Length

06:25	Jim	*Yeah*	
06:28	Sue	*Well, we want it to*	
		be able to support a	Support
		lot, so. We have to be	Number of components
		careful about how	
		much we use.	

Sue and Jim shifted their focus fourteen times in just under a minute and twenty seconds. Most of these shifts, nine out of fourteen, were larger forms of shifts. For example, at 05:32 Jim shifted from thinking about the direction the bridge should be built in, to thinking about the adequacy of the bridge's length. This is an example of a shift from overall design to task constraints. These microdevelopmental strands are relatively far apart from each other. Jim was making sure that the two bridge characteristics of direction and length were present within their joint problem space. Shift of focus provided two sources of variation: direction and length, which would need to be coordinated later if the bridge was going to have the right amount of length in the right direction.

The remaining five shifts were smaller ones. For example, at 05:11 Jim commented about the need for the bridge to have height (building in the vertical direction). Immediately following, at 05:13, Sue suggested that they first work in the horizontal direction to get across the gap and provide a foundation for later (perhaps vertical) building. Sue shifted the focus of their mutual attention only slightly. They were still within the category of overall design, but they were collecting attributes within that category that could later be coordinated. Shift of focus allowed this collection by way of an exploration of ideas.

Sue and Jim shifted focus within the task ninety-five times in the thirty-five minutes that they worked together. Most of the other groups produced considerably more shifts with the number ranging from 355 to seventy-two, and an average of 236 shifts across the pairs. Sue and Jim were not a very talkative pair, however, and the percent of shifts produced compared to their total number of comments was the highest of any pair at 94% (table 6.1).

Sue and Jim didn't keep up the pace of shifting demonstrated in the above excerpt; they clearly shifted focus less as they proceeded. This trailing off of the number of shifts as the activity progressed was seen in all the pairs. It seems that at the beginning of the activity shifts of focus were rapid because the task was unfamiliar and its essential attributes needed to be identified and explored. Table 6.2 shows how the rate of shifting foci changed by comparing the first ten minutes of each session with the last ten minutes.

Table 6.1 *Shifts of focus as a percentage of the task-related comments*

Grade	Pair	Shifts	Total	Percentage
5	Sally and Nick	355	450	79
5	Josh and Will	301	344	88
5	Beth and Mary	258	321	80
5	Ann and Pam	260	284	92
5	Sue and Jim	95	101	94
7	Ben and Victor	205	289	71
7	Leon and Scott	256	327	78
7	Alice and Ari	343	418	82
7	Heather and Jean	213	292	73
7	Amy and Hari	72	78	92
	Means	236	290	82

Table 6.2 *Number of shifts of focus in the first ten minutes compared to the last ten minutes*

Grade	Pair	First ten minutes	Last ten minutes
5	Sally and Nick	110	67
5	Josh and Will	95	55
5	Beth and Mary	79	33
5	Ann and Pam	88	54
5	Sue and Jim	53	12
7	Ben and Victor	102	25
7	Leon and Scott	92	51
7	Alice and Ari	137	68
7	Heather and Jean	95	40
7	Amy and Hari	33	14
	Means	88.4	41.9

Simple progress in skill levels was observed for only very short periods of time. Even when a relatively narrow focus was maintained these small shifts had an unexpected effect on levels of conversation complexity, as Alice and Ari demonstrated during a discussion of triangles.

They stuck to this topic relatively tightly and for a significantly long time (23 s) when compared to the conversations of the other student pairs. Even though they did stay with the topic of making triangles, there wasn't a progression in complexity of thought represented in their speech (figure 6.2). Alice and Ari decided quickly to make a three-dimensional

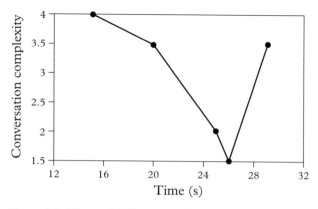

Figure 6.2 Alice and Ari's conversation levels.

large triangle of two large flat triangles at 15 s by joining them in the middle. Once that idea was established they began to think about the smaller details of the triangle's construction. Appropriately, their conversational structures became simpler through to 29 s when Ari clarified the idea of large triangles made of smaller ones.

The overall trend in their twenty-three-second conversation was for a small refocus on the construction technique and details even though the main focus was still triangles. This refocus was necessary to eventually build the idea into a bridge. Such shifts from global to specific were very common in all the working pairs of students. This pattern parallels the concept of integration and differentiation in knowledge construction proposed by many theorists (Fischer, 1980; Piaget, 1952/1974; Werner, 1948). Finally, a global idea expressed about large triangular forms was an integration complemented by the differentiation of specific construction details.

If this study had had a non-microanalytic focus, none of the above patterns of shifts in attention would have been noticed. More significantly, the constructive value of these shifts as evidenced by their patterns of use would not have been recognized.

Bridging

Bridging was another mechanism commonly used by these students to self-scaffold understanding construction. In her study of adults exploring the way small robots worked, Granott (1993) discovered conversational structures being used to help construct new ideas, *bridging*. These temporary structures suggested to participants the potential of a not yet finished new idea. By making the suggestion, usually by asking a question or providing a partially completed idea, people lead others and themselves to completing the new idea (Granott, Fischer, & Parziale, this volume). *Bridging* explains how people assemble simple ideas into more complex ones and how old ideas are adapted for a novel task. (To reduce confusion over terms, Granott's *bridging* will be italicized hereafter in this chapter to distinguish it from the marshmallow bridges of the task at hand.)

In this study, children used *bridging* mechanisms to project their ideas forward while shifts in focus provided the content for these "empty" thinking structures. By alternating these mechanisms children built the skeleton of a new idea with the *bridging* mechanism and then fleshed it out with particulars from shifts of focus. Watching the process closely and continuously provided evidence that children constructing understandings do not necessarily shift discontinuously from simple yet complete thinking structures to other complete but more complex thinking structures. Five forms of *bridging* were frequently used by these students: intention, term, format, question, and recast.

Bridging *intention* When using *bridging* intention people project a need or a possible idea to try. The students talked mostly of intentions:

| 10:34 | Amy | *Let's put two marshmallows together at each corner.* |
| 10:36 | Tom | *Let's put two toothpicks on each marshmallow.* |

In Granott's study, perhaps because the adults were reverse engineering already complete and functioning robots, participants were observing, experimenting, interpreting experimental results, hypothesizing, and theorizing in a much more balanced way than the students did in this study. The children here were building up their marshmallow bridges and each addition was based on an intention to try something new. It was not useful to the overall analysis to code each of these events.

Bridging *term* *Bridging* term was used with more discretion by the children in this study. It is the use of a word to represent a more complex understanding than was formerly used. Participants using this mechanism were struggling with the process of combining ideas and finding direction and were relying on a concept from another time or place for help. In other words, they were generalizing knowledge across domains. These children weren't always sure that the generalized concept could be applied to this task; they often just tried out some prior knowledge.

A pair of fifth-grade girls, Mary and Beth, provided clear and repeated use of the *bridging* term "sturdy" or "sturdier" as they built their bridge. Mary used the *bridging* term before their construction was any more than a one-toothpick-and-one-marshmallow unit:

> 02:06   Mary   *... it has to [be] sturdy.*

The bridge hadn't been built or tested across the table gap yet. But by using the term "sturdy" she was trying to anticipate a better understanding that would be required for success. The term was used to express this central concern throughout their work by both students. Mary, who used it first, only used it twice more, while Beth used it an amazing seventeen times in eighteen minutes.

The use of the term "sturdy" was associated many times by Beth and Mary with the testing of structural hypotheses: the use of stiffening "criss cross(es)"; and building in the vertical plane, " *... we'll make it higher, like sturdier.*" Sturdier was representing, in these examples, an empty idea structure based on a need,

$$\left[(???) \xrightarrow{\text{Sturdy}} (???) \right]$$

that later became filled in:

$$\left[(\text{ADDING})_{\text{CRISS-CROSS(ES)}} \xrightarrow{\text{Sturdy}} (\text{MAKES})_{\text{UNITS STABLE}} \right]$$

and

$$\left[(\text{BUILDING VERTICALLY})_{\text{MAKE IT HIGHER}} \xrightarrow{\text{Sturdy}} (\text{DISTRIBUTES})_{\text{(FORCE)}} \right]$$

Both of these situations demonstrate how a *bridging* term can be used to coordinate thinking structures to form a more complex one.

Bridging *format* Bridging format occurs when a person attempts to express a new understanding, but can only partially do so. At first glance the phenomenon might seem trivial. Yet, it is an obvious and prevalent mechanism in daily use by everyone in and out of schools: people start to say something, but can't quite finish the statement. These partial statements are self-constructed shells or frameworks within which simple understandings can be coordinated to form more complex ones.

Struggling to make their bridge stiffer, the two fifth-graders Ann and Pam experimented with the use of "crosses" placed across square structural units in three separate instances:

> 06:42   Pam   *We can do crosses here so it will stay.*
> 06:51   Ann   *We need crosses here so when you put on the top ...*

$$\left[\text{DO}_{\text{CROSSES}} \xrightarrow{\quad\quad} \text{IT}_{\text{WILL STAY}} \right]$$

$$\left[\text{WE}_{\text{NEED CROSSES HERE SO ....}} \xrightarrow{\quad\quad} (???) \right]$$

Pam expressed the reason for the use of the crosses, while Ann doesn't quite do so, although the sentence she started is in the format of an understanding. Ann attempted the transition to the next skill level as indicated by this *bridging* format.

Later, perhaps because of Ann's apparent lack of understanding, Pam justified the reason for the crosses differently, but this time incompletely:

> 07:49   Pam   *So it will be a little fashionable* (as she places more crosses).

$$\left[\text{(???)} \quad \text{———} \quad \textbf{SO IT}_{(\text{WILL BE A LITTLE FASHIONABLE})} \right]$$

Later, Ann still didn't quite state what their function was in an exchange with Pam, but again used a *bridging* format to attempt a transition:

> 08:59   Pam   *One more. I think two more. Two more stairs* (crosses).
>
> 09:02   Ann   *A couple more so that they ...*

Given the close nature of their joint work, Ann was perhaps signaling to Pam that she needed help to understand the use of the crosses.

Although the pair continued to add crosses to the structure, they failed to take full advantage of them in the bridge design until the very end. If they had had a complete understanding of the relationship between the crosses and the stiffness of their bridge, they could have expressed this to one another and built accordingly. Instead, the bridge didn't exhibit stiff building units oriented vertically against the force of gravity for eleven more minutes:

> 20:21   Pam   *Maybe if we hold it up like this and you put toothpicks up here and we put a line here. Maybe it will hold up.*
>
> 20:31   Ann   *I don't know 'cause it's adding weight to it.*
>
> 20:34   Pam   *No it isn't 'cause it will hold it up.*

At 21:00 Pam showed Ann how building vertically with crossed units provided stability and they both constructed this feature on the bridge.

Three critical points should be stressed about Pam and Ann's use of *bridging* format:

> Ann seemed to be using the format to get help
> Ann might also have been self-scaffolding (listening to herself partially construct the understanding)
> Pam made complementary format structures in response to Ann

Bridging *question* Perhaps the easiest *bridging* process to understand and find examples of is the *bridging* question. Questions abound
when people, especially children, are making rapid advances in understanding, as anyone with a four-year-old knows. The use of *bridging* questions during the collaboration for the bridge building seemed especially
important in directing partner's attention to a potential new understanding and in focusing partner's attention to the task.

Two seventh-grade girls, Amy and Hari, provide examples of both functions of using questions:

10:14	Amy	*Do you see what I am doing?*
12:36	Hari	*How did you make that triangle?*

The video shows Amy working alone on the bridge while Hari talks to a
neighboring pair of students. Amy at 10:14 tries to direct Hari's attention,
to get Hari to help, or to at least agree that what Amy is doing is right.
Hari's only reaction is to look at Amy at 10:14 and then to the bridge
and then to return to her conversation with the others. Amy's question
only got Hari's attention briefly, but this moment was enough to get her
further engaged spontaneously at 12:36.

At 12:36 Hari asked a question about the way that Amy was making
the bridge, showing her intention to get involved. She then proceeded to
put some marshmallows and toothpicks together, but seemed unsure of
duplicating Amy's work.

14:10	Hari	*How do you do this now?*
16:25	Hari	*Now how do you do this?*

At 14:10 Hari asks for guidance in building her section. She then does
well making the triangles, but at 16:25 asks for help in assembling the
triangles to form a larger section.

Amy's question led to Hari slowly becoming involved over a six-minute
period to the point where Hari was building a side section of the bridge
to match Amy's.

Bridging *recast* A *bridging* recast is when a idea is reformulated
from a past idea that has the same meaning and content. The recasted
idea is usually more specific to the task and often demonstrates a more
complex understanding.

Two seventh-grade boys in the following example had built a large
structure which sagged badly when they tried to put it between the tables.
At 13:25, at the questioning of his partner, Scott proposes a solution to

an observed problem. A recast at 13:30 reformulated his solution more specifically.

13:20	Scott	*Ooh, that's not going to work.*
13:23	Leon	*Why not?*
13:25	Scott	*Because, see, we'll have to flip the bridge over.*
13:28	Leon	*Why?*
13:30	Scott	*Because, see, what's going wrong is it's bending down that way. And see, that will allow it to bend down that way. So, what we need to do is flip the bridge over like that, so it won't bend down as easy.*
13:38	Leon	*All right, try it.*

Scott's idea is to take the sagged bridge and flip it upside-down, making an upward arching bridge that will resist sagging. His recast explains the effect that these actions will have on the bridge. The students in this study used recasts to advance the level of shared understanding by providing clearly coordinated ideas to build from.

Bridging *summary* The five types of *bridging* mechanisms were commonly alternated in use. For example, in the example above from Leon and Scott, Leon's first two statements are *bridging* questions. These questions led Scott to suggest a solution and then to specify the understanding that allowed the solution to be useful. Leon's last comment is a *bridging* intention, indicating that together they should try Scott's idea out.

Besides separate occurrences of *bridging* types, these transition mechanisms often occurred simultaneously. Exchanges can frequently fit the definition of two different types of *bridging*:

01:35	Will	*So you want to make it hexagonal basically?*

This statement could be coded as both a *bridging* term and a *bridging* question. Will was using the term *hexagonal* to imply a higher level idea. Both Will and his partner Josh used the term in the next few minutes of the activity, but had difficulty making the structure. They then tried to draw it, but they had trouble drawing a figure with six sides. At 01:35 neither Will nor Josh understood how to make a hexagon, but using the *bridging* term and working from an idea shell they later succeeded.

This statement (01:35) was also a *bridging* question. Will is asking if building a hexagon was what Josh was talking about. The question functioned as a means of clarifying a target, the building of a hexagon. Further, Will's comment was a *bridging* intention, since Will was stating what they should do next.

Table 6.3 *Maximum levels reached by student group*

Grade	Pair	Conversation	Marshmallow bridge
5	Sally and Nick	4	4.5
5	Josh and Will	3.5	5
5	Beth and Mary	4	5
5	Ann and Pam	3.5	4
5	Sue and Jim	3.5	5
7	Ben and Victor	3.5	5
7	Leon and Scott	4	5
7	Alice and Ari	4	5
7	Heather and Jean	4	5
7	Amy and Hari	3	5
	Means	3.7	4.85

The students in this study provided overwhelming evidence of *bridging* as a self-scaffolding mechanism but without their actually being watched continuously this evidence would have been overlooked.

Distributed cognition

Perhaps the most intriguing and unusual mechanism used by the students in their bridge building was distributed cognition. Apparently without conscious awareness of doing so, students caused the coordination of ideas not only in their own minds but also in the marshmallow bridges that they were building. Students actively used this spontaneous system to efficiently make decisions by allowing the physical interworking system of marshmallows and toothpicks to demonstrate how adaptive to the task a new idea was. The use of this strategy (what people commonly mean by solving a problem by "trial and error") relieved students of the need to understand why their designs worked and yet insured that new design features matched the task constraints. In fact, finished bridges coded on their own merits consistently demonstrated more complex ideas than were achieved at any point in student conversations (table 6.3). On the average the bridges demonstrated greater than a full level more in complexity than the maximum levels of conversations. This is not to say that the bridges are smarter than the young engineers who built them. Students used the bridges to coordinate ideas and these functional ideas accumulated in the bridges. These ideas did not have to be coordinated or accumulated in the builders' minds.

This finding has some profound implications wherever inference is made about the intelligence behind the making of a product. In education

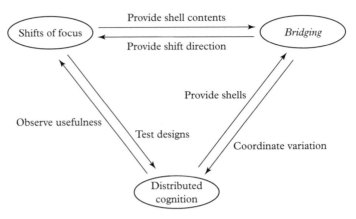

Figure 6.3 A task-solving system.

this finding suggests that if a student-completed project demonstrates a clever idea, it is a rash assumption to believe the creator of the project also had the clever idea. It could be that within the project the idea actually functioned so the idea was accepted without the need for conscious consideration by the student. These findings also suggest that in other fields of human study, in archeology for example, it might be folly to infer that special skills or intelligences resided in the minds of builders just on the evidence provided by their artifacts.

An integrated model: The task-solving system

The three constructive mechanisms (shift of focus, *bridging*, and distributed cognition) employed by the students did not act independently. Instead they spontaneously integrated into a system directed towards task success (figure 6.3). Each of the three mechanisms stimulated the function of the others by providing direction for idea searching (shift of focus), confirmation of ideas (distributed cognition), or idea structure (*bridging*).

Shifts of focus through real-time observations and retrieval of prior knowledge provided content for shells of ideas generated by *bridging* while *bridging* in turn provided direction for shifts of focus so that suitable task related ideas could be found. *Bridging* also provided incomplete ideas to test on the bridge, while the student who was observing the stability of the bridge received feedback from this observation and coordinated this feedback with the incomplete ideas to stimulate further *bridging*. Distributed cognition also tested ideas provided by shifts of focus and in return directed further shifts of focus.

One pathway in the model describes the link between shift of focus and *bridging* mechanisms. The function of *bridging* was to provide partially filled or empty ideas shells. As students shifted focus they identified attributes and variables and made observations that became the contents of empty or partially filled idea structures. In return the empty or partially empty bridging shells provided a target to direct shift of focus.

The function of this pathway can be further explained in terms of student activity. For example, a student commented that "*triangles are good*," thereby providing an empty shell for "triangle." They and their partner shifted focus to search for a variation of marshmallows connected to toothpicks that fit this empty shell. In return their partner, during their search, reported that "*toothpicks can go in at angles*," forming part of the necessary contents of the triangle idea.

A second pathway in the task-solving model connects *bridging* to distributed cognition. In one direction, *bridging* again provided empty or partially filled shells. This time the shell was not a coordinated activity of the students; rather, the interactions of design elements were tested on the students' bridges. In return the physical structure coordinated the interworking of the design features. For example, a student offered "*We need more support*" as an empty shell for a idea structure. In response some criss-crosses were added and the bridge was observed to be better supported. The design features interacted to demonstrate improved support. Therefore, the design feature was tested by observing the response of the physical system. In this way, variation coordinated through distributed cognition completed the empty shells.

The final pathway describes the connection between shifts of focus and distributed cognition. Again, shifts of focus are viewed here as the mechanism directing the students' attention. Shift of focus was involved when a coordination representing a design idea was not pursued fully, but instead was tested in the physical structure. In return, the success of the design in the physical structure was observed without the participants working out the understanding for themselves.

Shift of focus was also involved in guiding the observation of the testing of designs. When students placed a bridge built like a horizontal ladder across the table gap and watched to see if it was stable, they were actively using this pathway. Students looked to see if the design met the goals of the task.

The children, the task constraints, and the growing marshmallow bridge interacted to form this unique system. In other situations and with other people and products it can be expected that other systems may be similarly formed, perhaps from a mix of these or other mechanisms. These systems will be discovered only if researchers use microanalytic methods to continually observe changes in thinking as people interact with each other and their physical environments.

Educational implications

William James, who voiced concern about the practical uses of psychological theory in education, might have asked, do the findings of this study make any practical difference in the classroom (James, 1907, 1958)? In three areas they can make a difference: assessment methodology, mechanisms of learning, and systems of solving tasks.

Assessment methodology

The first and most important implication is that a dynamic analysis can be made of students constructing understanding in schools. Researchers and teachers using microanalytic methods can observe moment-to-moment change during an everyday classroom lesson. A teacher using microanalytic methods similar to those used here can also evaluate lessons to see if the thinking changes they seek to make are actually being made. This bridge-building activity had been used by many teachers for many years in the district where this study took place. These teachers widely assumed that their students were gaining a fairly comprehensive notion of what it takes to make a strong bridge. It is now clear that students are indeed learning during the activity, but they are mainly learning how to use the properties of the materials to be successful in the task, rather than an understanding of the way bridges function.

If educational systems began to use microanalytic methods in balance with posttests then perhaps more value would be given to the process of learning over the rote memorization of content.

Mechanisms of learning

The three mechanisms discovered and rediscovered in this study inform educational practice in several ways:

incomplete expression of ideas by students are positive signs that processes of change are being engaged in

students use manipulatives to shape their thinking in ways that might not be obvious

regression is not a negative sign, but instead can signal ideas being adapted to the novelty of a task

ideas have essential components that are content specific, meaning that generalization requires a reconstruction of ideas students changing their focus while solving a problem might be actively searching for sources of answers rather than venturing off task.

This list of ideas might change teachers' expectations about learning in their classrooms since at least some of them run counter to many teacher-held prior conceptions about learning. These ideas can also change students' perspectives on their own work and abilities, if they too are informed about these findings.

Systems of solving tasks

Educators and researchers are not as aware as they should be about spontaneous systems of construction that emerge during lessons in a classroom. These dynamic systems have been overlooked because, like the mechanisms of language use, they are practically invisible to learners, teachers, and researchers. Teachers need to know that during a lesson a repertoire of little known abilities and strategies spontaneously emerge.

References

Fischer, K. W. (1980). A theory of cognitive development: The control and construction of hierarchies of skills. *Psychological Review, 87,* 477–531.

Fischer, K. W., & Granott, N. (1995). Beyond one-dimensional change: Parallel concurrent distributed processes in learning and development. *Human Development, 38,* 302–314.

Granott, N. (1993). Microdevelopment of co-construction of knowledge during problem-solving: Puzzled minds, weird creatures, and wuggles. Doctoral dissertation, Massachusetts Institute of Technology, Cambridge, MA [on line]. Available: *http://theses.mit.edu:80/Dienst/UI/2.0/Composite/ 0018.mit.theses/1993-170/I?nsections=19*

Granott, N., Fischer, K. W., & Parziale, J. (this volume). Bridging to the unknown: A transition mechanism in learning and development.

James, W. (1907). *Pragmatism and four essays from the meaning of truth.* New York: World Publishing.

James, W. (1958). *Talks to teachers.* New York: Norman.

Parziale, J. (1995). Microdevelopment during an activity based science lesson: A pilot study. Unpublished qualifying paper. Harvard University, Cambridge, MA.

Parziale, J., & Fischer, K. W. (1998). The practical use of skill theory in the classroom. In R. J. Sternberg & W. M. Williams (Eds.), *Intelligence, instruction and assessment* (pp. 95–110). Hillsdale, NJ: Erlbaum.

Perkins, D. N. (1991). Schools of thought: The necessary shape of education. Unpublished manuscript, Project Zero, Harvard University, Cambridge, MA.

Piaget, J. (1952/1974). *The origins of intelligence in children* (M. Cook, trans.). Madison, CT: International Universities Press.

Teasley, S. D., & Roschelle, J. (1993). Constructing a joint problem space: The computer as a tool for sharing knowledge. In S. P. Lajoie & S. J. Derry (Eds.), *Computers as cognitive tools* (pp. 229–257). Hillsdale, NJ: Erlbaum.

Werner, H. (1948). *Comparative psychology of mental structures*. New York: International Press.

Part III

Micro- and macrodevelopment

7   Interacting time scales in personality (and cognitive) development: Intentions, emotions, and emergent forms

Marc D. Lewis

The relations between time scales of development, particularly microdevelopment and macrodevelopment, remain largely unexplored, both theoretically and empirically. How do processes in real time affect the laying down of shape and structure over developmental time? How do momentary events create novel forms or patterns that last for years or even a lifetime? The opposite causal direction is just as mysterious. How do longstanding patterns, only visible on a developmental scale, influence activity in real time, and very often in a way that serves to further entrench those patterns? Like the activity of a sculptor, small movements create lasting form that directs subsequent movements, as the sculptor comes to recognize the shape to which the medium gives rise. Yet there is no sculptor. Development may better resemble M. C. Escher's famous lithograph of two hands drawing each other: the form creates itself.

One of the most serious conundrums for cognitive developmentalists has been the integration of time scales of learning and development. When learning and development are simply viewed as different amounts of the same thing, theorists fail to look for the transformations through which they are related (Lerner, 1995). Conversely, when they are considered incommensurable, theorists tend to dismiss one and concentrate on the other rather than recognize their intrinsic complementarity (Granott, 1998). When learning and development are viewed as distinct yet complementary, their relationship is often assumed to be unidimensional and context-free, a perspective that obscures the multiple, nonlinear pathways that connect them (Fischer & Granott, 1995).

Interscale relations are just as troublesome in emotional and personality development, though they have not been the topic of as much discussion. Nobody knows why critical life events sometimes leave lasting traces, as when experiences of loss leave a personality scarred by anxiety, rage, or depression, and other times have no apparent impact (Magai &

The author thanks the Natural Sciences and Engineering Research Council of Canada for support during the writing of this chapter.

183

McFadden, 1995). Nor why attachment status, once consolidated in early childhood, can predict adult outcomes given environmental continuity yet fail do to so when environments change (Lamb, 1987; Thompson, 1998). These issues hint at the complexity of the mechanisms relating micro- and macrodevelopment, but they do not suggest directions for answering them.

To help solve such puzzles as these, it may be important to examine development using a framework that already includes principles for interscale relations. The dynamic systems (DS) framework, which views development as a process of self-organization, fits this category. This chapter presents a DS analysis of a particular interscale problem – the relation between emotions (lasting seconds), moods (lasting hours), and personality development (lasting years) – in order to illustrate mechanisms by which time scales of human development influence one another. In the first half of the chapter, I look at self-organizing systems in nature, dynamic systems approaches to human development, and principles for interscale relations in human and nonhuman systems. Then, before examining interscale relations in personality development, I point out parallels between personality and cognitive development defined by common mechanisms of intention, emotion, and action. I suggest that the tension between goals and actions is a fundamental organizer of interscale relations in both domains. In the second half of the chapter, I go on to sketch a new theory of personality development based on relations across three time scales. At each of these scales, I describe cognitive-emotional entrainment in the brain and then propose psychological processes that fit this description.

Interscale relations in self-organizing systems

Models of self-organization focus on the emergence of order from disorder, and in particular the emergence of complex, higher-order forms from simpler, lower-order components. Examples are the emergence of living microbes through the interaction of complex molecules, the emergence of stable ecosystems from interactions among its species, the emergence of social behavior out of the interactions of individual animals, and even the emergence of embryonic structure through the interaction of proliferating cells (Goodwin, 1993). These processes exemplify the convergence or crystallization of global organization from recurring interactions among simpler components, providing structure and pattern throughout nature.

The components of self-organizing systems are different for different kinds of systems. In physical systems, atoms and molecules interact to produce coherent forms such as lasers or stars. In biological systems, cells, metabolic components, and genes interact to produce the complex structures and behaviors that maintain life. In social systems, whether human or animal, individuals interact to produce group effects. In brains, neurons interact to produce electrochemical constellations underlying perception and cognition. What is common to all these kinds of systems is that energy (and information, or patterned energy) flows through the system from outside. Self-organizing systems are thus open systems. Moreover, energy flows as efficiently as possible through the elements of the system, across their connections with each other, and it is this flow that binds these elements into higher-order patterns (Prigogine & Stengers, 1984). Finally, in biological, social, and neural systems, these patterns serve a *function* that keeps energy and information flowing over time. Nourishment, sex, and tennis are familiar examples.

Dynamic systems (DS) terminology is a useful way to conceptualize and model self-organization, and this has been true in psychology as much as in the other sciences (Abraham, 1995; Vallacher & Nowak, 1997). In developmental psychology, DS approaches have flourished in the last few years, partly because developing systems are paradigmatic examples of emergent form, thus lending themselves easily to self-organization modeling (Keating & Miller, 2000; Lewis, 2000b). Dynamic systems theory is a mathematical tool for predicting the future states of systems that change continuously, and a number of developmental approaches utilize mathematical modeling (Newell & Molenaar, 1998; van Geert, 1991; van der Maas & Molenaar, 1992). Other approaches, however, incorporate DS ideas without the equations, relying instead on statistical methods of analysis (Fogel, Messinger, Dickson, & Hsu, 1999; Lewis, Lamey, & Douglas, 1999; Thelen & Ulrich, 1991; van der Maas, 1998). A thorough treatment of DS approaches is available elsewhere (Kelso, 1995; Thelen & Smith, 1994; van Geert, 1994; also see Thelen & Corbetta, this volume; van Geert, this volume) but a few key ideas are particularly important for the present discussion.

DS approaches depict higher-order forms as attractors on a state space, and they depict the character of the system as its collective tendencies to move toward these attractors (and away from other states). Attractors are states (or trajectories) to which the system evolves, rapidly, in real time, from other states that it may assume, and where it tends to remain for a while despite perturbations. In complex systems, this real-time evolution can be viewed as a process of self-organization at a very short time scale. The system is not instructed or directed to move to its attractor; rather, its movement is self-perpetuating and its journey is probabilistic (indeterminate), such that novelty and context always play a role in its moment-to-moment behavior (Thelen & Ulrich, 1991). The growth and development of the system itself can be depicted as self-organization at a longer time scale, spanning months and years. For Thelen and Smith (1994), this process is characterized as the creation or consolidation of attractors (or, the evolution of the state space describing the whole system). It is exemplified in motor development by learning to walk and reach and in cognitive development by the acquisition of perceptual and conceptual categories such as "hot" and "cold." Walking, reaching, "cold," and "hot" are new attractors that consolidate over developmental time and affect behavior in real time.

Thus, models of self-organization, and their instantiation in dynamic systems concepts, are intrinsically concerned with processes of change – literally, development – at different time scales, and especially with the relations between these time scales (van Gelder & Port, 1995). Real-time processes are generally equated with *microdevelopment* and developmental processes with *macrodevelopment* (Granott, 1998; Lewis, 1995; Thelen & Ulrich; 1991; van Geert, 1995). Indeed, change is synonymous with development in self-organizing systems, and this is true at all time scales from seconds and minutes (so-called real time) to eons spanning biological evolution. We now take a closer look at how self-organizing processes at the scale of microdevelopment (movement to a new or old attractor in real time) influence self-organizing processes at the scale of macrodevelopment (change and consolidation of the system's tendencies, its state space) – not only in psychological systems but in natural systems in general.

There are two directions of influence between scales of self-organization. First, small-scale (or short-term) emergent processes influence large-scale (or long-term) emergent processes. The key phenomenon at any scale is the emergence of novel, higher-order forms from recursive interactions among lower-order elements. These recursive interactions give rise to positive feedback loops. Positive feedback amplifies a subset of coordinations into a macroscopic pattern, replacing the previous organizational regime (Prigogine & Stengers, 1984). On a short time scale, these patterns are temporary arrangements of coupled elements, and they persist because they move energy through the system efficiently. They may last for only a few seconds or minutes, demonstrating emergence and persistence in real time. But how do such patterns recur across occasions, thus emerging and persisting at longer time scales such as development? A dominance ritual among monkeys in the zoo may emerge and persist for a few minutes because it couples individuals into a self-reinforcing pattern: a small number of angry monkeys scream at their cowering neighbors who frantically run about the cage, further irritating the dominant ones.

But how does a dominance hierarchy emerge and recur across many occasions, thereby giving the troop its unique family dynamics?

A universal consequence of self-organizing processes is their tendency to leave some trace behind them. Coupling in real time changes the elements and the connections among them. These changes facilitate similar couplings on subsequent occasions, so that active habits grow in strength and replace competing organizations (Thelen & Smith, 1994). Wherever water pools in the garden during a rain storm it is more likely to pool in future, fashioning a permanent puddle over time. Connection strengths in a neural network change and consolidate over a series of learning trials, giving rise to ensembles of units that behave as collectives (Rumelhart, Hinton, & McClelland, 1986). In the brain itself, neurons and neuronal assemblies coactivated within occasions become connected to form enduring maps over time (Edelman, 1987). These examples demonstrate how the temporary coupling of elements in a self-organizing system alters the elements, their connections with each other, and their relations with other levels of organization, such that similar patterns of coupling are facilitated in future.

This principle of recurrence and strengthening is absolutely ubiquitous in developing networks such as societies or brains. We may therefore represent it as an axiom: patterns of coupling initiate and reinforce certain *complementarities*, and those complementarities increasingly constrain subsequent coupling. To see how lasting complementarities grow out of episodes of coupling, picture a collection of individuals who sign up for a weekend workshop, perhaps directed toward personal growth or expressing the inner child. When the first exercise takes place, people form groups (that is, they "couple") for intimate discussions or dramatizations. The formation of groups is somewhat random on the first trial, because people are still strangers. During each exercise, however, people get to know each other and develop definite likes and dislikes; these serve to bring some people together and keep others apart the next time groups are formed. These likes and dislikes constitute a network of *complementarities*, both positive and negative, which constrains the way groups assemble over time. With each successive group exercise, coupling is less random and more constrained, guided by complementarities, while each episode of coupling reinforces those evolving complementarities.

The converse direction of influence is from larger (or longer) scales to smaller (or shorter) scales embedded within them. As seen in the last example, the emergence of large-scale patterns – complementarities – sets the parameters of self-organization at smaller scales, by shaping the structure and function of the parts, and the contingencies and connections between them (e.g., the exchange of smiles, gazes, and postural signals for our weekend interactants). This theme is also ubiquitous in the natural world, and biological evolution is a case in point. According to self-organization theorists, patterns of function and behavior emerge out of the interactions of species' traits and the genes that code for them (epistasis). For any generation, there is a variety of workable trait combinations, but the repertoire that provides these possibilities has already been selected by the species' evolution (Goodwin, 1993; Kauffman, 1995). Thus, species development at the scale of evolution provides the complementarities out of which behavior patterns self-organize in each animal's lifetime, including feeding patterns, mating patterns, and so forth. At an even larger scale, ecosystems – vast networks of complementarities – evolve over thousands or millions of years, but their influence is felt with each wave of reproduction and competition by all their resident species.

Getting back to human development, physiological, neural, behavioral, and communicative complementarities consolidate over years, and they increasingly constrain the kinds of self-organizing processes that transpire within seconds and minutes – from smiles to headaches. Momentary processes have only a limited range of possibilities owing to the structure and connections of the elements from which they arise. For the monkeys in the zoo, the dominance hierarchy that has evolved over months and years constrains the kind of social exchanges that can self-organize in a few seconds: who approaches, avoids, or hangs out with whom. For the brain, the patterning of synaptic connections that has converged over a lifetime constrains the perceptions, concepts, and expectancies that can emerge in any single situation. In general, when complementarities form among elements in a network, real-time patterns of activation are constrained by those complementarities, flowing along the lines of least resistance. These patterns of flow *are* the system's attractors, or dynamic equilibria. This characterization brings home the essence of a state space, the map of a system's tendencies or potentials. Such a map only makes sense if real-time behavior is governed by constraints that persist over a longer time scale.

Most important, these two directions of interscale causation form a macroscopic feedback loop in developing systems, as pointed out by developmental systems theorists for years (e.g., Gottlieb, 1991; Keating, 1990b; Sameroff, 1983). Real-time self-organization fashions complementarities over longer time scales, and these complementarities constrain subsequent real-time processes. According to Keating (1990b), cognitive/perceptual organizations that arise over development mediate the direction of information seeking and the interpretation of information in real time. Simultaneously, this real-time sense-making contributes to evolving developmental organizations. I have characterized this tightening spiral in terms of *cascading constraints* on developmental outcomes (Lewis, 1997). Activities become habits, as represented by attractors, while habits constrain activities that further reinforce those habits. Thus, the indeterminacy in a developmental path is progressively used up by successive occasions for thought and action (though developmental reorganizations certainly interrupt this sequence). These ideas of developmental feedback and cascading constraints necessarily span micro and macro scales, but they also refer to a common-sense vision of individual development: children fashion the styles which constrain their activities, leading to further refinements of those styles.

A paradigmatic example of macro-micro feedback and cascading constraints, and one to which we will return later in this chapter, is the developing brain. Brains have an enormous range of possibilities in early infancy: they include all the possibilities of all available futures. But brains fall into organized states with every act of perception and goal-pursuit. During these states, active synapses are strengthened or reinforced relative to nonactive synapses. When these states reemerge across situations, they progressively fashion a synaptic network that constrains subsequent actions, perceptions, and goals (Tucker, 1992). Moreover, the brain has been designed by evolution to capitalize on these interacting time scales and their mutual crystallization: neurons that do not become coupled in active assemblies literally die in the first two to six years of life, and unused synapses vanish over the lifespan (Greenough & Schwark, 1984; Schore, 1994; Tucker, 1992). In both cases, more active neighbors are left to call the shots. Thus, self-organizing brains are sculpted by increasingly specific individual learning experiences, they increasingly constrain the possibilities for learning, and the outcomes of this interscale loop become engraved in the neural flesh itself.

Having set out basic principles and mechanisms for interscale relations, this chapter is concerned, next, with modeling three interacting scales of self-organizing processes in personality development. Yet, for many readers of this volume, cognitive development is of primary interest, and principles of cognitive development may very well be necessary for explicating personality formation with precision. Could interscale relations in personality development be similar to those in cognitive development? In the following section I argue that the tensions between goals and obstacles, and the emotions and strategies that arise from those tensions, constitute a mechanism of emergence that may span domains of development as well as time scales within those domains.

Emotions, goals, strategies, and styles in cognitive and personality development

An obvious disparity between cognitive and personality development is that cognitive development is concerned with ongoing change and advancement whereas personality development is concerned with emerging continuity or sameness. Learning is often considered the microdevelopmental counterpart of cognitive development (Fischer & Granott, 1995) and emotion-related appraisals the microdevelopmental counterpart of personality development (Magai & McFadden, 1995). (An appraisal is defined as the rapid evaluation of a situation in terms of its relevance for oneself and one's goals, and it is generally considered necessary for producing an emotional response.) But how are personality and cognitive development similar? For both, characteristic structures, strategies, styles, approaches, and beliefs emerge in development and coalesce in individual repertoires. Thus, emergence is followed by accretion, consolidation, and continuity. For both, there are major transition points in the lifespan at which these acquisitions are reconfigured – stages of cognitive development and major maturational and life events for personality development. And for both, emotion may not only be the driver but also the organizer of interpretations that are used to make sense of the world.

Emotion is usually considered central to personality development and peripheral to cognitive development. However, emotion may serve the same function for both. Piaget and Vygotsky assumed that emotions are indispensable to cognitive development. More recently, Pascual-Leone has identified emotions and emotional biases as key factors that interact with attentional operators in fashioning new cognitive structures (e.g., Pascual-Leone & Goodman, 1979). Other neo-Piagetians have also integrated emotion into their theories of cognitive development, enabling them to analyze normative changes and individual differences in interpersonal and personality development (Case, 1988; Case, Hayward, Lewis, & Hurst, 1988; Fischer & Ayoub, 1996; Fischer, Shaver, & Carnochan, 1990). Research suggests that emotions constrain the contents of learning and cognitive development (Dore, 1989; Dunn, 1988) and that emotional differences predict differences in cognitive competencies (Estrada, Arsenio, Hess, & Holloway, 1987; Lewis, 1993a). In fact, rational thought and sustained attention appear to be impossible without emotional constraints (Damasio, 1994; Derryberry & Tucker, 1994). Whereas emotions such as interest and excitement are usually associated with learning and cognitive development (Renninger, Hidi, & Krapp, 1992), many other emotions may also serve to crystallize strategies, styles, approaches, and beliefs, and these emotions may be instrumental in fashioning individual differences in cognitive development. This topic has begun to be explored by cognitive developmentalists (Case et al., 1988; Fischer & Ayoub, 1996; Keating, 1990a; Lewis, 1993b) as well as personality theorists interested in learning styles (Cantor & Harlow, 1994; Dweck & Leggett, 1988), but these efforts are still quite preliminary.

The effect of emotion on cognition, in real time and development, is generally thought to be mediated by emotion regulation styles or strategies (e.g., Labouvie-Vief, Hakim-Larsen, DeVoe, & Schoeberlein, 1989; Keating, 1990a; Lewis, 1993a). From very early infancy, the way in which we regulate negative emotions, and even positive emotions, is also the way we tune our attention, seek information, perceive, think, and respond (Kopp, 1989; Rothbart, Ziaie, & O'Boyle, 1992; Thompson, 1991). For example, avoidant regulation attenuates attention to important aspects of situations, while an approach-and-overcome style increases it. However, emotion regulation is an abstract and slippery concept (Thompson, 1994). To get closer to the heart of the matter, it is useful to think of the relations between emotion, cognition, and development in terms of children's goals and the efforts they expend to achieve them. I suggest that the lag between the emergence of a goal and its resolution is always emotional, and the processes that take place during this lag – whether we call them "regulation" or something else – are the fundaments of cognitive *and* personality development.

Following Claparède, Piaget saw cognitive development as the result of effort – effort to equilibrate resolutions to contradictions, to overcome failures of assimilation, and to compensate for a lack of adaptation in general. According to Pascual-Leone (1987), cognitive development relies on the boosting of cognitive schemes in the process of overcoming obstacles; thus, for him, performance on misleading (difficult or nonobvious) situations is much more relevant to development than performance on facilitating tasks. This kind of effort is inevitably carried out in the service of action (or praxis), and it naturally presupposes an intention or goal. Moreover, efforts to pursue goals repeatedly over time give rise to strategies – ways of arranging skills in order to best assure success. Strategies are the basic units of cognitive development according to many contemporary theorists, and strategy changes are far more important than the learning of content per se (Siegler & Jenkins, 1989). Yet, strategies, executed effortfully in pursuit of goals may be just as central to personality development. Personality styles and characteristic behaviors have been viewed as the result of individual strategies for solving recurrent life problems (e.g., Cantor, Norem, Niedenthal, Langston, & Brower, 1987; Higgins, 1991). These strategies obviously become habitual and enduring, often long past the point when they have ceased being very productive. Interestingly, the staying power of old, even inferior, strategies is commonly observed in cognitive development as well (Siegler, 1997).

It seems, then, that goal-directed efforts and strategies are central to both personality and cognitive development. The next point to emphasize is that goals, efforts, and strategies depend on emotion. Emotion is what propels us to pursue goals in the first place, to select among competing goals, and to modify goals which have proven difficult to achieve (Oatley & Johnson-Laird, 1987). In fact, emotion has been singled out by personality theorists as the essential goad to strategy acquisition (Epstein, 1993; Higgins, 1987). Higgins (1991), like Piaget, views the resolution of inconsistencies as the force that drives development – in this case personality development – and emotional discomfort as its causal mechanism. I suggest that, during goal pursuit, while strategies are being formulated and applied to solving problems, emotions endure for some period of time and resonate with cognitive processes. For both cognitive and personality development, it is these enduring emotions that most influence the content and form of cognitive operations in real time and the acquisition of structures and strategies over development. In Piaget's (1974/1976) words, cognizance, or the elaboration of concepts, begins with the pursuit of a goal and becomes increasingly focused and intensive (as opposed to peripheral) when there is a "failure to achieve the goal" (p. 335). This failure must also be the occasion for extended emotional states.

Thus, for both cognitive and personality development, what is learned is learned between the emergence of a goal and its resolution. What is learned is sometimes construed as an appraisal or interpretation of the world, sometimes as a strategy or set of strategies for acting on the world. As we will see in the next section, there is no dichotomy from a neurobiological perspective. An appraisal includes strategies (as well as expected consequences and back-up strategies) and strategies presuppose an appraisal – they are *about* a particular situation. Most important, emotion is always guiding the effort, strategy, and appraisal, and it does so for prolonged periods when goals are not immediately satisfied. As a result, the type of emotion, the type of goal, and the capacity for achieving it are fundamental parameters for developing individual styles. In this way cognitive and personality development are not only similar, they are identical. It is just that goals not easily satisfied – being loved, escaping criticism, winning admiration, achieving safety from rejection – are the organizers of personality development. The emotions that accompany these goals are very often negative (cf. Higgins, 1987), and the lag between their emergence and their satisfaction tends to be lengthy, if not indefinite (which is why we often call them wishes). The goals pertinent to cognitive development are generally much more immediate, and the emotions that accompany them are usually not intensely negative and are very often positive.

Emotions, moods, and personality development: Time scales in brain and mind

In the previous section, similarities between cognitive and personality development were related to strategy formation and its resonance with emotions during prolonged efforts to achieve goals. According to principles of self-organization, these real-time activities ought to lay down patterns over development, patterns that feed back to real-time activities in an ongoing process of refinement. In the remainder of the chapter, a new theory of cognitive-emotional self-organization at interacting time scales (Lewis, 2000a) is used to model change and consolidation in personality development. However, it is worth keeping in mind that individual paths in cognitive development can probably be modeled in much the same way, and I will suggest some directions for doing so.

The theory addresses not only micro- and macrodevelopment, but also a middle time scale of mesodevelopment. I define microdevelopment as the scale at which an appraisal and an emotion rapidly emerge, along with an intention to act, and action is quickly executed – with little effort. This sequence usually takes no more than a few seconds. Mesodevelopment is defined as a period of minutes, hours, or even days, during which goal-directed actions are delayed, ineffective, or blocked, intentions to achieve goals persist over time, and appraisals and emotions remain "stuck" in mind. I view this enduring focus as roughly equivalent to mood (Lewis, 2000a). Mood is generally defined as a limited range of emotions accompanied by constrained or biased cognitive appraisals for an extended period of time (e.g., Frijda, 1993a). Note, however, that this is also the time scale of effortful problem solving in learning and cognitive development, during which one's "mood" is usually one of interest, excitement, and/or mild anxiety (Renninger, Hidi, & Krapp, 1992). Finally, macrodevelopment is defined as the scale at which personality dispositions emerge and consolidate over a course of months and years. We now examine how cognitive, emotional, and volitional processes become integrated or synchronized in the brain, at each of these time scales, and how they underpin the psychological processes of emotional experience and personality development (see table 7.1 for a summary).

Table 7.1 *Three interacting time scales in personality development, showing hypothesized neurobiological and psychological mechanisms*

	Emotional Interpretation	Mood	Personality
Developmental scale	micro	meso	macro
Typical duration	seconds	minutes–hours	months–years
Description	rapid convergence of cognitive interpretation with emotional state	lasting entrainment of interpretive focus with narrow emotional range	interpretive–emotional–behavioral habits specific to classes of situations
Dynamic systems formalism	attractor	modification, tuning, or entrenchment of state space	permanent structure of state space
Hypothesized neurobiological mechanism	cortico-limbic resonance mediated by orbitofrontal appraisal entrained with limbic circuits	lasting orbitofrontal–cortico-limbic–motor entrainment, perceptual preafference, sustained neurohormone release	selection and strengthening of cortico-cortical and cortico-limbic connections, synaptic pruning, loss of plasticity with age
Hypothesized psychological mechanism	cognition–emotion coupling in appraisal, rapid and successful goal-directed action	cognition–emotion coupling, goal preoccupation, inhibited or blocked action, strategy formation	cognition–emotion complementarities that arise from and constrain interpretation, strategy, and behavior in real time

Adapted from Lewis (2000a) by permission.

Microdevelopment in the brain

As noted earlier, emotion theorists define appraisal as the evaluation of a situation in terms of its relevance for oneself. Rapid evaluations or appraisals are considered the cognitive prerequisites for emotions. For example, an appraisal that something valued is lost, one is not capable of retrieving it, and nobody is there to help gives rise to the emotion of sadness. Appraisal theories of emotion claim that cognitive appraisals precede emotions (Smith & Ellsworth, 1985). However, brain research suggests that cognitive appraisals and emotions emerge more or less simultaneously, or, if the tie is to be broken, emotions probably come first.

One sense in which emotion precedes cognitive appraisal concerns the pathway from the thalamus, the waystation for perceptual input, directly to the amygdala, an important structure in the limbic system responsible for emotional conditioning. Through this pathway, coarse perceptual information triggers an emotion, or at least an emotion precursor, before the cortex has a chance to make sense of the stimulus or even to recognize it (LeDoux, 1992). The amygdala, in turn, is connected to many other brain structures, including a key area at the base of the prefrontal cortex called the orbitofrontal cortex (Rolls, 1999; Schore, 1994). The orbitofrontal area is one of a number of regions serving as a convergence zone for all cortical subsystems (Schore, 2000). That is, perception, association, expectancy, and motor rehearsal (each of which is a massively coupled system in itself) all become synchronized at the orbitofrontal cortex, precisely where raw emotional information enters from the limbic system.

The immediate purpose of this meeting of the waves is the regulation of the amygdala by the cortex. But its larger purpose is to marry cognition with emotion, rapidly, on-line, so that affective information can guide our thinking, perceiving, and action (e.g., Damasio, 1994). According to emotional neurobiologists (Derryberry & Tucker, 1994; Schore, 1994), the orbitofrontal cortex is where gist-like meanings are fashioned and entrained with emotion-mediating limbic circuits. Schore (2000) refers to this region as the locus of "orbitofrontal appraisals," and these appraisals are responsible for regulating limbic activation in the context of an *emergent meaning* for a given situation. This gist-like meaning is a key aspect of the appraisal process that has preoccupied emotion theorists for decades (cf. Frijda, 1993b). It arises from interactions among numerous perceptual, cognitive, and motor subsystems, and these remain continuously entrained with emotional circuitry in the limbic system (as well as lower structures such as the brain stem) in a globally stable configuration. Tucker (1992) refers to this entrainment as a co-emergent wholeness or resonance between cortical imagery and emotional activation. In DS terms, this state of resonance is an attractor to which the brain literally self-organizes, rapidly, in microdevelopment, in response to a triggering event or stimulus (Freeman, 1995; Schore, 1997).

The picture so far is of an emotional trigger mediated by a converging pattern in the orbitofrontal cortex where all cortical regions become coupled or synchronized in a gist-like appraisal. Walter Freeman takes this picture of co-emergence one step further, and links it with the chief biological function of emotion: action. According to Freeman (1995, 2000) cortico-limbic feedback or resonance emerges along with a global *intentional* state. This process begins in the hippocampus (another limbic structure, related to memory as well as emotion) and rapidly self-organizes across the entire brain. Action is initiated by this intentionality, fueled by emotion in the amygdala and other limbic structures, and articulated, rehearsed, and elaborated in the frontal and prefrontal cortices (Freeman, 1995; Tucker, 1992). Thus, the emergence of an appraisal is one aspect of a more comprehensive self-organizing configuration that includes emotion, intention, and action plans. As long as this configuration lasts, intention keeps the brain organized in the pursuit of a particular goal, thus remaining at or near a particular attractor (Freeman, 1995). This picture is consistent with Frijda's (1986) emphasis on action readiness as a key attribute of emotion.

Thus, the brain is a self-organizing system that converges to a highly ordered state in the presence of emotionally relevant events in microdevelopment, and goal-directedness holds the brain in this state for the time it takes to generate an action. But this orderly state is often short-lived. Evidence for this assertion comes from work on animals using multiple EEG sites to measure the coherence of brain waves across whole cortical regions (Skarda & Freeman, 1987). What these authors discovered was that animals' brains oscillate between order and chaos with the cycling of perception and action. EEG coherence (orderliness) is observed during the perception phase, while breath is inhaled, odors are recognized, and an intention is formed. But this coherence *dissipates* when action is initiated, leaving the brain in a *chaotic* "background" state from which new coherences can emerge in the next cycle (Freeman & Baird, 1987; Skarda & Freeman, 1987). Thus, an episode of cognitive-emotional self-organization at the scale of microdevelopment is completed by an action. The brain self-organizes to its attractor with the emergence of an intention, and that organization decays when action takes place. All this lasts only a second or two, leaving the animal in a state of adaptive disorganization so that it can quickly adjust to whatever comes next.

Microdevelopment in the mind

Cognitive scientists no longer doubt that the brain is a self-organizing system. Moreover, neural network modeling has provided a vivid empirical method for analyzing neural self-organization at different scales, consistent with the theme of this book and this chapter (cf. Elman, Bates, Johnson, Karmiloff-Smith, Parisi, & Plunkett, 1996; Mareschal & Thomas, in press). But can the mind – and particularly the emotional mind – also be characterized as self-organizing? We can begin to address this question by analyzing the emergence and consolidation of appraisal–emotion interactions in real time, then examining their relations to moods and personality across longer time scales. Self-organizing cognition–emotion interactions have been the focus of my own modeling (Lewis, 1995, 1997b; Lewis & Douglas, 1998) and research (Lewis, Lamey, & Douglas, 1999), and have also been addressed by the DS approaches of Fogel (1993), Izard, Ackerman, Schoff, & Fine (2000), and Scherer (2000). The theory that is presently under construction goes a few steps beyond these modeling efforts, looking specifically at interscale relations as the causal scaffold of all psychological structure.

According to this account, a cognitive appraisal or interpretation converges in real time from the coordination of (lower-order) elements such as concepts, associations, and perceptions, but it does so only in interaction with a consolidating emotional feeling state. The convergence of an appraisal amplifies and constrains emotion while emotion simultaneously directs and constrains attentional processes at work in appraisal (Lewis, 1995). In contrast to conventional appraisal theory, appraisals are not presumed to be independent of emotion, nor to precede emotion in time. Rather, I suggest that appraisals become coherent and stable only when an emotional state consolidates (cf. Frijda, 1993b). This sequence corresponds with what we know of underlying neural processes, whereby coherence depends on cortical entrainment with limbic activation, and cortico-limbic resonance is the endpoint rather than the beginning of an emotional episode. Thus, at the psychological level as well, appraisal and emotion are proposed to arise in tandem (cf. Buck, 1985) and stabilize through ongoing feedback.

The synchronization of appraisal and emotion can be described as a macroscopic coupling between the cognitive and emotional systems, giving rise to a coherent *emotional interpretation* (EI) in real time. Emotional interpretations are similar to Izard's (1984) affective-cognitive structures, but they are construed as temporary organizations rather than lasting structures. In an EI of blame, for example, the emotion of anger rapidly couples with the interpretation that someone is at fault. This macroscopic coupling subsumes more microscopic couplings among perceptual and cognitive constituents, paralleling the synchronization of cortical subsystems at the prefrontal (e.g., orbitofrontal) cortex. For example, the sense that someone is at fault results from couplings among an image of a person, an inference of harm, associations with a remembered persecutor (e.g., a big brother), and the attribution of intention. But these cognitive couplings would not cohere unless nested in a global coupling with the emotion of anger. Most important, an EI is a coherent psychological unit (like a mental model or a schema in conventional theories) that integrates attentional, interpretive, and emotional features in a seamless constellation until an action is initiated. Once action takes place, however, this psychological organization dissipates as the underlying neural systems become desynchronized and the mind wanders off. One rebukes a child who is blamed for making a mess and then goes back to folding the laundry and daydreaming.

Because EIs are higher-order forms, arising from couplings among lower-order cognitive and emotional constituents, they can be represented as attractors (at the psychological level as well as the neural level). Empirical methods for studying such attractors have yet to be developed for older children and adults. But research with infants shows real-time movement to attractors on a psychological state space defined by levels of distress and directions of visual attention (Lewis et al., 1999). Many of these attractors were found to be consistent across sessions within and across age periods, and more stable attractors (in real time) were more likely to be consistent across sessions. Stable attractors may thus represent recurrent EIs that express aspects of temperament or personality continuity even in infancy. Hypothetically, the presence of several attractors, representing several EIs, indicates a range of states to which interpretations can converge for the same individual. Thus, personality may be depicted as a cluster of probable cognitive-emotional states, indeterminate and variable in real time but stable over development (Lewis, 1997). However, before looking at personality development in greater detail, we move to the next time scale, mesodevelopment.

Mesodevelopment in the brain

In mesodevelopment, the orderliness of a brain that is ready for action may fail to dissipate, because the animal cannot engage in behavior that fulfills its intention. Rather than dissipate, I hypothesize that neural orderliness grows over a period of seconds, minutes, hours, and even days, as momentary appraisals coalesce into lasting interpretations, give rise to elaborate plans and strategies, and continue to perpetuate similar or compensatory intentions. This profile of self-organization fits the contours of a mood state that gathers over minutes or hours and finally solidifies like a fog bank that cannot be penetrated. What are the neural mechanisms responsible for this converging orderliness?

Freeman (1995, 2000) discusses a global circuit from the hippocampus through the prefrontal region to all sensory cortices as a "preafference loop" that strongly influences perception before it happens, and does so on the basis of goal-related expectancies entrained with motor rehearsal. Thus, extended goal states would necessarily maintain sensory-motor-affective patterns for long periods, the same synapses would fire continuously, and mechanisms of learning such as long-term potentiation would keep the cortex tuned to a selective class of inputs (Freeman, 1995). Such extended states also maintain the flow of particular neurohormones or neuromodulators (e.g., dopamine) from the brain stem. These chemicals act diffusely on large regions of cortex, enhancing particular synaptic connections and inhibiting others over long periods (Freeman, 1995; Panksepp, 1998). They directly promote the growth and maintenance of emotional states, specifically those related to aggression, withdrawal, abandonment, mating, caretaking, and other mammalian goals (Panksepp, 1998), and they are instrumental in long-term potentiation or learning.

Most important, neurohormones are released from the brain stem as a *consequence* of limbic activity mediating the construction and rehearsal of plans in frontal and motor cortex (Freeman, 1995; Panksepp, 1998). Thus, neurohormonal modulation could not be independent of specific *intentions*. Mesodevelopmental states of prolonged organization would therefore harness brain activity to an agenda, but one that might not be readily satisfied or abandoned. These states would have the potential to resonate for long periods, during which motor rehearsal and preafferent perceptual processes maintain each other, without a conclusive behavioral resolution. Moreover, as is typical of moods, these enduring states might eventually become consciously dissociated from their target or goal, perhaps as a result of exteroceptive or proprioceptive habituation.

Mesodevelopment in the mind

Retelling this story in psychological terms, we can now examine differences between short-lived appraisals and lasting moods and the means by which one leads to the other. Note that the term *mood* is being used loosely, to describe lasting states of cognitive-emotional organization. There are other definitions as well. That moods are characterized by reduced cognitive variance is supported by copious data on mood-congruent perception, interpretation, learning, and memory (e.g., Blaney, 1986; Isen, 1990). Moods also imply a limited range of long-lasting emotions or affects, though not necessarily a single, persistent emotion (Frijda, 1993a). For example, in an angry mood, resentment recurs often whereas interest, sadness, and happiness become rare events. Thus, mood can be depicted as a temporary refinement of the psychological state space, representing a cognitive-emotional bias: attractors are strengthened for some EIs and weakened or extinguished for others, and the range of trajectories between states becomes more limited (Lewis, 2000a).

As described earlier, psychological organization builds rapidly in an EI in microdevelopment, then rapidly dissipates when goals are achieved through actions. However, when actions cannot achieve goals, the goal state may persevere, and the organization of interpretation and emotion may persist for minutes, hours, days, or weeks (cf. Scheff, 1987; Teasdale & Barnard, 1993). In this way, an EI can lead to a mood when action is blocked, by either internally imposed inhibitions or externally imposed circumstances. For example, an insult leads to a rapidly self-organizing EI characterized by anger and shame and an impulse to retaliate. However, if the insult is from one's boss, retaliation is thwarted and anger and shame persevere, along with thoughts about how to teach the boss a lesson in the long run. Similarly, depression, depending on one's theoretical orientation, involves blocked goals for harming others, seeking affection, or escaping blame (generally, one's own), and anxious or worried moods involve the inability to escape from an uncertain threat. Note that positive mood states do not fit well with the present analysis. This is not surprising given the evidence for marked asymmetries between the cognitive consequences of positive and negative moods, with positive affect broadening attention and negative affect narrowing it (Derryberry & Tucker, 1994; Isen, 1990).

Thus, mood-like, mesodevelopmental states are constrained by an enduring intention or goal (or several competing goals), and this constraint can explain the cognitive and emotional narrowing that is typical of moods. Yet the elaboration of thoughts and feelings over time makes mood a *developmental* process, crystallizing over minutes, hours, or days, and very often gives rise to a rich and intricate (though often unpleasant) experience. Examples include the extensive and intricate patterns of interpretation that can build up in depressed and paranoid states, but even a simple grumpy mood becomes more articulated with time. Surprisingly, this kind of elaboration parallels *learning* in the context of cognitive development, when goal obstruction leads to effortful activity, linked insights, and strategy formation (Pascual-Leone, 1987; Siegler & Jenkins, 1989).

In the socioemotional realm, we tend to speak of unproductive rumination rather than insights and strategies. How might an emphasis on strategy formation change our understanding of moods?

In moods, not only does action (imagined or actual) fall short of achieving goals, but action tendencies continually arise as long as an emotional constellation remains in place. Thus, action is both urged and obstructed in moods. Where does this impasse lead? I suggest that, in socioemotional development just as in cognitive development, the prolonged focus on blocked goals leads to the formation and elaboration of strategies. These strategies, as well as the interpretations or insights in which they are embedded, return over many similar occasions of goal obstruction. Thus, strategies for achieving the desired goal, by getting around the obstacles blocking it, characterize mood in the mind, just as resonance between motor rehearsal and preafferent perception characterizes mood in the brain.

The hypothesis of a prolonged state of psychological organization, resulting from backed-up action, is congenial with theorists going back at least to Freud and continues to be verified empirically (Horowitz, 1998; Polivy, 1998). In this state, goal-related behaviors are rehearsed, new strategies fashioned, expected responses monitored, and contingencies checked and rechecked. Rumination is characterized by these mental activities, and research has demonstrated a reliable correlation between the tendency to ruminate and the endurance of depressive mood states (Nolen-Hoeksema & Morrow, 1991; Teasdale & Barnard, 1993). Instead of yelling at the boss or quitting in a rage, one endures the humiliations of the workplace and entertains increasingly elaborate plans for winning the lottery and resigning with a flourish. In this way, intentions that cannot be achieved resonate for long periods and cultivate elaborate contingency plans, often without one's awareness of their origins or their object.

Macrodevelopment in the brain

The relation between micro- and mesodevelopment was hypothesized to depend on one thing only: the inability to act effectively once a goal state has self-organized in the brain. If the goal cannot be abandoned, then the orderliness of intention, emotion, and appraisal persists, grows, and solidifies, and effort is directed toward finding a resolution, at least until the goal is satisfied or replaced by more pressing concerns. Thus, the lag between the emergence and satisfaction of a goal is the conduit between micro- and mesodevelopment, funneling orderliness from one time scale to the next. Earlier, however, I proposed that this lag is instrumental for macrodevelopment, generating emergent structure in personality and cognitive development. In fact, the conduit from micro- to mesodevelopment may *mediate* the emergence of structure in macrodevelopment. During the delay of goal satisfaction, effort breeds strategy formation and strategy modification, or in Piaget's words, the elaboration of cognizance. These *mesodevelopmental* processes, repeated across occasions, may then funnel orderliness from a scale of minutes and hours to a scale of years. In other words, a middle time scale may be a necessary stepping stone between microdevelopment and macrodevelopment.

Macrodevelopment can be viewed as the laying down of neural organization across occasions extending over months and years. In the case of personality development, it is characterized by a consolidating set of habits, traits, or beliefs that become predictable in familiar (and sometimes novel) situations. Yet it is obvious that the brain does not maintain any specific configuration continuously over development. This would be akin to holding a thought in mind permanently. What gets maintained is a set of neural complementarities that favor the recurrence of specific real-time patterns. We have already seen that lasting states of goal-directedness potentiate learning while neuromodulators enhance and maintain mood-like states. The outcome of this learning is the formation and strengthening of synapses that dispose the brain to repeat performances of the same appraisals, emotions, expectancies, and strategies, given the same frustrated goals, on future occasions.

As discussed earlier, it is axiomatic in self-organizing networks that patterns of coupling on each occasion establish and strengthen complementarities that guide similar patterns of coupling on subsequent occasions. While this should be true of any state of coherence in the brain, no matter how brief, it may be particularly important for the relation between mood and personality development, since mood states last much longer and involve more synaptic shaping than do brief EIs. With this synaptic shaping across occasions, the brain becomes more organized, more sensitive to particular triggers, falling more easily into its interpretive-emotional attractors, and perhaps yielding the same moods again and again (Harkness & Tucker, 2000). New or different moods can of course modify these synaptic complementarities and change the strength of habitual attractors. Indeed, this is the philosophy that often guides short-term antidepressive therapy (Kramer, 1994). But recurring moods of a particular character necessarily result in the strengthening of complementarities and the permanent engraving of the personality state space, as the cortex loses plasticity with age (Harkness & Tucker, 2000). Macrodevelopment can thus be represented as the consolidation of a neural state space, while mesodevelopment serves to tune, modify, or entrench that state space.

Neurodevelopmental theory and research lend support to this picture. First, it is generally assumed that psychological states perpetuate themselves across occasions through a variety of neuronal selection mechanisms (e.g., Edelman, 1987; Greenough & Schwark, 1984; Tucker, 1992). Second, developmentalists assume that temperamental differences, which often express themselves in mood-like states, guide the selection and strengthening of cortical connections by constraining experience, thus further refining individual styles (Derryberry & Rothbart, 1997). Third, the selective mechanisms underlying this process of crystallization appear to be centered in cortico-limbic areas where cognitive appraisals and emotional states resonate with each other (Freeman, 2000; Harkness & Tucker, 2000; Schore, 1994, 2000; Tucker, 1992). Fourth, neuromodulator action during prolonged affective states fashions entrenched habits (e.g., through long-term potentiation) that gradually supersede the brain's early plasticity (Panksepp, 1998; Schore, 1994). According to Harkness & Tucker (2000), more intense emotions and moods, reexperienced over many occasions, have the strongest effects, as when the recurrence of abuse or neglect early in life "kindles" depression or anxiety with increasing predictability. Finally, as discussed earlier, synaptic pruning and cell death eliminate connections that are underused, such that their more popular neighbors get even more of the action (Greenough & Schwark, 1984; Tucker, 1992). Thus, prolonged states of coupling not only enhance complementarities in the brain, but neurons or neuronal groups that remain (relatively) uncoupled lose their influence entirely.

Macrodevelopment in the mind

The idea that personality arises from cognition–emotion interactions is tied to theories of emotional development, though it also resonates with some mainstream personality theories (e.g., Higgins, 1987; Mischel & Shoda, 1995). Tomkins (1984) and Izard (1984) view personality as the construction of affective-cognitive or ideoaffective structures, arising through the child's most frequent or important experiences. These structures are defined as linkages between frequently felt emotions and accompanying cognitive interpretations, and they correspond with EIs in the present account. According to Malatesta & Wilson (1988), personality traits not only arise from such structures but are also expressed by them. This picture is consistent with the idea that consolidating complementarities in macrodevelopment both arise from and contribute to shorter-scale couplings.

Thus, the complementarities that underpin personality consolidation can be traced to the coupling of cognitive and emotional elements in EIs and moods. Through recurrent patterns of coupling, early complementarities are strengthened and entrenched, and the situations that induce them become experienced as similar. Perceptual associations, emotional conditioning, and conceptual generalizations extend this stamp of meaningfulness to other situations with shared features. These situations are then appraised and reacted to in the same way. Thus, personality stability comes to be reflected by interpretive and behavioral consistencies within broad classes of situations (Mischel & Shoda, 1995).

But what of the particular role of strategies generated during mood-like states? If mood-like states of goal preoccupation contribute the most to lasting complementarities, as argued in the last section, then strategy formation may be a particularly important factor in personality development. We have seen that strategies are of central importance in cognitive development, where effortful goal pursuit gives rise to new and varied means for achieving one's intentions. In personality development, strategies may serve exactly the same function, except that the implication of progress, through more powerful or more effective strategies, becomes arbitrary or irrelevant. Reference to goals and strategies in theories of personality development was briefly reviewed in the first half of this chapter. The present account goes on to emphasize that it is the cognitive-emotional resonance of mood-like states, resulting from repeatedly blocked goals in childhood, that propels the formation and reenactment of strategies that eventually crystallize in personality.

Recurrent strategies are either partially successful, temporarily successful, or seemingly successful in attaining goals. They thereby reduce some of the tensions or discrepancies building in the psychological system during mood-like states (cf. Higgins, 1991). By providing partial or relative equilibrium, strategies are good candidates for psychological attractors (van der Maas, 1998). As attractors, they express couplings that are recurrent and predictable over time: in this case couplings among cognitive appraisal, emotion, and plans. The jealous child, who cannot get rid of his little brother, finds strategies for denigrating or controlling him. He may tease him continually or call on his parents to chastise or punish him, thus achieving a partial, but only partial, fulfillment of his goal. Because the resolution is partial, the mood-like state of jealousy endures or recurs, giving rise to further refinements and elaborations of the same strategies. By later childhood or adulthood, this little boy's tendency to denigrate, chastise, or control may become characterological. The anxious child, who cannot achieve reassurance from a mother who is preoccupied, devises strategies of withdrawal to the safe haven of her room or her imagination. These strategies give a temporary sense of partial safety, and they grow in strength across occasions. By adolescence, this little girl no longer tries out these strategies; she lives by them. Withdrawal, as an organized state of thought, feeling, and action, has now moved from meso- to macrodevelopment.

Thus, the vehicle of personality is a network of complementarities that evolves over macrodevelopment with recurrent experiences, and these complementarities both arise from and give rise to particular interpretations coupled with particular emotions and strategies. The idea that such complementarities stem from thwarted intentions is essentially an update of Freud's view of personality as the "unfinished business" of need gratification (Thorne & Klohnen, 1993). As well, the notion of cascading constraints provides a heuristic for thinking about the refinement of interpretations, emotions, and strategies over development. Cascading constraints are evident within developmental periods, as children contend with recurring challenges in increasingly predictable ways. But they are also evident across periods, over the lifespan, as the resolution of each developmental passage constrains the negotiation of the next (Erikson, 1963; Kegan, 1982). It is in this way that early patterns of experience fashion longstanding interpersonal and cognitive habits (Keating, 1990a). Through these processes, personality self-organizes over many years, evolving from a set of potentials, through self-propagating patterns, to an entrenched set of tendencies in adulthood.

Conclusion: Interscale mechanisms in cognitive and personality development

According to this account, interactions between micro- and macrodevelopment are often, if not always, mediated by a scale of mesodevelopment, at least when emotion is part of the picture. Mesodevelopmental forms arise from sustained intentions that, in a sense, slow down the passage of real time, as attention is directed effortfully to what cannot be attained rapidly. How does this interscale mechanism play a similar role in cognitive and personality development yet give rise to a very different portrait of change and stabilization in each domain?

For cognitive development, the slowdown of mesodevelopment is characteristically productive, because temporary goal obstructions generate new strategies for overcoming barriers and discovering new solutions. These solutions feed up to macrodevelopment where they fashion a repertoire of enduring insights and skills. This repertoire, in turn, feeds down to microdevelopment where proceduralized competencies are executed with little effort. In the socioemotional realm, however, unsatisfied goals can continue to elude resolution indefinitely. The moods that converge around them in mesodevelopment generate strategies, but these strategies often take the form of rumination, wishful thinking, and goal substitution. These strategies feed up to macrodevelopment, fashioning a repertoire of beliefs, preferences, and emotional biases – i.e., personality. This repertoire, in turn, feeds down to microdevelopment where habitual feelings and appraisals emerge rapidly in the flow of everyday life. The difference between personality and cognitive development may thus reside in the impacts of different classes of goals, and the emotions and strategies that accompany them, rather than any fundamental difference in the mechanisms of change and stability.

References

Abraham, F. D. (1995). Dynamics, bifurcation, self-organization, chaos, mind, conflict, insensitivity to initial conditions, time, unification, diversity, free will, and social responsibility. In R. Robertson & A. Combs (Eds.), *Chaos theory in psychology and the life sciences* (pp. 155–174). Mahwah, NJ: Erlbaum.

Blaney, P. H. (1986). Affect and memory: A review. *Psychological Bulletin, 99,* 229–246.

Buck, R. (1985). Prime theory: An integrated view of motivation and emotion. *Psychological Review, 92,* 389–413.

Cantor, N., & Harlow, R. (1994). Social intelligence and personality: flexible life-task pursuit. In R. J. Sternberg & P. Ruzgis (Eds.), *Personality and intelligence* (pp. 137–168). New York: Cambridge University Press.

Cantor, N., Norem, J. K., Niedenthal, P. M., Langston, C. A., & Brower, A. M. (1987). Life tasks, self-concept ideals, and cognitive strategies in a life transition. *Journal of Personality and Social Psychology, 53,* 1178–1191.

Case, R. (1988). The whole child: Toward an integrated view of young children's cognitive, social, and emotional development. In A. D. Pellegrini (Ed.), *Psychological bases for early education* (pp. 155–184). New York: Wiley.

Case, R., Hayward, S., Lewis, M. D., & Hurst, P. (1988). Toward a neo-Piagetian theory of cognitive and emotional development. *Developmental Review, 8,* 1–51.

Damasio, A. R. (1994). *Descartes' error.* New York: Avon.

Derryberry, D., & Rothbart, M. K. (1997). Reactive and effortful processes in the organization of temperament. *Development and Psychopathology, 9,* 633–652.

Derryberry, D., & Tucker, D. M. (1994). Motivating the focus of attention. In P. Niedenthal & S. Kitayama (Eds.), *The heart's eye: Emotional influences in perception and attention* (pp. 170–196). San Diego: Academic Press.

Dore, J. (1989). Monologue as reenvoicement of dialogue. In K. Nelson (Ed.), *Narratives from the crib* (pp. 231–260). Cambridge, MA: Harvard University Press.

Dunn, J. (1988). *The beginnings of social understanding.* Cambridge, MA: Harvard University Press.

Dweck, C. S., & Leggett, E. L. (1988). A social-cognitive approach to motivation and personality. *Psychological Review, 95,* 256–273.

Edelman, G. M. (1987). *Neural Darwinism.* New York: Basic Books.

Elman, J. L., Bates, E. A., Johnson, M. H., Karmiloff-Smith, A., Parisi, D., & Plunkett, K. (1996). *Rethinking innateness: A connectionist perspective on development.* Cambridge, MA: MIT Press.

Epstein, S. (1993). Implications of cognitive-experiential self-theory for personality and developmental psychology. In D. C. Funder, R. D. Parke, C. Tomlinson-Keasey, & K. Widaman (Eds.), *Studying lives through time: Personality and development* (pp. 399–438). Washington, DC: American Psychological Association.

Erikson, E. H. (1963). *Childhood and society.* New York: Norton.

Estrada, P., Arsenio, W. F., Hess, R. D., & Holloway, S. D. (1987). Affective quality of the mother-child relationship: Longitudinal consequences for children's school-relevant functioning. *Developmental Psychology, 23,* 210–215.

Fischer, K. W., & Ayoub, C. (1996). Analyzing development of working models of close relationships: Illustration with a case of vulnerability and violence. In G. G. Noam & K. W. Fischer (Eds.), *Development and vulnerability in close relationships* (pp. 173–199). Mahwah, NJ: Erlbaum.

Fischer, K. W., & Granott, N. (1995). Beyond one-dimensional change: Parallel, concurrent, socially distributed processes in learning and development. *Human Development, 38,* 302–314.

Fischer, K. W., Shaver, P. R., & Carnochan, P. (1990). How emotions develop and how they organise development. *Cognition and Emotion, 4,* 81–127.

Fogel, A. (1993). *Developing through relationships: Origins of communication, self, and culture.* Chicago: University of Chicago Press.

Fogel, A., Messinger, D., Dickson, K. L., & Hsu, H. (1999). Posture and gaze in early mother-infant communication: Synchronization of developmental trajectories. *Developmental Science, 2,* 325–332.

Freeman, W. J. (1995). *Societies of brains.* Hillsdale, NJ: Erlbaum.

Freeman, W. J. (2000). Emotion is essential to all intentional behaviors. In M. D. Lewis & I. Granic (Eds.), *Emotion, development, and self-organization: Dynamic systems approaches to emotional development* (pp. 209–235). New York: Cambridge University Press.

Freeman, W. J., & Baird, B. (1987). Relation of olfactory EEG to behavior: Spatial analysis. *Behavioral Neuroscience, 101,* 393–408.

Frijda, N. H. (1986). *The emotions.* Cambridge, UK: Cambridge University Press.

Frijda, N. H. (1993a). Moods, emotion episodes, and emotions. In M. Lewis & J. M. Haviland (Eds.), *Handbook of emotions* (pp. 381–403). New York: Guilford.

Frijda, N. H. (1993b). The place of appraisal in emotion. *Cognition and Emotion, 7,* 357–387.

Goodwin, B. (1993). Development as a robust natural process. In W. Stein & F. J. Varela (Eds.), *Thinking about biology* (pp. 123–148). Reading, MA: Addison-Wesley.

Gottlieb, G. (1991). Experiential canalization of behavioral development: Theory. *Developmental Psychology, 27,* 4–13.

Granott, N. (1998). We learn, therefore we develop: Learning versus development – or developing learning? In M. C. Smith & T. Pourchot (Eds.), *Adult learning and development: Perspectives from educational psychology* (pp. 15–34). Mahwah, NJ: Erlbaum.

Greenough, W. T., & Schwark, H. D. (1984). Age-related aspects of experience effects upon brain structure. In R. N. Emde & R. J. Harmon (Eds.), *Continuities and discontinuities in development* (pp. 69–91). New York: Plenum.

Harkness, K. L., & Tucker, D. M. (2000). Motivation of neural plasticity: Neural mechanisms in the self-organization of depression. In M. D. Lewis & I. Granic (Eds.), *Emotion, development, and self-organization: Dynamic systems approaches to emotional development* (pp. 186–208). New York: Cambridge University Press.

Higgins, E. T. (1987). Self-discrepancy: A theory relating self and affect. *Psychological Review, 94,* 319–340.

Higgins, E. T. (1991). Development of self-regulatory and self-evaluative processes: Costs, benefits, and tradeoffs. In M. R. Gunnar & L. A. Sroufe (Eds.), *The Minnesota symposia on child psychology, Vol. 23: Self processes and development* (pp. 125–165). Hillsdale, NJ: Erlbaum.

Horowitz, M. J. (1998). *Cognitive psychodynamics: From conflict to character.* New York: Wiley.

Isen, A. M. (1990). The influence of positive and negative affect on cognitive organization: Some implications for development. In N. Stein, B. Leventhal, & T. Trabasso (Eds.), *Psychological and biological processes in the development of emotion* (pp. 75–94). Hillsdale, NJ: Erlbaum.

Izard, C. E. (1984). Emotion-cognition relationships and human development. In C. E. Izard, J. Kagan, & R. B. Zajonc (Eds.), *Emotions, cognition and behavior* (pp. 17–37). Cambridge: Cambridge University Press.

Izard, C. E., Ackerman, B., Schoff, K., & Fine, S. (2000). Self-organization of discrete emotions, emotion patterns, and emotion–cognition relations. In M. D. Lewis & I. Granic (Eds.), *Emotion, development, and self-organization: Dynamic systems approaches to emotional development* (pp. 15–36). New York: Cambridge University Press.

Kauffman, S. (1995). *At home in the universe: The search for the laws of self-organization and complexity.* New York: Oxford University Press.

Keating, D. P. (1990a). Charting pathways to the development of expertise. *Educational Psychologist, 25,* 243–267.

Keating, D. P. (1990b). Developmental processes in the socialization of cognitive structures. In *Development and learning: Proceedings of a symposium in honour of Wolfgang Edelstein on his 60th birthday.* Berlin: Max Planck Institute.

Keating, D. P., & Miller, F. K. (2000). The dynamics of emotional development: Models, metaphors, and methods. In M. D. Lewis & I. Granic (Eds.), *Emotion, development, and self-organization: Dynamic systems approaches to emotional development* (pp. 373–392). New York: Cambridge University Press.

Kegan, R. (1982). *The evolving self: Problem and process in human development.* Cambridge, MA: Harvard University Press.

Kelso, J. A. S. (1995). *Dynamic patterns: The self-organization of brain and behavior.* Cambridge, MA: Bradford/MIT Press.

Kopp, C. B. (1989). Regulation of distress and negative emotions: A developmental view. *Developmental Psychology, 25,* 343–354.

Kramer, P. D. (1994). *Listening to prozac*. New York: Penguin.

Labouvie-Vief, G., Hakim-Larsen, J., DeVoe, M., & Schoeberlein, S. (1989). Emotions and self-regulation: A life-span view. *Human Development, 32,* 279–299.

Lamb, M. E. (1987). Predictive implications of individual differences in attachment. *Journal of Consulting and Clinical Psychology, 55,* 817–824.

LeDoux, J. E. (1992). Emotion and the amygdala. In J. P. Appleton (Ed.), *The amygdala* (pp. 339–351). New York: Wiley.

Lerner, R. M. (1995). The place of learning within the human development system: A developmental contextual perspective. *Human Development, 38,* 361–366.

Lewis, M. D. (1993a). Early socioemotional predictors of cognitive competency at four years. *Developmental Psychology, 29,* 1036–1045.

Lewis, M. D. (1993b). Emotion-cognition interactions in early infant development. *Cognition and Emotion, 7,* 145–170.

Lewis, M. D. (1995). Cognition-emotion feedback and the self-organization of developmental paths. *Human Development, 38,* 71–102.

Lewis, M. D. (1997). Personality self-organization: Cascading constraints on cognition-emotion interaction. In A. Fogel, M. C. Lyra, & J. Valsiner (Eds.), *Dynamics and indeterminism in developmental and social processes* (pp. 193–216). Mahwah, NJ: Erlbaum.

Lewis, M. D. (2000a). Emotional self-organization at three time scales. In M. D. Lewis & I. Granic (Eds.), *Emotion, development, and self-organization: Dynamic systems approaches to emotional development* (pp. 37–55). New York: Cambridge University Press.

Lewis, M. D. (2000b). The promise of dynamic systems approaches for an integrated account of human development. *Child Development, 71,* 36–43.

Lewis, M. D., & Douglas, L. (1998). A dynamic systems approach to cognition–emotion interactions in development. In M. F. Mascolo & S. Griffin (Eds.), *What develops in emotional development?* (pp. 159–188). New York: Plenum.

Lewis, M. D., Lamey, A. V., & Douglas, L. (1999). A new dynamic systems method for the analysis of early socioemotional development. *Developmental Science, 2,* 458–476.

Magai, C., & McFadden, S. H. (1995). *The role of emotions in social and personality development: History, theory, and research*. New York: Plenum.

Malatesta, C. Z., & Wilson, A. (1988). Emotion/cognition interaction in personality development: A discrete emotions, functionalist analysis. *British Journal of Social Psychology, 27,* 91–112.

Mareschal, D., & Thomas, M. S. C. (in press). Self-organization in normal and abnormal cognitive development. In A. F. Kalverboer, & A. Gramsbergen (Eds.), *Brain and behavior in human development: A source book*. Dordrecht: Kluwer.

Mischel, W., & Shoda, Y. (1995). A cognitive-affective system theory of personality: Reconceptualizing situations, dispositions, dynamics, and invariance in personality structure. *Psychological Review, 102,* 246–268.

Newell, K. M., & Molenaar, P. C. M. (1998). *Applications of nonlinear dynamics to developmental process modeling*. Mahwah, NJ: Erlbaum.

Nolen-Hoeksema, S., & Morrow, J. (1991). A prospective study of depression and distress following a natural disaster: The 1989 Loma Prieta earthquake. *Journal of Personality and Social Psychology, 61*, 115–121.

Oatley, K., & Johnson-Laird, P. N. (1987). Towards a cognitive theory of emotions. *Cognition and Emotion, 1*, 29–50.

Panksepp, J. (1998). *Affective neuroscience: The foundations of human and animal emotions.* New York: Oxford University Press.

Pascual-Leone, J. (1987). Organismic processes for neo-Piagetian theories: A dialectical causal account of cognitive development. *International Journal of Psychology, 22*, 531–570.

Pascual-Leone, J., & Goodman, D. (1979). Intelligence and experience: A neo-piagetian approach. *Instructional Science, 8*, 301–367.

Piaget, J. (1974/1976). *The grasp of consciousness: Action and concept in the young child.* Cambridge, MA: Harvard University Press. (Originally published 1974.)

Polivy, J. (1998). The effects of behavioral inhibition: Integrating internal cues, cognition, behavior, and affect. *Psychological Inquiry, 9*, 181–204.

Prigogine, I., & Stengers, I. (1984). *Order out of chaos.* New York: Bantam.

Renninger, K. A., Hidi, S., & Krapp, A. (1992). *The role of interest in learning and development.* Hillsdale, NJ: Erlbaum.

Rolls, E. T. (1999). *The brain and emotion.* Oxford: Oxford University Press.

Rothbart, M. K., Ziaie, H., & O'Boyle, C. G. (1992). Self-regulation and emotion in infancy. In N. Eisenberg & R. A. Fabes (Eds.), *New directions for child development, No. 55* (pp. 7–23). San Francisco: Jossey-Bass.

Rumelhart, D. E., Hinton, G. E., & McClelland, J. L. (1986). A general framework for parallel distributed processing. In J. L. McClelland, D. E. Rumelhart, & the PDP Research Group (Eds.), *Parallel distributed processing: Explorations in the microstructure of cognition* (pp. 45–76). Cambridge, MA: MIT Press.

Sameroff, A. J. (1983). Developmental systems: Contexts and evolution. In P. H. Mussen (Series Ed.), & W. Kessen (Vol. Ed.), *Handbook of child psychology, vol. 1* (pp. 237–294). New York: Wiley.

Scheff, T. J. (1987). Creativity and repetition: A theory of the coarse emotions. In J. Rabow, G. Platt, & M. Goldman (Eds.), *Advances in psychoanalytic sociology* (pp. 70–100). Malabor, FL: Krieger.

Scherer, K. R. (2000). Emotions as episodes of subsystem synchronization driven by nonlinear appraisal processes. In M. D. Lewis & I. Granic (Eds.), *Emotion, development, and self-organization: Dynamic systems approaches to emotional development* (pp. 70–99). New York: Cambridge University Press.

Schore, A. N. (1994). *Affect regulation and the origin of the self: The neurobiology of emotional development.* Mahwah, NJ: Erlbaum.

Schore, A. N. (1997). Early organization of the nonlinear right brain and development of a predisposition to psychiatric disorders. *Development and Psychopathology, 9*, 595–631.

Schore, A. N. (2000). The self-organization of the right brain and the neurobiology of emotional development. In M. D. Lewis & I. Granic (Eds.), *Emotion, development, and self-organization: Dynamic systems approaches to emotional development* (pp. 155–185). New York: Cambridge University Press.

Siegler, R. S. (1997). Concepts and methods for studying cognitive change. In E. Amsel & K. A. Renninger (Eds.), *Change and development: Issues of theory, method, and application* (pp. 77–97). Mahwah, NJ: Erlbaum.

Siegler, R. S., & Jenkins, E. (1989). *How children discover new strategies*. Hillsdale, NJ: Erlbaum.

Skarda, C. A., & Freeman, W. J. (1987). How brains make chaos in order to make sense of the world. *Behavioral and Brain Sciences, 10*, 161–195.

Smith, C. A., & Ellsworth, P. C. (1985). Patterns of cognitive appraisal in emotion. *Journal of Personality and Social Psychology, 48*, 813–838.

Teasdale, J. D., & Barnard, P. J. (1993). *Affect, cognition, and change: Re-modelling depressive thought*. Hillsdale, NJ: Erlbaum.

Thelen, E., & Corbetta, D. (this volume). Microdevelopment and dynamic systems: Applications to infant motor development.

Thelen, E., & Smith, L. B. (1994). *A dynamic systems approach to the development of cognition and action*. Cambridge, MA: Bradford/MIT Press.

Thelen, E., & Ulrich, B. D. (1991). Hidden skills: A dynamic systems analysis of treadmill stepping during the first year. *Monographs of the Society for Research in Child Development, 56(1)* (Serial No. 223).

Thompson, R. A. (1991). Emotional regulation and emotional development. *Educational Psychology Review, 3*, 269–307.

Thompson, R. A. (1994). Emotion regulation: A theme in search of definition. In N. A. Fox (Ed.), The development of emotion regulation: Biological and behavioral considerations. *Monographs of the Society for Research in Child Development, 59(2–3)* (Serial No. 240).

Thompson, R. A. (1998). Early sociopersonality development. In W. Damon (Series Ed.), & N. Eisenberg (Vol. Ed.), *Handbook of child psychology, Vol. 3: Social, emotional, and personality development* (5th edn., pp. 25–104). New York: Wiley.

Thorne, A., & Klohnen, E. (1993). Interpersonal memories as maps for personality consistency. In D. C. Funder, R. D. Parke, C. Tomlinson-Keasey, & K. Widaman (Eds.), *Studying lives through time: Personality and development* (pp. 223–253). Washington, DC: American Psychological Association.

Tomkins, S. S. (1984). Affect theory. In K. R. Scherer & P. Ekman (Eds.), *Approaches to emotion* (pp. 163–195). Hillsdale, NJ: Erlbaum.

Tucker, D. M. (1992). Developing emotions and cortical networks. In M. R. Gunnar & C. Nelson (Eds.), *Minnesota symposia on child psychology, Vol. 24: Developmental behavioral neuroscience* (pp. 75–128). Hillsdale, NJ: Erlbaum.

Vallacher, R. R., & Nowak, A. (1997). The emergence of dynamical social psychology. *Psychological Inquiry, 8*, 73–99.

van der Maas, H. L. J. (1998). The dynamical and statistical properties of cognitive strategies: Relations between strategies, attractors, and latent classes. In K. M. Newell & P. C. M. Molenaar (Eds.), *Applications of nonlinear dynamics to developmental process modeling* (pp. 161–176). Mahwah, NJ: Erlbaum.

van der Maas, H. L. J., & Molenaar, P. C. M. (1992). Stagewise cognitive development: An application of catastrophe theory. *Psychological Review, 99*, 395–417.

van Geert, P. (1991). A dynamic systems model of cognitive and language growth. *Psychological Review, 98*, 3–53.

van Geert, P. (1994). *Dynamic systems of development: Change between complexity and chaos*. New York: Prentice Hall/Harvester Wheatsheaf.

van Geert, P. (1995). Dimensions of change: A semantic and mathematical analysis of learning and development. *Human Development, 38,* 322–331.

van Geert, P. (this volume). Developmental dynamics, intentional action, and fuzzy sets.

van Gelder, T., & Port, R. F. (1995). It's about time: An overview of the dynamical approach to cognition. In R. F. Port & T. van Gelder (Eds.), *Mind as motion: Explorations in the dynamics of cognition* (pp. 1–43). Cambridge, MA: MIT Press.

8 How microdevelopment creates macrodevelopment: Reiterated sequences, backward transitions, and the Zone of Current Development

Nira Granott

What creates development? This question has intrigued researchers for centuries. Traditional cross-sectional and longitudinal methods, which compare abilities at specific points in time, capture global developmental trends. However, these methods cannot explain how development occurs, because the mechanisms and patterns that underlie development are manifested in the developmental *process,* not at single points in time. By contrast, on-line activity within context can capture transitions and change. On-line activity that evolves is called microdevelopment – i.e., development during short time spans (usually ranging from minutes and hours to weeks or a few months). By giving access to the developmental process, analysis of microdevelopment can identify developmental patterns that suggest how development occurs.

This chapter describes a developmental model that relates micro- and macrodevelopment. The model suggests that development evolves through reiterated microdevelopmental sequences (Granott, 1993a). Each sequence develops within a specific context. Three types of variability operate within and across sequences. (1) *Backward transitions* that form temporary regressions followed by progress. (2) *Ordered fluctuations,* bounded within a developmental range – a Zone of Current Development (ZCD). (3) *Reiteration* of processes. The three processes have several functions that promote developmental progress. The attributes of the model are demonstrated by a study on the microdevelopment of adults' scientific inquiry.

The author thanks Edith Ackermann, Kurt Fischer, Sheldon White, Seymour Papert, Jim Parziale, Paul van Geert, Esther Dromi, Larry Cauller, and Richard Golden for their feedback and contribution to earlier versions of these ideas. Writing of this chapter was supported by National Science Foundation (Grant SBR-9818959), Texas Higher Education Coordination Board TARP grant, Timberlawn Psychiatric Research Foundation grant, and University of Texas at Dallas. The work reported here was also supported by the Media Laboratory at Massachusetts Institute of Technology, LEGO Systems A/S, and the National Science Foundation (Grant #851031-0195).

Process-oriented approaches: A new view of development

Most developmental theories describe development as a series of stages, each building on the achievements of previous ones. Traditional theories link stages to age. Within a stage, the underlying abilities are considered as even. Variability in performance is treated as "noise" caused by measurement errors.

By contrast, researchers who adopt a process-oriented approach view variability as a characteristic developmental attribute. Variability is a most prominent finding in a multitude of studies that use diverse tasks in different content areas, and is considered as an inherent part of change (Miller & Coyle, 1999). It appears in different aspects of activities. For example, Miller and Coyle indicate that variability appears not only in strategy production, but also in its effectiveness. Coyle & Bjorklund (1997) suggest that variability is the rule rather than the exception: children use a mixture of recall strategies over trials and they often change the combination of strategies that they use. Van Geert (1997) points out that short-term fluctuations and the effect of control variables on long-term development depend on the developmental level, and midterm fluctuations are a genuine property of performance. A person-in-context has a range of scores, with different degrees of characteristicness (different values on a characteristic variable; see van Geert, this volume). Thelen & Smith (1994) maintain that variability is a source of adaptive forms in development. Variability in developmental aspects is not incidental, but is part of a larger self-organization. For example, transitions in interlimb coordination often match transitions in the development of new postural milestones (Thelen & Corbetta, this volume). Siegler (1996, this volume) suggests that development proceeds as a series of overlapping waves, representing different ways of thinking. Changes in the distribution of waves explain developmental progress. Goldin-Meadow and colleagues (e.g., 1993) show that during transitional periods, there are mismatches between information conveyed in gesture and in speech. Fischer & Bidell (1998) attribute variability to differences between high- and low-support supplied by the social environment. Kuhn (this volume) highlights variability in a meta-level of operation as the locus of most developmental change. Miller & Coyle (1999) indicate that variability does not only characterize transitional states in children's development, but rather seems to be a general characteristic of human behavior, prevailing within a person as well as between persons.

Variability is also found in the levels on which people operate at a given period of time (see Granott, Fischer, and Parziale, this volume). Several researchers found that people function simultaneously on different levels in relation to different variables. For example, Siegler (1996, this volume) shows that children use different strategies, some more developed than others, at the same session and even in relation to the same problem. Kuhn (this volume) finds similar variability in strategy use. Coyle & Bjorklund (1997) find that children use multiple recall strategies even within each trial. Goldin-Meadow finds that different knowledge is expressed simultaneously in gesture and in speech (e.g., Goldin-Meadow & Alibali, this volume). Thelen and colleagues (e.g., Thelen & Smith, 1994; Thelen & Corbetta, this volume) show differences in the development of different indicators, like infant kicking, stepping, or reaching, at the same period of time. Granott (1993a) suggests that knowledge structures coexist. At the same period, a person may use different knowledge structures in relation to different aspects of a task. Variability, then, is found across ages, in different domains, contents, and tasks. Altogether, the shifting view about variability is so substantial that several researchers regard it as a paradigm shift (Granott, 1998c; Lee & Karmiloff-Smith, this volume; Thelen & Smith, 1994).

The model presented in this chapter highlights the developmental functions of variability. According to the model, variability is not only a prevalent and characteristic developmental attribute: variability within and across microdevelopmental sequences creates progress in macrodevelopment.

A microdevelopment model of progress and change

The model presented here focuses on the microdevelopment of thinking and discovery that evolves in relation to complex problems. Discovery, Klahr (2000) suggests, involves diverse processes related in a hierarchical structure that encompasses search hypothesis space, test hypothesis space, and evidence evaluation (see Klahr's model of Scientific Discovery as a Dual Search, or SDDS). When a problem is complex, additional spaces may involve selecting which data to encode, how to represent the data, and how to analyze the observations. Participants' behavior may deviate from rational, logical inferences: they may abandon confirmed hypotheses and maintain disconfirmed ones (ibid., pp. 201–215). The model presented in this chapter analyzes the microdevelopment of such processes that involve complex problems and often do not seem logical.

An underlying assumption of the model, which is supported by the findings reviewed earlier, is that knowledge structures coexist. If at the same period of time a person may operate on substantially different levels in relation to different developmental variables, the analysis should differentiate between developmental variables. It should focus on each developmental variable separately, disregarding the developmental levels that the same person may exhibit at the same time in relation to other variables. Therefore, the model focuses on change in a specific variable during microdevelopment.

It is suggested that development evolves through a series of microdevelopmental sequences, each defined for a specific developmental variable. When people encounter an unfamiliar or a difficult problem, they often start processing the problem at a level lower than the developmental levels they exhibit when solving familiar or easy problems. Such a backward transition to lower levels usually marks a beginning of a new microdevelopmental process, related to that specific problem. As people continue to solve the problem, they use higher levels and their microdevelopment shows progress. Progress is rarely smooth and unidirectional: it shows much variability within a developmental range and reiterative construction of higher and lower knowledge levels. A series of microdevelopmental sequences creates generalization and transfer of knowledge across contents and domains, while making knowledge more robust and valid within specific content areas. Different types of variability operate in microdevelopment and have an important role for stimulating and supporting progress (Granott, submitted). These processes operate at all ages.

Types of variability within and across sequences

A *microdevelopmental sequence* is a set of successive values of a developmental variable that undergoes change during an activity in context. The values of the developmental variable reflect developmental levels. A level is the smallest unit that shows increased ability as measured according to a developmental theory. In short-term development, some sequences have a trend of growth (although not all sequences; see Granott, 1998a). These sequences evolve in relation to the corresponding variable, whereas other variables may neither change nor show a different pattern of change. Although a sequence is defined per a specific aspect of an activity in context, it is suggested that these processes prevail across contexts, contents, tasks, and domains.

A sequence with a trend of growth represents developmental progress, yet even a progressive sequence consists of different types of variability, clustered into three main types: backward transitions, ordered fluctuations within a developmental range, and reiteration.

1. Backward transitions and progress Microdevelopmental sequences often include backward transitions, with regressions to lower developmental levels that are followed by progress (Granott, 1991a, 1993a, 1994a). The regressions may appear only in the developmental variable for which the sequence is defined. The extent of backward transitions and subsequent progress depends on the social and task contexts and on the person's abilities in other domains and tasks. There are three types of backward transitions.

(a) Initial backward transitions. When people at all ages encounter a new, somewhat unfamiliar task, they often cannot immediately start processing the task at their highest developmental levels. Their highest levels are the most demanding and are based on reorganization of lower-level structures. If the task is not immediately understood, lower levels have to be reconstructed within the context of the task before people can construct higher levels within that context. Therefore, first they regress to adapt their knowledge structures to the task's attributes and process the task through lower levels. This backward transition refers only to a specific variable (e.g., understanding the problem). At the same time the person uses high levels of knowledge in relation to other aspects of the task (e.g., social interaction, communication skills, strategies of scientific inquiry) and other tasks. Backward transition to lower levels makes the task more intuitively interpretable and facilitates further progress. For example, Karmiloff-Smith & Inhelder (1974) asked children to balance blocks with asymmetric weight distribution. Younger children (eighteen to thirty-nine months) pressed with a finger on the blocks' point of contact. Older children (four to six years) started with regression (backward transition) and began their exploration in a similar way, which gave them sensorimotor feedback about the blocks' attributes. Then, they progressed to more successful strategies.

More unfamiliar and complex tasks generate a stronger initial regression to allow processing the problem, which cannot be processed at as high levels as simpler and familiar tasks. Help and explanations from others (e.g., parents, teachers, or experts) may minimize the extent of initial regressions. An explanation can clarify the task, make it more easily understood, and allow processing it through higher levels of knowledge during the following progress.

Initial backward transitions are not rare. In experiments, they often cause researchers to use an initial warm-up period to familiarize participants with the experimental task.

Subjective experiences and the "eye of the beholder." Regressions often occur because of subjective rather than objective difficulties. Familiarity of a problem is in the "eye of the beholder." A problem may seem unfamiliar to one and familiar to another, especially when one attunes to surface rather than structural similarities (e.g., Chi, Feltovich, & Glaser, 1981). The difficulty of a task may vary for different people or even for the same person at different times. Backward transitions reflect the subjective way a person perceives a task, not its objective analysis.

(b) Intermediate backward transitions embedded within progress. After an initial regression, progress is not smooth. Backward transitions are evident even within a process with an average growth. Sometimes intermediate regressions are triggered by difficult external conditions. Often, however, intermediate backward transitions reflect neither objective difficulties nor incidental occurrences, but an internal reorganization of knowledge. Intermediate regressions, which occur within progressive processes, are often characterized by regrouping, interrelating disconnected knowledge, processing new information, or developing new interpretations. These backward transitions enable further progress.

Backward transitions occur on the verge of new discoveries either within the task context or in other domains or developmental variables. The pending breakthrough demands much of the person's mental and emotional resources and therefore causes a temporary backward transition. This backward transition is apparent before major progress: it precedes and prepares for change and predicts a spurt of growth.

Backward transition may occur also when the problem conditions change and the solution becomes more challenging. The change may require regression to assist in processing the problem. Sometimes, new interpretations may lead to wrong solutions. Then, progress depends on backward transitions, returning to interpretations that appeared earlier. Intermediate backward transitions are prevalent in development. They appear at any age, in many developmental processes characterized by a U-shape curve (Strauss, 1982).

(c) Backward transitions after leaps forward. When excessive leaps are premature and not supported by current understanding, they destabilize knowledge (Granott, submitted). Because the corresponding observations cannot be interpreted, the leap may result in questioning previous interpretations. Therefore, backward transition often follows, facilitating the comparison of prior and new understanding, and raising interpretations that reconcile old and new perspectives. Mild leaps precede mild backward transitions, whereas extreme leaps may require extreme regressions to re-establish understanding.

The functions of backward transitions. Backward transitions are not incidental: they serve several fundamental functions (Granott, 1992, 1993a). (1) Creating access to new problems or domains: Construction of lower developmental levels facilitates processing an unfamiliar task and enables development in an area where knowledge is missing. (2) Stimulating progress: When lower-level structures are constructed through initial backward transition, they can support further understanding and development. (3) Enabling developmental breakthroughs: Backward transitions free capacity for a pending discovery, thereby enabling a highly demanding breakthrough. (4) Re-stabilizing knowledge: When excessive leaps destabilize understanding, backward transitions can amend the setback. Regressions test the context of leaps in relation to prior understanding through simpler structures, thereby re-stabilizing knowledge. (5) Validating knowledge: Backward transitions reexamine prior observations and interpretations, validating or modifying previously constructed knowledge.

Development never occurs as a continual progress without backward transitions. Steps forward and backward allow alternation of effort and rest, progress and stability, wild guesses and testing.

2. Ordered fluctuations within a shifting developmental range: The Zone of Current Development Progressions and regressions cause substantial variability. However, within a microdevelopmental sequence, variability is bounded within a developmental range (see van Geert, this volume). For example, a three-year-old who tries to balance blocks usually uses strategies that fluctuate over a range of developmental levels. Across time, a sequence can be viewed as a moving window that covers a range of developmental levels. The moving window represents the order in variability. In progressive sequences, the window shifts from lower to higher levels across time (see figure 8.1).

I labeled the developmental range "the Zone of Current Development," or ZCD (Granott, 1993a, 1994b, 1995), in tribute to Vygotsky's (1978) Zone of Proximal Development (ZPD). Vygotsky defines the ZPD as the distance between the actual (current) developmental level, as determined by the child's abilities when operating independently, and potential development expected in the near future, as determined by the child's abilities when guided by an adult. The ZCD is a range of *current* developmental levels – a range in which a person operates in a given sequence, at a given period of time and context. The ZCD indicates the focus of current developmental efforts. The width of the ZCD may vary. Fluctuations downward create its lower bound, and upward – its upper bound. Variability within the microdevelopmental sequence, then, creates and determines the attributes of the ZCD.

A special type of ordered fluctuations is the mechanism of bridging (Granott, 1992, 1993a, Granott, Fischer, & Parziale, this volume;

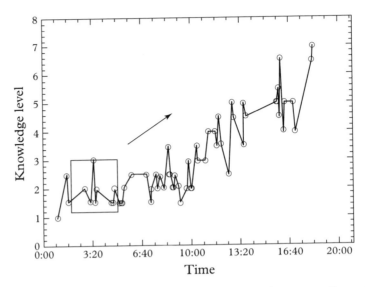

Figure 8.1 Ordered fluctuations within a bounded range – a Zone of Current Development (ZCD): Microdevelopmental progress as a moving window that shifts up across time.

Parziale, this volume; see the analysis of bridging in creating breakthroughs in high-level thinking in Fischer & Yan, this volume). Bridging encompasses lower and higher levels, linking current knowledge and future target structures. In a systematic way that is common to several bridging forms, bridging constructs shells that outline missing knowledge and incorporates different levels.

The functions of ordered fluctuations. Ordered fluctuations within a bounded range have several important functions. (1) Creating a focused developmental effort: Fluctuations within a range of levels put these levels at center stage and create a focus for current knowledge construction. (2) Making knowledge more flexible and amenable to change: Fluctuations across knowledge levels prevent knowledge from being "stuck" at a given level, bound to a single perspective, or limited to one interpretation. (3) Reinforcing and strengthening knowledge: Fluctuations strengthen new knowledge by anchoring it to previous understanding. (4) Stimulating progress: While downward fluctuations anchor knowledge, upward fluctuations reach up to higher levels and pave the way for progress.

3. Reiteration The construction of knowledge in development is a reiterative process. For example, a child who tries to balance blocks does not do it once or twice, but several times. Reiteration occurs at all ages. As a basic developmental mechanism, reiteration appears from early age: circular reactions (Baldwin, 1894/1968; Piaget, 1952) are examples of reiterations during infancy (Granott, 1993a). Reiteration operates in four ways.

(a) Reiterated construction of a specific level. One way in which microdevelopment is constructed is by reiterating activities at each developmental level. An activity can be repeated as is or with some modifications. People reconstruct each level over and over, often in relation to changing conditions, slight variations in the problem, and while attending to different aspects of the situation.

(b) Reiterated patterns within segments. The microdevelopmental process reiterates itself not only at single levels but also as patterns of fluctuations across levels. A single sequence can be parsed into segments with similar patterns. Different analyses may show different patterns (Granott, 1998c, Baron & Granott, submitted).

(c) Reiterated fluctuations along the ZCD. Fluctuations are also reiterated along a sequence. Up-and-down shifts repeatedly appear within the ZCD. In the ZCD shifting developmental range, these fluctuations are reiterated over and over.

(d) Reiteration of sequences. A microdevelopmental sequence is context-specific. An unfamiliar content, a difficult task, or a new domain may trigger a new sequence. When people change their activity, if the problem becomes too difficult, they regress to lower levels in order to start processing the problem before continuing to progress. Changes in the problem parameters, such as its definition, materials, or goals, can create new sequences that restart with backward transitions and reiterate the sequence. While slight changes can be integrated within ongoing explorations in the current sequence, major changes trigger a new sequence.

Reiteration across people. In social contexts, reiterations can occur across individuals. Interacting partners repeat each other's actions and statements (Granott, 1993b). Clearly, these reiterations give social support, but they also have an important developmental function. For example, by reiterating a partner's statement, a person reconstructs and internalizes the knowledge just constructed by the partner (Granott, 1996). This process occurs across ages, developmental levels, and degrees of asymmetry in knowledge and expertise. It appears in interactions among peers with similar knowledge, or with a more capable partner, as in parent–child or expert–novice interaction.

The functions of reiteration. Reiterations have several important functions. (1) Generalizing and expanding knowledge: During reiterations, processes are often repeated with some modifications, giving an opportunity to reprocess different aspects of the task. Variations generalize and broaden the newly constructed knowledge. (2) Making knowledge more cohesive: Reiterating the construction of specific levels over and over turns knowledge into an interrelated whole. (3) Strengthening knowledge: Reiterations reinforce knowledge construction by repeating it over and over. Reiterations strengthen knowledge just as several seams at about the same place strengthen the connection between two pieces of cloth sewn together. (4) Testing and re-testing knowledge: Reiterations of activities weed out random occurrences. They can confirm previous understanding or refute it while leading to alternative interpretations.

Backward transitions, ordered fluctuations, and reiterations prevail within and between people. When people co-construct knowledge together, they share with each other backward transitions, ordered fluctuations, and reiterations, thereby aligning their microdevelopmental sequences with each other and operating at the same developmental range. In this way, the three types of variability also assist co-development in social context (Granott, 1998b, 1999).

Interrelations between micro- and macrodevelopment

Following backward transitions to simpler processing modes, new structures are constructed on the basis of the initial structures, and development can take off. It is suggested that the following progress has some similarity with the microdevelopmental sequence, because the same underlying mechanisms operate on both scales. The initial structures that develop during backward transition are interrelated and self-organized into increasingly higher structures through the same developmental mechanisms that operate in macrodevelopment. As in fractals, such a process can create similar patterns across scales (Granott, 1993a, in preparation). Therefore, after backward transition, when the sequence progresses, its microdevelopment creates patterns similar to those that appear in macrodevelopment.

It is important to underscore the assumption that knowledge structures coexist. At the same time, a person may operate on different levels in relation to different developmental indicators. Backward transitions in a microdevelopmental sequence and its similar patterns with macrodevelopment refer only to the specific developmental indicator for which the sequence is defined. While people may regress in relation to a specific variable, their other abilities, skills, and behavior may remain intact or even show progress.

Several factors influence the way a microdevelopmental sequence progresses. One is the person's highest macrodevelopmental level in relation to other tasks and contexts. This developmental level, which varies with age, can be defined as the current highest microdevelopmental level a person uses in any context and domain. The highest macrodevelopmental level sets a temporary upper bound on microdevelopmental sequences within specific contexts. On the other hand, during microdevelopment, discoveries can break through this upper bound and extend the highest macrodevelopmental level upward.

Contextual attributes influence the progress that follows initial backward transitions in microdevelopment, as they do in macrodevelopment. Social environments give feedback that can facilitate progress. Similarly, physical environments give directive feedback through experimentation with the task materials (see for example Parziale, this volume). When social and physical environments are rich and stimulating, easily accessible, allowing diverse activities, and do not constrain the person's agency and initiative, they promote microdevelopmental progress (Granott, 1998a).

At the same period of time, a person may construct different microdevelopmental sequences in relation to different domains, social contexts, tasks, and aspects of a task. These domains, contexts, tasks, and aspects may have different degrees of difficulty and unfamiliarity. Therefore, the corresponding sequences may have diverse shapes, with different backward transitions (initial, intermediate, or following leaps) and progress, ZCDs, and reiteration.

In the next part of the chapter, several attributes of the model are demonstrated in a study on adults' microdevelopment. Initial findings confirm the predictions of the model also when using other methods of analysis (Baron & Granott, submitted), different developmental variables (Granott, under review), during microdevelopment related to a different task (Granott & Baron, 2001), and in the microdevelopment of developmentally delayed children (Greenwald & Granott, in preparation).

Attributes of the microdevelopment model in a study of robotic "wuggles"

In a study on collaborative problem-solving and scientific inquiry, graduate students were asked to discover and explain the operation of unfamiliar Lego robots nicknamed "wuggles" (Granott, 1993a, 1998a). There were a few variations of the wuggles, with different combinations of sensors and logic bricks, reacting to light, sound, and touch with different movement patterns. The participants explored the robots collaboratively as groups or ensembles that co-construct knowledge together (Granott, 1998b). Ensembles changed in size as the participants moved freely from one group and robot to another. Within each ensemble, partners spontaneously shared their observations, thoughts, and understanding while co-constructing their knowledge.

The ensembles' conversations provided rich data about processes of development and change. Continuous video and audio recording documented all the activities in their entirely. Conversations were analyzed by using Fischer's (1980) skill theory. In the study, the formal definitions of levels from skill theory were applied to the specific context of the robots (see appendix). In addition to identifying skill levels, the continuous documentation allowed the discovery of bridging – a transition mechanism that creates progress to higher levels (Granott, 1993a, 1994b; Granott, Fischer, & Parziale, this volume). To analyze the microdevelopment of the participants' understanding, their collaborative discourse was transcribed. Statements related to understanding the robots were analyzed and coded according to their skill level. The latter formed a scale of knowledge levels related to the specific context of the robots. The sequence of knowledge levels, indicated by the participants' statements, was analyzed and then plotted across time.

Variability – incidence or systematic pattern? Backward transitions, ordered fluctuations, and reiterations

The study tests whether variability is incidental and reflects measurement errors, as treated in traditional methodology, or whether it has the functions and attributes described by the microdevelopmental model. Specifically, in contrast with incidental variability, does variability show backward transitions, ordered fluctuations, and reiterations?

Initial backward transition At the beginning of the study, Ann and Donald explored a wuggle that responded to sound with a complex sequence of movements. Although they noticed changes in the wuggle's movement, the changes were not clear at first. They referred to the robot's movement in an implicit, vague, and undefined way (e.g., "this one is doing what it was doing"). By the same token, it was not immediately obvious what had triggered the changes (e.g., "I tried to experiment with if it would [...] react if it's hitting the ... Let's see, if it started up here ..."). Ann and Donald did not differentiate between attributes of the object and their own action on it (e.g., mistakenly inferring "now I've broken it, hmm"). They did not describe actions that affected the robot (e.g., "Oh! What – why. That's the o– that's what I was ..."). With some practice, Ann and Donald did control the robot's movement in a sensorimotor way by touching its sensor or clapping, without understanding how it functioned or whether it responded to sound or touch. The ensemble

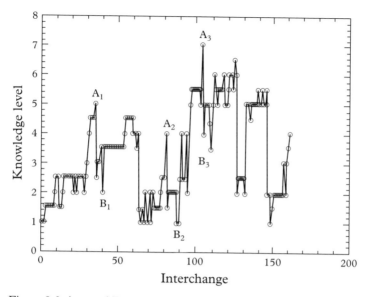

Figure 8.2 Ann and Donald's activity: Incidental variability and insubstantial progress?

started co-constructing their knowledge about the robot through an initial backward transition, regressing to levels 1–2, which parallel skills that usually appear in early development (see figure 8.2). While their understanding of the wuggle indicated such low levels, they clearly exhibited high abilities in every other aspect of the activity. They showed advanced scientific inquiry skills, like isolating variables when dealing with a complex problem; they used high representations and abstractions in their communication skills, and they exhibited highly sophisticated social skills (Granott, 1993a, 1998a; Fischer & Granott, 1995). Within the activity, then, the microdevelopmental sequence that was defined for the specific aspect of understanding the robot's functioning started with substantial backward transition.

Negligible progress, disorder, and incidental variability? Even though the process started with backward transition, without systematicity in the process the initial backward transition might have been incidental. Therefore, next, the attributes of variability following the initial backward transition are analyzed.

Ann and Donald's microdevelopment consisted of much variability and up-and-down fluctuations: peaks preceded troughs, which preceded other peaks, and so forth (e.g., A_1, B_1, A_2, B_2, A_3, B_3 in figure 8.2).

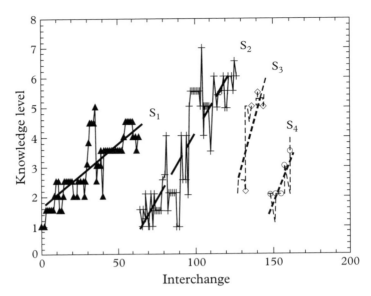

Figure 8.3 Reiteration of sequences in Ann and Donald's activity: Each sequence involved a change in the problem's parameters and started with an initial backward transition.

Moreover, there was not much progress during their microdevelopment (an autoregressive analysis indicates a negligible rate of growth; $b = 0.012$; $SSE = 323.6$; $R^2 = 0.85$).[1] Their microdevelopment seems to be disappointing and consist of substantial measurement errors. Was there indeed no progress in the ensemble's understanding of the robot?

Order and progress: Reiteration of microdevelopmental sequences An in-depth analysis of Ann and Donald's activity indicated that the ensemble redefined the problem several times, reiterating their microdevelopmental sequences. The activity presented in figure 8.2 actually consisted of four different microdevelopmental sequences, each related to a new variant of the problem (see figure 8.3).

In the first sequence (sequence S_1), Ann and Donald started exploring their robot. As their explorations continued, they identified that the robot responded to sound and defined its movement (e.g., "its regular thing is clockwise, and its stopping thing is counterclockwise"). They developed advanced understanding of the sounds it responded to (e.g., "it's a sharp

---

[1] Skill levels are treated as a quantitative measure (interval/ratio scale). See Cohen & Cohen, 1983.

[sound] of either the clapping and the snapping, it's more sharp noise, right? I'm talking pretty loudly here, right, and it's not, and there's background noise and it's not picking that up at all"). They also started to explore the way the sensor functioned. Then, they disconnected one of the robot's wires and inadvertently connected it differently. The robot's pattern of movement changed, and the ensemble faced a new, unfamiliar pattern that created a new problem. This triggered a new sequence (S_2), in which Ann and Donald were trying to understand the new pattern. Again they started by vague reference to the movement (e.g., "the thing is schizophrenic") and without identifying the causes ("I wonder what we're doing to it"). And, as earlier, they continued by constructing higher-level understanding (e.g., Donald: "these are probably two separate, ah, gears, and ..." / Ann: "and the sensor is telling you which switch ... is setting it to"). Later, they decided to write notes and summarize their understanding. The new goal redefined the process and, again, created a new sequence (S_3) that started from lower and evolved to higher levels. Still later, the ensemble rewired the robot. They thought they reinstated the previous wire connection, but the robot again started to "behave" differently. The unfamiliar pattern created yet a new problem and triggered a new sequence (S_4). The fourth sequence stopped when another participant joined and asked them about the robot's operation. The question generated yet another sequence for the new ensemble (not presented in the figure). Microanalysis of the ensemble's activity shows, then, that when the parameters of the problem changed, the ensemble started a new sequence. Through reiterated sequences, they generalized their knowledge across the changing context.

Each sequence started with initial backward transition and continued with progress. While the analysis of the whole activity indicated insubstantial progress and much variability, each of the four sequences in figure 8.3 showed a high rate of growth and lower variability ($b_1 = 0.047; b_2 = 0.09; b_3 = 0.184; b_4 = 0.136; SSE = 84.7, R^2 = 0.96$). The accelerated progress that followed initial backward transitions could be detected only by identifying sequences within the activity. Without differentiating between microdevelopmental sequences, the analysis would have erroneously indicated that the ensemble made almost no progress. In contrast, distinction between the sequences showed remarkable progress in their microdevelopment. Parsing an activity into microdevelopmental sequences is a crucial step and, if skipped, may fundamentally bias the results (Granott, 1995).

Although parsing the activity into sequences reduced variability, there was still much variability in each sequence (see figure 8.3). What was the reason for this variability? Why did Ann and Donald not focus on one knowledge level at a time and progress to a higher level only after establishing its predecessor?

Why variability? Reiteration within and across levels Even after making a discovery, often Ann and Donald were still puzzled. They tested and sometimes doubted their discovery, tried alternative explanations, and made rediscoveries before establishing their knowledge. During the process of discoveries and rediscoveries, they often repeatedly constructed the same level. They also reiterated a pattern of up-and-down fluctuations, making both lower-level statements and higher-level distinctions (Granott, 1995). Why did they do it?

When Ann and Donald tried to discover the causality underlying the robot's movement, they had to find out which factors (e.g., claps, touch, bouncing against a box, light) were relevant and affected the robot and which were not. They reiterated their activities in order to make these distinctions. Moreover, even when they repeated an action under the same conditions, their conversation indicated that often they paid attention to different aspects of the problem. Correspondingly, they changed their way of thinking about the problem. Repeated trials often generated up-and-down fluctuations across different levels of knowledge related to different aspects of the problem.

The conditions under which Ann and Donald explored the robot changed too, either when the robot changed its location, or when environmental stimuli changed. Sometimes, previous observations supported their understanding and facilitated progress to higher levels. At other times, they encountered difficulties in explaining ongoing observations and had to rework their understanding at the same level in relation to the changing occurrences. Occasionally they suggested alternative hypotheses, which did not hold (e.g., "So, you don't think it's where the noise comes from"). They raised vague interpretations ("I mean, I don't know ..., all I'm saying is that it just changes directions, where it stops, and then that puts, that sets it up in a different position to start the next time") – which eventually were replaced by rediscoveries. Therefore, reiterating the construction of knowledge levels often required careful reconstruction at a similar level as well as up-and-down fluctuations, constructing anew lower and higher levels.

An example from the activity of another ensemble, Marvin and Kevin, demonstrates the necessity of reconstructing knowledge at a specific level, as well as reiterating the up-and-down fluctuations within a segment. Marvin and Kevin explored a robot that responded to light. Having discovered a causal relation between shadow and a change in the robot's "behavior," the ensemble had difficulty in reassessing the causality when the robot was in a different location. Although they changed light-and-shadow conditions around the robot, they could not make it move. They redirected lamps near the robot and flashed light on it with a flashlight, but the robot did not respond, which they could not understand ("So what happened?"). Since there were several environmental conditions that operated on the robot simultaneously (e.g., several light and shadow sources in its proximity), sometimes they misidentified the condition that triggered the robot's response. For example, the robot did not respond to a shadow from a notebook they were holding above it. This puzzled them too ("what happens here?"). But as the conditions changed (one of them moved away), they found the reason: "Oh, my shadow did it."

While noticing new stimuli or observing new responses with unknown causality, Marvin and Kevin's statements showed lower levels of knowledge. At the same time, statements that related to previously identified causal relations indicated higher knowledge levels. For example, they differentiated between the effects of various light sources (e.g., a flashlight versus an ambient light), different shadows (like shadows made by different objects or their own shadows), diverse actions ("if you follow it in a certain direction ..."; "but if you did it this way ..."), and different types of robot movements ("that's a sort of bouncing back and forth").

The variability in the ensemble's knowledge levels could not be explained away by variability in the occurrences (i.e., a task analysis with a scale of task complexity). For example, an obvious factor like one's shadow (when shadow had been discovered as a factor many statements previously) created a setback. On the other hand, in a previous similar study (Granott, 1991b, 1993a), a complex response like fast oscillation on a shadow edge triggered an initial discovery in another ensemble. Yet that ensemble continued to explore simpler conditions long after their discovery.

By contrast, the detailed microgenetic examination of the ensemble's actions and conversations did shed light on the reasons for variability. It indicated that variability reflected meaningful struggle to understand the observed phenomena. Variability represented genuine fluctuations in the level of understanding the robots' functioning. The constructed levels fluctuated up and down in direct relation with new observations, new questions, and even with a need to reconstruct knowledge in relation to the same observations and questions. Variability across knowledge levels was an inherent part of the developmental process. Focusing on different aspects of the problem, the changing conditions, previously identified factors, or newly discovered aspects created variability. Knowledge

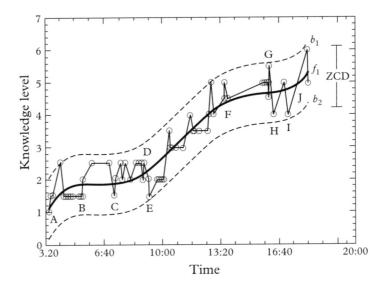

Figure 8.4 Ordered fluctuations: The ZCD in Marvin and Kevin's activity.

previously gained seemed to be lost and reconstructed anew over and over, sometimes with subtle variations, under different conditions, in relation to various questions, or with attention to different details. These fluctuations across levels did not reflect objective task difficulties, but inherent attributes of the knowledge-construction process.

Ordered fluctuations and the Zone of Current Development Although there was much variability within the microdevelopmental sequences, there was order in the variability. During the ensembles' microdevelopment, knowledge levels did not fluctuate across all possible levels. Instead, the fluctuations were bounded: at a given time, knowledge levels tended to fluctuate within a Zone of Current Development.

Figure 8.4 demonstrates the ZCD in Marvin and Kevin's activity. In the figure, a line connecting the data points represents the microdevelopmental sequence. A fifth-order polynomial (f_1) shows the progression of the microdevelopmental sequence. The broken lines b_1 and b_2 mark the ZCD around f_1 (at a range of $\pm \alpha$ around f_1).[2] While the ensemble's statements indicated substantial fluctuations, these fluctuations were contained within the ZCD range.

[2] In this sequence, $\alpha = 0.625$ SD at each side of f_1, the standard deviation computed by collapsing the five sequences.

Marvin and Kevin's activity demonstrates the functions of reiterations within the ZCD. Reiterations within a range of levels helped the ensemble focus on these levels and establish them. For example, after starting the sequence with a level 1 statement, the ensemble's activity consisted of fluctuations between levels 1.5 and 2.5 (segment AE). The fluctuations focused on and evolved around level 2. Knowledge became more flexible by repeated variation of these levels and reiteration of bridging levels (1.5, 2.5). The fluctuations reinforced level 2 by anchoring it to level 1.5 and facilitated progress to level 3 by generating bridging transitions (level 2.5). The strong setting from below and above established level 2 and created robust knowledge that supported accelerated progress (segment EF). This progress, too, focused on a specific range and included fluctuations that anchored the newly constructed knowledge from below and above.

Reiterated patterns within segments Marvin and Kevin's microdevelopmental sequence evolved through repeated up-and-down fluctuations, creating reiterated patterns within segments of the microdevelopmental sequence. Sometimes, the progression–regression pattern appeared within a given range and created an overall plateau in the ZCD (e.g., in segments BC, FG). At other times, the fluctuations created parts with accelerated growth within the ZCD (segments AB, EF, IJ).

Intermediate backward transitions Although the ZCD had a general trend of growth, it also included intermediate backward transitions. Segments DE and GH demonstrated such regressions. Both segments appeared toward the end of a plateau and preceded an accelerated growth in the ZCD. At E, the ensemble declared a vague intention, indicating a lower level than they had stated for a while. This statement directed further exploration and, in this sense, reorganized their activity and thinking. Through their subsequent exploration, the ensemble increasingly constructed higher levels in an accelerated progress (segment EF). At points H, I the ensemble tried a new variant of the hypothesis, about which they had not constructed prior knowledge. The suggestion, which was discarded, also created an intermediate backward transition to a lower level. This hypothesis was replaced by reassessment of prior knowledge and led to further progress. The last example demonstrates backward transition that did not lead to fruitful discovery. Instead, subsequent progress was based on returning to prior interpretations.

Micro- and macrodevelopment: Reiterated patterns across developmental scales The stepwise progression, which is typical to development

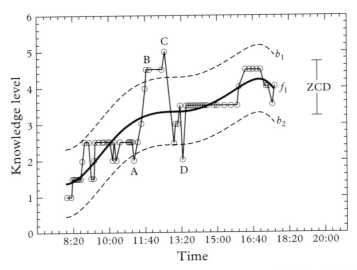

Figure 8.5 Ann and Donald break through their ZCD: A stabilizing backward transition following an exaggerated leap.

across the life span according to stage theories, appeared in Kevin and Marvin's sequence. In the ensemble's microdevelopment, the ZCD had the shape of a step function, creating a pattern similar to macrodevelopment.

Ann and Donald's sequences, too, paralleled the macrodevelopmental sequence (see figures 8.3, 8.5). In each sequence, their microdevelopment started at levels 1 or 2 and progressed to relatively high levels. When changes in the parameters of the problem created a new microdevelopmental sequence, they reiterated the knowledge-construction process through a pattern similar to the macrodevelopmental sequence.

When progressing fast is too fast: Breaking through the ZCD and intermediate backward transitions Ann and Donald's sequences demonstrated fast growth. However, fast progress may be too fast. Figure 8.5 presents Ann and Donald's first sequence (which appears as S_1 in figure 8.3). The ZCD delineates the same α range as in figure 8.4 around a fifth-order polynomial (f_1). The section around points B, C indicates an extreme upward shift, exceeding the ZCD. Ann and Donald "jumped to conclusions" and made a leap that was not supported by their understanding at the time. The leap destabilized their knowledge; they doubted their initial interpretation of the causality underlying the wuggle's movement.

Intermediate backward transition appears both before and after the leap, at points A, D, correspondingly. Point A shows intermediate backward transition that accompanies scarce capacity while preparing for a change. Point D presents backward transition that follows a destabilizing leap. At D, the ensemble wondered and re-tested whether the robot indeed responded to sound ("Is it reacting to the voice at all?"), a level 2 they had established much earlier. This intermediate backward transition helped them re-stabilize their knowledge. Having established again that the robot responded to sound, the ensemble continued their progress.

A similar phenomenon – big leaps unsubstantiated by current understanding – appeared twice again in Ann and Donald's explorations (figure 8.2, points A_2 and A_3) and on both occasions triggered substantial intermediate backward transitions (points B_2 and B_3). These examples demonstrate the destabilizing effect of fluctuations that exceed the ZCD, the re-stabilizing function of intermediate backward transition, and its importance for enabling further progress.

The activities described in this part of the paper demonstrate the claims of the microdevelopment model. After summarizing the attributes of the model, I review findings and theoretical explanations with similar attributes in other researchers' work, which corroborate the proposed model.

Summary and discussion: A microdevelopmental explanation of how development occurs

The microdevelopment model explains development as series of microdevelopmental sequences, each defined for a specific developmental indicator. Sequences often start with backward transitions and then progress. Three major processes create variability that enables progress and change in development: backward transitions, ordered fluctuations bounded within a range, and reiterations. Backward transition is a facilitator and precursor of progress. Ordered fluctuations mark a Zone of Current Development (ZCD) – a range of knowledge levels that is the focus of current development. Reiterations repeat patterns within and across sequences. The three types of variability operate to facilitate progress and have crucial functions for development.

In an unfamiliar context, microdevelopmental sequences show patterns similar to macrodevelopment, in the specific indicators for which they are defined. Microdevelopmental sequences are context specific, and at about the same period a person's sequences can span different developmental levels in relation to different tasks, contexts, contents, and domains. Development evolves in this way at all ages, but throughout development, breakthroughs in microdevelopment reach increasingly higher levels. The child's highest macrodevelopmental level is the current highest level the child achieved in microdevelopment in any area and domain. This level is extended during the following microdevelopmental breakthrough, which may occur in any domain.

Support from findings and theories of other researchers

In the literature, there is evidence supporting the attributes of the microdevelopment model in other researchers' findings and theoretical explanations. Their work, which is related to diverse ages, tasks, and domains, gives credence to the model and suggests its generality.

The functions of variability A few researchers suggest that variability enables developmental progress. For example, Siegler indicates that children who show greater variability of reasoning learn more (Siegler, 1996, this volume). Siegler also suggests that variability in thinking allows infants, children, and adults to make discoveries about their environments (Siegler, 1994). Goldin-Meadow and colleagues study variability expressed in mismatches between information conveyed in gestures and speech. They show that mismatches reflect a transitional period and are likely to predict learning (e.g., Goldin-Meadow & Alibali, this volume; Goldin-Meadow, Alibali, & Church, 1993). Thelen and Smith (1994) suggest that variability is adaptive. However, Thelen and Corbetta (this volume) note that the reasons why variability appears are still poorly understood, which highlights the need to analyze variability, its patterns, and its functions.

Initial backward transition and its functions The phenomenon of initial backward transition is supported by findings of other process-oriented studies. For example, in a study cited earlier, Karmiloff-Smith and Inhelder (1974) maintain that older children's initial strategy was "clearcut regressions to earlier patterns" (ibid., p. 200). In a similar vein, Kuhn, Amsel, and O'Loughlin (1988), in their analysis of the development of scientific thinking skills, state that the initial performance of many adults is similar to that of children (ibid., p. 205). Vygotsky notes that laboratory conditions can provoke a microgenetic process that turns back to its initial stages (1978, pp. 61–62). The enabling function of initial regressions is supported by Werner's analysis of the orthogenetic principle in development. Werner highlights the ability to "regress to a point from which new development can take place" (1957, p. 130). In other words, regression makes developmental progress possible, as suggested in the model proposed here.

Intermediate backward transition, its causes and functions Findings comparable with intermediate backward transitions are also reported in the literature. For example, intermediate backward transitions appear before progress in individuals' learning curves in Gelman, Romo, & Francis' chapter (this volume). Intermediate backward transitions appear also when children produce a more mature strategy, which creates a temporary regression in their recall (Miller & Seier, 1994). Fischer & Yan (this volume) found backward transitions in their analysis of the evolution of Darwin's thought. Siegler & Jenkins (1989) indicate that prior to discovering the min strategy (counting up from the larger addend), children exhibited long solution times (i.e., regression): the average solution time was twice as long as their average for the whole experiment (ibid., p. 67). Longer solutions characterized the trial on which children made the discovery as well as the trial that immediately preceded it. The regression in children's performance manifested also in false starts, slow counting, and verbal descriptions that became less articulate. The sequence that Goldin-Meadow & Alibali (this volume) propose shows intermediate backward transition during the mismatched period.

Siegler and Jenkins suggest that longer solution trials and less articulate descriptions reflect intense cognitive activity that requires more mental resources (1989, pp. 69; 109). Goldin-Meadow and colleagues advance a similar explanation, showing that during the mismatch period, when children solve the problem, they entertain more than one idea, which consumes cognitive resources. Van Geert's analyses of growth modeling (1994) indicate overshoots and subsequent troughs ("leaps and dips") when a supported grower temporarily exceeds its carrying capacity. Based on models of connected growers, Van Geert (1997) also indicates that an increase in a conceptual strategy may cause a decrease in another, owing to limited resources. The claim about the compensating effect of intermediate backward transitions is supported, then, by findings and modeling in relation to diverse contexts.

Reiterations The reiterative nature of discovery appears in Siegler & Jenkins' (1989) findings: children discovered and rediscovered the min strategy. Reiterations were analyzed as circular reactions in infant development (Baldwin, 1894/1968; Piaget, 1952), as indicated earlier. Reiterative cycles of stages appear in Piaget's and neo-Piagetian theories (e.g., Case, 1985; Fischer, 1980). Van Geert's growth modeling shows cycles, for example, in resource allocation (1994). Thelen & Smith (1994) analyze cycles of perception–action–perception. Lewis (this volume) indicates reiteration as recurring patterns in development (e.g., recurring emotional interpretations that manifest in stable attractors, recurrent structures that manifest in personality traits). Parziale (1997, this volume) finds reiterative bridge construction (as children changed strategies, they dismantled their bridge and restarted differently). Reiteration appears, then, in different ages, activities, and contexts.

Similarity of processes at different time scales Lewis (this volume) analyzes bi-directional influences across scales of self-organization. Thelen & Smith (1994) propose that similar self-organizing processes occur in a time scale of minutes or seconds as well as on the ontogenetic time scale. They also view variability as a source of adaptive new forms in real time, ontogenetic, and phylogenetic time. Werner (1957) suggests an orthogenetic principle of differentiation and hierarchical integration, which applies to micro- and macrodevelopment. These suggestions support the idea of some parallelism in patterns across scales.

A developmental sequence that applies across ages Karmiloff-Smith (1986, 1992) suggests a representational redescription model, which specifies a sequence of phases, progressing from implicit to increasingly more explicit knowledge. At the same age and period, a person can be at different phases in relation to different domains. Karmiloff-Smith demonstrated this attribute in research findings related to different ages and domains, as suggested by the current model as well.

A developmental range Van Geert (this volume) suggests a range of scores that cover different degrees of characteristicness of an attribute. Van Geert shows ranges in moving average and maximum and minimum of percentile ranges of several indicators.

Specifying and explaining processes suggested in the literature

Werner (1957) suggests that development evolves through progressions and regressions and states that oscillatory activity in terms of progression and regression is an important developmental principle. The microdevelopment model specifies the process of progressions and regressions and its functions. The model suggests that progressions and regressions occur through reiteration at different scales – as patterns in segments within sequences, in ordered fluctuations along a sequence, and in reiterations of sequences.

The microdevelopment model explains another perplexing phenomenon: lack of transfer (e.g., Determan & Sternberg, 1993). From the beginning of the twentieth century (Thorndike & Woodworth, 1901), many studies found that people at different ages do not transfer learned knowledge to new problems and tasks. The microdevelopment model suggests that when people develop new knowledge, they cannot simply transfer knowledge from one set of problems to another (Granott, 1993a). Even small variations of the problem can make it obscure for a learner. The model also proposes a remedy, predicting that if learners are encouraged to explore the modified task through backward transition, they will reconstruct their knowledge through a brief microdevelopmental sequence.

As indicated earlier, ongoing studies confirm the predictions of the microdevelopment model in other populations, age groups, contents, and types of analyses. The generalization of the model has to be tested further. However, where the model applies, backward transitions, ordered fluctuations, reiterations, and the context specificity of reiterated sequences have important implications: when abilities are sampled at widely separated points in time, they may belong to different sequences. To support valid comparisons of these abilities, more information is needed about their microdevelopment.

Appendix: Examples for defining skill theory levels in the robot context (selected levels)

Skill structures in this appendix follow the conventions of skill theory formatting (see Fischer, 1980): Sets inside brackets constitute a single skill. Mapping is denoted by a line; system by a horizontal bidirectional arrow. Sensorimotor sets appear in boldface capital letters; representational sets in italic capital letters. Subscripts add information about the set.

Skill theory level	Underlying structure of levels	Level definition in the robot context
SM2 (second sensorimotor level)	*Mapping between sensorimotor sets:* Controlling an interrelation between two sensorimotor sets. $$[\textbf{ACTION}_1 \text{—} \textbf{PERCEPTION}_2]$$ or: $$[\textbf{PERCEPTION}_1 \text{—} \textbf{PERCEPTION}_2]$$ E.g., an infant touches a mobile to make it move: $$[\textbf{TOUCH}_{\text{A MOBILE}} \text{—} \textbf{MOBILE}_{\text{MOVES}}]$$	*Mapping between sensorimotor sets:* Controlling an interrelation between two sensorimotor sets. E.g., a person performs certain actions to bring about a certain movement of the robot: $$[\textbf{TOUCH}_{\text{A ROBOT}} \text{—} \textbf{ROBOT}_{\text{MOVES}}]$$
SM3 (third sensorimotor level)	*A system of sensorimotor sets:* Coordinating variations in one sensorimotor set with variation in another sensorimotor set. $$\left[\textbf{ACTION}_{1b}^{1a} \longleftrightarrow \textbf{PERCEPTION}_{2b}^{2a}\right]$$	*A system of sensorimotor sets:* Coordinating variation in one sensorimotor set with variation in another sensorimotor set.

E.g., an infant coordinates variation in throwing objects and objects falling:

$$THROW \longleftrightarrow SPOON \begin{bmatrix} \text{A SPOON FROM HIGH CHAIR} & \text{FALLS DOWN} \\ \text{A SPOON ON TOP OF HIGH CHAIR} & \text{STAYS ON HIGH CHAIR} \end{bmatrix}$$

E.g., a person coordinates variations of actions with variations in the movement of the robot:

$$PUT \longleftrightarrow ROBOT \begin{bmatrix} \text{FINGERS IN FRONT OF ROBOT} & \text{DOES NOT CHANGE DIRECTION} \\ \text{FINGERS ABOVE ROBOT} & \text{CHANGES DIRECTION} \end{bmatrix}$$

REP2 (second representational level)

Mapping between representational sets: Constructing an interrelation between two representational sets.

$$[REPRESENTATION_1 \text{ —— } REPRESENTATION_2]$$

Mapping between representational sets: Constructing an interrelation between two representational sets.

E.g., a baby holds a block, talks on pretend phone, and represents hearing his father's answers on the phone:

$$\left[REPRESENT_{\text{TALKING ON PRETEND PHONE}} \text{ —— } REPRESENT_{\text{LISTENING TO DADDY'S ANSWERS}} \right]$$

E.g., a person constructs a causal mapping between representation of stimuli that can activate a sensor and representation of the robot's (previously observed) pattern of movement:

$$\left[REPRESENT_{\text{ENVIRONMENTAL STIMULI THAT AFFECT THE ROBOT'S SENSOR}} \text{ —— } REPRESENT_{\text{THE ROBOT'S PATTERN OF MOVEMENT}} \right]$$

References

Baldwin, J. M. (1894/1968). *Mental development in the child and the race: Methods and processes.* New York: Kelley.

Baron, M. I., & Granott, N. (submitted). Consistent estimation of early and frequent change points.

Case, R. (1985). *Intellectual development: Birth to adulthood.* New York: Academic Press.

Chi, M. T. H., Feltovich, P. J., & Glaser, R. (1981). Categorization and representation of physics problems by experts and novices. *Cognitive Science, 5,* 121–152.

Cohen, J., & Cohen, P. (1983). *Applied multiple regression/correlation analysis for the behavioral sciences.* Hillsdale, NJ: Erlbaum.

Coyle, T. R., & Bjorklund, D. F. (1997). Age differences in, and consequences of, multiple- and variable-strategy use on a multitrial sort-recall task. *Developmental Psychology, 33,* 372–380.

Determan, D. K., & Sternberg, R. J. (Eds.) (1993). *Transfer on trial: Intelligence, cognition, and instruction.* Norwood, NJ: Ablex.

Fischer, K. W. (1980). A theory of cognitive development: The control and construction of hierarchies of skills. *Psychological Review, 87,* 477–531.

Fischer, K. W., & Bidell, T. R. (1998). Dynamic development of psychological structures in action and thought. In R. M. Lerner (Ed.), *Handbook of child psychology* (pp. 467–561). New York: Wiley.

Fischer, K. W., & Granott, N. (1995). Beyond one-dimensional change: Multiple, concurrent, socially distributed processes in learning and development. *Human Development, 38,* 302–314.

Fischer, K. W., & Yan, Z. (this volume). Darwin's construction of the theory of evolution: Microdevelopment of explanations of variation and change in species.

Gelman, R., Romo, L., & Francis, W. S.(this volume). Notebooks as windows on learning: The case of a science-into-ESL program.

Goldin-Meadow, S., & Alibali, M. W. (this volume). Looking at the hands through time: A microgenetic perspective on learning and instruction.

Goldin-Meadow, S., Alibali, M. W., & Church, R. B. (1993). Transitions in concept acquisition: Using the hand to read the mind. *Psychological Review, 100,* 279–297.

Granott, N. (1991a). From macro to micro and back: On the analysis of microdevelopment. Paper presented at the *21st Annual Symposium of the Jean Piaget Society,* Philadelphia, PA.

Granott, N. (1991b). Puzzled minds and weird creatures: Phases in the spontaneous process of knowledge construction. In I. Harel & S. Papert (Eds.), *Constructionism* (pp. 295–310). Norwood, NJ: Ablex.

Granott, N. (1992). Microdevelopmental puzzle and the mechanism of cognitive growth: Alternative pathways, parallel access, and co-existing structures. Paper presented at the *22nd Annual Symposium of the Jean Piaget Society,* Montreal, Canada.

Granott, N. (1993a). Microdevelopment of co-construction of knowledge during problem-solving: Puzzled minds, weird creatures, and wuggles.

Doctoral dissertation, Massachusetts Institute of Technology, Cambridge, MA [on line]. Available: *http://theses.mit.edu:80/Dienst/UI/2.0/Composite/0018.mit.theses/1993–170/1?nsections=19*.

Granott, N. (1993b). Patterns of interaction in the co-construction of knowledge: Separate minds, joint effort, and weird creatures. In R. Wozniak & K. W. Fischer (Eds.), *Development in context: Acting and thinking in specific environments* (pp. 183–207). Hillsdale, NJ: Erlbaum.

Granott, N. (1994a). From macro- to micro and back: An analysis and explanation of microdevelopment. The Microdevelopment Laboratory, University of Texas at Dallas.

Granott, N. (1994b). On the mechanism of cognitive change: Transition mechanism in microdevelopment and the "Zone of Current Development." Paper presented at the *24th Annual Symposium of the Jean Piaget Society*, Chicago, IL.

Granott, N. (1995). The dynamics of problem solving: Rediscovery, variability, and the complexity of making sense. The Microdevelopmental Laboratory, University of Texas at Dallas.

Granott, N. (1996). How to analyze the co-construction of knowledge? A dynamic approach. Paper presented at the *Annual Meeting of the American Educational Research Association*, New York.

Granott, N. (1998a). We learn, therefore we develop: Learning versus development – or developing learning? In C. Smith & T. Pourchot (Eds.), *Adult learning and development: Perspectives from educational psychology* (pp. 15–34). Mahwah, NJ: Erlbaum.

Granott, N. (1998b). Unit of analysis in transit: From the individual's knowledge to the ensemble process. *Mind, Culture, and Activity: An International Journal, 5(1)*, 42–66.

Granott, N. (1998c). A paradigm shift in the study of development. *Human Development, 41(5–6)*, 360–365.

Granott, N. (1999). The complexity of development: Interplay of factors. Paper presented at the *29th Annual Symposium of the Jean Piaget Society*, Mexico City: Mexico.

Granott, N., & Baron, M. (2001, April). Unconscious discoveries, mindful insights, and knowledge: Change point analysis of problem solving. Poster presented at the Biennial Meeting of the Society for Research in Child Development, Minneapolis, MN.

Granott, N., Fischer, K. W., & Parziale, J. (this volume). Bridging to the unknown: A transition mechanism in learning and development.

Karmiloff-Smith, A. (1986). From meta-processes to conscious access: Evidence from children's metalinguistics and repair data. *Cognition, 23(2)*, 95–147.

Karmiloff-Smith, A. (1992). *Beyond modularity: A developmental perspective on cognitive science*. Cambridge, MA: MIT Press.

Karmiloff-Smith, A., & Inhelder, B. (1974). If you want to get ahead, get a theory. *Cognition, 3*, 195–212.

Klahr, D. (2000). Exploring science: The cognition and development of discovery processes. Cambridge, MA: MIT Press.

Kuhn, D. (this volume). A multi-component system that constructs knowledge: Insights from microgenetic study.

Kuhn, D., Amsel, E., & O'Loughlin, M. (1988). *The development of scientific thinking skills.* San Diego, CA: Academic Press.

Lee, K., & Karmiloff-Smith, A. (this volume). Macro- and microdevelopmental research: Assumptions, research strategies, constraints, and utilities.

Lewis, M. D. (this volume). Interacting time scales in personality (and cognitive) development: Intentions, emotions, and emergent forms.

Miller, P. H., & Coyle, T. R. (1999). Developmental change: Lessons from microgenesis. In E. K. Scholnick, K. Nelson, S. A. Gelman, & P. H. Miller (Eds.), *Conceptual development: Piaget's legacy* (pp. 209–239). Mahwah, NJ: Erlbaum.

Miller, P. H., & Seier, W. S. (1994). Strategy utilization deficiencies in children: When, where, and why. In H. W. Reese (Ed.), *Advances in child development and behavior, Vol. 22* (pp. 107–156). New York: Academic Press.

Parziale, J. (1997). Microdevelopment during an activity based science lesson. Unpublished doctoral dissertation, Harvard Graduate School of Education, Cambridge, MA.

Parziale, J. (this volume). Observing the dynamics of construction: Children building bridges and new ideas.

Piaget, J. (1952). *The origins of intelligence in children* (M. Cook, trans.). Madison, CT: International Universities Press.

Siegler, R. S. (1994). Cognitive variability: A key to understanding cognitive development. *Current Directions in Psychological Science, 3(1),* 1–5.

Siegler, R. S. (1996). *Emerging minds: The process of change in children's thinking.* New York: Oxford University Press.

Siegler, R. S. (this volume). Microgenetic studies of self-explanation.

Siegler, R. S., & Jenkins, E. (1989). *How children discover new strategies.* Hillsdale, NJ: Erlbaum.

Strauss, S. (Ed.). (1982). *U-shaped behavioral growth.* New York: Academic Press.

Thelen, E., & Corbetta, D. (this volume). Microdevelopment and dynamic systems: Applications to infant motor development.

Thelen, E., & Smith, L. B. (1994). *A dynamic systems approach to the development of cognition and action.* Cambridge, MA: MIT Press.

Thorndike, E. L., & Woodworth, R. S. (1901). The influence of improvement in one mental function upon the efficiency of other functions. *Psychological Review, 8,* 247–261.

van Geert, P. (1994). *Dynamic systems of development: Change between complexity and chaos.* New York: Harvester Wheatsheaf.

van Geert, P. (1997). Variability and fluctuations: A dynamic view. In E. Amsel & K. A. Renninger (Eds.), *Change and development: Issues of theory, method, and application* (pp. 193–212). Mahwah, NJ: Erlbaum.

van Geert, P. (this volume). Developmental dynamics, intentional action, and fuzzy sets.

Vygotsky, L. S. (1978). *Mind in society: The development of higher psychological processes.* Cambridge, MA: Harvard University Press.

Werner, H. (1957). The concept of development from a comparative and organismic point of view. In D. B. Harris (Ed.), *The concept of development: An issue in the study of human behavior* (pp. 125–148). Minneapolis: University of Minnesota Press.

9 Macro- and microdevelopmental research: Assumptions, research strategies, constraints, and utilities

Kang Lee and Annette Karmiloff-Smith

Introduction

Over the last half century, developmental research has undergone tremendous change. Our knowledge of how children develop in the physical, neurological, cognitive, and social domains has advanced greatly. In some areas, progress has been so extensive that old theories have been abandoned and textbooks completely rewritten (e.g., infant perceptual and cognitive development). Other advances are evident in the emergence of entire fields that did not even exist two or three decades ago (e.g., developmental neuroscience: Johnson, 1999; developmental connectionism: Elman, Bates, Johnson, Karmiloff-Smith, Parisi, & Plunkett, 1996). Still other, relatively "old" areas have moved in novel directions that have revealed new facts about how children develop (e.g., motor skills: Thelen, 1995; language: Markman, 1991; memory: Bruck & Ceci, 1999).

Theoretical approaches to developmental research have also changed dramatically in the past fifty years. For instance, in cognitive development research, radical behaviorism was replaced by Piagetian constructivism in the 1950s and 1960s, which itself was challenged by symbolic information processing theorists in the 1970s. The assumptions of symbolic information processing theories were later contested by connectionist theorists and domain-specificity theorists in the 1980s and 1990s. Nativist theories are also again in vogue after being marginalized for nearly a century. In addition, dynamic systems approaches derived from chaos theory in mathematics and thermodynamic research have been introduced to account for certain patterns of child development (Thelen & Smith, 1994; van Geert, 1991).

This chapter is prepared with a grant from the British Council's Young Researchers Programme and a grant from the Natural Science and Engineering Research Council of Canada to Kang Lee and program and project grants from the British Medical Research Council to Annette Karmiloff-Smith. We would like to thank Alejo Freire, Nira Granott, and Jim Parziale for their constructive comments and suggestions on earlier versions of this chapter.

243

Despite significant advances in knowledge and theory about child development, the general methods used to study developmental change have not radically changed. Only two basic paradigms exist: a macrodevelopmental approach and a microdevelopmental approach. Examples of the macrodevelopmental approach are the conventional cross-sectional and longitudinal methods. The microdevelopmental approach was pioneered by Inhelder and her colleagues in Geneva, and Vygotsky, Luria, and their colleagues in Russia. Examples of this approach are microgenetic methods and dynamic systems methods.

It has been suggested that the difference between the two approaches lies mainly in the density of data collection: macrodevelopmental methods resemble taking snapshots, while microdevelopmental methods are like making a movie (Siegler & Crowley, 1991). From this perspective, the former may be inferior to the latter because the former lacks detailed information about how developmental change occurs. In this chapter, we argue that the difference between the two approaches is more fundamental than variation in data collection frequencies. In our view, differences between macro- and microdevelopmental approaches are analogous to that between Newtonian and quantum physics. These two paradigms operate under fundamentally distinct assumptions, which lead to dramatically different research designs, data collection strategies, and data analysis methods. Owing to variations in basic assumptions, macro- and microdevelopmental approaches each have unique constraints and hence are useful for answering different developmental questions. Despite fundamental differences between macro- and microdevelopmental approaches, the approaches complement, rather than compete with, each other. We believe that our understanding of developmental change in children will necessarily be limited if we rely exclusively on one or the other of the two approaches. To achieve a deeper understanding, we must adopt a new research paradigm that combines the best aspects of both the methods.

Fundamental assumptions

There exist both similarities and differences between macro- and microdevelopmental approaches in their basic assumptions regarding what developmental research is about and how it should be conducted. Both approaches hold a similar view that the goal of developmental research is to reveal, describe, and explain systematic, age-related changes in behavior and psychological functioning of children, either as a group or as individuals. Both approaches also presuppose that this goal can be achieved with the use of scientific, empirical methods. That is, developmental researchers can study child development in much the same manner as physicists study physical objects and biologists study living organisms. Based on this presupposition, developmental researchers, regardless of whether they take the macro- or microdevelopmental approach, assume that: a) developmental phenomena can be objectively observed and observations can be replicated independently, b) developmental phenomena are quantifiable in terms of some meaningful units, c) one can manipulate a developmental phenomenon such that factors that cause certain developments to occur can be identified, and d) the principles of scientific reasoning can be applied to the description and explanation of any developmental phenomena.

While agreeing on these basic assumptions, macro- and microdevelopmental approaches differ greatly in several additional but equally fundamental assumptions. These differences can be characterized in terms of how each approach deals with the following issues: a) main focus of research, b) nature of causal relationship between developmental and independent variables, c) measurement model to quantify this relationship, and d) measurement errors.

Macrodevelopmental approach

The macrodevelopmental approach advocates that research should focus on the discovery of common patterns in behavior and psychological functioning of a general child population. Therefore, researchers taking the macrodevelopmental approach tend to focus on a group of children rather than any specific child. Even when studying individual differences, they tend to focus on differences between subgroups of children (e.g., group difference based on gender, race, personality type). From this perspective, individual-specific characteristics are considered idiosyncratic. They offer no useful information about the common pattern of development in children, and may even add noise to the data.

The macrodevelopmental approach assumes that the relationship between a developmental variable (DV) and independent variables (IVs) is linear. The central thesis of this assumption is that a developmental variable will not act as an independent variable that contributes to subsequent systematic changes in the developmental variable itself. Also, for a particular developmental variable, the nature of the relationship between the DV and IVs remains the same from one child to another and from one age to another. Because of the linearity assumption, the macrodevelopmental approach adopts the following General Linear Model for data collection and analysis:

$$Y = a_0 + a_1 X_1 + \ldots + a_n X_n + \text{INTs} + \text{Es} + \text{Er}$$

where Y is a developmental variable, a_1-a_n are scaling factors, X_1-X_n are independent variables, INTs are interactions between independent variables, Es is systematic measurement error, and Er is random error.

According to the General Linear Model, the goal of data collection and analysis is to minimize systematic and random errors of measurement and to identify the scaling factors such that the "true" linear relation between the DV and IVs can be established. To minimize systematic errors, researchers design studies that eliminate experimenter biases and procedural confounds, and that maximize measurement reliability and validity.

To minimize random errors, repeated testing of the same children is the most ideal: random errors should even out after a sufficiently large number of repeated measurements. However, in developmental studies, particularly those involving young children, fatigue and learning often make repeated testing both unfeasible and problematic. For example, children become better at the same task as time goes by. Fatigue or boredom, on the other hand, decrease children's performance on the same test over a period of time. To circumvent this problem, the macrodevelopmental approach makes the critical assumption that individual-specific characteristics are random errors, and differences between same-aged children of the same subgroup (e.g., sex, race) are random variations. Such variations are analogous to variations of repeated measurements taken from a single child. Hence, the mean of single measurements taken from a sufficiently large number of children, like the mean of a sufficiently large number of measurements taken from one child, should also even out the random errors. Once systematic and random errors are controlled for, one can obtain estimates of parameters that determine the "true" linear relationship between a DV and IVs. It should be noted that the General Linear Model does not suggest that the model can only account for the cumulative pattern of development. It is also applicable to curvilinear patterns of development because these patterns are special cases of the General Linear Model and can be transformed to fit the model (see figure 9.1a).

Microdevelopmental approach

Microdevelopment is a relatively new methodology in developmental psychology. The manner in which the approach addresses developmental questions is so novel and radically different from the macrodevelopmental approach that some authors believe it marks a significant paradigm shift in the field (Granott, 1998a; Smith & Thelen, 1993). While advocates of this new approach do not suggest abandoning the macrodevelopmental

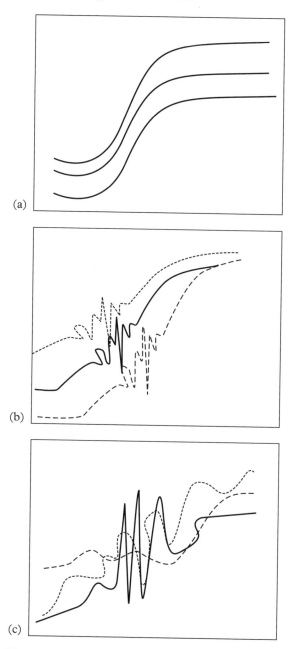

Figure 9.1 Three types of developmental changes: Cumulative change (a), re-organizational change (b), and self-organizational change (c).

approach, they argue that the traditional approach alone is inadequate to capture the essence of the dynamics of development (Kuhn, 1995; Siegler, 1997; Thelen & Smith, 1994). From the perspective of the microdevelopmental approach, development is an on-going process of self-organization (Thelen & Smith, 1994) or re-organization (Karmiloff-Smith, 1993a). Any particular pattern of development is the outcome of interactions between a child, his or her developmental history, and the ever-changing environment around the child. Although this interactionist view of development is hardly new theoretically, most developmentalists have not applied interactionist principles to their empirical research. The microdevelopmental approach, in contrast, offers methodological frameworks in which a truly interactionist study can be implemented.

The microdevelopmental approach is in fact comprised of two similar, yet distinctive approaches: the microgenetic approach and the dynamic systems approach. The microgenetic approach has been used to study notational development (Karmiloff-Smith, 1981), language development (Karmiloff-Smith, 1979), reasoning (Kuhn, Schauble, & Garcia-Mila, 1992), and problem-solving (Fischer & Granott, 1995; Karmiloff-Smith & Inhelder, 1974; Siegler & Crowley, 1991; Siegler & Chen, 1998). The dynamic systems approach has been implemented mainly in the areas of motor development (for a review, see Thelen, 1995), but is now being expanded to developmental research in learning (Cooney & Troyer, 1994), reasoning (Rabinowitz, Grant, Howe, & Walsh, 1994), language acquisition (van Geert, 1991), communication (Fogel & Thelen, 1987), and emotional development (Lewis, 1995). Although both approaches share certain features (see below), they differ in other fundamental aspects, and are discussed separately.

Microgenetic approach Research paradigms pertinent to the current form of the microgenetic approach date back to the early days of developmental psychology (see Catan, 1986, for review). In the past three decades, the Genevan group has been using this approach to further the investigation of transitive phenomena of cognitive development that the traditional Piagetian method had failed to address (e.g., Karmiloff-Smith & Inhelder, 1974; see Karmiloff-Smith, 1993b for a review). These researchers have used the method to reveal qualitative changes during scheme formation and transition in various problem-solving situations. There has also been a recent increase in interest in the microgenetic method among developmentalists in countries outside Europe studying problem-solving and concept formation (Siegler, 1995; Siegler & Crowley, 1991). Furthermore, researchers have also begun to use microgenetic methods to study issues other than problem-solving (e.g., Kuhn et al., 1992; Granott, 1998b). Findings from various domains indicate that this paradigm is a promising tool for studying systematic developmental changes.

Unlike the macrodevelopmental approach's focus on group developmental patterns, the microgenetic approach's emphasis is on individual children. Both inter- and intra-individual variation are considered a source of meaningful information about developmental change. High inter-individual variation of children at the same age suggests that these children may be at different phases of developmental change, so that researchers are encouraged to examine the developmental trajectory of each child separately. High intra-subject variation indicates that qualitative developmental changes may be taking place. Hence, in order to capture the pattern of change and factors that engender such change, special attention is paid to periods of individual development where intra-individual variability is high.

In the microgenetic approach, it is assumed that a child's developmental history may affect subsequent development. According to Karmiloff-Smith (1993a), the impact of the earlier developmental history of children on their later development is realized via a mechanism of re-organization: when and only when a developmental variable reaches a certain level does a qualitative change take place in the relationship between a developmental variable and independent variables. This assumption leads to a different measurement model from that adopted by the macrodevelopmental approach. For the macrodevelopmental approach, as age increases, there may exist different values of IVs and hence different values of a DV, but the parameters ($a_1, a_2, \ldots$, and $b_1, b_2, \ldots$) that determine the relationship between the DV and IVs do not change. In the General Linear Model of the macrodevelopmental approach, it is the parameter of the linear equation that determines whether a developmental change is linear (which shows a cumulative pattern) or log-linear (showing a step-wise pattern) or exponential (showing a sharp ascending or descending pattern); the values of independent variables only determine the quantitative level of the developmental variable. In contrast, the microgenetic approach assumes that the nature of the relationship between a DV and IVs may change before and after a developmental transition. Hence, one General Linear Model may capture the relationship before the transition but not that during or after the transition. For this reason, the microgenetic approach allows researchers to use different linear models to describe the relatively stable developmental states before and after a developmental transition. During these periods, inter- and intra-individual variation is considered measurement error. In contrast, for the period of transition, the microgenetic approach treats intra-subject variability as a manifestation of the developmental change that is taking place and inter-subject variability as an indication that different children are at different phases of transition.

Dynamic systems approach The dynamic systems approach is based on dynamic systems theory (DST), or chaos theory, that originated in the study of the evolution of complex physical systems over time (e.g., gas, fluid). Space limitation does not permit an extensive discussion of the dynamic systems theory itself and its application to developmental psychology. Interested readers should consult Thelen & Corbetta (this volume) or Thelen and Smith (1994). In a nutshell, DST views an individual as a complex system of inter-related and mutually interacting components. The system as a whole may develop qualitatively owing to self-organization. That is, new forms may emerge not because of qualitative changes in individual components, but rather as a result of changes in the relations between the system components. Further, and more importantly, DST assumes that the developmental course of a child is influenced not only by multiple internal and external factors but also by the child's developmental history. There are two consequences of this assumption: first, a child's developmental course becomes intrinsically nonlinear; second, the child's developmental course is also inevitably unique and different from that of any other child.

To explain this point, let us consider the following two simple equations:

$$Y(t_{i+1}) = a + b X(t_i)$$
$$Y(t_{i+1}) = a + b X(t_i) + c Y(t_i)$$

where $Y(t_i)$ and $Y(t_{i+1})$ are dependent variables (e.g., reading ability) at time t_i and t_{i+1}, a, b, and c are scaling parameters, and $X(t_i)$ is an independent variable (e.g., exposure to print materials) at time t_i. The first equation is a linear model with two critical characteristics: first, different values for a and b change the quantitative relation of Y and X but not the pattern of the relation; second, for a specific a and a specific b, Y at t_i is independent of Y at t_{i-1} that precedes it and Y at t_{i+1} that follows it. In other words, no matter what the initial state of the system (Y_0 or Y_0'), a given $X(t_i)$ should always yield the same outcome Y. This is to say, the model is linear and deterministic. In contrast, the second model does not have these two characteristics because of the addition of $Y(t_i)$ to the right side of the equation. Now, different scaling parameters (a, b, and c)

result in qualitatively different patterns of evolution over time. We may call this feature "dependence on specific parameters," which is a typical characteristic of a non-linear system.

In addition, in some situations and for a given set of parameters, a, b, and c, slightly different initial states of $Y(t_i)$ and $Y'(t_i)$ may result in entirely different patterns of evolution of the system over time. For example,

$$Y(t_i) = a + bX(t_i) + cY(t_{i-1})$$
$$Y'(t_i) = a + bX(t_i) + cY'(t_{i-1})$$
$$Y(t_i) \neq Y'(t_i)$$

This "dependence on initial states" is another typical characteristic of a nonlinear system.

The dynamic systems approach applies DST to the empirical investigation of child development. In keeping with DST's general principles, the dynamic systems approach assumes that the relation between a DV and IVs is nonlinear. In other words, a DV itself may contribute to an individual's subsequent development. Hence, the following measurement model is used:

$$DV_{t+1} = f(DV_t, a_1IV_1, \ldots, a_nIV_n) + Es + Er$$

where DV_{t+1} is a developmental variable at time $t + 1$, $f(DV_t, a_1IV_1, \ldots, a_nIV_n)$ is a patterned combination of independent variables and the developmental variable at an earlier point in time, a_i is a scaling factor, Es is systematic error, and Er is random error.

Based on this nonlinear measurement model, researchers not only have to minimize and control for systematic and random errors, but also must differentiate between these errors and inter- and intra-individual variation that is part and parcel of a nonlinear developing system. With regard to inter-individual variation, because different individuals may have different initial conditions of development, their developmental patterns are inevitably distinctive (owing to the "dependence on initial states" characteristic). Also, because the relationship between the independent variables may vary from one individual to another (owing to the "dependence on specific parameters" characteristic), different developmental patterns result. Intra-individual variation is also not necessarily a "measurement error." A main reason for such variation to exist is that a child's developing system is perturbed and destabilized by new conditions, and various existing components of the developing system are undergoing self-organization to reach a new stable state. Hence, intra-individual variability is an inherent characteristic of a nonlinear system that is in transition from one developmental level to another. For this reason, the dynamic systems approach focuses on the specific period when there is high intra-subject variability. It is believed that inspecting this period may reveal whether a qualitative developmental change is indeed taking place, and if it is, what engenders the change.

Research strategies

Macrodevelopmental approach

Two major research strategies are derived from the macrodevelopmental approach: the longitudinal method and the cross-sectional method. The longitudinal method requires researchers to observe a group of same-aged children repeatedly over an extended period of time, with the same observational procedures and measurements. By doing so, researchers can reveal how children as a group develop over time. To achieve this outcome, the longitudinal method requires researchers to obtain a representative, sufficiently large and unbiased sample of children from the population. A large and unbiased sample should reveal the size of the inter-individual variation (e.g., sample standard deviation) and even out random errors caused by this variation. Consequently, the "true" value of the developmental variable at a particular point in time can also be estimated (e.g., sample mean). To avoid intra-individual variations that are viewed to be short-term, random fluctuations, longitudinal study requires the interval between data collection sessions to be large enough that data collected at different sessions reflect permanent changes in children.

While the longitudinal method provides information about the sequence of major developmental milestones, it has some major disadvantages: a) it is time consuming and costly, b) participant attrition may occur (which may result in biased results as time goes by), and c) children become over-exposed to the same procedures and measurements (which may result in them losing motivation to participate, becoming fatigued with the study, or becoming test-wise).

The cross-sectional method requires the researcher to obtain a representative sample of participants and divide them into age groups. The same measurements or observations are administered to all participants over a short span of time. The cross-sectional method has been the choice of most contemporary developmental researchers because it has several important advantages over the longitudinal method. First, it allows for inexpensive and efficient developmental data collection. A cross-sectional study only requires participants to be tested once. It minimizes above-mentioned problems (e.g., subject attrition). Second, researchers can quickly embark on a series of follow-up studies to test new hypotheses arising from the results of earlier studies. Third, a set of well-established, General-Linear-Model-based statistical methods and computer programs are readily available for analyzing cross-sectional data. Also, because contemporary researchers are most familiar with these statistical methods, research findings derived from such methods can be widely understood and evaluated. Finally, the cross-sectional method is well suited for establishing developmental milestones of children at different ages.

It should be noted that to gain the above-mentioned advantages, the cross-sectional method has to make an auxiliary assumption. It assumes that differences between age groups are developmental differences. That is, it is assumed that the performance of children in a younger age group will be statistically the same as that of an older age group once the former group reaches the latter age. However, this assumption may not hold when cohort effects exist. Participants from different age groups may be exposed to different historical events and experiences, and hence perform differently on the same task owing to historical, not developmental, reasons. For this reason, the sequence and timing of developmental milestones obtained from cross-sectional studies must be interpreted with caution, unless cohort effects are empirically ruled out (e.g., using the cross-sequential design).

Microdevelopmental approach

Microgenetic approach Researchers have used a number of methods to implement the assumptions and principles of the microgenetic approach. These methods share similar data collection strategies. For example, all microgenetic methods require a researcher to focus on an individual, in effect conducting a case study (or multiple case studies when more than one individual is involved). These microgenetic methods also require high data sampling density such that a child's behavior or psychological functioning can be traced from the onset of a developmental transition to a relatively stable state. Data sampling frequency can be as high as every second, or every trial or every movement that the child makes. Further, as mentioned earlier, all microgenetic methods tend to focus on intra- and inter-individual variations.

While sharing the same data collection strategy, the existing microgenetic methods also differ from each other in the procedure researchers use to achieve their specific research goals. One of the major goals of microgenetic research is to capture in detail how a developmental variable changes qualitatively in an individual from one developmental level to another. Ideally, the individual would be observed intensively in the natural setting during a critical period of time. This period extends from the initial point when the qualitative change has yet to occur, to the point when the individual has reached a new level of development. In reality, such a strategy would be both impractical and inefficient because many qualitative changes take months or even years to complete. Dense sampling of individuals would be not only costly and time-consuming but also highly intrusive to participants' own daily activities. Also, a large amount of information collected through dense data sampling may not be relevant to the research issue in question. To avoid these problems, researchers normally use strategies that simulate a natural developmental course in an accelerated manner.

One strategy (the natural task procedure) involves researchers introducing a task that an individual encounters in the natural course of development (e.g., learning how to add or subtract). The task is, however, introduced at the point when it is above the individual's current developmental level. The individual is exposed to the task; the amount or intensity of exposure over several weeks may be comparable to that occurring naturally in a span of several months or years. In this strategy, the tasks are generally designed so that there is minimal experimenter intervention. The child is generally provided with a goal and allowed to explore freely the ways to achieve the goal. The experimenter does not provide direct feedback as to whether the participant is successful. The experimenter's task is only to maintain the participant's interest in the task and engage him or her in achieving the goal. A study is terminated not at the point when a developmental variable reaches a new level but when it becomes stabilized.

An example of this strategy is a study by Siegler and his associates (Siegler & Jenkins 1989; Siegler & Crowley, 1991) who investigated young children's acquisition of addition strategies. In particular, they were interested in how children acquire and use the min strategy that involves counting up from the larger addend the number of times indicated by the smaller addend. Over a period of eleven weeks, they provided children with an extensive number of single-digit addition problems (e.g., $6 + 3$, $2 + 7$) and observed their use of various strategies to solve them. A number of discoveries were made. For example, there was a high level of variability in children's strategy use, both in terms of the number of strategies and in terms of relative frequencies of the use of each method by different children. Children tended to use concurrently several strategies to solve addition problems. Their discovery of the min strategy was not made when they encountered difficult problems or failures but often when they had been successful in using existing strategies. Also, the discovery of such a more efficient strategy as the min strategy did not instantly lead to its wide generalization and the abandonment of the old, less efficient strategies. These findings, the researchers believe, could be generalized to account for children's discovery and use of the same addition strategies in the natural setting where they may experience the same number of addition problems over a much longer period of time.

A second strategy (the novel task procedure) is similar to the natural task procedure, except that it introduces a task that an individual has not previously encountered and may never actually encounter naturally. However, structurally and functionally, the task resembles a natural task that is the actual focus of research. The advantage of using the second strategy is that one can rule out the influence of prior experience on performance during investigation. Hence, the procedure can introduce novel tasks that are either above or compatible with the children's developmental level. In the former case, information about how an individual develops from an initial level on the novel task to a qualitatively different and relatively stable level of development is assumed to mimic the developmental course of an individual in dealing with the natural task. In the latter case, the procedure is used for examining how children adapt their existing knowledge and behavior to new situations.

For example, Karmiloff-Smith (1981) investigated how children adapt their notations as their mastery of a task progresses. She asked children to play a novel game in which they acted as an "ambulance driver" who needed to drive a patient from the patient's home to the hospital as quickly as possible and without going astray in various cul-de-sacs. Children were allowed to practice on the correct route many times. They were also instructed to take notes to help them remember the correct route. As the experiment progressed, children naturally became more and more efficient in reaching the "hospital." During the same time, children's notations also changed. Contrary to previous thought that children tended to change strategies when encountering failure, Karmiloff-Smith discovered that children often stopped using notation methods that had been producing success on the driving game and began using alternative approaches instead. Note that this discovery could not have been made with the use of macrodevelopmental methods because their data sampling intervals are too sparse (also see Karmiloff-Smith, 1985 for other examples).

Microgenetic methods have also been developed to delineate factors that may contribute to qualitative change. Accelerated simulation strategies are again used, with some modifications. According to one strategy (Granott, 1998b), participants interact either with peers or with more advanced partners (parents or older siblings). Children and their partners are often not given any specific instruction about how to interact and are allowed to act freely. This procedure simulates the natural social situations in which many developments take place. The focus of this procedure is on the effect of social interaction on the child's development. Another strategy is a training procedure in which the experimenter acts as an instructor. The child is provided with certain training about how to proceed on the task, and feedback about whether the child has succeeded. This procedure stresses the role of instruction and learning in the child's development. With different forms of instruction, factors that contribute to the development can be delineated.

Regardless of procedures used, a microgenetic study has to address several methodological issues that are crucial to the attainment of meaningful developmental results. First, the microgenetic approach must establish that the seemingly systematic changes observed in one participant are not individual-specific, idiosyncratic ones. In order to rule out this possibility, one common strategy is to use the same experimental procedure with a number of different individual children. If the same, or similar patterns of change are seen from one child to another, these patterns are considered to be general. This, however, does not necessarily indicate that the patterns of change reflect the genuine systematic change in a particular developmental variable. The results may still be task-specific or context-specific. Two solutions have been used to overcome this limitation. One is to use a traditional transfer paradigm (e.g., Kuhn, 1995). This paradigm involves observing or training a participant in one task, and introducing a new task when the participant's performance reaches a certain level. If the child applies the newly acquired strategies to the new task, the generalizability of the change is established. The other solution involves providing the child with two different tasks simultaneously. The child's performance is tracked session by session to determine whether a similar change takes place with reference to both tasks.

Dynamic systems approach The fundamental assumptions of the dynamic systems approach, especially the nonlinearity assumption, have significant implications for data collection strategies. First, non-linearity requires a dynamic systems study to focus on a specific child. Second, owing to the "dependence on initial states" characteristic of the non-linearity assumption, researchers are required to track the child from an initial state and over an extended period of time. A longitudinal case study with dense data sampling is therefore needed. Third, the dynamic systems approach requires multiple measures be taken. This is based on the assumption that the pattern of changes in several variables, not necessarily changes in a specific variable, may engender a qualitative developmental change in an individual. Fourth, because of the use of a case study paradigm, the conventional, macrodevelopmental strategies for dealing with random error cannot be used (e.g., group means). Instead, to minimize measurement errors, the dynamic systems approach requires researchers to take the same measurement intensively during the same session (e.g., giving a child multiple trials). Finally, intra-individual variation in a developmental variable between different sessions may indicate that the developmental variable is undergoing qualitative changes from one level of development to another. However, this variation may also be due to random fluctuations or to the fact that the developmental variable has reached a stable state, which by nature is variable (e.g., a strange attractor state where a DV may vary in a chaotic fashion). Both experimental procedures and mathematical modeling must be used to delineate the nature of intra-individual variations across sessions.

In addition to these basic requirements, Thelen and Ulrich (1991) have identified several issues that one must consider in conducting a dynamic systems study. They suggest that researchers must first identify the appropriate developmental variable of interest, which must be both well defined and observable; it cannot be a derived construct. Second, they discuss how to characterize appropriately the behavioral attractor states (i.e., states where the developmental variable becomes relatively stable). Identification of such attractor states is important because it helps researchers determine the span of a child's developmental history which is to be observed and the time scale for each set of observations (e.g., days, weeks, months). Thelen and Ulrich recommend the use of the conventional macrodevelopmental methods for such a purpose.

The third issue is how to describe appropriately the dynamic trajectory of the developmental variable. Researchers must use a longitudinal method at appropriately dense sampling intervals to capture the time scale of relevant change in the developmental variable. In addition, changes in independent variables must be observed concurrently. A fourth issue is how to identify correct points of transition. Points of transition signify the emergence of a new form of the developmental variable. Thelen and Ulrich (1991) have suggested that researchers pay particular attention to the period where a new form of the developmental variable emerges or the DV has a high level of variability. Transitions are critical because when a developmental variable is in transition, the critical variables (i.e., control variables) that engender the transition can be more easily identified. In order to discover the relevant control variables, Thelen and Ulrich suggest that the researcher measure changes in a number of independent variables along with the collective variable, thereby obtaining multiple response measures. Once the point of transition and control variables have been identified, researchers can manipulate control parameters to generate transitions experimentally and to examine the causal relationship between the developmental variable and the control variable. It should be noted that the above issues identified by Thelen and Ulrich (1991) are concerned with the data collection aspect of using the dynamic systems approach to investigating changes. Dynamic systems approach can also be used for data analysis and modeling (for details, see van Geert, this volume) and for guiding data interpretation and explanation (for details, see Lewis, this volume).

Constraints

Macrodevelopmental approach

Macrodevelopmental methods have several common methodological constraints. First, both the longitudinal and cross-sectional methods ignore the impact of the child's developmental history on later development. For this reason, cross-sectional and longitudinal methods may be useful for studying and explaining age-related changes when the impact of the history of a dependent variable on itself is negligible. However, they are inadequate when a dependent variable is significantly influenced by its own earlier states. Second, because intra-subject variation is regarded as random error, researchers using macrodevelopmental approaches tend to take pains to develop tasks to which children will give consistent and reliable responses. Tasks that produce highly variable responses are viewed as a design flaw and often discarded. One negative consequence of this pursuit of highly reliable tasks is that a whole set of genuine developmental phenomena that are variable by nature may be missed or ignored. For example, it was originally thought that young children will abandon a less efficient addition strategy once a more efficient strategy is discovered. However, as mentioned earlier, Siegler and Crowley (1991) discovered that children's use of old and new addition strategies are highly variable. Sometimes they use a familiar yet not efficient strategy and at some other times they opt for a new, efficient strategy. With time, the more efficient strategies tend to win over the older strategies. However, both new and old strategies co-exist for extended period of time and older strategies may never be abandoned. Such high variability, according Siegler and Crowley (1991), is the rule rather than exception in children's problem-solving process.

Third, with regard to inter-individual variability, researchers using the macrodevelopmental approach tend to treat it as a phenomenon that is not as informative and meaningful as inter-individual commonality. They often make tremendous efforts to minimize its impact either methodologically or statistically. Methodologically, researchers develop tasks that will obtain similar results from children of the same age group. Statistically, when reporting the performance of each age group and developmental differences between them, researchers tend to use central tendency measures (e.g., mean, median, mode) instead of variability measures (e.g., standard deviation). As a direct consequence of such emphasis, developmental researchers today tend to focus on large effect developmental phenomena (e.g., number conservation, false belief understanding) where inter-subject variability is relatively small. This strategy is, however, insensitive to developmentally meaningful phenomena that have high inter-subject variability unless a large sample size is used.

Microdevelopmental approach

Microgenetic method The microgenetic method is of course not devoid of limitations. First, although it provides a fine-grained picture of certain systematic changes, this picture is obtained at the expense of considerable time, money, and effort. Second, dense data sampling may produce artifacts attributable to repeated testing. Third, while viewing variability as an index of meaningful development is a novel and perhaps important theoretical contribution of the microgenetic approach to developmental study, it also poses a methodological challenge. Certain variability in behavior may indeed reflect a "developmentally meaningful" change in the individual, but other variability may simply be a result of random variation, or non-random changes in the individual that are of no theoretical significance. The microgenetic method has yet to develop procedures to differentiate these sources of variability.

Another related methodological problem is the lack of mathematical tools for data summary and modeling. Microgenetic data tend to be categorical (e.g., the absence or presence of a certain strategy) or involve repeated measures (Siegler & Crowley, 1991). More importantly, individuals' responses tend to differ in many ways. For example, suppose a group of children are asked to complete a problem-solving task. One child may take five sessions to progress from one level of performance to another, while another child may take ten sessions. In addition, some strategies used by one child may not be used by another. Even when children use the same strategies, the order in which they are explored may differ. Individual differences therefore make it difficult to combine data from different children. At present, many researchers who use the microgenetic method tend to either resort to a descriptive (sometimes biographical) account of an individual child's behavioral changes or use descriptive statistics (e.g., frequency count). These two ways of data reporting do not satisfy the presently dominant General-Linear-Model-based paradigm of experimental research. Hence, new mathematical or statistical tools are required for processing microgenetic data. The lack of these tools at present remains a major obstacle for microgenetic studies to be accepted by mainstream developmentalists.

Dynamic systems method The dynamic systems method also has several constraints. First, like the traditional longitudinal method, the dynamic systems method is both time consuming and costly. Second, the method's non-linearity assumption requires a researcher to collect data regarding as many independent variables as possible, and about both the initial and current states of development. Gathering all such information in a single study is not always possible and practical. The problem space must therefore be reduced to a manageable size and one must select relevant initial developmental states and variables. At present, the dynamic systems method itself does not offer any solutions about how to make such selections. Third, the dynamic systems method's requirement for dense data sampling has a high risk of measurement interference.

Further, the volume of data collected from a dynamic systems study may pose an enormous challenge for analyses as it must be analyzed on an individual-by-individual basis. Grouping individual data would violate the fundamental assumptions of the dynamic systems approach. Mathematical modeling is a possible solution. However, additional theoretical assumptions are required before the data can be fitted with a mathematical model. This is because the dynamic systems method itself is atheoretical about the relationship between a developmental variable and independent variables. Also, the same set of dynamic systems data may be fitted with different mathematical models. Hence, researchers must determine, a priori, how many and which parameters are needed in the model, and how the variables of the model are related to each other. Unfortunately, such a priori determination of a nonlinear model is not only very difficult but also may bias the interpretation of the observed data.

Utilities

Any developmental research must answer three fundamental questions: What develops? How does development occur? Why does development occur? To answer the first question, researchers must identify various developmental milestones and describe how these milestones are ordered along the dimension of age. The second question requires researchers to identify factors that engender development and establish a causal relationship between a developmental variable and factors that contribute to change in the developmental variable. Answering the "why" question requires an explanation of mechanisms that underlie the causal relationship between a developmental variable and development-engendering factors.

It would be wrong to ask whether macro- or microdevelopmental methods are better suited for answering any of the above questions, or even whether one method is generally superior to the other. In our view, macro- and microdevelopmental methods are each suited to address all three questions. The difference in utility of these methods seems to lie in a) the kind of assumptions and compromises that researchers are prepared to make in order to answer the three questions, b) the nature of the developmental change to be investigated, and c) the extent to which the developmental issue in question has been understood. Let us examine these issues in turn.

First, no developmental research method is perfect. All existing macro- and microdevelopmental methods are constrained by the fact that the targets of these methods are children with lives that extend beyond being subjects of study. Researchers are limited in terms of access to child participants, how much time they can spend with them, and what they can do with them. All developmental research methods, in one way or another, are designed to get the best information from children within such limitations. To do so, assumptions must be made, which, as we discussed above, inevitably entail compromises.

Because both advantages and disadvantages are associated with each developmental research method, no one method is generally better than another. Rather, the choice of method depends on the nature of developmental change to be investigated. There are several major forms of developmental change. One is a cumulative change: as age increases, the developmental variable changes steadily as a function of cumulative change in the independent variables. In terms of the pattern of such development, it can take a linear or curvilinear form (see figure 9.1a). The critical characteristic of cumulative development is that as age increases, the nature of the relationship between the developmental variable and independent variables remains the same. Because the assumptions of macrodevelopmental methods are consistent with this type of change, these methods are well suited to studying it.

The second major type of change is a so-called re-organizational change (figure 9.1b). Such change occurs when qualitative change takes place in one or more independent variables (e.g., a new independent variable emerges or an existing independent variable reaches a critical point).

Re-organizational change results in a qualitatively different form of the developmental variable as well as a qualitatively new relationship between the developmental variable and the independent variables. Therefore, the new relationship must be described by a mathematical model that differs qualitatively from the one describing the old relationship. One characteristic of a re-organizational change is that the developmental variable is highly variable during transition. The microgenetic method seems to be the most ideal method to study this type of development.

The third major type of change is a self-organizational change (see figure 9.1c). A self-organizational change, like a re-organizational change, results in a new form of the developmental variable. However, unlike in a re-organizational change, in a self-organizational change the existing independent variables do not change qualitatively. In addition, the actual relationship between the developmental and independent variables remains qualitatively the same (hence the same mathematical model can be used to describe the system before, during, and after transition). A self-organizational change occurs because of the fact that an individual's developmental history plays an important part in the change of a developmental variable. One of the characteristics of a self-organizational change is that inter-individual variability is high: different individuals may have entirely different developmental trajectories and each individual's developmental pattern is related to his or her initial level of development. For this reason, the dynamic systems method is best suited for studying self-organizational changes.

Ideally, researchers would know what type of developmental change is involved when embarking on a research project, so that an appropriate research method could be chosen. This, however, is normally not the case. The answer to this question can be obtained only when both macro- and microdevelopmental methods are simultaneously used. However, because the cross-sectional method is the most efficient among all developmental methods, it is often recommended that the method be used initially when developmental phenomena are least understood. The cross-sectional method can reveal major differences between age groups, which in turn suggests that a developmental change may take place between these ages. A small-scale longitudinal study is then carried out. Instead of covering a whole age spectrum, the longitudinal study, informed by the cross-sectional method, needs only to focus on the ages where a developmental change is suspected to take place.

If the longitudinal study confirms the existence of the developmental change, inspection of inter- and intra-individual variability is required. High variability between and within children may indicate a non-cumulative form of change in the developmental variable. At this point, additional cross-sectional studies are needed to delineate critical independent variables that may contribute to the change. With sufficient information about the timing of transition in the developmental variable and relevant independent variables, a microgenetic study or dynamic systems study can be launched, focusing on the ages when variability is high. For reasons of efficiency, we recommend that a microgenetic study be conducted prior to the dynamic systems study. Because the microgenetic method simulates change in an accelerated manner, it normally takes less time than the dynamic systems method, which requires tracking the developmental variable on a real-time scale. Once the microgenetic method confirms high inter-individual variability in a simulated situation, a dynamic systems method may be launched. This method should provide information about real-time developmental transitions. Also, with perturbation procedures, the dynamic systems method can reveal experimentally critical variables responsible for qualitative change in a developmental variable. With sufficient data, one can identify whether a developmental change is a re-organizational change (when the onset of, or qualitative change in, an independent variable engenders the change) or a self-organizational change (when no apparent qualitative change has taken place in any of the independent variables).

Only with the use of all these methods can we begin to have an adequate description of the developmental trajectory of a developmental variable, the factors that contribute to age-related change, and the mechanisms responsible for the change. It is clear that answering the "what," "how," and "why" questions about a single developmental variable cannot be achieved in isolation. It has to be a concerted effort by a community of researchers. A collective endeavor, however, requires researchers to share similar assumptions and values. In other words, they have to work within the same paradigm. Currently, developmental research is dominated by the macrodevelopmental approach, in terms of the conceptualization of research questions, research design, data analysis, and interpretation of findings. Only a limited number of studies have been done from the microdevelopmental perspective.

A paradigm shift is indeed needed (Granott, 1998b). However, the paradigm shift does not require that the macrodevelopmental approach be abandoned in favor of the microdevelopmental approach. A new paradigm should reflect the strength of these two approaches. We believe that the continuing improvement of the macrodevelopmental methods and the maturation of the microdevelopmental methods together will bring us closer to answering the three basic questions of child developmental research: What develops? How does development occur? Why does development occur?

References

Bruck, M., & Ceci, S. J. (1999). The suggestibility of children's memory. *Annual Review of Psychology, 50,* 419–439.

Catan, L. (1986). The dynamic display of process: Historical development and contemporary uses of the microgenetic method. *Human Development, 29,* 252–263.

Cooney, J. B., & Troyer, R. (1994). A dynamic model of reaction time in a short-term memory task. *Journal of Experimental Child Psychology, 58,* 200–226.

Elman, J. L., Bates, E. A., Johnson, M. H., Karmiloff-Smith, A., Parisi, D., & Plunkett, K. (1996). *Rethinking innateness: A connectionist perspective on development.* Cambridge, MA: MIT Press.

Fischer, K. W., & Granott, N., (1995). Beyond one-dimensional change: Parallel, concurrent, socially distributed processes in learning and development. *Human Development, 38,* 302–314.

Fogel, A., & Thelen, E. (1987). Developmental early expressive and communicative action: Reinterpreting the evidence from a dynamic systems perspective. *Developmental Psychology, 23,* 747–761.

Granott, N. (1998a). A paradigm shift in the study of development. *Human Development, 41,* 360–365.

Granott, N. (1998b). Unit of analysis in transit: From the individual's knowledge to the ensemble process. *Mind, Culture, and Activity, 5,* 42–66.

Johnson, M. H. (1999). Developmental neuroscience. In M. H. Bornstein & M. E. Lamb (Eds.), *Developmental psychology: An advanced textbook* (4th edn.) (pp. 199–230). Mahwah, NJ: Erlbaum.

Karmiloff-Smith, A. (1979). Micro- and macrodevelopmental changes in language acquisition and other representational systems. *Cognitive Science, 3,* 91–117.

Karmiloff-Smith, A. (1981). Getting developmental differences or studying child development? *Cognition, 10,* 151–158.

Karmiloff-Smith, A. (1985). From metaprocesses to conscious access: Evidence from children's metalinguistic and repair data. *Cognition, 23,* 95–147.

Karmiloff-Smith, A. (1993a). Self-organization and cognitive change. In M. H. Johnson (Ed.), *Brain development and cognition: A reader* (pp. 532–618). Oxford, UK: Blackwell Publishers.

Karmiloff-Smith, A. (1993b). Beyond Piaget's "epistemic subject": Inhelder's microgenetic study of the "psychological subject." *Archives de Psychologie, 61,* 247–252.

Karmiloff-Smith, A., & Inhelder, B. (1974). If you want to get ahead, get a theory. *Cognition, 3,* 195–212.

Kuhn, D. (1995). Microgenetic study of change: What has it told us? *Psychological Science, 6,* 133–139.

Kuhn, D., Schauble, L., & Garcia-Mila, M. (1992). Cross-domain development of scientific reasoning. *Cognition and Instruction, 9,* 285–327.

Lewis, M. (1995). Cognition-emotion feedback and the self-organization of developmental paths. *Human Development, 38,* 71–102.

Lewis, M. D. (this volume). Interacting time scales in personality (and cognitive) development: Intentions, emotions, and emergent forms.

Markman, E. M. (1991). The whole-object, taxonomic, and mutual exclusivity assumptions as initial constraints on word meanings. In S. A. Gelman & J. P. Byrnes (Eds.), *Perspectives on language and thought: Interrelations in development* (pp. 72–106). New York: Cambridge University Press.

Rabinowitz, F. M., Grant, M. J., Howe, M. L., & Walsh, C. (1994). Reasoning in middle childhood: A dynamic model of performance on transitivity tasks. *Journal of Experimental Child Psychology, 58,* 252–288.

Siegler, R. S. (1995). Children's thinking: How does change occur? In F. E. Weinert & W. Schneider (Eds.), *Memory performance and competencies: Issues in growth and development* (pp. 405–430). Hillsdale, NJ: Erlbaum.

Siegler, R. S. (1997). Concepts and methods for studying cognitive change. In E. Amsel & K. A. Renninger (Eds.), *Change and development: Issues of theory, method, and application. The Jean Piaget symposium series* (pp. 77–97). Mahwah, NJ: Erlbaum.

Siegler, R. S., & Chen, Z. (1998). Developmental differences in rule learning: A microgenetic analysis. *Cognitive Psychology, 36,* 273–310.

Siegler, R. S., & Crowley, K. (1991). The microgenetic method: A direct means for studying cognitive development. *American Psychologist, 46,* 606–620.

Siegler, R. S., & Jenkins, E. (1989). *How children discover new strategies.* Hillsdale, NJ: Erlbaum.

Smith, L. B., & Thelen, E. (Eds.) (1993). *A dynamic systems approach to development: Applications.* Cambridge, MA: MIT Press.

Thelen, E. (1995). Motor development: A new synthesis. *American Psychologist, 50,* 79–95.

Thelen, E., & Corbetta, D. (this volume). Microdevelopment and dynamic systems: Applications to infant motor development.

Thelen, E., & Smith, L. B. (1994). *A dynamic systems approach to the development of cognition and action.* Cambridge, MA: MIT Press.

Thelen, E., & Ulrich, B. D. (1991). Hidden skills: A dynamic systems analysis of treadmill stepping during the first year. *Monographs of the Society for Research in Child Development, 56* (Serial No. 223), 1–35.

van Geert, P. (1991). A dynamic systems model of cognitive and language growth. *Psychological Review, 98,* 3–53.

Van Geert, P. (this volume). Developmental dynamics, intentional action, and fuzzy sets.

Part IV

Context

10 Notebooks as windows on learning: The case of a science-into-ESL program

Rochel Gelman, Laura Romo, and Wendy S. Francis

Introduction

Our efforts to study the acquisition of new knowledge, especially in the areas of mathematics and science, take advantage of a combination of methods. These include experiments, controlled training studies, and qualitative analyses of videotaped classroom learning. In addition, we have been developing ways to treat the classroom as an in situ learning laboratory. Here we focus on a particular example, a science-into-ESL (English as a Second Language) classroom that functioned as a concept and language learning laboratory.

A key research goal was to gather "on-line" data on whether students moved on to and along relevant learning paths during the course of a semester. Given the classroom setting, we wanted these to be inconspicuous "probes" rather than more traditional learning test trials. Our solution shares important aspects of the microgenetic method, the topic of this book. We requested that students keep notebooks and make regular entries that could function as learning experiences for them and probes as to whether learning was happening over time. Notebook entries are a common feature of how scientists work, especially when it comes to trying to keep track of experiments and evolving ideas. They also have served historians of science as documents for analyzing the conditions of conceptual change. As we shall see, notebooks have the potential to serve researchers' efforts to obtain on-line information about students' progress in a non-intrusive manner. Thus, they can function both as a

An early report of the Science-into-ESL project was presented in a master's thesis by Romo (1993). The work covered here was supported by several funding sources, including grants from the Linguistic Minority Research Institute, University of California; the US Office of Education; and an NSF LIS grant entitled "Learning in Complex Environments by Natural and Artificial Systems." Correspondence about the chapter can be addressed to Rochel Gelman.

This chapter is dedicated to Anne Brown. She and her husband Joe Campione were ever-present conversationalists and cheerleaders from the very outset of the science-into-ESL project.

learning opportunity for students and as a research tool for investigators of concept and language acquisition.

Our commitment to a constructivist theory of concept acquisition motivated us to achieve on-line peeks at students' accomplishments (or lack of accomplishments) as their term progressed. Since learners are active participants in their own conceptual development, we cannot assume that they and their instructors will share a common interpretation of the lessons and related learning exercises. The knowledge and language skills they bring to a given subject influence what they attend to and how they interpret offered data. When the to-be-learned material is not readily related to what is already known, there is a risk that the inputs are ignored or even misinterpreted (Bartlett, 1932). Hence, it is critical to have ways to peek regularly at what, if anything, about the curriculum is being learned.

The science-into-ESL program featured here was developed by a team of high-school ESL and science teachers in collaboration with members of our university research team. A major goal of the program was to move ninth-grade students (fourteen and a half to sixteen years of age; median fifteen years) far enough along in their use and understanding of science in English so that they could take regular tenth-grade science classes, even though they had not completed their ESL course sequence. Of course, the program also had to increase students' overall English proficiency. At the time of study, ESL students at high schools in the Los Angeles Unified School District (LAUSD) were required to finish at least four semesters' worth of ESL instruction before starting science classes. This had the effect of limiting their opportunity to take enough years of high-school science courses to meet admission requirements to many colleges and other advanced levels of training.

The science-into-ESL curriculum used many of the lessons of cognitive science (see Bransford, Brown, & Cocking, 1999; Gelman & Gattis, 1995, for reviews). Every effort was made to ensure that students were active participants in their own learning, and that they engaged in guided discovery (Brown & Campione, 1996). In addition to being able to read newly prepared reading text materials about science topics, the students had opportunities to do collaborative experiments, make entries in their science notebooks, interpret data, talk and write about science, use computers, and interpret the course materials. Further, a group of bilingual UCLA undergraduates were present during voluntary after-school periods. Not only did the notebook requirement allow us to build in non-evaluative exercises that we could use to monitor students' learning over time, but it also fit with one of the desiderata of the course, this being that the students be able to do science and communicate about what was covered in readings and classroom lectures.

Monitoring learning in a classroom, given a constructivist perspective

Learners, be they infants, children, or adults, are not passive recipients of their environments. We all contribute to our own conceptual development by virtue of the fact that we use existing knowledge structures, no matter how skeletal they might be. Mental structures both require and contribute to epigenetic interactions with their environment. Without conscious effort, we more readily notice and remember those aspects of the environment that are related to available mental structures. Our ever-present tendency to assimilate data that are related to existing conceptual structures is often a good thing. Domain-relevant paths lead learners to inputs that are consistent with the structure of the domain to be learned; domain-irrelevant paths do not. Thus, existing structures of mind help novices move on to learning paths that are domain-relevant rather than domain-irrelevant.

There is a potential downside to the constructivist nature of our minds, namely, that it is always possible that beginning and novice learners will ignore and/or misinterpret their environments. Where mental structures have to be acquired de novo – as is surely the case for topics such as Newtonian mechanics, the theory of evolution, the stock market, etc. – learners have to acquire domain-relevant structures in addition to content (see Brown, 1990). Efforts to provide instruction in these domains must recognize and overcome a crucial challenge: learners may assimilate inputs to existing conceptual structures even when those inputs are inconsistent with existing structures and intended to force accommodation and conceptual change (Slotta, Chi, & Joram, 1995; Gelman, 1993, 1994). For this reason, students are often at risk of failure to learn mathematics or science. If we leave them to their own devices, they are biased to assimilate classroom inputs about fractions to their counting-based number theory. For example, they are likely to assume that $1/56$ is less than $1/75$ because 56 is less than 75. The risk of a mismatch between our intended inputs and what the learners take on is much increased when what is to be learned does not share structure with what is already known (Gelman, 1994; Gelman & Williams, 1998).

If the to-be-learned data do not map to an existing structure, the conditions are conducive for them to be regarded as irrelevant and therefore ignored (Stigler & Fernandez, 1995), or misinterpreted as relevant to an existing knowledge structure (Hartnett & Gelman, 1998). In the former case, learners fail to move on to the target learning path. In the latter case, they might even move on to the wrong learning path, one that encourages the development of misconceptions. These considerations highlight the need to have tools to determine whether learners move on to relevant learning paths when they are offered inputs meant to nurture new learning.

There is growing evidence that microgenetic studies – ones that probe for the kinds of hypotheses, language, and strategies children use at different points in the course of acquisition – contribute to efforts to understand concept development (e.g., Karmiloff-Smith & Inhelder, 1974/75, as well as the chapters by Goldin-Meadow & Alibali, Granott, Kuhn, Siegler, and Parziale in this volume). They are especially suited to gaining insight about the initial and changing nature of children's interpretations of inputs for learning. We had this advantage in mind when we set the goal of developing a version of such microgenetic analyses to chart learning paths in a school setting over the course of a semester. To do so we had to deal with three challenges.

The science-into-ESL materials were likely to be rather novel for many in the class. Therefore, despite extensive efforts to achieve a superb curriculum, it was not reasonable to expect the students to achieve learning with full understanding in a ten-week term. Mastery of the scientific concepts taught in high school can take many years. Acquisition of what Gelman and Williams (1998) dub "non-core domains" requires the assembly of new conceptual structures as well as the domain-relevant knowledge, and lengthy formal instruction is often required (see for example Bransford et al., 1999; Carey, 1991; Chi, 1992; Chi, Glaser, & Farr, 1988; Kuhn, 1970). We knew it would be foolhardy to expect the students to achieve learning with understanding. Therefore, we needed a design plan that differed from those microgenetic studies that track the evolution of strategy preference and deployment as learners converge on an endpoint, a correct solution, or a target learning plateau. The challenge then was to have ways to monitor whether students were at least attending to, and beginning to learn about, their lessons. A second challenge was to find a way to deal with the fact that, compared to most microgenetic studies, the time frame of our study was much expanded, indeed, to a full academic term. Finally, we knew that we could not achieve the level of experimental control that is a key feature of microgenetic studies. Still, our variant of the microgenetic method had to allow us to monitor whether or not students were moving on to and along relevant learning paths. Our search then was for a method that would provide a window on whether students were traversing learning paths which led toward science-relevant knowledge and language. As indicated, we responded to these challenges by taking advantage of a central feature of the science-into-ESL curriculum we were involved with – the students kept scientific notebooks. This was part of the plan to engage students in doing, talking, and reporting science.

Writing: A window on conceptual and language learning paths

The acquisition of scientific language and scientific concepts constitutes two sides of a coin; each is integrally dependent on the other (Kuhn, 1970; Halliday & Matin, 1993). When it comes to learning about technical domains, it is not stretching matters too far to treat science language learning as a form of second language learning. It is not just that the languages of science and mathematics are filled with specialized terms that derive their meaning from the domain within which they operate. There is also the problem that some everyday terms have completely different meanings. For example, the word "conductor" refers to the leader of an orchestra when used in everyday English. However, in the language of science "conductors" are substances or bodies that have the capacity to transmit or carry heat, electricity, etc. Within mathematics terms like "multiply" and "add" are more like false cognates; they do not have the same meaning in mathematics as they do in the natural language. They do not always mean "increase" or "get bigger," as shown in the result of multiplying two fractions or adding two negative numbers. Things are equally tricky when we consider the meaning of "add" when liquids are being combined. When one adds two cups of water to three cups of water, the result is five cups, but when one adds a 10 °C cup of water to another 10 °C cup, the resulting temperature is 10 °C. These examples illustrate that terms cannot always be treated as equivalent across different domains. Bransford et al. (1999) offer many further examples of the fact that learning about concepts and the specialized language (and notational system) of a domain go hand in hand. Such considerations reinforced our view that we would be able to probe whether students were moving on to and along a learning path that was related to the learning activities, by looking at their developing use of the domain-relevant scientific language.

Our decision to encourage students to write and ask questions about what they had been taught was also motivated by the finding that the study of explanations has provided researchers with a window into transitional states of students' mathematical and scientific understanding (Gelman, 1991; Hartnett & Gelman, 1998; Siegler & Jenkins, 1989). In addition, as individuals acquire knowledge about a topic, their ability to communicate and write about that topic progresses. For example, Siegler & Jenkins (1989) found that as children discover new strategies for addition problems their explanations are less articulate, that is, they use incomplete sentences, pause more often while talking, and engage in multiple starts and stops. These are taken to be indications that they are thinking about new and old strategies simultaneously. Related findings are provided by

Goldin-Meadow, Alibali, Church, & Breckinridge (1993). When children are in a transitional state of learning, the hand gestures that they use to describe their understanding of a math problem are often incongruent with their speech. This is because one kind of math strategy is being conveyed nonverbally while another competing strategy is conveyed through their verbal communication (Goldin-Meadow et al., 1993). Gelman and her colleagues have also illustrated the power of having students write about their understanding of to-be-learned concepts at different points in the learning process. Fourth- and fifth-grade children (nine- to eleven-year-olds) who were at different ability levels provided qualitatively different written answers when asked "why are there two numbers in a fraction?"

The foregoing examples illustrate another important point, this being that both mathematical understanding and language use differ as a function of how much students know about math. The same is true for learning about science. For example, Anderson and Shifrin (1980) demonstrated that when students acquire organized knowledge about spiders, they both understand and recall the salient features of a passage after reading it. Those who do not know about spiders recall poorly and have little understanding of the text.

Bransford et al. (1999) also review the growing evidence that teachers can benefit from clues about students' evolving and changing interpretations and understandings of the material being taught. An example of this comes from Stigler's analyses of video-taped lessons of elementary school mathematics teachers in Japan. The teachers made extensive use of students' changing explanations within and across lessons as a way to monitor students' progress. Stigler and his colleagues' characterization of the students' evolving solutions to problems brought out the fact that the students in the class often started out with different kinds of answers that covered a variety of areas. Over the course of classroom discussions, the teacher explored students' errors with them. Teachers then used these errors to guide students towards correct solutions and, from our point of view, move them on to relevant learning paths. (Stigler & Hiebert, 1999).

Aims and setting of the present study

As indicated, the curriculum was designed to embed science instruction into a ninth-grade ESL class in a public high school in the Los Angeles area. The high school which served the students in this study accommodates approximately 3,000 students, 20% of whom are designated as "Limited English Proficient." The school is in relatively good condition and has good sports fields as well as outdoor spaces. The great majority of the students in the school's ESL program speak Spanish, having come primarily from Mexico and El Salvador. Korean-speaking students comprise the next largest group; however, the program also serves students who speak Russian, Persian, Armenian, Tagalog, Vietnamese, Hebrew, Thai, Cantonese, and Mandarin. Many of the students traveled long distances from their homes on LAUSD school buses that picked them up at their neighborhood school. The data presented in this report were collected in an intermediate-level ESL2 class during the first semester in which the Science-into-ESL program was implemented.

Every effort was made to take into account the emerging views on how to apply the findings about the nature of conceptual learning to the design of classroom instruction. An effective program for preparing students with the relevant background for learning new science concepts requires more than just having them memorize terms or lists of facts (e.g., Beck & McKeown, 1989; Carey, 1988; Dooling & Lachman, 1971; Glynn, Yeany, & Britton, 1991). The ability to repeat the definitions of terms does not guarantee a correct understanding of the concepts (e.g., Osborne & Cosgrove, 1983; Stepans, Dyche, & Beiswenger, 1988). Therefore, it is important to attempt to relate classroom reading and other instruction materials and tools around a plan to develop into class an organized knowledge base of related concepts. It was agreed that the program would do well to concentrate on a limited number of topics in some depth. Topics from the biological and physical sciences that met school system guidelines, including those in the *California State Board of Education Science Framework* (State of California, 1990), were organized into a ten-unit program that focused on the conceptual themes of variability, energy, interdependence, and change. These were featured in the reading materials prepared for the classes (Meck & Gelman, 1992).

Materials were ordered to have latter lessons build on earlier ones. When it seemed warranted, several units were devoted to a topic. The titles of the initial ten units were: 1. Sun; 2. Photosynthesis; 3. Respiration; 4. Local Winds; 5. Temperature and State; 6. Buoyancy and Density; 7. Water Cycle; 8. Food Energy; 9. Organs and Organisms; 10. Interactions and Ecosystems. Each unit consisted of:

i. an *initial reading* designed to focus the student on the core concept(s) of the unit and to provide the linguistic means to respond appropriately to a short pretest for that unit
ii. a short *pretest* of a representative core concept presented in the initial reading; for the teachers, a *listing of the core concepts and vocabulary* around which each of the units was built

iii. a *main reading* that incorporated the core concepts and vocabulary into a text. This was paired with reading comprehension and second language development exercises

iv. a *laboratory exercise* focusing on the core concepts and including both demonstrations and experiments that the students did in groups, using inexpensive materials brought from home or a grocery. For each laboratory exercise, there was a teacher-oriented set of instructions

v. a *review* involving language and concept development exercises

vi. a short *follow-up test* to complement item ii, the short pretest

vii. a *journal notebook* for students to keep track of their classwork (see below)

Given the findings that opportunities to do science improve the likelihood of learning science (Brown & Campione, 1996), we created groups of "experimenters." Students were assigned to groups for conducting experiments, talking about them, and recording their observations. These groups also prepared their findings to report to the class, and the teacher was encouraged to engage students in guided question-answering opportunities. Also, as indicated, notebooks were an integral part of the students' participation in the class. They were used to make notes about a variety of learning experiences, including the preparation of graphs and other scientific figures, record keeping and analysis of experimental data, lessons on science vocabulary, reviews, and question-asking. Two examples of the kinds of notebook entries students made to record their experiments are show in a schematized version in figure 10.1. Figure 10.2 illustrates the kind of writing activities that were part of the review sessions that ended a unit.

The review session for a unit started with a group discussion during which the group generated a list of ten to twenty science terms relevant to the unit's theme. After the class agreed on the list of relevant terms, students were given approximately fifteen minutes to construct concept maps in their notebooks. In this exercise, students drew lines to link concepts that they thought to be related to each other. Subsequently, they were given fifteen minutes more to write up to ten sentences to describe how they had inter-related the concepts in their concept maps. The sentences that students did write became the focus of our analyses of whether students' knowledge of the concepts and language of science had indeed moved on to a learning path by the end of the second half of the course.

We turn to an extended consideration of the kinds of analyses we did with the review sentences. We also present some standard outcome measures. However, evaluation of the curriculum itself is not the main focus

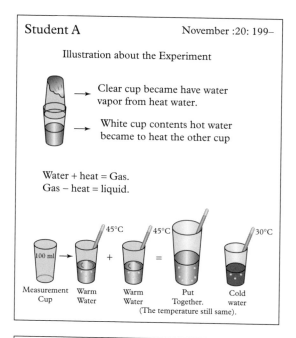

Student A   November :20: 199–

Illustration about the Experiment

→ Clear cup became have water vapor from heat water.

→ White cup contents hot water became to heat the other cup

Water + heat = Gas.
Gas – heat = liquid.

| Measurement Cup | Warm Water | Warm Water | Put Together. | Cold water |

100 ml → 45°C + 45°C = 30°C

(The temperature still same).

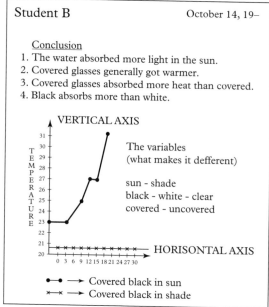

Student B   October 14, 19–

Conclusion
1. The water absorbed more light in the sun.
2. Covered glasses generally got warmer.
3. Covered glasses absorbed more heat than covered.
4. Black absorbs more than white.

VERTICAL AXIS

T E M P E R A T U R E

31 30 29 28 27 26 25 24 23 22 21 20

The variables
(what makes it defferent)

sun - shade
black - white - clear
covered - uncovered

HORISONTAL AXIS

0 3 6 9 12 15 18 21 24 27 30

●–● → Covered black in sun
×—× → Covered black in shade

Figure 10.1 Redrawn examples of the kind of notebook records that Students *A* and *B* made for the experiments they did to accompany their reading. (Students' spelling and grammatical errors have not been corrected.)

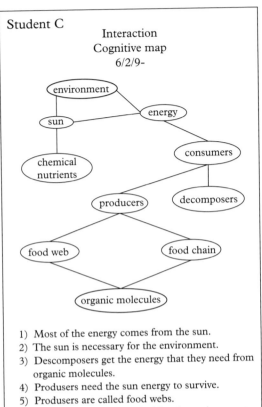

Student C

Interaction
Cognitive map
6/2/9-

1) Most of the energy comes from the sun.
2) The sun is necessary for the environment.
3) Descomposers get the energy that they need from organic molecules.
4) Produsers need the sun energy to survive.
5) Produsers are called food webs.
6) Chemical nutrients are bad for the environment.
7) Descomposers need organic molecules to survive.
8) Consumers need chemical nutrients.
9) Not all the energy come from the sun.
10) Consumers need food chain.

Figure 10.2 A redrawn example of a notebook entry for a given review session. (Students' spelling and grammatical errors have not been corrected.)

in this chapter. It is instead to show that investigators can use students' notebooks to accomplish some of the key advantages of the microgenetic method, namely, that notebooks are windows into which to regularly peek at "on-line" learning (or non-learning) over an extended period of time and in a regular classroom setting. The kinds of on-line measurements that we have been developing need not be tied to a particular instantiation of a programmatic effort to embed relevant science learning materials into an ESL program.

Analyzing the progression of students' ideas: The written sentences

A total of thirty students were enrolled for at least some part of the term. Of the thirty students, eight either moved, started the semester late, or were excessively absent. The notebooks of the remaining twenty-two students who were present throughout the semester provided the corpora for our analyses.

The writing exercises for Units 1 and 10 were excluded from analysis because the first unit served as practice and the last unit was separated from the other nine units by a holiday break. The remaining eight units yielded a database of 1,271 sentences. Of these sentences, thirty-seven (all produced by the same student) were judged to be inappropriate, in that they stated simply which terms in the map could be connected, without describing the relationship. Two independent coders evaluated whether or not each of the remaining 1,234 sentences was comprehensible and what the intended message was. The coders' classifications matched in 98% of the cases (Cohen's $k = 0.89$). Consensus was reached on all discrepancies, resulting in the exclusion of eighty-one sentences (6.6%) from further coding, whereupon the remaining body of codeable data contained 1,153 sentences.

Some students did not complete the task of writing ten sentences in the time allotted. Students who consistently wrote at least five sentences in every exercise were assigned to a High-Production group. The other students were assigned to a Low-Production group, the rationale being that students less fluent in English might perform differently owing to the extra mental effort it requires for them to produce language (Francis, 1999). Half of the twenty-two students generated at least five sentences during each review; the other half of the students consistently wrote fewer than five sentences in every exercise. Because this difference in production might lead to different levels of overall performance, it was used as a blocking variable in the statistical analyses. For the purposes of analysis, the groups that produced more than five sentences per exercise were called the "High-Production Group" and those who produced fewer were called the "Low-Production Group." As it turned out, the levels of performance of these two groups did not differ for most variables and effects analyzed. Therefore results for the High- and Low-Production students are reported separately only when differences or interactions were present.

Figure 10.3 contains examples of individual students' tendencies to produce multi-clause sentences as a function of successive curriculum units. Although the shapes of the individual learning curves vary across students, overall students tended to generate sentences that were more

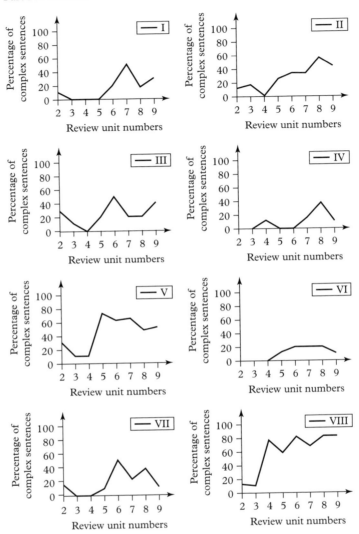

Figure 10.3 Eight individuals' learning curves for percentage of complex sentences as a function of review unit. Unit 1 is not included because it was used to introduce the exercise.

structurally complex in the latter half of the science course. The tendency to move forward was our first clue that the review sentences possibly contained more specific science information as a function of experience. We will return to the matter of the possibility of different acquisition functions in the discussion. Now we focus on ways to measure whether the students

Table 10.1 *Concept specificity coding system and examples*

Level	Content specificity category	Examples of student sentence productions
1	Properties or category membership	The sun is a star. Sunlight has different colors. Stars have their own heat. Vapor is a type of gas.
2	Needs or sources	Energy comes from the sun. All plants need energy. Our body needs a lot of carbohydrates.
3	Mechanics or functions	The sun gives energy to the plants. Animals breathe oxygen. Air is always pulled by gravity. Green plants make food from the sunlight.
4	Conditions or purposes	A hot air balloon is sometimes dangerous, because it has gas in it. All plants need energy in order to survive. Hot air goes up, because it is less dense. When we add heat energy to the water, it causes the water to change temperature.

were on relevant learning paths at least by the second half of the term. To accomplish this goal we designed a coding system to quantify both (1) the syntactic complexity of the sentences and (2) the amount of conceptual information expressed in the sentences over time (see table 10.1).

Analysis of sentence syntactic structure

The sentence structure analyses focused on two variables relevant to writing sentences with complex ideas: 1) the use of embedded clause structures and 2) the inclusion of prepositional phrases. The first kind of complexity in sentence structures is common in scientific language, such as "if you boil water, it vaporizes" (Celce-Murcia & Larsen-Freeman, 1983). Therefore to describe specific concepts, the students would need to develop their skills in writing these kinds of sentences. The addition of prepositional phrases serves to expand the number of concepts expressed within a sentence.

Each sentence was coded as either *simple* or *complex*. A *simple* sentence was made up of a single main clause (e.g., "All plants need energy"). A *complex* sentence was made up of at least one main clause and one embedded clause (e.g., "All plants need energy in order to survive"). Sentences joined together simply by coordinating conjunctions (e.g., "and," "or") were counted and coded as separate sentences. Each sentence was coded for whether or not it contained any prepositional phrases. For each student, the proportion of complex and simple sentences and the proportion of sentences containing at least one prepositional phrase was calculated for each half of the course.

The total number of sentences produced in the first and second halves of the course were 555 and 598, respectively. The mean proportion of complex sentences increased from 13% in the first half to 31% in the second half ($F(1, 19) = 38.068$, $MSE = 0.009$, $p < 0.001$). The average proportion of sentences containing one or more prepositional phrases also increased from 34% in the first half to 48% in the second half of the course ($F(1, 19) = 14.95$, $MSE = 0.01$, $p < 0.001$). These results indicate that the sentences in the latter half of the course were made up of complex phrase structures, a condition in English for writing more conceptually informative prose. The next set of analyses addressed whether the syntactic complexity of the sentences served this purpose.

Analysis of conceptual information

Students described and explained how the science concepts/terms related to one another in a variety of ways across sentences. In the analysis, four categories were identified (see table 10.1). At the most general level, *Properties or Category Membership* (Level 1) sentences described attributes associated with at least one entity. Next, *Needs or Sources* (Level 2) sentences described a simple relationship of two or more entities needing one another, or one deriving from the other (e.g., energy sources or food sources). *Mechanics or Functions* (Level 3) sentences provided more information by describing how entities act or operate on other entities, but no reasons or conditions were specified. The most conceptually informative sentences, *Conditions or Purposes* (Level 4) sentences, explained conditions and circumstances for how and why entities, substances, or processes were related to one another. Table 10.1 shows examples of sentences that students produced in each of these four categories. Two independent raters coded the conceptual information of each sentence, which ranged from general (Level 1) to more conceptually informative (Level 4). Agreement on classifications into the four categories was 94% (Cohen's $k = 0.92$). Consensus was reached on all discrepancies.

Table 10.2 shows the distribution of sentences across the four category levels. In the first half of the course (Units 2 through 5), the most prevalent kind of sentence was a *Properties or Category Membership* sentence ($M = 47\%$). It seems that during the first half of the course students mostly attended to properties of entities and wrote general definitions.

Table 10.2 *Average proportion (standard deviation) of sentences at each concept specificity level*

Level	Content specificity category	1st half of course	2nd half of course
1	Properties or category membership	0.47 (0.14)	0.26 (0.13)
2	Needs or sources	0.15 (0.14)	0.12 (0.10)
3	Mechanics or functions	0.20 (0.09)	0.25 (0.11)
4	Conditions or purposes	0.18 (0.13)	0.37 (0.18)

In the second half of the course (Units 6 through 9), *Conditions or Purposes* sentences were most prevalent ($M = 37\%$). Students shifted their focus from describing general attributes of entities to describing specific conditions, reasons, or circumstances governing relationships among entities.

To further analyze this pattern, an *average concept specificity* measure was computed for each student for each half of the course. This measure was derived by summing products of category levels and their corresponding proportions.[1] This weighted average provided a useful way to compare performance across the two halves of the course (though it clearly has only ordinal, not interval scaling properties). Average concept specificity scores increased from 2.08 in the first half to 2.72 in the second half [$F(1, 19) = 113.92$, $MSE = 0.033$, $p < 0.001$], indicating that students expressed more specific ideas about the science terms in the second half of the course. This change reflects an increase in the production of *Conditions or Purposes* sentences from 18% of all sentences in the first half to 37% of all sentences in the second half. All but one student produced several examples of this type of sentence. Thus, it appeared that as students became familiar with the properties and functions of entities, they shifted to writing more sentences about why and for what purpose these entities stood in relationship to one another. It is important to note that although the proportion of attribution sentences decreased from the first half to the second half, the students continued to write some definitional sentences, perhaps because they were introduced to novel concepts in new units or were still clarifying the older ones.

What kinds of conditions, reasons, or circumstances were described in these *Conditions or Purposes* sentences? Again, because this was an English course and not a regular science course, we did not expect the ideas to be extremely sophisticated. Overall, the students wrote mostly

[1] For example, for a student who produced 15% Level 1, 20% Level 2, 30% Level 3, and 35% Level 4 sentences, the weighted average would be calculated as follows: $(1 \times 0.15) + (2 \times 0.20) + (3 \times 0.30) + (4 \times 0.35) = 2.85$.

about conditions or reasons (Category Level 4) associated with mechanics or functions of things (60% of 336 sentences). For example, students explained that "When we add heat energy to the water, it causes the water to change temperature." Nineteen percent of the sentences provided reasons or conditions for needs and sources (e.g., "Plants need water, carbon dioxide, and sunlight for photosynthesis"). Twenty-one percent of the sentences described conditions or circumstances for a property or a category membership (e.g., "The balloon has gas when it has air"). Agreement on these subcategories was 92% (Cohen's $k = 0.87$).

Accuracy of the content

To measure the accuracy of the sentence content, each sentence was scored on a scale from 0 to 4, with higher numbers indicating a more accurate display of conceptual understanding. Scale anchor points were $0 = $ no display of understanding; $1 = $ mostly unclear and inaccurate; $2 = $ about half correct and half incorrect; $3 = $ mostly clear and accurate; $4 = $ clearly accurate display of understanding. Two coders, who had assisted in the classroom, worked together to score the accuracy of each sentence. They agreed on 90% of the cases.

For each student, an average accuracy score was computed for each half of the course by dividing the total score across the units by the total number of sentences (i.e., weighting each sentence equally). On average, students' sentences were scored as mostly clear and accurate, a score of approximately 3. The production groups differed in their patterns of content accuracy across the two halves of the course ($F (1,19) = 14.21$, $MSE = 0.03$, $p < 0.001$). Accuracy of the Low-Production Group did not change significantly from the first to the second half of the course (from $M = 2.93$ to $M = 2.83$), but they did maintain their level of accuracy. In contrast, the High-Production Group improved significantly in accuracy from the first to the second half of the course (from $M = 2.90$ to $M = 3.20$, $p < 0.005$), suggesting that students who could produce more sentences showed higher levels of science accuracy.

Ability to explain new phenomena: The unit quizzes

Although the content of students' sentences was mostly accurate, one could argue that students could have been simply repeating facts that they had heard in class. To rule out this alternative explanation for their high level of content accuracy, we compared the students' scores to another source of written data – their explanatory answers to the posttest quizzes that accompanied each unit. The quizzes were designed, as part of the curriculum, to measure whether students could transfer their knowledge of key concepts of the units to explain novel scientific phenomena. The questions and the target answers had not been reviewed in the curriculum, although an analogous situation might have been discussed. Thus, these tests provided us with a written measure of the students' understanding of the science material that could not have been simply copied or repeated from class materials or discussions. For example, following the unit on buoyancy and density, the students read the following passage and were asked to write a few sentences to explain the various phenomena described.

Hot air balloons are dangerous but very exciting. Sometimes, we can see only one balloon high in the air, and sometimes we can see many balloons together. The people who ride a balloon stand or sit in a large basket below the balloon. As they move through the air, pushed by the winds, they fall gently and slowly toward the ground. When the people in the basket want to go up, they turn on a burner below the balloon and for a short time shoot a hot flame up into it. The balloon slowly climbs higher. After a while, the balloon again goes slowly toward the ground. How does a hot air balloon work? The mouth of the balloon is open to the air – there is nothing inside the balloon except air. What causes the balloon to go up?

Students' responses to these questions were scored independently by the ESL instructor and by a teaching assistant, who agreed on 94.5% of their ratings. Two points were given for responses in which the science information was clearly accurate with respect to the question; one point was given if most but not all of the science information was accurate; and zero points were given if the science information was clearly inaccurate.

For each student, a percentage score was computed across all completed unit posttest quizzes by dividing the sum of their unit quiz scores by the number of unit quizzes completed ($M = 33\%$, $SD = 22\%$). All of the students completed at least seven quizzes. We reasoned that if students were learning more about science concepts, and they could describe their understanding accurately in their sentences, they should also be able to provide coherent, accurate responses to questions on the unit quizzes. Indeed, the quiz scores and the content accuracy scores were highly correlated ($r = 0.79$, $p < 0.001$). This result provides some independent evidence against the explanation that the accurate concepts expressed in students' sentences were merely copied or repeated without understanding.

Requests for more science information

At the end of each unit, the instructor asked students to write down any questions they had about the material and what they would like to learn

Table 10.3 *Examples of specific "why" and "how" questions asked by students[a] (corrected for spelling and simple grammar)*

- why we can't drink the water in the ocean because when you put water in a pot and put salt, we can drink the water
- why people can't live underwater and why other animals can't live on the land
- why the dirt gets cold more faster than water
- how the winds go around
- why if we eat a lot of calories, we will get fat
- how come hot air goes up and changes to cold air
- how a tree can live in the winter
- why any object with density that is greater than water will sink and any object whose density is less than water will float
- how do we know that green plants have covered our planet for over a billion years?
- why can't we breathe in the water?
- why is the sun very hot?
- if gravity pulls everything's down including the air, why doesn't it kill us?
- how can a tree pick up water from his root?
- how do living things get energy from food?
- I would like to find out if there is someone in space like ET.
- what would happen if a space man takes off their clothes in space?

[a] Some students failed to ask questions, despite the instructions for this exercise. Some examples of what these students wrote are included here.

about in the future. All of the students provided at least one request for additional specific information about a scientific process or phenomenon (e.g., "Why are the hot air and cool air different weights?" or "How do the stars make their own light?") over the course. Most of the questions were about why or how things function, take place, or come to be (72%). Some examples of the students' questions (corrected for spelling and simple grammar) are presented in table 10.3. The remaining responses included general statements either restating the title of the unit (e.g., "I don't understand about local winds"), or general comments about wanting to learn more science (e.g., "I would like to learn more about respiration"). Two independent raters coded the number of specific information requests for each of the students (Cohen's $k = 0.98$ for each question). The mean number of information requests for each of the twenty-one students (missing data on one student) was computed across all completed units, with a maximum possible score of 18 ($M = 9.52$, $SD = 5.01$).

A correlational analysis was performed to examine the relationship of the number of specific information requests to the concept specificity and correctness scores from the sentences. Students who asked more specific kinds of questions also included more correct information in their sentences ($r = 0.46$, $p < 0.05$), although asking specific questions was not related to sentence concept specificity. Furthermore, increased specific question-asking was reliably associated with students having more correct science explanations in the unit quizzes ($r = 0.56$, $p < 0.01$). Overall, it seems that students who gained a better understanding of the material were also able to ask more thoughtful, focused questions about the science topics throughout the course.

Question-asking may also be considered an indicator of students' interest in science or motivation to learn science. Indeed, there was a marginally positive correlation between how many specific questions the students asked and their ratings on a seven-point scale ($M = 5.6$, $SD = 1.0$) of how interested they were in learning science ($r = 0.42$, $p = 0.057$). Although the number of specific questions did not predict whether or not they took a mainstream science class the following year, there was interesting relation to the grades of the twelve students who did go on to take science. Those students who had asked more questions about the science material in our program the previous year did better in their regular science courses the next year ($r = 0.62$, $p < 0.05$). The mechanism for this relationship could be motivation, or it could be that the students continued to ask specific questions in their regular science classes to clarify their understanding.

English grammar skills

A main concern among the ESL instructors at the school was that the new science curriculum would use up valuable class time that would otherwise be dedicated to basic grammar drills and exercises and that their students would fall behind in learning English. Given our plans for coding the sentences, we gained information that addresses these concerns (Francis, Romo, & Gelman, in press). A brief discussion of the English language-learning results is included in this section.

To start, we simply scored whether each of the 1,153 sentences contained a grammatical error or not. The number of sentences in each half of the course that were free of grammatical errors was divided by the total number of sentences in each half to obtain the proportion of sentences that were completely grammatical in each half. The percentage of error-free sentences decreased from 35% in the first half to 24% in the second half of the course (F (1, 19) $= 10.03$, $MSE = 0.01$, $p < 0.01$). As expected, the ESL students had problems producing sentences with correct morphosyntax throughout the semester. In

Table 10.4 *Correlations among the five main concept and language variables across students*

	Content accuracy	Clause complexity	Preposition frequency	Whole-sentence grammaticality
Content specificity	0.73^c	0.80^c	0.62^b	0.07
Content accuracy		0.78^c	0.52^a	0.24
Clause complexity			0.49^a	0.35
Preposition frequency				0.24

$^a p < 0.05$; $^b p < 0.005$; $^c p < 0.001$

particular, students made errors in applying subject–verb agreement, auxiliary and modal verbs, prepositions, and determiners. The increase in sentences with grammatical errors was most likely due to the increase in opportunities to make more errors as the students wrote longer and more complex sentences. Surely many of us have extremely accomplished colleagues who do and write science in English but who nevertheless fail to include an obligatory determiner or mix up their use of "he" and "she," and so on. Although we expected the students to continue to have persistent problems producing correct morphosyntactic constructions, we thought it possible that these kinds of grammatical errors would not be related to students' learning of information about science.

Relationships among the conceptual and language variables

The results of the analyses reported in the previous sections motivated us to examine the relationships among the conceptual and linguistic variables. We selected five variables for a correlational analysis: *Content Specificity* (scaled from 1 to 4), *Content Accuracy* (scaled from 0 to 4), *Clause Structure or Complexity* (simple or complex), *Frequency of Prepositional Phrases* (none as opposed to one or more), and *Whole-Sentence Grammaticality* (correct or incorrect). These relationships were examined to reveal which features tend to go together to characterize individual students' ideas and written expression.

For the correlational analysis, we obtained the average score assigned to each of the five variables across all the sentences produced by each student. (For variables based on dichotomous classifications, the averages correspond to proportions.) Table 10.4 shows the correlations among the five variables. It can be seen that students who wrote about specific complex ideas also wrote more accurate ideas. Students who wrote more specific and/or accurate ideas also used complex sentence structures that contained more embedded clauses and more prepositional phrases. It appears that students generated sentence structures that were useful, and sometimes necessary, to explain the conditions, circumstances, reasons or purposes of scientific phenomena.

In contrast, whole-sentence grammaticality was not significantly associated with any of the content or sentence structure variables. It is important to note, however, that the directions of these nonsignificant correlations were positive – one cannot say that students who express specific complex or accurate ideas or who use more embedded clauses and prepositional phrases were compromised on their morphological marking. That is, there was no trade-off between learning science and learning English morphology, or between learning to use complex sentence structures and learning English morphology.

The fact that overall grammatical accuracy score is a poor predictor of one's ability to engage in learning about science-relevant concepts and communication skills deserves special attention. For all students in the ESL program, including those in ours, took the LAUSD's end-of-semester evaluation exam, which is a multiple-choice test on English grammar. Our students' scores were comparable to those of former ESL students who were taught the standard ESL curriculum by our teachers. Much to the relief of the ESL instructors, the students who participated in this program performed as well as had previous ESL2 students (Gelman, Meck, Romo, Meck, Francis, & Fritz, 1995). True, the ESL scores mean that learning about science did not come at the cost of learning English grammar as indexed by expected levels of performance on standardized ESL tests. However, if the only measure used to assess students' progress were these tests, then the students in our program would not have had an opportunity to start on to science learning paths. Given that 64% of the students in our study actually went on to take a tenth-grade science course that is taught in English with English textbooks, our analyses of different aspects of language illustrate the importance keeping in mind the fact that "language" is not a unidimensional domain.

Some final thoughts

There is an overarching lesson about the kinds of results presented here, one that dovetails well with the patterns of results presented in a number of chapters in this book. This is that the acquisition of knowledge is a multi-faceted matter, so much so that different measures taken at the same time even can diverge, conflict, or disagree. In our case, we show that students' ability to write about science-relevant concepts improved from the first half to the second half of the course. So did their ability

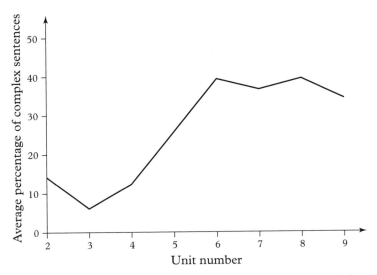

Figure 10.4 The learning curve that results when the individual data points in figure 10.3 are averaged.

to write with complex sentences of the kind that support the expression of if–then and causal scientific content. Still, this does not mean that the production of these sentences was perfectly correct at the syntactic level. Indeed, whole-sentence grammaticality was not correlated with any of our content or sentence structure measures. This means that, for example, students who earned relatively high scores on measures of conceptual complexity still could have made errors regarding determiners, plural markers, and even subject–verb agreement.

As indicated, this chapter has focused on the idea that students' science notebooks provide a rich data source for monitoring what, if anything, students are starting to learn about. The analyses we presented illustrate the feasibility of this approach; however, these are by no means the only analyses that can be done. We chose to focus on first-half/second-half analyses. Some will ask why we did not do group, trial-by-trial analyses. An example of such an analysis would be like that shown in figure 10.4, where we show the average learning curve for the eight individual curves shown in figure 10.3. The averaged data give the impression that use of complex sentences improved rather gradually, starting around Unit 4. However, if we compare figures 10.3 and 10.4, it becomes clear that this is not true for all of the individuals represented in figure 10.3. That is, it seems as if the different students had different acquisition curves. The average curve obscures this. It is because there is an obvious first-half/second-half difference across the individuals that we started at this level of comparison.

Now we have some ideas about the kinds of things that students were or were not learning to write about in the Science-into-ESL program. We expect that future analyses could help us get a closer picture of the possible relationships between the ability to use the kinds of syntactic structures that support the expression of scientific knowledge and the learning of the scientific knowledge itself. Indeed, we think it could be possible to focus on the students' entries for their science experiments. The examples in figure 10.1 are quite characteristics of the notebooks as a set. This encourages us to consider whether to provide the opportunity to track the students' use of graphs, notational systems, experimental materials, and interpretation of experiments.

We end with a word of caution. It is unlikely that any kind of notebooks can be used to monitor learning paths and their shapes. It is extremely important to think about the kinds of entries that students might make and how these facilitate the joint goals of moving students on to learning paths and having a way for teachers and experimenters to peek to see if this is happening.

References

Anderson, R. C., & Shifrin, Z. (1980). The meaning of words in context. In R. J. Spiro, B. C. Bruce, & W. F. Brewer, (Eds.), *Theoretical issues in reading comprehension.* Hillsdale, NJ: Erlbaum.

Bartlett, F. (1932). *Thinking: An experimental and social study.* New York: Basic Books.

Beck, I. L., & McKeown, M. G. (1989). Expository text for young readers: The issue of coherence. In L. B. Resnick (Ed.), *Knowing, learning, and instruction: Essays in honor of Robert Glaser* (pp. 47–67). Hillsdale, NJ: Erlbaum.

Bransford, J. D., Brown, A. L., & Cocking, R. R. (Eds.) (1999). *How people learn: Brain, mind, experience and school.* Washington, DC: National Academy of Sciences.

Brown, A. L. (1990). Domain-specific principles affect learning and transfer in children. *Cognitive Science, 14,* 107–133.

Brown, A. L., & Campione, J. C. (1996). Psychological theory and the design of innovative learning environments: On procedures, principles, and systems. In L. Schauble & R. Glaser (Eds.), *Contributions of instructional innovation to understanding theory* (pp. 229–270). Hillsdale, NJ: Erlbaum.

Carey, S. (1988). Why John and Jane aren't learning science. In *Science and public policy seminars.* Federation of Behavioral, Psychological, and Cognitive Sciences. Washington, DC: American Psychological Association.

Carey, S. (1991). Knowledge acquisition: Enrichment or conceptual change? In S. Carey & R. Gelman (Eds.), *Epigenesis of mind: Studies in biology and cognition.* Hillsdale, NJ: Erlbaum.

Celce-Murcia, M., & Larsen-Freeman, D. (1983). *The grammar book: An ESL/EFL teacher's course.* Rowley, MA: Newbury House.

Chi, M. (1992). Conceptual change within and across ontological categories: Examples from learning and discovery in science. In R. Giere (Ed.), *Cognitive models of science: Minnesota studies in the philosophy of science.* Minneapolis, MN: University of Minnesota Press.

Chi, M. T. H., Glaser, R., & Farr, M. J. (Eds.) (1988). *The nature of expertise.* Hillsdale, NJ: Erlbaum.

Dooling, D. J., & Lachman, R. (1971). Effects of comprehension on retention of prose. *Journal of Experimental Psychology, 88,* 216–222.

Francis, W. S. (1999). Analogical transfer across languages in English–Spanish bilinguals. *Journal of Memory and Language, 40,* 301–329.

Francis, W. S., Romo, L., & Gelman, R. (in press). Syntactic structure, grammatical accuracy, and content in second-language writing: An analysis of skill learning and on-line processing. In R. R. Heredia & J. Altarriba (Eds.), *Bilingual sentence processing.* n.p.: Elsevier.

Gelman, R. (1991). Epigenetic foundations of knowledge structures: Initial and transcendent constructions. In S. Carey & R. Gelman (Eds.), *Epigenesis of mind: Essays on biology and cognition* (pp. 293–322). Hillsdale, NJ: Erlbaum.

Gelman, R. (1993). A rational-constructivist account of early learning about numbers and objects. In D. Medin (Ed.), *Learning and motivation, Vol. 30* (pp. 61–96). New York: Academic Press.

Gelman, R. (1994). Constructivism and supporting environments. In D. Tirosh (Ed.), *Implicit and explicit knowledge: An educational approach* (pp. 55–82). Norwood, NJ: Ablex.

Gelman, R., & Gattis, M. Lee (1995). *Trends in educational psychology in the United Statess. Recent trends and developments in educational psychology: Chinese and American perspectives.* Paris, France: UNESCO.

Gelman, R., Meck, G., Romo, L., Meck, B., Francis, W., & Fritz, C. O. (1995). Integrating science concepts into intermediate English as a second language (ESL) instruction. In R. F. Macías & R. G. García-Ramos (Eds.), *Changing schools for changing students: An anthology of research on language minorities, schools, and society* (pp. 181–203). Santa Barbara, CA: UC Linguistic Minority Research Institute.

Gelman, R., & Williams, E. (1998). Enabling constraints for cognitive development and learning: Domain specificity and epigenesis. In W. Damon (Series Ed.), & D. Kuhn & R. S. Siegler (Vol. Eds.), *Handbook of child psychology, Vol. 2: Cognition, perception, and language* (5th edn., pp. 575–630). New York: Wiley.

Glynn, S. M., Yeany, R. H., & Britton, B. K. (1991). A constructive view of learning science. In S. M. Glynn, R. H. Yeany, & B. K. Britton (Eds.), *The psychology of learning science* (pp. 3–19). Hillsdale, NJ: Erlbaum.

Goldin-Meadow, S., & Alibali, M. W. (this volume). Looking at the hands through time: A microgenetic perspective on learning and instruction.

Goldin-Meadow, S., Alibali, M. W., & Church, R. Breckinridge (1993). Transitions in concept acquisition: Using the hand to read the mind. *Psychological Review, 100,* 279–297.

Granott, N. (this volume). How microdevelopment creates macrodevelopment: Reiterated sequences, backward transitions, and the Zone of Current Development.

Halliday, M. A. K., & Martin, J. R. (1993). *Writing science: Literacy and discursive power.* Pittsburgh, PA: University of Pittsburgh Press.

Hartnett, P. M., & Gelman, R. (1998). Early understandings of number: paths or barriers to the construction of new understandings? *Learning and Instruction: The Journal of the European Association for Research in Learning and Instruction, 8,* 341–374.

Karmiloff-Smith, A., & Inhelder, B. (1974/75). If you want to get ahead, get a theory. *Cognition, 3,* 195–212.

Kuhn, D. (this volume). A multi-component system that constructs knowledge: Insights from microgenetic study.

Kuhn, T. S. (1970). *The structure of scientific resolutions.* Chicago, IL: University of Chicago Press.

Meck, G. H., & Gelman, R. (1992). *Interrelated science concepts in English as a Second Language: A science content text for intermediate level ESL instruction.* Draft, Department of Psychology, UCLA.

Osborne, R. J., & Cosgrove, M. M. (1983). Children's conceptions of the changes of state of water. *Journal of Research in Science Teaching, 20,* 825–838.

Parziale, J. (this volume). Observing the dynamics of construction: Children building bridges and new ideas.

Romo, L. F. (1993). Science concept development and language proficiency in ESL instruction. Unpublished master's thesis. University of California, Los Angeles.

Siegler, R. S. (this volume). Microgenetic studies of self-explanation.

Siegler, R. S., & Jenkins, E. (1989). *How children discover new strategies.* Hillsdale, NJ: Erlbaum.

Slotta, J. D., Chi, M. T. H., & Joram, E. (1995). Assessing students' misclassifications of physics concepts: An ontological basis for conceptual change. *Cognition & Instruction, 13,* 373–400.

State of California (1990). *California State Board of Education Science Framework.* Sacramento, CA: California Publication.

Stepans, J. I., Dyche, S., & Beiswenger, R. (1988). The effect of two instructional models in bringing about a conceptual change in the understanding of science concepts by prospective elementary teachers. *Science Education, 72,* 185–195.

Stigler, J. W., & Fernandez, C. (1995). Learning mathematics from classroom instruction: Cross-cultural and experimental perspectives. In C. A. Nelson (Ed.), *Basic and applied perspectives on learning, cognition, and development. The Minnesota Symposia on Child Psychology, Vol. 28* (pp. 103–130). Mahwah, NJ: Erlbaum.

Stigler, J., & Hiebert, J. (1999). *The teaching gap.* New York: Simon & Schuster.

11 Darwin's construction of the theory of evolution: Microdevelopment of explanations of variation and change in species

Kurt W. Fischer and Zheng Yan

The process of building new knowledge can seem mysterious, and microdevelopmental analysis shows great promise for unpacking some of that mystery (Dunbar, 2001; Fischer, 1980b; Granott, 1998; Klahr, 2000; Werner, 1948). How do people bootstrap themselves and others to build new knowledge? Performing such analysis, however, requires obtaining detailed information about how people build knowledge and skill in real time. Tracking changes with assessments that are performed only at widely separated intervals – the norm in developmental research – makes the process seem mysterious. For knowledge that leads to conceptual revolutions, such as Charles Darwin's theory of evolution by natural selection, the mystery appears deep and impenetrable.

Despite its obvious promise for illuminating the construction of knowledge, microdevelopmental research has been generally neglected (a state that this book will hopefully help to remedy). Collecting data can be difficult, requiring intensive commitments of time and energy. The person being observed may not learn or develop any new skill or understanding, making the effortful data collection useless. Even if the person does learn something new, studying important learning moments is difficult, because the most important kinds of learning are typically not recognized until after they are complete. Study of the building of culturally new, creative knowledge is frequently impossible, because the importance of the knowledge is not recognized until after it has been constructed.

Fortunately this mystery can be illuminated for the theory of evolution, because Darwin himself recorded in detail his construction of

The work on which this chapter is based was supported by grants from Mr. and Mrs. Frederick P. Rose, Harvard University, and NICHD grant #HD32371. The authors thank Eric Fischer, Nira Granott, Jane Haltiwanger, Karen Kitchener, Arlyne Lazerson, Juliana Paré-Blagoev, and Samuel P. Rose for contributions to the theory and research. Special thanks to Howard Gruber, on whose biography of Darwin this chapter is centrally based.

We dedicate this chapter to the memory of our friend and colleague Robbie Case, who died too young in the midst of a good, strong, productive life.

the theory of evolution as he was building it. The significance of these data is enormous, because evolution is obviously the most important new theory in biology in modern times. Darwin regularly recorded notes describing his thoughts and observations during the several years during which he first constructed the theory of evolution, thus unknowingly tracing his own construction of the theory (Barrett, 1974, 1980; Barrett, Gautrey, Herbert, Kohn, & Smith, 1987; DeBeer, Rowlands, & Skramovsky, 1960). He recorded these notes for his own purposes, to further his research and theory-building. The notes were all written early in his adult life, between 1832 and 1839, the period when he constructed the theory; and they culminated in a series of notebooks specifically about "the transmutation of species" and related issues written between 1837 and 1839. Many years passed until 1859, when he finally published his earthshaking book, *On the origin of species by means of natural selection, or the preservation of favoured races in the struggle for life*. For Darwin, the process of initial construction of the theory was long, slow, and full of emotion and turmoil, reflecting the usual course for acquisition or creation of complex knowledge (Gardner, 1993; Gruber, 1973).

In his remarkable book *Darwin on man*, Howard Gruber describes in detail Darwin's creation of the theory of evolution. When I (Fischer) first read Gruber's description shortly after its publication, the microdevelopmental process leapt from the page. It helped that Gruber himself had studied with Piaget and frequently used developmental concepts to inform his description. Still, I was surprised at how closely Darwin's construction of the theory corresponded with the higher levels of development of abstractions beyond what Piaget and Inhelder called "formal operations" (Inhelder & Piaget, 1955/1958; Piaget, 1983). Darwin's construction of explanations of variation and change in species amounts to a case study of adult skill development, unusual because of the novelty and importance of the knowledge constructed.

In 1980 one of us had presented the first formulation of development of levels beyond formal operations into early adulthood (Fischer, 1980b), an account followed by related models by others (Basseches, 1984; Case, 1985; Commons, Richards, & Armon, 1984; Kitchener & King, 1990). Gruber's description of Darwin's painstaking pathway to evolution fits the levels for abstract skills amazingly well (see also Keegan, 1989).

Processes of building new theory: Micro- and macrodevelopment together

Contrary to stereotypes about sudden creative insight, Darwin took a full eight years to develop his theory, building day by day a huge number of smaller skills about biological variation and adaptation that he eventually transformed through creation of the principle of evolution by natural selection. People commonly believe that creative new ideas come suddenly – as a kind of bolt from the blue or inspiration – but the evidence indicates that the process of creating new ways of thinking is long and slow, depending on lengthy processes of microdevelopment of component skills (Gruber, 1989). Parts of the novel knowledge system may come suddenly, such as solutions to single, well-defined problems within the broader knowledge domain, but even those solutions have been prepared by lengthy cognitive work beforehand.

For new ways of thinking, such as evolution (or impressionism in painting or relativity in physics), a long and complex process of learning and thinking is required before a person can produce what is essentially a new point of view – a new way of looking at many problems, a new theory. Indeed, the gradualness of this construction is not limited to original creations but applies to any form of expertise dealing with richly textured problems. A rule of thumb is that becoming an expert in a new field requires five to ten years of skill construction, which combines many microdevelopmental processes with longer-term cognitive reorganization of component skills (Ericsson & Charness, 1994; Gardner, 1993).

The construction of the theory of evolution by Darwin fits this model well, and analyzing it requires considering development as involving simultaneously both microdevelopment (change in understanding over a matter of seconds, minutes, hours, or days) and macrodevelopment (change over months and years), as skills are gradually constructed and reconstructed. Indeed, the time frame is less important to the distinction between micro- and macrodevelopment than the processes involved. Microdevelopment involves combining, differentiating, and reorganizing specific skills in particular tasks and contexts, as well as generalizing them. Macrodevelopment begins with the many skill changes wrought by microdevelopment over an extended period and adds long-term changes in capacity and framework. For detailed analysis of actual skill construction like Darwin's, there is no simple distinction between micro- and macrodevelopment but only a broader developmental analysis that subsumes both types of processes.

Traditionally there has been a sharp distinction between macrodevelopment based on longitudinal assessment over long time spans such as years and microdevelopment or learning based on short-term changes. However, assessment only at widely separated intervals makes almost impossible the analysis of the constantly evolving process of constructing complex skills or knowledge systems. The approach that we take, called "dynamic skill theory," shares with dynamic systems theory an emphasis on common processes of change across both short and long time courses. In addition, the recent surge of research on microdevelopment has convincingly demonstrated its power for analyzing short-term change and relating it to macrodevelopment, although researchers still disagree about the most useful tools for analyzing microdevelopment (Case & Okamoto, 1996; Dunbar, 2001; Fischer & Bidell, 1998; Kuhn, 1995, Granott & Parziale, this volume; Siegler, 1996; van Geert, 1998).

Fundamental variability of skills

Understanding development of skills and expertise in an adult requires first recognizing the enormous variability in each individual in the complexity level of skill and understanding at different moments. This pervasive variability characterizes even single, coherent domains, such as understanding coral reef formation or analyzing the functions of the shapes of birds' beaks (two domains where Darwin made important contributions). Much adult activity takes place at surprisingly low skill levels, while some activity occurs at high levels (Fischer & Granott, 1995; Granott, 1993a). Low levels are common when a person encounters a novel or unfamiliar task or when a task is not challenging, requiring only low-level functioning (Fischer, 1980b; Fischer, Yan, McGonigle, & Warnett, 2000).

Even for long-term development, people evidence substantial variability, with the upper limit on skills varying as a function of contextual support, as illustrated in figure 11.1 for optimal and functional levels in adolescence and early adulthood (Fischer, Rotenberg, Bullock, & Raya, 1993; Kitchener, Lynch, Fischer, & Wood, 1993). Assessments that support high-level functioning through priming and practice produce a high upper limit on performance, called the "optimal level." Assessments that provide no such support produce a low upper limit, called the "functional level." The gap between optimal and functional levels is termed the "developmental range." The same person routinely produces skills that vary up and down within this range, showing a different "stage" depending upon whether the context provides support for high-level functioning. Key components of support are familiarity with a task and immediate priming of its key components.

Optimal level commonly shows stage-like spurts in performance at specific ages, as illustrated in figure 11.1, whereas functional level does not show systematic spurts. The four levels of abstractions emerge at approximately ten, fifteen, twenty, and twenty-five years of age, respectively, for single abstractions (Ab1), abstract mappings (Ab2), abstract systems (Ab3), and systems of abstract systems (Ab4), which form principles.

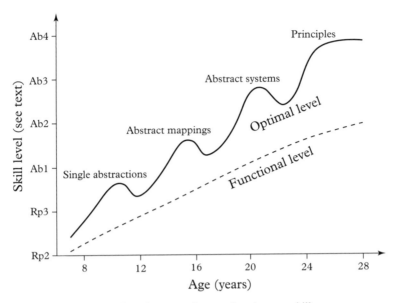

Figure 11.1 Developmental range for abstract skills.

Before the development of abstractions, earlier levels of concrete representations develop and lay the foundation for abstractions, such as representational mappings (Rp2) and representational systems (Rp3), which emerge at approximately four and six and a half years. Based on research on spurts in relevant skills, these ages of emergence appear to be relatively stable across people for familiar domains that are important to a person or that are facilitated by education (Fischer, Pipp, & Bullock, 1984; Fischer & Rose, 1994).

Darwin constructed the main tenets of his evolutionary theory when he was between twenty-two and thirty years of age, the period during which the highest level of abstract skills typically emerges. Each of the four levels of abstractions will be explicated later in terms of development of Darwin's thinking about variation and evolution.

In ordinary activities, people show great variability in skill level over short time periods, only occasionally functioning at their upper limit, and this variability is essential to the processes of construction of new skills. Contrary to the common cognitive image of people as scientists or philosophers functioning with high-level logic, people live in a practical world in which they routinely adapt their activities to fit the immediate demands of each situation (James, 1975; Peirce, 1878; Wittgenstein, 1953). Much of the time, the tasks that people face do not require high-level skills. From an ecological perspective, low-level activity fulfills important adaptive functions for coping with simple, concrete realities, such as preparing dinner, eating, conversing about the day's activities, and washing dishes. More complex, abstract activities such as explaining variations in species, diagnosing problems with a car engine, or analyzing the problems with political institutions have an important place in human cultures, although they are not required for most daily activities.

Dropping to a low level to build new skills

For both concrete tasks and abstract ones, construction of a new understanding (microdevelopment) starts with a sharp drop in the complexity level of skill, usually far below both functional and optimal levels. To build new skills or to change old ones to fit a new task, people must move their skill *backward* to a low level in a given domain in order then to gradually construct a higher-level skill. Without this process of regression and reconstruction, skills remain stuck in old forms at a higher level that is adapted to a prior situation, not to the new one that is required (Fischer et al., 1993). That is, staying at a high level fixes lower-level skill components in old forms, while building new high-level skills requires first reworking lower-level ones by moving down to action at those lower levels and thus rebuilding components to eventually make possible the required new high-level skills. That is, to adapt to new situations, people need to move down to a lower level so that they can reorganize their skills at that level for the new situation.

Granott (1993b, 1998, this volume) has described compellingly how people produce these backwards transitions in order to adapt to new tasks and reconstruct their activities and understandings. Faced with a Lego robot for the first time, adults routinely regressed to egocentric sensorimotor actions that had many similarities to infants' activities, failing to differentiate their own actions from properties of the robot. Granott found that even when adults seemed to have constructed a higher-level skill for understanding a robot, minor changes in the situation produced regression once again, with a further need for new reconstruction. They thus showed repeated scalloping – building gradually to a higher-level skill and then falling back down, building gradually again and once more falling back down, and so forth.

Yan (1998) found similar backwards transitions when graduate students learned how to use a computer to do simple statistical analyses over four class sessions as part of a course (Fischer et al., 2000). The students developed backwards to single representations (not all the way to actions) and then gradually built new more complex skills. For example,

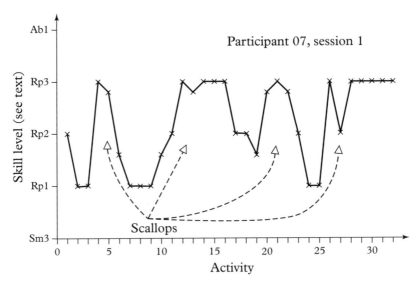

Figure 11.2 Learning a statistics operation. *Sources*: Yan, 1998, 2000.

figure 11.2 shows this process of repeated scalloping in the skills of one student in her first class session. She began at a low level, moved up to a higher level as she solved one subtask, moved down again to a lower level with a new subtask and then built up to a higher level for it, and so forth. Note that she demonstrated only representational systems (Rp3) as her highest skill, even though other evidence showed that she commonly used higher levels of abstraction when appropriate in class. Similar patterns of skill levels obtained for other students too. Because the computer task required only representational systems and perhaps occasional single abstractions, people used skills at those levels, not superfluous higher ones.

The microdevelopmental process of repeating skill construction with variations (scalloping) pervades learning of new skills. These recurring growth spurts are similar to the circular reactions that pervade young children's activities, as they repeat an activity many times with the apparent goal of mastering it (Baldwin, 1894; Piaget, 1936/1952; Wallon, 1970). Similarly Darwin showed repeated reconstruction of understanding as he built the theory of evolution – rediscovering, for example, the principle of natural selection repeatedly until finally he could generalize it to become a central building block of his theory. At several separate places in his notebooks he described the core principle of evolution by natural selection, but the early versions did not stick with him. Instead he seemed to lose the significance of the principle and then had to invent it again later.

Granott and her colleagues Fischer and Parziale (this volume) also describe how people bootstrap their activities during microdevelopmental regressions to low-level skills, using a process called "bridging," in which they establish a target shell to guide people's efforts to learn a task or solve a problem. In bridging, people function at two levels simultaneously – the (low) level at which they perform a new or problematic task and the (higher) level of a bridging shell to mark the kind of skill they seek to build. The shell includes empty slots, like algebraic unknowns, to be filled in through activities with the task. In Granott's study of Lego robots, for example, one dyad used a shell based on the concept of "reaction." Framing the robot as producing a reaction, they set up a shell that initially had two unknowns – the input that caused the reaction and the change in activity that came from the reaction. Typically a shell is based on prior knowledge about related tasks, linking the known and the new and thus facilitating understanding the new. Teachers, mentors, or friends can provide a bridging shell (Case & McKeough, 1990; Dunbar, 2001; Ericsson & Charness, 1994; Rogoff, 1993), and people often provide shells for themselves.

Solving novel tasks seems to require bridging shells to guide the creation of new knowledge, as when Darwin sought a naturalistic explanation for variations and changes in species. In the early part of his voyage on the *Beagle*, he used concepts from geology as bridging shells – for example, the theory of formation of coral reefs. Later he used some of his own earlier conceptions, such as the theory of coral reefs, as bridging shells for his later work. Through many such microdevelopmental processes of building specific skills to solve specific problems, he gradually laid the foundation for the macrodevelopmental transformation of his thinking through the integrative principle of evolution by natural selection. Within each shorter period he built many individual understandings through microdevelopmental processes, with the long-term result being construction of a novel, revolutionary framework for understanding variation and change in living things. Each of the following four sections outlines some of the microdevelopmental changes through which Darwin built specific understandings at each of the four skill levels, ultimately leading to the macrodevelopmental construction of the theory of evolution.

Darwin's starting point: The social context of understanding variations

Like all scientists, Darwin began with the viewpoints of his time, which he learned from his highly educated family and at school. Many scientists were studying nature, and their study was structured by a Christian belief system concerning creation, a nearly universal belief in a narrow interpretation of the Biblical account of creation: The Earth and its inhabitants were the products of a Creator, who made the world in six days about 6,000 years earlier. One purpose of much science was to document and catalogue the marvels of physical and organic nature in order to demonstrate the supreme intelligence and necessary existence of the Creator, who devised such intricate and perfect structures and creatures. Eventually, Darwin built a different view, showing how the imperfections and irregularities found everywhere in living organisms indicate that the design of nature was achieved not by an omniscient inventor but by a groping evolutionary process. He began, however, with the standard scientific view of his time.

In 1831–32, before the twenty-two-year-old Darwin began his major scientific work during his voyage as the naturalist on the British naval ship *HMS Beagle*, he thought of the world in terms of the conventional religious beliefs of his day: There were two separate worlds, the Physical World of rocks, minerals, gases, and the like, and the Organic World of plants, animals, and human beings. God created the two worlds separately, on different days during the week of creation, and they remained separate in their fundamental nature. He created the two worlds in perfect balance, with each creature having a specific place and role in the physical world. There was no fundamental interaction between the two worlds beyond the fit that God had ordained, no basic change in one caused by the other.

Each of these concepts – the physical world and the organic world – required a minimum of a Level Ab1 single abstraction, a skill level that sustains the formation of intangible concepts, such as consistency, justice, physical world, or organic world (Fischer, Hand, & Russell, 1984). The concept for physical world, denoted by the skill structure

WORLD
PHYSICAL

involves nonliving materials, such as rocks, soil, water, and air. The concept of organic world, denoted by the skill structure

WORLD
ORGANIC

involves living things, such as plants, fish, and farm animals. The concept of Creator was also a single abstraction at its simplest,

CREATOR
DIVINE

involving a notion of God not simply as a (concrete) king sitting on his throne in the skies, but instead as an intangible agent who somehow created the physical and organic worlds. Starting with these relatively simple abstractions, Darwin and his peers could build up more complex skills, such as understandings about relations between the Creator's actions or intentions and properties of the physical and organic worlds. However, at their simplest and by themselves, the concepts of physical and organic worlds required only two single abstractions. These concepts represented the primary starting point for Darwin's eventual creation of the theory of evolution by natural selection.

The general skill levels for Darwin's construction of the theory of evolution by natural selection are outlined in figure 11.3. Abstractions develop through four main optimal levels, indicated in the left-hand column. The skill structures in the table are defined broadly to emphasize Darwin's general conceptions about how the organic and physical worlds interact. Here in the text, on the other hand, the skill structures are defined more specifically with concepts about the organic and physical worlds that Darwin actually used, such as death of an animal (organic world) or growth of a mountain (physical world). In skill formulas words in large capital letters denote abstract concepts, while words in small capitals below or above the large ones denote specific characteristics or subsets of those concepts. Lines and arrows denote relations between abstractions that are characteristic of different levels.

At age twenty-two, as Darwin was about to begin his work on species variation and evolution, he was not limited to these simple concepts, these single abstractions about variation in the world, but he already had more sophisticated skills. Based on the norms for emergence of levels of abstraction, he could use skills involving relations between abstractions (abstract mappings and systems), especially for familiar topics and in supportive contexts. The capacity to construct abstract systems coordinating several abstractions typically emerges at about age twenty, while that for coordinating such systems in terms of general principles does not usually emerge until age twenty-five (Fischer & Rose, 1994; Kitchener et al., 1993). In some domains, he was already sophisticated about biology and geology, and he used these areas of high-level skill to provide microdevelopmental bridges to help him construct understandings of species variation and evolution. During the voyage of the *Beagle* his capacity to construct and understand principles for coordinating abstract systems emerged and developed. Late in the voyage and in the following three years, he vividly demonstrated this capacity in his extensive discussions in his notebooks about principles for making sense of variations and adaptations across species.

Level	Skill	Major events	Dates

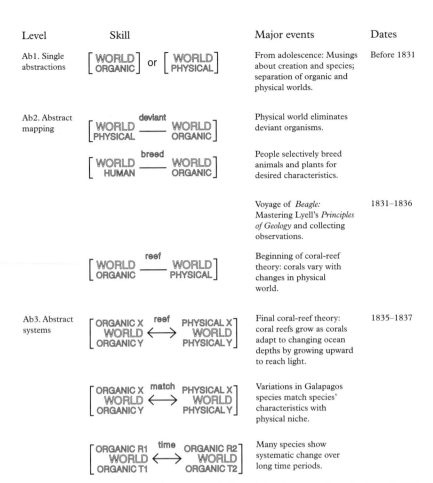

Ab1. Single abstractions — WORLD ORGANIC or WORLD PHYSICAL — From adolescence: Musings about creation and species; separation of organic and physical worlds. — Before 1831

Ab2. Abstract mapping — WORLD PHYSICAL —deviant— WORLD ORGANIC — Physical world eliminates deviant organisms.

WORLD HUMAN —breed— WORLD ORGANIC — People selectively breed animals and plants for desired characteristics.

Voyage of *Beagle:* Mastering Lyell's *Principles of Geology* and collecting observations. — 1831–1836

WORLD ORGANIC —reef— WORLD PHYSICAL — Beginning of coral-reef theory: corals vary with changes in physical world.

Ab3. Abstract systems — ORGANIC X WORLD ORGANIC Y ←reef→ PHYSICAL X WORLD PHYSICAL Y — Final coral-reef theory: coral reefs grow as corals adapt to changing ocean depths by growing upward to reach light. — 1835–1837

ORGANIC X WORLD ORGANIC Y ←match→ PHYSICAL X WORLD PHYSICAL Y — Variations in Galapagos species match species' characteristics with physical niche.

ORGANIC R1 WORLD ORGANIC T1 ←time→ ORGANIC R2 WORLD ORGANIC T2 — Many species show systematic change over long time periods.

Figure 11.3 Development of Darwin's theory of evolution (1831–1839): A general overview. *Sources for historical information*: Barrett, 1974; Darwin, 1859; Keegan, 1989; Gruber, 1981.

Note: Skill structures in this figure emphasize relations between physical and organic worlds in the various phases of Darwin's work. The structures in the text diagram the actual skills, specifying components from physical and organic worlds that Darwin actually coordinated. Each set in abstract skills is designated by words in outline capital letters, with the main set or agent indicated by larger letters and the categories or subsets indicated by smaller letters. A skill structure is delimited by brackets, and relations between sets are denoted by lines or arrows. Level Ab1 skills involve single sets, Level Ab2 mapping skills are denoted by a single line relating sets, Level Ab3 system skills by a two-headed arrow between sets, and Level Ab4 by a two-headed double-line arrow between sets. Words in lower-case letters next to a line or arrow define the relation. Further explanation of skill structures and notations can be found in Fischer, 1980a; Fischer & Rose, 1994.

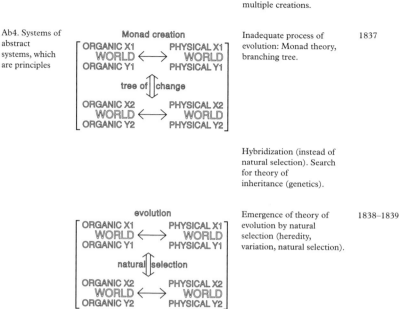

Ab4. Systems of abstract systems, which are principles

Struggling with idea of multiple creations.

Inadequate process of evolution: Monad theory, branching tree.

1837

Hybridization (instead of natural selection). Search for theory of inheritance (genetics).

Emergence of theory of evolution by natural selection (heredity, variation, natural selection).

1838–1839

Figure 11.3 *(cont.)*

Foundations: Geological evolution and the organic world

The first break in the existing point of view about variation and evolution came from geologists, who were finding it difficult to reconcile large classes of geological facts with the Biblical stories of creation and the flood. In particular, the *Principles of geology*, published by Darwin's mentor Charles Lyell in three volumes between 1830 and 1833, demonstrated that the geological time scale was much longer than 6,000 years. The publication of Lyell's books was a crucial event in Darwin's life. In December of 1831 Darwin sailed on the *Beagle* to help with its mission of charting the coastal geology of South America and making various other scientific and navigational measurements. He took along Lyell's first volume to read and use as he studied geological formations and organic life in the many locations he visited during the five-year voyage, including the Galapagos Islands that he later made famous for its variety of species.

During the several years following publication of this landmark geological work, many scientists came to agree with Lyell's conclusions about earth's physical changes, including that the time elapsed since creation of the physical world was much more than 6,000 years. The consensual interpretation became that God had created a set of universal natural laws that accounted for the geological changes. The geological changes characterized the physical world, however, and were not seen as implying anything about changes in the organic world. Acknowledging that natural laws operate on rocks was vastly different from acknowledging that they operate on human beings. A common argument was that the Earth was created first and then, some time later, the Creator made plants, animals, and people. Here is where the analysis of Darwin's thinking about evolution begins.

A central idea from geology that pervaded Darwin's work on evolution was gradualism: Universal natural laws produce gradual change in small amounts but, over long periods of time, the small changes add up to make enormous changes (Keegan, 1989). In geology, small, gradual changes combine to create powerful qualitative changes, such as strata of soil and even mountains and seas. In biology, Darwin gradually applied the same principle, eventually extending gradualism to explain enormous changes in the organic world over long periods.

Darwin assimilated Lyell's geological principles during the voyage of the *Beagle* and made extensive field observations in many locations in South America. Gradually he began to recognize that there were important interactions between the physical world and the organic world. In constructing his new skills for understanding organic and physical variations, he built on his earlier understandings of two kinds of interactions – the death of defective or deviant creatures, and selective breeding of animals and plants by people. Each of these skills he built through a series of microdevelopmental steps.

Regarding the death of deviant organisms, when an animal, plant, or person has a major physical defect, that organism will usually die or fail to reproduce. A sparrow born with defective wings, a deer with part of a leg missing, a monkey that is blind, or a cactus with no chlorophyll will quickly die in their natural environments. Because of the nature of the physical world in which particular organisms live, major physical defects lead to death. Darwin understood that in this way the physical world acts on the organic world to eliminate deviants, a skill structure denoted as

$$\begin{bmatrix} \text{WORLD} & \xrightarrow{\text{deviant}} & \text{ORGANISM} \\ \text{REQUIRE} & & \text{DEATH} \end{bmatrix}$$

This skill was a Level Ab2 abstract mapping relating characteristics of the physical world (requirements for survival) to characteristics of the organism (death from deviance from requirements), as shown in figure 11.3. The relation of the two worlds also required a differentiation of the organic world into two distinct types, deviant and normal (not shown in figure 11.3),

$$
\left[\begin{array}{ccc} \text{ORGANISM} & \xrightarrow{\text{differ}} & \text{ORGANISM} \\ \text{NORMAL} & & \text{DEVIANT} \end{array} \right]
$$

a distinction that later facilitated Darwin's use of the concept of natural selection.

Before Darwin's theory, scientists interpreted this relation between the physical world and the organic world in a way that required no change in the conception of two separate worlds. Since the Creator had devised all creatures to fit their particular environmental niche, deviants would naturally die. There was still no true interaction between the physical and organic worlds.

The second understanding that Darwin built on was selective breeding of animals and plants (which he later studied himself in a hobby of selectively breeding pigeons). Within the organic world, when breeders wanted pigeons with a particular characteristic, such as large chests to provide more meat for eating, they would selectively breed several generations of pigeons with larger chests and thus produce offspring with large chests. In general, people (a special part of the organic world according to the Christian framework) could produce major changes in desired characteristics through such selective breeding,

$$
\left[\begin{array}{ccc} \text{PERSON} & \xrightarrow{\text{breed}} & \text{ORGANISM} \\ \text{SELECT} & & \text{CHANGED} \end{array} \right]
$$

This kind of human selection eventually proved to be a useful bridge to help Darwin think about inheritance and natural selection in evolution. In this way his skills for understanding both deviant organisms and selective breeding served later as bridging shells to guide his construction of skills for analyzing evolution by natural selection.

During the *Beagle* voyage, Darwin's interest at first was in geology, and his first major step toward conceptualizing the pervasive interaction between organic and physical worlds involved geological formations – coral reefs – which commonly form large rock-like barriers in the ocean in the vicinity of islands or continental coasts. During the voyage, Darwin confirmed Lyell's observations and hypotheses about coral reefs, and gradually began to build his theory of coral reef formation and evolution, which, by the end of the voyage, he had built into a broad theory that is still valid today. The theory built on the observation that corals, which are living organisms that live in huge colonies, actually construct the reefs through their shells, with the colonies creating massive rock formations.

In its simplest form, this concept involved a Level Ab2 mapping of the organic world of the coral on to the physical world of ocean reefs: Changes in the organic world of corals produce changes in the physical world of reefs,

$$\left[\begin{array}{ccc} \text{ORGANISM} & \xrightarrow{\text{change}} & \text{WORLD} \\ \text{CORAL} & & \text{REEF} \end{array} \right]$$

This simple conception neglected any back-and-forth relation between the organic and physical worlds, focusing only on one dimension of the relation between coral organisms and physical reefs in the ocean, but still it established a clear link of organic world affecting physical world, moving beyond the separation that pervaded common belief. Of course, Darwin moved rapidly beyond this simple conception to a sophisticated analysis of the interplay of influences in the formation of coral reefs.

Central theme: Relations among variations in organic and physical worlds

By the end of the *Beagle* voyage, Darwin had constructed a sophisticated multi-dimensional theory that went beyond Lyell's ideas to explain both the formation of coral reefs and their evolution over long geological time periods. This theory also presaged the theory of evolution by natural selection, with its dynamic interaction of physical and organic worlds along multiple dimensions. Of course, Darwin did not recognize these connections initially but had to gradually construct understandings of the sophisticated interactions embodied in variation and evolution in species. His new skills involved several dimensions of variation in organism and world and thus required Level Ab3 abstract systems, which typically emerge for optimal level at about twenty years of age (Fischer & Rose, 1994).

The coral-reef theory specified variations in land masses, sea floors, water depth, sunlight under water, reef height, and coral growth. Corals grow only in relatively shallow, sun-lit waters, and each generation of organisms builds its hard skeleton on the foundation of skeletal remains laid down by preceding generations. As land masses rise over hundreds and thousands of years, the floor of the sea nearby slowly recedes, making the water deeper and lowering a reef under more water. To stay close enough to the surface of the sea to obtain the sunlight they need to survive, new corals must grow on top of the skeletons of dead corals, and thus coral reefs slowly form on top of previous generations of corals.

Dealing with the several dimensions and components of coral-reef variation and evolution required several related abstract systems. In one skill, the lowering of the reef into deeper water (because of subsidence of the sea floor) leads gradually to death of the old coral and growth of new coral on top, which in turn produces a higher reef,

$$\begin{bmatrix} \text{GROWTH} & & \text{HIGHER} \\ \text{CORAL} & \xrightarrow{\text{larger}} & \text{REEF} \\ \text{DEATH} & & \text{LOWER} \end{bmatrix}$$

Another part of the dynamic interaction in coral-reef formation is that the depth of the ocean floor varies with the height of the land mass nearby (two aspects of the physical world). The ocean floor lowers as an island rises in the Pacific Ocean or as mountains grow on the western coast of South America,

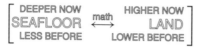

$$\begin{bmatrix} \text{DEEPER NOW} & & \text{HIGHER NOW} \\ \text{SEAFLOOR} & \xleftrightarrow{\text{math}} & \text{LAND} \\ \text{LESS BEFORE} & & \text{LOWER BEFORE} \end{bmatrix}$$

Consequently coral reefs tend to form where there has been a visible upwelling of land and a corresponding drop in the ocean floor.

The interaction between ocean floor and upwelling of land involves a relation of compensation or match, in which the rising of the land corresponds to the dropping of the ocean floor. The interaction between coral growth and reef formation also involves a correspondence, but one that involves adaptation, a central process in evolution. The corals adapt to the changing light conditions relating to ocean depth. Such nonobvious correspondences and adaptations were essential to Darwin's work on geological and biological evolution, grounding his many later achievements in biological explanation: Variations in the organism involve adaptations to variations in the physical world where the organism lives. Coral reefs adapt to sinking ocean floors by growing to heights that keep them at the right depth from the surface in order to obtain the sunlight that they need to grow. This kind of adaptational argument became central in Darwin's theory and research.

Along with the coral-reef theory, Darwin also began to build an interactive view of variations across species. During the *Beagle* voyage, he made extensive notes about the many animals and plants he saw and the many specimens that he collected. His notes describe, for example, the variations in species that he saw from island to island in the Galapagos. The notes were concerned primarily with cataloguing, classifying, and describing what he had seen; but he also began to attempt seriously to explain his observations.

One key example involved the adaptations of the beaks of the many species of Galapagos finches to their feeding habits. For finches – and eventually, Darwin saw, for other organisms – the physical and organic worlds were intimately related. Darwin observed that each species of finch had a type of beak that fit its needs for obtaining the kind of food it ate. For example, small tree finches have small thin beaks that are effective for catching the insects that they eat, while woodpecker finches have large thick beaks that fit the needs of hammering holes in wood,

$$\begin{bmatrix} \text{INSECTS} & & \text{THIN} \\ \text{FOOD} & \overset{match}{\longleftrightarrow} & \text{BEAK} \\ \text{TREE} & & \text{THICK} \end{bmatrix}$$

Darwin found similar adaptive matches everywhere he looked, and he described and explained many such adaptations throughout his long career as a biologist. Birds' and bats' wings are adapted to the kinds of flying that they need to do in their species' specific niche. Monkeys' legs and arms are adapted to the kinds of locomotion that they use in their niche. Many earlier scholars had noted some such matches and marveled at God's creation of such matches, but Darwin built a framework for analyzing the matches in order to understand adaptation and evolution. This pattern of adaptive match became an essential building block for the theory of evolution by natural selection.

Once Darwin had built skills for complexly relating the organic world of coral to the physical world of reefs, the variations in beaks of species of finch to their sources of food, and other explanations of variations among species, he could use these skills as microdevelopmental bridging shells to guide his construction of the broader theory of evolution. Darwin began to realize that organisms undergo physical and behavioral changes that allow them to adapt to variations and shifts in their environments. Also, from fossil finds, he knew that some species had changed dramatically over time, and others had died out completely. Here was another piece of the picture, skills that related changes in species over time. For example, he hypothesized that all the species of Galapagos finches might have come from one species that happened to fly to the island, reproduced, and then changed over time to take on many different forms,

$$\begin{bmatrix} \text{FINCH 1} & & \text{FINCH 1A} \\ \text{PAST} & \overset{change}{\longleftrightarrow} & \text{PRESENT} \\ \text{FINCH 1} & & \text{FINCH 1B} \end{bmatrix}$$

With many pieces of the puzzle in hand, Darwin now struggled to construct a theory that would explain all that he had learned. How and why did these adaptations and eliminations of species take place? As he searched for solutions, he used the coral-reef theory, the examples of adaptive variation, and other analyses to support building broader explanations of adaptive variation.

Resolution: Principles for unifying and explaining systematic variations

As the *Beagle* voyage came to an end in 1836, Darwin continued to work toward finding a principle to coordinate and explain his many observations of species variation and adaptation. In his microdevelopmental struggle Darwin created not only successful explanations but also ones that failed. He labored mightily, for example, with concepts of multiple creation, as well as multiple extinction. What if God had created new species several times, not just once, with each creation producing animals and plants especially adapted to particular environmental niches? What if somehow many organisms had died out at one particular time, as described in the Biblical story of the flood? He was struggling to construct a principle that would tie together the many adaptive variations into a coherent whole and explain them. That is, he was striving to build a Level Ab4 skill, a system of abstract systems integrated in terms of a broad principle, as shown in figure 11.3.

All Darwin's first attempts at creating a general principle to explain variation and adaptation proved unsatisfactory. One of the principles that he tried was hybridization – that interbreeding between species somehow produced new species – but for this and other processes of inheritance he was at a major disadvantage because of the virtual nonexistence of genetic knowledge in his lifetime.

Despite the failure of these first attempts at principles, some of them turned out to be productive mistakes. Although the explanations failed in themselves, they sometimes created useful bridges that helped Darwin in his later work. One particularly interesting principle that he tried in 1837 and abandoned was monad theory, which provided important concepts for his eventual success in building the theory of evolution by natural selection (Gruber, 1981). A monad is a hypothetical entity that Darwin considered to explain multiple creations and extinctions. At some historical point, a monad (like a small germ cell with a fixed life span) comes into existence, engendering a new species. The species reproduces and radiates into many distinct species, inhabiting different parts of the physical world. Eventually, however, the life span of the monad is reached, and all species coming from the monad become extinct.

Darwin considered monad theory briefly because it could perhaps explain the exuberant radiations of new species as well as the massive extinctions that fossils seemed to show. For example, if the original species of Galapagos finch was a monad, then over time it would engender new species for different niches in the islands through the process of growth along a monadic tree,

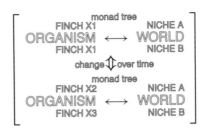

That is, the first finch species would change over time into several new species that fit into different niches.

Darwin knew that this principle was extremely speculative. Although he was publicly circumspect about speculation and careful always to present concepts in terms of the empirical evidence for them, in private he freely searched for concepts to explain species variation and adaptation. Before long, he rejected monads, but in the meantime the idea had given him a powerful new tool. When he thought about how monads might grow new species, he began to draw tree diagrams to capture the radiation of species. Although he eventually concluded that monads do not exist, he kept the idea that species radiate into new species in tree- and bush-like patterns over long periods of time.

Darwin's notebooks show that he created this tool, the tree of evolutionary change, as a result of his brief efforts to use monads to create a principle to explain multiple creations and extinctions. His work on coral reefs also served as a bridging shell to this tool, as when he said in his notebook, "the tree of life should perhaps be called the coral of life, base of branches dead, so that passages cannot be seen" (Gruber & Barrett, 1974, p. 143). Once again, microdevelopment occurs through bridging, in which a shell created for one set of skills (monad theory or coral-reef theory, respectively) can be adapted to support construction of another set of skills (evolution by natural selection).

In late 1838 and early 1839 Darwin gradually worked out the solution, the theory of evolution by natural selection. In an important event in 1838, he read Thomas Malthus' *Essay on population*, which argued that every species, including human beings, is capable of reproducing itself at a much greater rate than its physical surroundings can support. Darwin had encountered this idea in earlier years, reading scientific descriptions of the superfecundity of species. During his travels on the *Beagle*, he had seen many examples of species reproducing excessively and competing for resources.

During several months of intense microdevelopmental construction, Darwin put together all the concepts to build the principle of evolution by natural selection: The high rate of reproduction, he realized, leads to competition for the means to survive and reproduce – a struggle for existence – which in turn results in natural selection of the species members who fit the requirements of the physical world.

Even with this important realization, however, he did not simply build the principle in one day. Over several months he seemed to understand it several times, based on what he wrote in his notebooks, but he was not quite able to sustain the new skill and make it work consistently. By early 1839, he had built and rebuilt the skills for the principle so frequently that he could sustain the principle as a generalization across many domains, and the theory of evolution came into existence.

The notebooks and other records show that repeated reconstruction and eventual generalization occurred for a number of key components of Darwin's framework. For example, the concept of the tree of life receded for some time after its first flowering, so that despite the evidence in his notebooks Darwin himself eventually attributed it to some time after 1844 (*Autobiography*, pp. 120–121, cited in Gruber & Barrett, 1974, p. 117).

The principle of evolution by natural selection requires a Level Ab4 skill that systematically relates various abstract systems involving variations in organisms and their physical worlds. For example, Galapagos finches' beaks are well adapted to their particular environmental niche because the finches evolved that adaptation through natural selection. The first finches to migrate to the islands were not specifically adapted to the niches there, and through selection their descendants gradually evolved adaptations specific to distinct environmental niches (A and B in the formula),

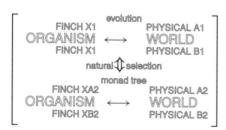

This is the essence of the evolutionary principle. The characteristics that organisms possess show variations, which are somehow inherited. Darwin did not know about genetics, which had not yet been discovered, but he knew that people could practice selective breeding (artificial selection) with animals and plants, like pigeons, dogs, cows, and wheat. Because of the high rate of reproduction, organisms compete for limited physical resources, such as food, water, and shelter. Natural selection occurs because those that compete more successfully are more likely to survive and reproduce, passing on their inherited characteristics to their offspring. Evolution will thus occur as a matter of course through the mechanism of natural selection.

Note that a number of factors contribute to evolution (including many more than those explicitly mentioned here) and they are coordinated through the principle of evolution by natural selection. Darwin's and other scientists' specific skills involve not just one principle of evolution, but a number of related principles dealing with variation, adaptation, competition, inheritance, and much more. Darwin spent the rest of his scientific life elaborating principles by which the factors of evolution worked in diverse domains, and other scientists continue that endeavor today. The whole edifice of modern biology is built on the foundations of Darwin's evolution by natural selection, which he constructed initially over a period of eight years between 1831 and 1839.

A note on socioemotional repercussions of Darwin's theory

This essay focuses on microdevelopment in Darwin's construction of the theory of evolution, but there is another story that needs to be mentioned – the socioemotional side of Darwin's efforts. Emotions and social relationships played a central role in Darwin's efforts from start to finish. He began with the traditional Christian view of creation, and he knew that many people, including his mother and other family members, would be upset by the new view that he was creating. Just as he was reaching a stable formulation of the principle of evolution by natural selection in 1838, he had a vivid dream of being executed. He knew that his theory would be bitterly attacked when it was published and that his life and the lives of his family might be endangered. That seems to be the main reason that he delayed publishing his theory of evolution from 1838 to 1859.

Along with these anxieties, Darwin was simultaneously excited by the theory and methods that he was creating to understand species variation and change. He made it his life's work to build not only the theory of evolution but a wide range of branches of biology that are informed by it. Even in the twenty-first century, it is hard to find a part of biology that was not shaped powerfully by Darwin's projects. In constructing these many scientific achievements, Darwin embodied the processes of circular reaction and bridging – repetition of problem-solving over and over with variations, and use of skills from past successes as bridging shells for new problems. From 1838 until his death in 1882, Darwin worked on dozens of projects that not only elaborated the theory of evolution but also applied it to a wide range of topics, ranging from barnacles to human facial expressions. These later works were important in themselves, each elaborating new explanatory principles for a domain of science. They were also essential to the eventual success of the theory, making evolution ever more difficult to dismiss. Without them the grand theory of evolution would have been less powerful, less creative, and less successful (Gruber, 1981).

Conclusion: Development of deep understanding

Micro- and macrodevelopmental analysis of Darwin's construction of the theory of evolution illuminates how new knowledge is constructed. Darwin gradually built his skills for analyzing variation and change in organisms in relation to variation and change in the physical world. The entire sequence required eight years for the full formulation of the theory, with many microdevelopmental fits and starts along the way. He even built important concepts, such as natural selection and the tree of life, and then could not sustain them and had to build them again. In the long term, Darwin moved from the level of simple abstractions about the Organic World, the Physical World, and the Creator through three further levels of coordinating and differentiating abstractions until he could unify them all in terms of the principles of evolution by natural selection.

In building many distinct abstract skills for particular biological problems, such as the formation of coral reefs and the adaptation of finches' beaks, he built new knowledge by using some of his previous skills to form bridging shells. This repeated bridging construction in microdevelopment allowed him eventually in macrodevelopment to formulate broad principles that incorporated the earlier skills as special instances. For example, the theory of coral reefs had the formal structure of evolution implicit in it, specifying how coral organisms adapted to long-term changes in the physical world (lowering of the ocean floor) and simultaneously changed the physical world through their own activities (forming coral reefs). Darwin used this theory to bootstrap his later work, seeing the evolution of species as a tree of evolutionary life, similar to corals growing upward in the ocean on top of their ancestors.

Eventually, and gradually, he created the broad principles of evolution, the deep understanding that subsumed coral-reef theory as a specific case. None of the general principles themselves were realized in one moment, but Darwin constructed and reconstructed them until they became stable skills that he could use consistently and explain to other scientists, as Howard Gruber describes eloquently in his insightful book *Darwin on man*.

References

Baldwin, J. M. (1894). *Mental development in the child and the race.* New York: Macmillan.

Barrett, P. H. (1974). *Darwin's early and unpublished notebooks.* New York: Dutton.

Barrett, P. H. (1980). *Metaphysics, materialism, and the evolution of mind: Early writings of Charles Darwin.* Chicago: University of Chicago Press.

Barrett, P. H., Gautrey, P. J., Herbert, S., Kohn, D., & Smith, S. (1987). *Charles Darwin's notebooks, 1836–1844: Geology, transmutation of species, metaphysical enquiries.* Ithaca, NY: Cornell University Press.

Basseches, M. (1984). *Dialectical thinking and adult development.* Norwood, NJ: Ablex.

Case, R. (1985). *Intellectual development: Birth to adulthood.* New York: Academic Press.

Case, R., & McKeough, A. (1990). Schooling and the development of central conceptual structures: An example from the domain of children's narrative. *International Journal of Educational Psychology, 8,* 835–855.

Case, R., Okamoto, Y., Griffin, S., McKeough, A., Bleiker, C., Henderson, B., & Stephenson, K. M. (1996). The role of central conceptual structures in the development of children's thought. *Monographs of the Society for Research in Child Development, 60(5–6)* (Serial No. 246).

Commons, M. L., Richards, R. A., & Armon, C. (1984). *Beyond formal operations: Late adolescent and adult cognitive development.* New York: Praeger.

Darwin, C. R. (1859). *On the origin of species by means of natural selection, or the preservation of favoured races in the struggle for life.* London: John Murray.

DeBeer, M. J., Rowlands, M. J., & Skramovsky, B. M. (1960). Darwin's notebooks on transmutation of species. *Bulletin of the British Museum (Natural History) Historical Series, 2*(2, 3, 4, 5).

Dunbar, K. (2001). What scientific reasoning reveals about the nature of cognition. In K. Crowley, C. D. Schunn, & T. Okada (Eds.), *Designing for science: Implications from everyday, classroom, and professional settings* (pp. 115–140). Mahwah, NJ: Erlbaum.

Ericsson, K. A., & Charness, N. (1994). Expert performance: Its structure and acquisition. *American Psychologist, 49,* 725–747.

Fischer, K. W. (1980a). Learning and problem solving as the development of organized behavior. *Journal of Structural Learning, 6,* 253–267.

Fischer, K. W. (1980b). A theory of cognitive development: The control and construction of hierarchies of skills. *Psychological Review, 87,* 477–531.

Fischer, K. W., & Bidell, T. R. (1998). Dynamic development of psychological structures in action and thought. In R. M. Lerner (Ed.), *Handbook of child psychology, Vol. 1: Theoretical models of human development* (5th edn., pp. 467–561). New York: Wiley.

Fischer, K. W., & Granott, N. (1995). Beyond one-dimensional change: Parallel, concurrent, socially distributed processes in learning and development. *Human Development, 38,* 302–314.

Fischer, K. W., Hand, H. H., & Russell, S. L. (1984). The development of abstractions in adolescence and adulthood. In M. Commons, F. A. Richards, & C. Armon (Eds.), *Beyond formal operations* (pp. 43–73). New York: Praeger.

Fischer, K. W., Pipp, S. L., & Bullock, D. (1984). Detecting discontinuities in development: Method and measurement. In R. Emde & R. Harmon (Eds.), *Continuities and discontinuities in development* (pp. 95–121). New York: Plenum.

Fischer, K. W., & Rose, S. P. (1994). Dynamic development of coordination of components in brain and behavior: A framework for theory and research. In G. Dawson & K. W. Fischer (Eds.), *Human behavior and the developing brain* (pp. 3–66). New York: Guilford Press.

Fischer, K. W., Rotenberg, E. J., Bullock, D. H., & Raya, P. (1993). The dynamics of competence: How context contributes directly to skill. In R. H. Wozniak & K. W. Fischer (Eds.), *Development in context: Acting and thinking in specific environments. The Jean Piaget symposium series* (pp. 93–117). Hillsdale, NJ: Erlbaum.

Fischer, K. W., Yan, Z., McGonigle, B., & Warnett, L. (2000). Learning and developing together: Dynamic construction of human and robot knowledge. In J. Weng & I. Stockman (Eds.), *Development and learning: Proceedings of an NSF/DARPA workshop* (pp. 50–59). Cambridge, MA: AAAI/MIT Press.

Gardner, H. (1993). *Creating minds.* New York: Basic Books.

Granott, N. (1993a). Microdevelopment of co-construction of knowledge during problem-solving: Puzzled minds, weird creatures, and wuggles. Doctoral dissertation, Massachusetts Institute of Technology, Cambridge, MA [on line]. Availabe: *http://theses.mit.edu:80/Dienst/UI/2.0/Composite/0018.mit.theses/1993-170/1?nsections=19.*

Granott, N. (1993b). Patterns of interaction in the co-construction of knowledge: Separate minds, joint effort, and weird creatures. In R. H. Wozniak & K. W. Fischer (Eds.), *Development in context: Acting and thinking in specific environments* (pp. 183–207). Hillsdale, NJ: Erlbaum.

Granott, N. (1998). We learn, therefore we develop: Learning versus development – or developing learning? In M. C. Smith & T. Pourchot (Eds.), *Adult learning and development: Perspectives from educational psychology* (pp. 15–34). Mahwah, NJ: Erlbaum.

Granott, N. (this volume). How microdevelopment creates macrodevelopment: Reiterated sequences, backward transitions, and the Zone of Current Development.

Granott, N., & Parziale, J. (this volume). Microdevelopment: A process-oriented perspective for studying development and learning.

Gruber, H. E. (1973). Courage and cognitive growth in children and scientists. In M. Schwebel & J. Raph (Eds.), *Piaget in the classroom.* New York: Basic Books.

Gruber, H. E. (1989). The evolving systems approach to creative work. In D. B. Wallace & H. E. Gruber (Eds.), *Creative people at work: Twelve cognitive case studies* (pp. 3–24). New York: Oxford University Press.

Gruber, H. E. (1981). *Darwin on man* (2nd edn.). Chicago: University of Chicago Press.

Gruber, H. E., & Barrett, P. H. (1974). *Darwin on man* (1st edn.). New York: E. P. Dutton.

Inhelder, B., & Piaget, J. (1955/1958). *The growth of logical thinking from childhood to adolescence* (A. Parsons & S. Seagrim, trans.). New York: Basic Books. (Originally published 1955.)

James, W. (1975). *Pragmatism and the meaning of truth*. Cambridge, MA: Harvard University Press.

Keegan, R. T. (1989). How Charles Darwin became a psychologist. In D. B. Wallace & H. E. Gruber (Eds.), *Creative people at work: Twelve cognitive case studies* (pp. 107–125). New York: Oxford University Press.

Kitchener, K. S., & King, P. M. (1990). The reflective judgment model: Ten years of research. In M. L. Commons, C. Armon, L. Kohlberg, F. A. Richards, T. A. Grotzer, & J. D. Sinnott (Eds.), *Adult Development 3: Models and methods in the study of adolescent and adult thought* (pp. 62–78). New York: Praeger.

Kitchener, K. S., Lynch, C. L., Fischer, K. W., & Wood, P. K. (1993). Developmental range of reflective judgment: The effect of contextual support and practice on developmental stage. *Developmental Psychology, 29(5)*, 893–906.

Klahr, D. (2000), with Dunbar, K., Fay, A. L., Penner, D., & Schunn, C. D. *Exploring science: The cognition and development of discovery processes*. Cambridge, MA: MIT Press/Bradford.

Kuhn, D. (1995). Microgenetic study of change: What has it told us? *Psychological Science, 6*, 133–139.

Peirce, C. S. (1878). How to make our ideas clear. *Popular Science Monthly, 12(January)*, 268–302.

Piaget, J. (1936/1952). *The origins of intelligence in children* (M. Cook, trans.). New York: International Universities Press. (Originally published 1936.)

Piaget, J. (1983). Piaget's theory. In P. H. Mussen (Series Ed.), & W. Kessen (Vol. Ed.), *Handbook of child psychology, Vol. 1: History, theory, and methods* (pp. 103–126). New York: Wiley.

Rogoff, B. (1993). Children's guided participation and participatory appropriation in sociocultural activity. In R. Wozniak & K. W. Fischer (Eds.), *Development in context: Acting and thinking in specific environments* (pp. 121–154). Hillsdale, NJ: Erlbaum.

Siegler, R. S. (1996). *Emerging minds: The process of change in children's thinking*. New York: Oxford University Press.

van Geert, P. (1998). A dynamic systems model of basic developmental mechanisms: Piaget, Vygotsky, and beyond. *Psychological Review, 105*, 634–677.

Wallon, H. (1970). *De l'acte à la pensée [From action to thought]*. Paris: Flammarion.

Werner, H. (1948). *Comparative psychology of mental development*. New York: Science Editions.

Wittgenstein, L. (1953). *Philosophical investigations* (G. E. M. Anscombe, trans.). Oxford, UK: Oxford University Press.

Yan, Z. (1998). Measuring microdevelopment of understanding the VMS-SAS structure: A developmental scale pilot. Unpublished qualifying paper, Harvard Graduate School of Education, Cambridge, MA.

Yan, Z. (2000). Dynamic analysis of microdevelopment in learning a computer program. Unpublished doctoral dissertation, Harvard Graduate School of Education, Cambridge, MA.

12 Developmental dynamics, intentional action, and fuzzy sets

Paul van Geert

One of the most striking findings of microdevelopmental studies is the existence of a considerable degree of variability in a person's performance levels (Crowley, Shrager, & Siegler, 1997; Fletcher, Huffman, Bray, & Grupe, 1998; Kuhn, Garcia-Mila, Zohar, & Andersen, 1995; Kuhn, 1995; Nakatani, 1995; Siegler, 1995). In addition, variability itself seems to vary between persons and conditions too (Alibali, 1999; Goldin-Meadow, Alibali, & Church, 1993). Still another finding is that individuals differ among one another in the way they reach a developmental outcome or in the way they show the psychological property under scrutiny (for instance, the use of a particular cognitive strategy) (Siegler, 1994, 1995, 1997; Siegler & Shipley, 1995; Siegler & Chen, 1998; Lautrey, 1993; Lautrey & Caroff, 1996).

The standard view on variability – which I shall confine to fluctuations in a person's level across time – is that it is more closely related to the notions of error and deception than to the idea of truth. The psychologist is like Narcissus, who looks at his face mirrored by the water of a pond that is touched by a gale of wind. The wrinkles he sees are those of the water, not of his face. If we study a property such as a person's level of skill, knowledge, intelligence – all alleged internal properties – we look at that property through some medium, for instance a test, an observation of spontaneous behavior, and so forth. We assume that the medium itself suffers from influences that have nothing to do with the property we want to see, like the gale of wind that wrinkled the water and that is completely independent of Narcissus' face itself. In this way, the testing medium is assumed to distort the image of the tested variable by adding the effects of coincidental influences. Consequently, most of the differences found between repeated measures of the same underlying variable should be attributed to – uninformative – variation in those coincidental factors.

This view is based on three underlying axioms. The first, which I shall call the *axiom of specificity*, says that psychological properties are internally presented in a highly specific, "crisp" form. A child has a grammatical rule or not, has an object concept with specific properties, has a unique,

319

true level on an underlying variable, such as spatial ability, numerical ability and so on. The second, which I shall call the *axiom of linearity*, says that observable performance is the sum of effects caused by many variables acting independently.[1] The third axiom, the *axiom of causality*, states that the variable that is measured must also be the internal cause of the measure. For instance, if we measure an infant's object concept by observing the infant's behavior in a particular experimental setup, the object concept is the (non-unique) internal cause of the infant's behavior (non-unique in the sense that, in view of the second axiom, other variables may also contribute).

These axioms express a view on the causes of human action and performance that has emerged in close correspondence with the standard theory of psychological measurement, the historical roots of which begin in the nineteenth century with Lambert Quételet. Against this view I present one that has its roots in a more phenomenological approach and that combines intentionalist psychology with dynamic systems theory, ecological psychology, and fuzzy logic. I define action and performance as the unfolding in time of an intentional relationship between an actor (and his or her co-actors) and an object (set) in the broadest possible sense of the word, both immersed in an ambient environment (see van Geert, 2000, for a more elaborate explanation of the framework). The nature of intentional relationships requires us to make a distinction between the immanent object and the transcendent object. The immanent object is the object as it is present in or constituted by the act of the actor, whereas the transcendent object is the "real" object, beyond the actor. It is important to note that the notion of "object" refers to the whole spectrum ranging from actual physical objects to "abstract" objects such as concepts, numbers, etc. Finally, the participating factors cannot be defined but in a fuzzy way (in the technically precise sense of fuzzy logic).

In this framework, the causes of human actions, performance, skills, and knowledge lie in the process of a temporal interplay between three groups of factors. The first are the properties of the transcendental object(s) that allow for certain kinds of intentional action to take place. The second are the properties of the subject that enable him or her to intentionally relate to the object (in the broad sense of the word) in question; the third are the properties of the ambient context and environment in which the intentional action takes place. In the context of the present chapter, two things are important. The first is that these causal factors are characterized by fuzzy and dynamic boundaries. Because they come

---

[1] This form of linearity or additivity does not preclude the possibility of interaction effects. Interaction effects amount to conditional relationships among otherwise independent variables.

about as a result of the time-governed interplay among the factors, it is impossible – not only in practice but also in principle – to draw a sharp line between the factors or to specify their properties in a "crisp" way. Second, if we measure a person's psychological properties, we must, by necessity, also invoke the objects – again in the broadest possible sense of the word – and the contexts in which these psychological properties make sense, so to speak, and which are characteristic of the person in question. This is similar to saying that a person's abilities are devoid of meaning if they are not specified in terms of a context that offers a particular affordance to these abilities and, similarly, that the notion of affordance is meaningless if it is not specified in terms of a person or organism with the ability to make use of these affordances. Note that this inherent mutuality between person and context still enables us to make a distinction between state- and trait-related properties through comparing the relative contribution of the person and the context. All this may sound very philosophical – and it is very philosophical after all – but in the remainder of this chapter I shall try to demonstrate that this notion of the dynamic nature of psychological properties leads to a different view of the nature of psychological measurement.

Scores as fuzzy numbers

If we start from the notion of a *true score* on an underlying variable we can represent the true score as a single point on a (semi-)continuous dimension. The latter is nothing but the variable whose value we have measured. If s_i is a child's *true* score on variable S at time t_i, we can also assert that s_i is the child's *characteristic* score at t_i because, trivially, the score s_i characterizes the child at that particular moment.

Usually, however, what we mean by "true score" is not the score at any specific moment in time. For instance, if the test has been administered at t_i we want the score to reflect the child not only at t_i, but at some considerably more extensive time frame around t_i. That is, we do not want the notion "true score" to refer to *trivially true score* (a score without measurement errors based on errors such as miscounting scores or overlooking cases and that refers to the subject's score level at the time and occasion of the test administration only: see van Geert, 1997). We know, however, that repeated testing will almost never yield exactly similar scores. Frequently repeated testing, for instance in a microdevelopmental design, almost unequivocally hints at a *range* of successive scores, with an upper and a lower bound. This range may show properties of a normal distribution around a mean or it may not do so. But even if there exists something like a normal distribution, it is not automatically

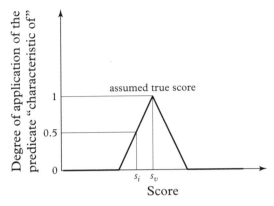

Figure 12.1 Degree of characteristicness of an assumed true score s_v and scores with assumed measurement error (e.g. the observed score s_i).

the case that its central tendency (in the limit) is the true value, whereas all other values boil down to deviations due to measurement errors.

Let us assume that the child's true score (whatever that may be) is s_v and that a test yields the score s_i which is just a little different from s_v. We have just identified the true score s_v as the child's characteristic score because it correctly characterizes the child with respect to his current position on variable S. But is a slightly different score s_i *not* characteristic of the child? Nobody would say it isn't, provided the difference from s_v is not too big. Maybe s_i is just a little less characteristic of the child than the allegedly true score s_v. If s_i were to be very different from s_v – for instance an extremely low score caused by the fact that the child who's taking the test is suffering from a bad headache – we would most likely say that s_i is *not* characteristic of the child, or that it is *very uncharacteristic* of the child to obtain a score like this. What we implicitly admit here is that the property "being characteristic of" is a property that has a *continuous set membership function*. That is, the degree to which a property is characteristic of a particular person may vary. For instance, if the alleged true score – still assuming it exists – has a membership value of 1 to the set "is characteristic of this child," a slightly different score s_i has only a very slightly lower membership value, depending on its distance from s_v (see figure 12.1). However, the concept of a single true score, i.e. a single point on the variable dimension, reflects a metaphysical stance, i.e. a statement about the nature of reality that can only be assumed. I have argued that, in view of the nature of the causes, psychological properties such as skills, abilities, knowledge or concepts are properties that apply to persons in a fuzzy way. That is, it makes no sense to try to determine exactly what a person's level is on a specific psychological variable, since whatever the cause that generates this level, it is itself a fuzzy set. A fuzzy set is characterized by the fact that its members belong to the set with varying degrees of membership (Nguyen & Walker, 1997; Ross, 2000; Altrock, 1995). For instance, an IQ of 95 can have a membership degree of 0.50 to the set "Person X's IQ." In standard set theory, an IQ score either does or does not belong to the set "Person X's IQ" (and standard score theory adds to this statement that this set has only one member, namely that person's true IQ score).

If we test a child repeatedly, for instance in a microdevelopmental study, we observe a *range* of scores. I have explained elsewhere (van Geert, 1997) that the width and temporal variability of that range is a significant property of development itself. For instance, if we test a largely automatized skill, the range will be significantly narrower from that of a highly controlled skill, which is considerably more vulnerable to perturbations and fatigue. The fact that the skill is so vulnerable to intervening factors such as attention and effort is an important characteristic of that particular skill. It is also plausible that, close to an acceleration in the rate of growth of a skill, the width of the score range will temporarily increase. That is, it is likely that the forthcoming jump or transition is preceded by an increase in the variability of the responses, i.e. a widening of the characteristic range (Savelsbergh, van der Maas, & van Geert, 1999; van Geert, Savelsbergh, & van der Maas, 1999; van Geert, 1997).

In view of the preceding remarks, it seems considerably more natural and informative to replace the truthfulness dimension ("*x* is the true score") by a characteristicness dimension ("how characteristic is *x* of this particular person?"). Instead of assuming there exists something like a true score we specify *a range of scores that differ in their degree of characteristicness of a particular person at a particular period (and eventually of a particular range of contexts)*. None of these scores is more "true" than any other score: they just differ in how characteristic they are of a particular person (figure 12.2; note that the reference to a true score s_v has now been replaced by a reference to scores s_l and s_u which correspond with the lower and upper bounds of the scores that have a maximal degree of characteristicness).

Using the entire variable range to specify the characteristic score range of a child (or subject, for that matter) has a number of interesting advantages. First of all, we are able to specify the width of the range and make use of the fact that this is a property that is of developmental importance and that adds to the information we can use when making predictions, for instance. Second, it is also possible to specify various types of score distribution. For instance, when a child is on the verge

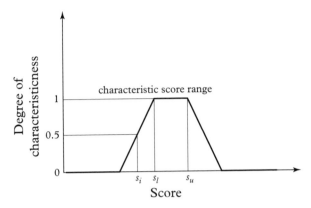

Figure 12.2 A score specified as a range with varying degrees of characteristicness; the scores s_l and s_u represent the lower and upper bounds of the range with characteristicness 1 (maximal characteristicness). In this example, the observed score s_i has a degree of characteristicness of 0.5.

of making a discontinuous jump, the score distribution upon repeated measurement could easily be bimodal (van der Maas & Hopkins, 1998; Hosenfeld, van der Maas, & van den Boom, 1977a, 1997b; van der Maas & Molenaar, 1992; Alibali, 1999; Goldin-Meadow, et al., 1993). In principle, various types of bimodality are possible (for instance two tops of unequal height or overlapping distributions (see figure 12.3).

Note that the principle of continuous membership degrees can also be applied to the characteristicness dimension itself, in a way that is customarily applied in fuzzy logic, where class membership values are related to ordinary linguistic qualifiers. For instance, we can divide the characteristicness dimension into four overlapping regions, for instance "highly characteristic of," "mildly characteristic of," "mildly uncharacteristic of," and "highly uncharacteristic of." The overlapping regions act as mappings between categorical predicates, such as "highly typical of" – which we commonly use in natural language – and fuzzy class membership. The advantages of such mapping have been amply discussed in fuzzy logic textbooks (Kosko, 1993, 1997; Nguyen & Walker, 1997; Ross, 2000; Altrock, 1995). It has been shown that fuzzy logic mappings can approximate any non-linear relationship between variables if the relationship can be expressed in the form of sets of linguistically formulated rules (Castro, 1995; Kosko, 1997). Examples of such rules are, "if a person's spatial ability is very high, he or she is likely to solve a specific

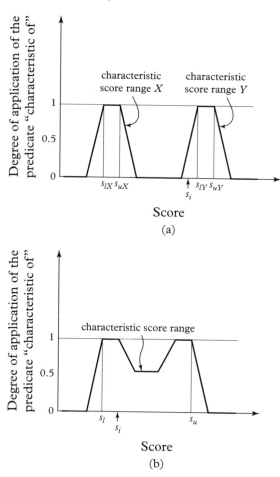

Figure 12.3 Two examples of bimodal score ranges; in example (a), the ranges are disjunct, scores falling in between the ranges are highly uncharacteristic and are likely not to occur; in example (b), the ranges are conjunct; scores between the ranges of maximal characteristicness are moderately characteristic.

problem X." In fuzzy logic, such intuitively meaningful rules can obtain an explicit mathematical formulation and be combined into networks of rules (fuzzy associated memories). Thus, by applying fuzzy logic and fuzzy rules it is possible to specify any type of complex prediction that accounts both for person- and context-specific properties (figures 12.4 and 12.5).

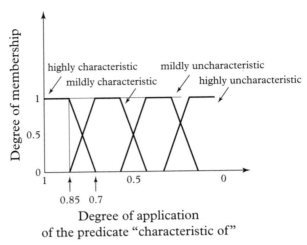

Figure 12.4 Score ranges map differentially on to linguistic categories (e.g. "highly characteristic of" applies with maximal membership to values between 1 and 0.85, for instance, and with zero membership to values lower than 0.7).

Scores, developmental levels, and context specificity

A person's level on an underlying skill, capacity or psychological variable is traditionally viewed as a covert property of the person. It follows from the standard axioms explained in the first part of this chapter that the overt expression of that skill or capacity, i.e. the expressed level, is consequently seen as the confounding effect of a particular context on the underlying, true level. Thus, an observed score is the sum of an underlying true score – an essential property of a subject – and a contingent factor, the present context. I have argued that this view expresses a particular ontology where properties are treated as true essentials. I have introduced an intentionalist ecological psychology, which views the causes of intentional actions as the confluence of various co-defining causal sources, namely causal factors in the intentional object, in the subject having the intentional relationship, and in the context. In this view, it is impossible to isolate one set of causes and treat them as having an intrinsic causal meaning. A specific internal causal factor, for instance, is a causal factor because it is consistent with some particular external factor. I referred to the notion of affordance as an illustration of the fact that causes are relationally defined, or, more precisely, defined in terms of a relationship that unfolds in time. In this way, external and context factors are essential parts of the causal makeup of an ecology that allows for the emergence of fuzzy sets of intentional actions.

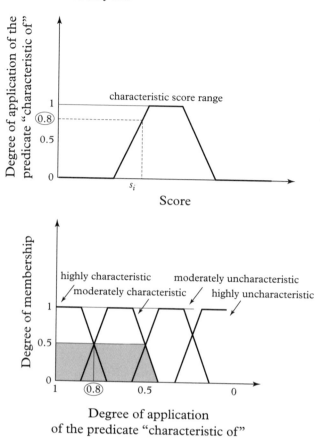

Figure 12.5 Scores map differentially on to various linguistic categories; the score s_i has a degree of characteristicness of 0.8 and a degree of membership of 0.5 to the linguistic categories "moderately characteristic of" and "highly characteristic of."

At first sight, it seems impossible to reckon with contextual variation when establishing the score or level of a subject on a particular skill or capacity: There exists an infinite range of contexts and each context appears to affect the resulting score in a particular way. The standard solution to this problem is to discard context variation and to measure a person's level in a highly formalized and standardized context, which is the context of standard testing. Contexts, however, are not entirely coincidental or contingent. They are, to various degrees, typical of specific persons or specific developmental levels or stages. This conclusion follows directly from the principle that contexts provide affordances and that affordances are co-defined by abilities and vice versa. For instance, grown-ups regularly exert their skills and capacities in a professional context where they either work alone, or with colleagues who have an approximately similar mastery level of the skill or skills at issue, or within the framework of a collegial team where a range of expertise is distributed across the team members. The problems that adult experts are facing are adapted to their particular expertise, but the difficulty or complexity of those problems is determined by what comes along, so to speak. A medical doctor, for instance, is confronted with problems of arbitrary complexity, depending upon whatever diseases his or her patients present for diagnosis and cure. It is also characteristic of adults that they often have to solve problems under high time pressure, stressful conditions or competition from others, and that the consequences of their performance are – sometimes literally – of vital importance. Children, on the other hand, are characteristically confronted with problems that are deliberately adapted to their developmental level and are given with the purpose of teaching them and helping them acquire better skills. Those problems are characteristically of a kind that has been solved already or for which model solutions are available. Children characteristically perform in the context of educational help, that is, help given by a more competent person with the explicit aim of improving the child's ability. On the other hand, it is also characteristic of children that they are asked to solve problems independently or do so in the context of tests or similar procedures intended to diagnose their capacities (Greeno 1997, 1998).

Note that by "characteristic" I do not necessarily mean "with high frequency" or "highly probable" or anything else that primarily relates to a frequency distribution. By "characteristic" I trivially mean, "that which characterizes a person (or a situation) in contrast with another person (or situation)." For instance, it is possible that in solving problems both adults and children use a kind of concrete operational strategy most of the time. Adults, however, are capable of applying formal operational strategies in a limited range of contexts, whereas children are in general not able to do so. In this case, we may call formal operational thinking characteristic of adults, not because it is their habitual way of thinking, but because the presence of such – eventually rather infrequently exercised – thinking distinguishes adults from children and is thus characteristic of adults.

These examples are not pretending to be universally applicable to either adults or children. However, they do illustrate an important point, namely that it is possible, at least in principle, to make a general, fuzzy judgment of the characteristicness of a context or type of context for a specific individual person, group of persons, or type of person (e.g. children vs. grown-ups, toddlers vs. schoolchildren, and so forth). For instance, a problem-solving situation where the person is being helped by a more competent other person in the context of instruction is highly typical or characteristic of a child (at least of the type of child that most regularly features in standard developmental research). The same context is only weakly characteristic of an adult (with a whole range of exceptions not explicitly specified). Note that fuzzy logic enables us to quantify linguistic qualifiers such as "highly" or "weakly" in terms of prototypical degree-of-membership functions and to specify decision nets that allow us to simplify complex predictive relationships between measured variables and possible outcomes.

Let me now return to the problem of the context specificity of a skill level, a capacity or any score on an underlying psychological variable, for that matter.

If not otherwise specified, a skill level representation as in figure 12.2 in principle entails all possible contexts for which the expression of that skill makes (reasonable) sense. Technically, the membership function is the intersection of the degrees of characteristicness of all possible scores on the variable (skill, capacity, test, . . .) at issue on the one hand and of the degrees of characteristicness of all reasonably relevant contexts on the other hand. The relevance of contexts is specified by various criteria. For instance, it depends on the affordances a context offers for the measured skill, ability or concept at issue (the context is relevant to the degree it offers specific affordances for the measured ability). Relevance may also depend on culturally and socially determined tasks, for instance contexts of education for younger people and contexts of work for adults.

To continue the context issue, let us imagine a child who is presented with an intelligence test administered under highly adverse conditions (whatever they may be). Imagine that we find an IQ score of 90 that is highly characteristic for that particular condition. Assume that a score of 90 is highly characteristic of this particular child in this particular adverse condition. That is, the degree of characteristicness of the score 90 for this particular child and condition is (approximately) 1. However, it is reasonable to assume that the present adverse test condition is highly *un*characteristic of the normal conditions under which the child is supposed to function. Let us say that the predicate "highly uncharacteristic" corresponds with a degree of "characteristicness" of 0.2 (that value, as any value in fuzzy logic, can eventually also be represented as a fuzzy value itself). Let S be the degree of characteristicness (d) of the score m (S is 1, for this particular person and context) and C be the degree of characteristicness of the context (for this particular person). The degree of characteristicness of this score in this particular context is defined as

$$(S \wedge C)(d_m) = \min \{S(d_m), C(d_m)\} = \min \{1, 0.2\} = 0.2$$

Stated differently, the degree of characteristicness of the score m for this particular child is the disjunction set of S and C, which is equal to the smallest value, which is 0.2. (Note that in fuzzy logic, the disjunction is defined as the minimal degree-of-membership value of the elements in the disjunction.) The principle can also be illustrated by the reverse case. Assume there exists a highly characteristic context (e.g. doing a math exam in a classroom setting, where $C(d_m) = 1$). Next assume that a pupil who is not very good at math obtains a score that is considerably higher than the scores he or she usually gets or that we expect from that pupil. Let us say that this rather unexpected score can be given a degree of characteristicness of 0.2 (for instance, a score m that is far above the child's average expected score; $S(d_m) = 0.2$). According to the disjunction principle, the degree of characteristicness of score m is the minimum, 0.2

Whereas the combination of a particular score with a particular context obeys the fuzzy disjunction principle, the combination of various pairs of scores and their contexts follows the fuzzy conjunction or union principle. The importance of combining such pairs follows from the fact that scores (e.g. on a spatial abilities test) are assumed to differ across contexts and that such differences in contexts are likely to occur with any particular subjects. Or, to put it differently, it is important, psychometrically speaking, to know how scores across different contexts can be combined in order to yield a score that is characteristic of a specific person. Assume a highly unlikely context C_i (e.g. $C_i(d) = 0.1$) and a score m on a test obtained in that context by a particular child. Assume also that this score is moderately characteristic of this particular context (and this particular child; $S_i(d_m) = 0.5$). From the disjunction principle it follows that the degree of characteristicness of m is the minimum of both DoCs (degrees of characteristicness), namely 0.1. In addition, assume that there exists a far more likely context, say with degree of characteristicness of 0.8, and assume also that the same score m is very typical ($S(d) = 1$) of that context (for a particular child, that is). The DoC for that score in that context is, again according to the disjunction principle, 0.8 (the minimum of 1 and 0.8). What is the DoC of m for this particular child for *the two contexts*? It is easy to see that, if a property is expressed in a less characteristic context and the same property is also displayed in a more characteristic context, the characteristicness of that property must be that of the most characteristic context. Thus, for the given DoC values in the two separate contexts, the DoC of the combined contexts must be 0.8, which is the result of the fuzzy *union* (or conjunction) of the context-score pairs, which is defined as the maximum of the members of the union set:

$$(S \vee C)(d_m) = \max\{S(d_m), C(d_m)\} = \max\{0.8, 0.2\} = 0.8$$

By generalizing this latter principle, any degree of characteristicness function, for instance the one represented in figure 12.2, can be considered as the intersection of all possible contexts with all possible scores characteristic of those contexts. Put differently, the degree-of-characteristicness format allows us to specify the score distribution of a particular subject *for all possible contexts*, since both the scores and the contexts map on the same degree-of-characteristicness dimension and can be combined by union and intersection operations.

Let me try to specify the practical implications of this way of representing scores by giving a number of examples. It is perfectly natural for a teacher, for instance, to say "This student could very well achieve a level m on this particular exam, but it is highly doubtful that this will ever happen since he would have to invest quite some effort in preparing himself and I hardly expect him to ever do that." Assuming that the linguistic qualifiers of the type "very well," "highly doubtful" etc. can be mapped on to a single DoC value (it is more realistic to assume that they should be mapped on to a fuzzy range, but that won't change the principle), what the teacher says can be logically represented as

✓ There exists a student P ("this student")
✓ There exists a context "spending considerable effort in preparation for an exam" with a DoC of 0.1 ("is highly doubtful")[2]
✓ For that context, there exists a score, m, with a DoC of 1 ("could very well achieve")
✓ Hence, the DoC of m for P, $P(d_m) = \min\{(C(d), S(d) = 0.1\}$

Here's an example of a – probable – underachiever with an occasional peak performance:

This student usually performs on a rather mediocre level, but if he gets motivated – which does occur every now and then – his test levels will be among the best. If he were willing to spend a little more effort on preparing for his exams, his scores would be fairly good actually, but there's very little chance he will ever do so.

---

[2] Note that the DoCs (degrees of characteristicness) are just reasonable estimations, specified with no other aim in mind than to illustrate a general principle.

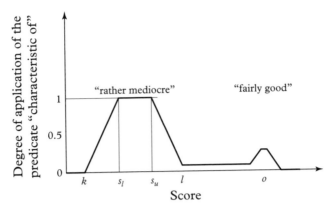

Figure 12.6 An imaginary score distribution of an underachieving student, who is supposed to be able to function on a "fairly good" level if he or she were willing to put in more effort; the high-effort condition is considered to have a low degree of characteristicness for the student at issue; the student's most characteristic scores are between s_l and s_u.

This description can be formalized as

✓ There exists a student P
✓ Whose highly characteristic scores ($S(d) = 1$) range from k to l (provided k and l mark the boundaries of what we consider to be the range "rather mediocre")
✓ When a relatively rare situation occurs ($C(d) = 0.3$, being motivated to put more effort into preparing for the exams), his characteristic score ($S(d) = 1$) will be o (in the range "fairly good"), which is considerably higher than l
✓ Hence, the range of scores characteristic of P will probably take the form of a bimodal distribution, as depicted in figure 12.6.

What I want to show with these examples is that it is possible to formalize, in a relatively simple and intuitive way, natural statements about abilities or skills that explicitly relate to dynamic and context-specific aspects. I do not imply that such formalizations make those natural statements more "scientific" or true. They remain to be demonstrated empirically, by experiment, testing or observation. The main reason behind formalizing ability statements in ways that include contextual and dynamic aspects is that the latter constitute an essential aspect of abilities in the broadest sense of the word.

Representing change, growth, and development by fuzzy numbers

We have seen that the notion of fuzzy scores requires two variables (see for instance figure 12.1). One variable specifies the property we have measured (for instance, intelligence, the level of a reasoning skill, etc.) and which we can specify in the form of a test score. The other variable specifies the "characteristicness" of the values of the first variable for a given subject or group (for instance, with regard to a particular person, the score range between 115 and 125 is highly characteristic, whereas scores higher than 135 and lower than 95 are completely uncharacteristic). The question I shall address in this section concerns the application of this general model, first, to representing change, growth, and development and, second, to the attribution of qualitative properties.

To begin with the latter, developmental psychologists are used to attributing qualitative milestones instead of just specifying development in terms of a score on a single underlying variable. The latter does occur – for instance when we ascribe a mental age score to a child – but we are more often concerned with specifications such as "this child has mastered the understanding of conservation," "this child is in the one-word stage," "this adolescent is able to apply formal operational logic to quantitative problems," and so forth. Take for instance the property "understanding the conservation principle." From a representational view, which sees knowledge as a representation of a principle, rule or state of affairs, a representation is either present or not. If it is present, the child has the competence to act according to the representation (e.g. understand a conservation problem). Whether the child will actually display the competence depends on intervening factors, for instance context and performance properties. According to this view, there is no partial understanding of a rule, principle or concept: it is either there or not. Partial understanding – if any occurs – results from the intervention of additional factors, such as memory limitations or adverse contexts. In the alternative view that I sketch in this chapter, understanding – or ability in general, for that matter – is partial and context dependent by its very nature (but it is so to various degrees). The representation of ability – including the presence of concepts, rules, and so forth – in terms of degrees of characteristicness allows one to formalize the partial, dynamic, and context-specific nature of ability in an intuitively appealing way. I shall try to illustrate this point with an example on the understanding and measurement of the Piagetian concept of conservation.

A typical way of measuring conservation understanding is by administering a conservation test, for instance the Goldschmidt–Bentler Test

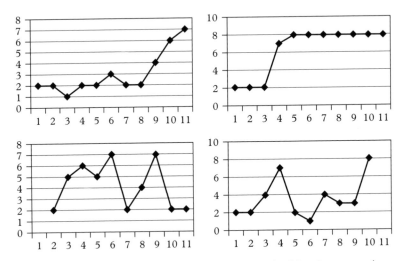

Figure 12.7 Longitudinal data from van der Maas' conservation study (1993). *Top*: two examples of orderly change (sudden jump); *bottom*: two examples of scores with strong fluctuations. The horizontal axis specifies time in the form of successive measurements; the vertical axis represents the number of conservation questions answered correctly.

(GBT). It consists of twelve concrete conservation questions that are scored correct or incorrect and so yield a score that varies between zero and twelve. How does the GBT ruler correspond with the qualitative attribution "understands conservation"? Does the latter imply that a child must have all twelve questions correct? What does a score of nine out of twelve, for instance, imply with regard to the attributed understanding of conservation? In a longitudinal study of conservation, van der Maas (1993) found both stepwise developmental patterns and strong fluctuations. With the latter, children often "regress" to considerably lower scores after having reached a score that would otherwise function as a criterion for conservation understanding (figure 12.7). This situation is also typical of microdevelopmental research, which employs a comparable approach in terms of frequently repeated assessment of a skill level or ability.

In order to solve questions similar to the conservation example, developmentalists have often reverted to the distinction between competence and performance. This distinction is conceptually similar to the notion of a true score and a measure that is like an error-laden approximation of the latter. However, the most natural and probably also most descriptively adequate solution is to consider the presence of a rule, or a concept or understanding, for that matter, as a fuzzy property of the person, instead

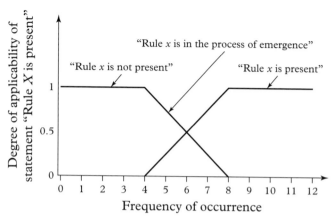

Figure 12.8 Scores on a criterion variable (e.g. a frequency of occurrence of a particular linguistic form x in a sample of 100 utterances) map differentially on to a degree of applicability of the statement "Linguistic rule x is present"; in the example, the statement "Linguistic rule is present" applies with a degree of applicability of 1 if the number of occurrences is eight or more; if the number of ocurrences is between four and eight, the statement applies with increasing degrees of applicability and would probably be described as "is in the process of emergence."

of a crisply defined state. The justifications for this approach are, first, that the brain, as a neural network, is a structure that approximates a rule to an arbitrarily large or small extent (see for instance Elman's notion of partial knowledge [Elman, 1990; Elman, Bates, Johnson, & Karmiloff-Smith, 1996]). Second, cognition is by its very nature always embodied and situated, which implies that a person's state of knowledge is a function not only of that person's brain, but also of the context in which that knowledge locally and temporarily functions. In summary, the presence of a rule, concept or understanding can be conceptualized as a fuzzy membership function across a ruler that specifies some observable criterion (a test score, for instance). The simplest membership distribution consists of two overlapping ranges, one for "is present," the other for "is not present" (figure 12.8).

Developmental ranges in longitudinal datasets

Longitudinal data sets with dense measurements are ideally suited for applying the concept of fuzzy score ranges. I shall discuss an example taken from a longitudinal study of emotional state behavior in infancy (de Weerth & van Geert, 1998; de Weerth, van Geert, & Hoijtink, 1999).

We collected data from four infants between birth and about one year and one month (about sixty-three consecutive weeks). The data consisted of weekly observations of crying (frequency and total duration), fretting/fussing, body contact, and smiling during a total of three hours. Each data set consists of about sixty-three measurements and thus represents a dense longitudinal series, for instance on cry duration. If one inspects the raw observation data, the variability of the data from week to week immediately strikes the eye. How can such data be used to characterize changes in cry duration during, for instance, the first year of life? One possibility would be to calculate averages, for instance, an average of cry duration during the first month, the second and so on. Another, slightly more sophisticated way consists of plotting a moving average across a time window of, for instance, six weeks. By doing so, however, one loses an important source of information, namely the obvious variability of the amount of cry duration over the weeks. At first sight, it seems as if the degree of variability decreases with increasing age. Elsewhere, we have argued that such a decrease indeed occurs with infants in the first year of life and that such a decrease amounts to a developmentally relevant phenomenon (de Weerth et al., 1999). We could of course also plot a moving standard deviation across the same time window as the moving average. A plot of a moving standard deviation alone, however, is not directly visually appealing or conceptually transparent. What we would like to see is how the range within which cry duration – or any other variable for that matter – varies, changes across time. For instance, does that range have a constant width, independent of age? Does it increase or decrease? Is such increase or decrease linear or nonlinear (e.g. an increase followed by a decrease followed by an increase)?

In the preceding sections we have argued that a score on a variable should in fact be replaced by a characteristic range. For every value of the variable in question we can attribute a degree of characteristicness, similar to the degree of membership used in fuzzy logic. On a longitudinal level, we may assume that the variability range characteristic of a specific age changes with time. Can the longitudinal data be employed to reconstruct such a changing range?

Looking at an infant's cry duration at week 6, for instance, it is natural to take into account his cry duration figures at surrounding weeks, for instance weeks 3, 4 and 5, and 7, 8 and 9. We could use these surrounding weeks to calculate the moving average. We can just as well use this set of surrounding weeks to estimate the upper and lower boundaries of the range of variability during this particular period. For the sake of simplicity we shall assume that everything that falls within these upper and lower boundaries is characteristic of the child during the time frame in question.

The simplest way to specify the lower and upper boundaries is to take the maximum value of the cry duration value of this particular seven-week period as that period's upper level and the minimum value as its lowest level. A disadvantage of this procedure is that if an extreme maximum or minimum occurs, it is likely to dominate the moving maximum or minimum plot for an entire seven-week period. Following the reasoning of the preceding sections, it is also likely that such an extreme value cannot be considered highly characteristic of the child's current range of cry duration – or any other variable for that matter. However, since that value occurs, it should not be abandoned, since it provides interesting information, namely information about extreme scores (see figure 12.9). A more sophisticated way of specifying the width of the – changing – range of values is to plot suitable moving percentile values. Still another way to plot a developmental range and which is advisable if the size of the window is relatively small (for instance five to seven data points) is to take a moving window (of, for instance, five or seven data points) and to plot the smallest value in the window, the smallest but one, the smallest but two, etc. up to the biggest value. This method uses no other values than those actually present in the data and therefore provides the fairest representation of what the data actually contain. This visual pattern is in agreement to what we found in our statistical analysis of variability across the first year of life, namely a significant decrease in variability (de Weerth et al., 1999).

However, we should first check how the scores are dispersed across the score range. That is, if we specify a range, it should be a real range, and not an artifact of the fact that we plot moving minima and maxima. For instance, if we apply the moving window technique to a simple linear increase (1 2 3 4 5 6 7 8 9 . . .), we will obtain an artificial range (1 to 5, 2 to 6 etc. if we take a time window of five points). The values in the linear set, however, are anything but dispersed in a range: they follow a strict line. We wish to calculate a dispersion coefficient that is 0 for all data that are ordered along a strict line and 1 for all data that are exclusively located at extreme values (e.g. 1-5-1-5-1-5 etc.). An equation that does this is the following. Let w_j be a "window" of j consecutive values, v_i the middle value of that window and n the number of windows under consideration. We define the coefficient of dispersion d as follows:

$$d = \left[\left(\sum_1^n \left\{ \frac{\max \left\{ \dfrac{v_i - \min(w_j)}{\max(w_j) - v_i} \right\}}{\sum_1^n (\max(w_j) - \min(w_j))} \right\} \right) - 0.5 \right] \cdot 2 \quad (12.1)$$

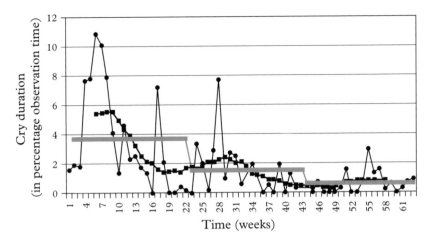

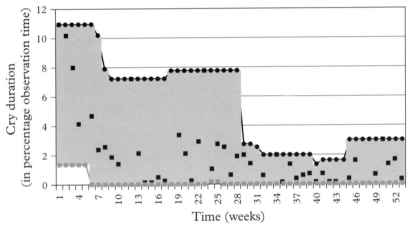

Figure 12.9 Weekly observations of cry duration in a child aged between two and sixty-three weeks. *Top*: raw data compared with moving average and periodical average; *bottom*: raw data compared with moving maximum and moving minimum. *Top*: —●—, cry%; —■—, moving averages; —▢—, periodical averages; *bottom*: —●—, max. cry%; ■, data; —▢—, min. cry%.

The coefficient of dispersion, which is computed with equation (12.1), is 0.58. This value is close to what we obtain with an even distribution of scores between the maxima and minima. One of the advantages of the present equation over a standard deviation, for instance, is that it varies between 0 and 1. Another is that it will specify a bimodal distribution as a value close to 1 (1 in the extreme) even if the modes of the distribution are highly unequally divided over the maximum and the minimum mode.

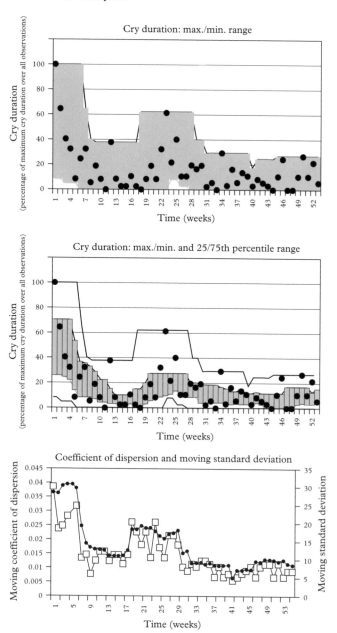

Figure 12.10 Maximum, minimum, and percentile ranges of cry duration in an infant during the first sixty-four weeks; *bottom*: a comparison between moving dispersion levels and moving standard deviations (window = eleven weeks). –□–, dispersion; –●–, s.d.

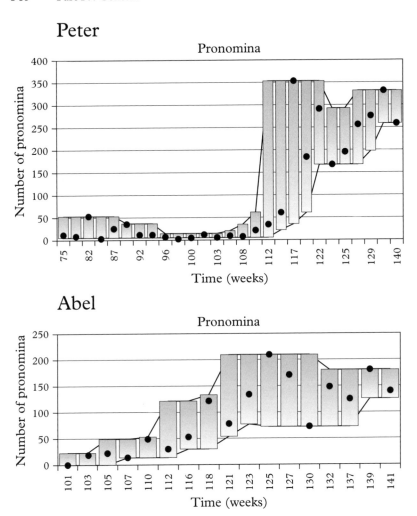

Figure 12.11 Maximum and minimum ranges of pronomina use in Peter and Abel.

One may wonder if the minimum and maximum boundaries specify cry frequencies which we can still consider characteristic of the child. Given that those "extreme" frequencies occur anyhow and also given the fact that the extremes change across development, we may characterize the local maxima and minima as scores that are at least "moderately characteristic." Let us say those minima and maxima have a degree of characticsness of 0.5. Since the coefficient of dispersion (0.58) is close to one that is characteristic of an even distribution, it is reasonable to assume that scores that fall within the 25th and the 75th percentile can be considered "highly characteristic" of the child. Assuming the maximum and minimum levels are reasonably specified as "moderately characteristic," we can specify a fuzzy band of cry frequencies across the first year (figure 12.10). In addition to plotting the ranges, one may also graph the coefficients of dispersion for every consecutive time window (see equation 12.1). The coefficients tell us how "eccentric" the observed cry frequencies were in the corresponding time window. The sequence of coefficients shows the changes in variability across the time span covered by the time series at issue.

A second study that I shall briefly describe concerns an observational study of the use of so-called "function" words (prepositions, pronouns, articles, etc.) in eight children in the age range of approximately one and a half to three years (Ruhland & van Geert, 1998). Figure 12.11 shows the maximum and minimum ranges of pronomina use in two children, Abel and Peter. The way the ranges change differs considerably, suggesting that Peter makes a more jump-like transition in his use of pronomina.

To conclude, in this chapter I have argued that the causes of developing performance are in fact a fuzzy and distributed set. Variability across time is one of the indicators of this fuzziness, which is not a matter of error or unsystematic variance but an inherent property of the developing and functioning person. I have discussed the notion of ranges of scores over time and I have shown how the notion of fuzziness nevertheless allows for a precise quantitative treatment. My main objective has been to argue that longitudinal or time series data of development should first be viewed at the level of the information they actually contain and should not be too rapidly reduced to averages or similar measures that often conceal important aspects of the data.

References

Alibali, M. W. (1999). How children change their minds: Strategy change can be gradual or abrupt. *Developmental Psychology, 35,* 127–145.

Altrock, C. von (1995). *Fuzzy logic and neurofuzzy applications explained.* Upper Saddle River, NJ: Prentice Hall.

Castro, J. L. (1995). Fuzzy logic controllers are universal approximators. *IEEE Transactions on Systems, Man, and Cybernetics, 25,* 629–635.

Crowley, K., Shrager, J., & Siegler, R. S. (1997). Strategy discovery as a competitive negotiation between metacognitive and associative mechanisms. *Developmental Review, 17,* 462–489.

de Weerth, C., & van Geert, P. (1998). Emotional instability as an indicator of strictly timed infantile developmental transitions. *British Journal of Developmental Psychology, 16,* 15–44.

de Weerth, C., van Geert, P., & Hoijtink, H. (1999). Intraindividual variability in infant behavior. *Developmental Psychology, 35,* 1102–1112.

Elman, J. L. (1990). Representation and structure in connectionist models. In G. T. M. Altmann (Ed.), *Cognitive models of speech processing: Psycholinguistic and computational perspectives* (pp. 345–382). Cambridge, MA: MIT Press.

Elman, J. L., Bates, E. A., Johnson, M. H., & Karmiloff-Smith, A. (1996). *Rethinking innateness: A connectionist perspective on development.* Cambridge, MA: MIT Press.

Fletcher, K. L., Huffman, L. F., Bray, N. W., & Grupe, L. A. (1998). The use of the microgenetic method with children with disabilities: Discovering competence. *Early Education and Development, 9,* 357–373.

Goldin-Meadow, S., Alibali, M. W., & Church, R. B. (1993). Transitions in concept acquisition: Using the hand to read the mind. *Psychological Review, 100,* 279–297.

Greeno, J. G. (1997). Theories and practices of thinking and learning to think. *American Journal of Education, 106,* 85–126.

Greeno, J. G. (1998). The situativity of knowing, learning, and research. *American Psychologist, 53,* 5–26.

Hosenfeld, B., van der Maas, H. L. J., & van den Boom, D. C. (1997a). Indicators of discontinuous change in the development of analogical reasoning. *Journal of Experimental Child Psychology, 64,* 367–395.

Hosenfeld, B., van der Maas, H. L. J., & van den Boom, D. C. (1997b). Detecting bimodality in the analogical reasoning performance of elementary schoolchildren. *International Journal of Behavioral Development, 20,* 529–547.

Kosko, B. (1993). *Fuzzy thinking: the new science of fuzzy logic.* New York: Hyperion.

Kosko, B. (1997). *Fuzzy engineering.* Upper Saddle River, NJ: Prentice Hall.

Kuhn, D. (1995). Microgenetic study of change: What has it told us? *Psychological Science, 6,* 133–139.

Kuhn, D., Garcia-Mila, M., Zohar, A., & Andersen, C. (1995). Strategies of knowledge acquisition. *Monographs of the Society for Research in Child Development, 60* (Serial No. 245).

Lautrey, J. (1993). Structure and variability: A plea for a pluralistic approach to cognitive development. In R. Case & W. Edelstein (Eds.), *The new structuralism in cognitive development: Theory and research on individual pathways* (pp. 101–114). Basel: Karger.

Lautrey, J., & Caroff, X. (1996). Variability and cognitive development. *Polish Quarterly of Developmental Psychology, 2,* 71–89.

Nakatani, K. (1995). Microgenesis of the length perception of paired lines. *Psychological Research/Psychologische Forschung, 58,* 75–82.

Nguyen, H. T., & Walker, E. A. (1997). *A first course in fuzzy logic.* Boca Raton, FL: CRC Press.

Ross, T. J. (2000). *Fuzzy logic with engineering applications.* New York: McGraw-Hill.

Ruhland, R., & van Geert, P. (1998). Jumping into syntax: Transitions in the development of closed class words. *British Journal of Developmental Psychology*, *16*, 65–95.

Savelsbergh, G., Maas, H. van der, & Geert, P. L. C. van (1999). *Non-linear developmental processes*. New York: Elsevier.

Siegler, R. S. (1994). Cognitive variability: A key to understanding cognitive development. *Current Directions in Psychological Science*, *3*, 1–5.

Siegler, R. S. (1995). How does change occur: A microgenetic study of number conservation. *Cognitive Psychology*, *28*, 225–273.

Siegler, R. S. (1997). Beyond competence – toward development. *Cognitive Development*, *12*, 323–332.

Siegler, R. S., & Chen, Z. (1998). Developmental differences in rule learning: A microgenetic analysis. *Cognitive Psychology*, *36*, 273–310.

Siegler, R. S., & Shipley, C. (1995). Variation, selection, and cognitive change. In T. J. Simon & G. S. Halford (Eds.), *Developing cognitive competence: New approaches to process modeling* (pp. 31–76). Hillsdale, NJ: Erlbaum.

van der Maas, H. L. (1993). Catastrophe analysis of stagewise cognitive development. Amsterdam: Faculty of Psychology, University of Amsterdam (academic dissertation).

van der Maas, H. L. J., & Hopkins, B. (1998). Developmental transitions: So what's new? *British Journal of Developmental Psychology*, *16*, 1–13.

van der Maas, H. L., & Molenaar, P. C. (1992). Stagewise cognitive development: An application of catastrophe theory. *Psychological Review*, *99*, 395–417.

van Geert, P. (1997). Variability and fluctuation: A dynamic view. In E. Amsel & K. A. Renninger (Eds.), *Change and development: Issues of theory, method, and application* (pp. 193–212). Mahwah, NJ: Erlbaum.

van Geert, P. (2000). Time, change and intentional action in a dynamic framework: On the nature of psychological causes and measurement. Unpublished manuscript, University of Groningen.

van Geert, P. L. C., Savelsbergh, G., & van der Maas, H. (1999). Transitions and non-linear dynamics in developmental psychology. In G. Savelsbergh, H. van der Maas, & P. L. C. van Geert (Eds.), *Non-linear developmental processes* (pp. 11–20). New York: Elsevier.

Author index

Page numbers in *italics* refer to the list of references at the end of each chapter.

Subject index

Page numbers in **bold** indicate definitions.